SWAMI VIVEKANANDA

MESSIAH OF RESURGENT INDIA

P.R. BHUYAN

ATLANTIC
PUBLISHERS & DISTRIBUTORS

Published by
ATLANTIC PUBLISHERS AND DISTRIBUTORS
B-2, Vishal Enclave, Opp. Rajouri Garden, New Delhi-110027
Phones : 25413460, 25429987, 25466842

Sales Office
7/22, Ansari Road, Darya Ganj, New Delhi-110002
Phones : 23273880, 23285873, 23280451
Fax : 91-11-23285873
web : www.atlanticbooks.com
e-mail : info@atlanticbooks.com

ISBN 81-269-0234-5

Typeset at
APD Computer Graphics, Delhi
Printed in India at
Nice Printing Press, Delhi

DEDICATED TO

The sacred memory of our parents—
Late Heramba Narayan Bhuyan
Late Swarnamayee Bhuyan

FOREWORD

A spiritualist, a mystic and a monk, Swami Vivekananda did not participate in the nationalist movement, yet within a short span of life, by his work and ideas, he immensely contributed to the growth of national consciousness in modern India. He wanted to build up a new India through a spiritual upheaval. Though steeped in India's religious tradition and heritage, Vivekananda was free from dogmatism and sectarian exclusiveness. He denounced social superstitions, caste system, untouchability and backward status of women in the strongest possible language. He tried to rouse the dormant strength and faculty of our people and make them feel that, they were a nation. "I am an Indian, every Indian is my brother." "The ignorant Indian, the poor and destitute Indian, the Brahmin Indian, the pariah Indian is my brother." "The Indian is my brother, the Indian is my life, India's gods and goddesses are my God. India's society is the cradle of my infancy, the pleasure garden of my youth, the sacred heaven, the Varanasi of my old age." "The soil of India is my highest heaven, the good of India is my good." These are a few of the patriotic utterances of the patriot-saint. Swami Vivekananda was a staunch critic of the British rule and held it responsible for the degeneration of India. His ideas greatly inspired those who subsequently endeavoured to emancipate India from the foreign rule.

Growth of nationalism all over the World is attributed to the Western influence. Dr. Bhuyan has shown how

Vivekananda's nationalism has grown out of Indian roots, how it is moral and spiritual in character and, therefore, basically different from Western nationalism which is materialistic, imperialistic and exploitative. At the same time he has shown the wider cosmopolitan dimension of Vivekananda's nationalism. Like that of Aurobindo Ghosh and Mahatma Gandhi, his nationalism was broad and humanitarian and he believed that a free India has a great spiritual mission for the whole world.

Under the able guidance of an erudite scholar like Professor Benudhar Pradhan, Dr. P.R. Bhuyan has made a commendable intellectual exercise by collecting and analysing the ideas of Swami Vivekananda in all details and ramifications. I sincerely feel that his work will be appreciated and evaluated by those who are interested in Swamiji and Indian Renaissance and nationalism.

ATUL CHANDRA PRADHAN
Professor
Department of History,
Utkal University, Vani Vihar,
Bhubaneswar, Orissa

PREFACE

Notwithstanding the fact that Swami Vivekananda is a saint *par excellence* who championed the cause of Sanatana Hindu Dharma and its culture, he is acclaimed, the world over as "the Patriot Saint" and "The Patriot Prophet" of modern India. As opposed to a political philosopher or a politician, who deals with the concept of nationalism, Swami Vivekananda, a thorough mystic, dealt with Hinduism as the grand heritage of India. At home and abroad in all his speeches and writings he championed the cause of the ancient Hindu religion and its sublime culture. Such championship of the cause of Hinduism and its culture led to the awakening of India from stupor into which she had fallen before and after the British conquest and fostered among the Indians a consciousness of their identity as a nation. It, too, gave a rude shock to British imperialism in India and went a long way to prepare the ground for the movement for India's Independence in the long run.

A humble bid has been made in this book to explore Swami Vivekananda's concept of nationalism.

The book has been divided into eight chapters. The first chapter is entitled, "Evolution of Nationalistic Personality of Swami Vivekananda." Born in a religious Bengali family of wide repute, Swami Vivekananda grew up to feel a severe commotion in his heart. Swami Ramkrishna Paramahansa, his spiritual preceptor, pacified the young aspirant and initiated him to the task of alleviating the misery from the world. With the mission in life, he wandered all over India as a mendicant.

But his heart bled to see the poor and wretched lot of the Indian masses everywhere. He attributed such misery of the Indian masses to the British imperialistic exploitation and in course of time turned a nationalist *par excellence.* When he attended the Parliament of Religions at Chicago in 1893, and won universal approbation for old Hinduism and its culture, it galvanized the drooping spirit of the Indians to a mystical height and fostered in them a sense of nationalism. On his return from the West his triumphal march from Colombo to Almora also aroused the Indian masses against all lethargy and prostration that had beset our national life under the British rule. Evolution of Swami Vivekananda from mere a child of a religious family to the height of a spiritual nationalist has been vividly depicted in course of this chapter.

The second chapter bears the title "Basis of Swami Vivekananda's Nationalism." Unlike Western nationalism, which is secular in nature Swami Vivekananda's nationalism is based on religion, which is the life-blood of the people of India. Indian spiritual culture, which has a humanising and civilizing mission for the world also provides a basis for Swami Vivekananda's nationalism. Further his nationalism is based upon his deep concern for the masses as masses constitute the source of all vitality of the nation. To Swami Vivekananda freedom and equality, through which man expresses himself, is the birth right of every man. As such it should be made the basis of Indian nationalism. Spiritual integration of the world on the basis of universal brotherhood is another basis of Swami Vivekananda's nationalism. Non-attachment, non-covetousness and non-possessiveness, which serve as the antidote of capitalism, also constitute the basis of Swami Vivekananda's nationalism. "Karma Yogo" which is nothing but a system of ethics, intended to attain freedom — both political and spiritual through unselfish and good work, also subscribes to the basis of Swami Vivekananda's nationalism. Veneration for women, the most cardinal feature of our culture and civilization is the final basis of Swami Vivekananda's nationalism. All these have been highlighted in detail in course of this chapter.

The third chapter bears the title "Nature of Swami Vivekananda's Nationalism." Swami Vivekananda's nationalism unlike that of the West which is purely materialistic and secular, is spiritual in nature, emphasising on spirituality as the secret of all strength of our national life. His nationalism is also didactic in nature with a deep moral tone, giving much stress on character-building and man-making. Besides his nationalism is also socialistic in nature, that aims at eradicating gross inequalities of wealth from the society. His nationalism is also reformative in character that seeks to do away with all socio-religious dogmatism and superstitions. Expansion of spiritual knowledge to other parts of the world, what India calls her spiritual mission, also characterise Swami Vivekananda's nationalism. Organic nature of Swami Vivekananda's nation and nationalism with emphasis on religion and spiritualism as the vitality of such organism cannot be overlooked. Swami Vivekananda's nationalism also seeks to revive the grand old Vedic culture and discourages the blind imitation of the Western culture. Lastly Swami Vivekananda's nationalism is universalistic and cosmopolitan in character. All these points have been elaborately discussed in course of this chapter.

The fourth chapter bears the title "Special Features of Swami Vivekananda's Nationalism." Religiosity or spirituality which is the core of Indian cultural heritage, constitutes one of the special features of Swami Vivekananda's nationalism.

Universalism, a cardinal feature of Hindu religion and its culture, is also a speciality with Swami Vivekananda's nationalism. Another unique aspect of Swami Vivekananda's nationalism is its spirit of renunciation instead of self-aggrandisement. Nation-building through educational reconstruction constitutes another hallmark of Swami Vivekananda's nationalism. Besides, unity in the midst of diversity also forms another speciality of Swami Vivekananda's nationalism. Above all Swami Vivekananda's nationalism is marked by deep and intense humanism that aims at redemption of entire mankind, ground down under the formidable wheel of Western imperialism. All these points have been substantiated in detail in course of this chapter.

The fifth chapter deals with "Swami Vivekananda's Nationalism and National Freedom." Swami Vivekananda, a mystic *par excellence*, though did not involve himself in the freedom struggle, his nationalistic spirit and proclamations provided impetus for the freedom struggle.

Swami Vivekananda's emphasis on sense of patriotism, love of the masses, character-building and man-making produced some men with strong commitment for national freedom. That apart, his advocacy for spiritual unity promoted the spirit of national unity and thus aided freedom struggle.

Swami Vivekananda's projection of India on the world scenario as a land of superior culture and civilization to that of the West inflamed the nationalistic zeal of the people of this country for freedom struggle.

Swami Vivekananda's stress on political freedom as the essential prerequisite of spiritual freedom or freedom of soul also gave further impetus to freedom struggle.

Swami Vivekananda's reference to the events of Indian invasion by the foreign powers along with the present nefarious policy of British imperialism, galvanised the nationalistic spirit of the Indian people from which national freedom struggle also received tremendous inspiration.

Lastly, Swami Vivekananda's cult of Shakti-worship influenced Extremist Movement as a part of Indian freedom struggle. All these points have been dealt with in detail in course of this chapter.

The sixth chapter bears the title "Swami Vivekananda's Nationalism *vis-a-vis* Western Nationalism." Swami Vivekananda's nationalism like Western nationalism was a product of Renaissance and Reformation. The only difference being whereas Western nationalism was a product of Renaissance and Reformation in the West, Swami Vivekananda's nationalism emerged out of the impact on him of Indian Renaissance and Reform Movements of 19th century. Like Western concept of nationalism Swami Vivekananda's nationalism is based on the principle of self-determination. But his concept of nationalism differs radically from the Western concept of nationalism. In the first place whereas the Western concept of nationalism is purely secular in tone, Swami Vivekananda's nationalism is religious and spiritual in character. Besides, whereas Western Nationalism is mainly concerned with material advancement of the nation devoid of moral tone, Swami Vivekananda's nationalism is deeply moralistic, and is characterised by deep moral aspiration. That apart, whereas Western nationalism has flourished on colonialistic and imperialistic exploitation of the economically underdeveloped parts of the world Swami Vivekananda was a critic of colonialistic and imperialistic exploitation. Above all whereas Western nationalism is aggressive and belligerent in nature and is based on capitalistic greed Swami Vivekananda denounced them. He tried to leaven his nationalism by religious and spiritual conquest and emancipation of the poor and the downtrodden. All these points have been exhaustively developed in course of this chapter.

The seventh chapter is entitled "Swami Vivekananda's Nationalism and Imperialism." Swami Vivekananda as an impassioned nationalist was a bitter critic of imperialism and condemned outright the imperialistic greed of the West. India's poverty and backwardness he considered to be the direct consequence of British imperialistic exploitation. As a lover of mankind as a whole he earnestly desired liberation of all peoples and all nations over the world from the clutches of imperialism. Hence, he advocated shedding of fearlessness and commencement of struggle for the liberation of India from the grip of imperialism. He called upon the Indians to cultivate muscles of iron and nerves of steel to put an end to British imperialism. All these points have been highlighted in course of this chapter.

The eighth chapter bears the title "Nationalism of Swami Vivekananda, Sri Aurobindo Ghose and Mahatma Gandhi." Swami Vivekananda, Sri Aurbindo Ghose and Mahatma Gandhi had, as opposed to the moderate nationalists identical objective in the sense that all the three had as the end of this nationalism, Swaraj for the country. For them Swaraj was the birth right of every people and every nation. All the three were basically spiritual personalities and believed in the rich spiritual heritage of India. Hence, their nationalism is spiritual in tone and temper. They felt that India has a spiritual mission for the whole world and that mission can be fulfilled only when India attains her nationhood. They realised the tremendous importance of education for building up a mighty nation and advocated Indianisation of educational system with its emphasis on spiritual basis of education and education through the medium of mother-tongue. All the three were great humanists apart from being nationalists. As a matter of fact their nationalism emanated from their deep sense of humanism. Hence, their nationalism did not suffer from narrowness and exclusiveness, but is marked by universalistic fervour and intense desire for effecting welfare of mankind. Although all the three were spiritual personalities their nationalism is secular in nature in the sense that all believed in the spirit of mutual toleration by people of different faiths. That they felt shall strengthen the nation by unifying people of different religious beliefs. All these points have been discussed elaborately in course of this chapter.

In preparing this book I have adopted historical, comparative and analytical methods of study.

In my enterprise to explore the nationalistic dimension of a spiritual colossus like Swami Vivekananda, I am profoundly indebted to my revered guide Dr. Benudhara Pradhan, former Professor and Head of Department, Utkal University, Vani Vihar, Bhubaneswar and the present Dean of Studies and Research of the Institute of Gandhian Studies, Wardha, whose counsel not only inspired me with abundant enthusiastic impulse for initiative and impetus for adventure, but has sustained me along the tracts of a fabulous spiritual giant with nebulous political horizon, of the period of Indian Renaissance. At my voyage's end, with the overwhelming joy of accomplishing the avowed mission, I am too full of obeisant gratitude for my guide Dr. Benudhara Pradhan, who has stood by me all along as a guardian angel through many a rough terrains and weathered many shocks and shivers, travails and trials of the inclement weather and adverse surrounding.

My thanks are due to the authorities of the Library of Utkal University, Vani Vihar, Bhubaneswar; Library of Jawaharlal Nehru University, New Delhi; National Library, Kolkata; Library of Ramkrishna Mission's Cultural Institute, Golpark, Kolkata; Library of Ramkrishna Math & Mission, Howrah and the Library of the Institute of Gandhian Studies, Wardha from which I have gathered the facts and formulated the ideas for my work.

My hearty thanks are due to the dynamic Principal of my college — Dr. P. Patra and my erudite colleague-brothers who have extended their kind co-operation for completing this book.

I owe thanks to Sri Ajay Kumar Senapati, Propritor, Padmabati Technical Institute, Chitrada, Mayurbhanj, who has unhesitatingly taken the troubles of typing and re-typing the entire work so meticulously.

I am greatly beholden to my senile old parents for their blessings and wishes, to my revered mother in particular, who shared all the hazards of unfurling the sail of my mission-bound vessel but no more alive to share the hilarity of reaching the destination for which my heart sinks in sorrows bedewing my eyes with tears. I am equally beholden to my brothers for their enormous goodwill that has gone a long way to inspire and influence me to accomplish the goal.

Station Bazar, Baripada, P.R. BHUYAN
Mayurbhanj, Orissa State

CONTENTS

1

Evolution of the Nationalistic Personality of Swami Vivekananda

(i) The Contemporary Age

Swami Vivekananda was born in an age when India was rotting under the formidable weight of British imperialism. The intention of the imperial power was to retain their hold over India by hook or by crook in disregard of the socio-religious and politico-economic crises in India. The British nefarious intention can be best summed up as, "...from Robert Clive to Winston Churchill one of the supreme objective of the British race was the preservation of the Eastern possession, if not for all time certainly for as long as the nation had the right to retain."[1] The loss of India was beyond their comprehension. On the contrary the British had a determination not to leave India to Indians.[2] As a consequence of such British imperial policy and the Western influence the channels of Indian culture were getting shrivelled and dry. The vast sub-continent had become moribund, decadent and effete. The creative and assimilative spirit of Indian civilization had reached the lowest ebb. The intellectual life of India had become dull and sluggish. Knowledge was petrified. The society with all its evils was like a pool of stagnant water. The traditional charm of Indian social life was on the wane.

The Western civilization and culture challenged the old values and beliefs of India. As a consequence the old rites and rituals, customs and traditions gradually decayed. All the institutions — social, religious, political and economic — were collapsing at a terrifying speed. Literally India was in a melting point. As a reaction there arose two divergent schools of thought

— the conservatives and the radicals. B.N. Luniya writes, "On the one side there were conservatives, who clung to the superstitions and lifeless rigidity of traditions. They sought to strengthen the forces of orthodox. On the other hand there was gradually rising in social prominence, a group of educated Indians, lured by the Western ideas. They looked to the West for guidance and inspiration. They advocated extreme radical policy. They tried to explain the hollowness of Indian religion and society."[3]

As a reaction against the threat of complete collapse of Indian socio-economic-political system, there occurred in 1857 the first war of India's independence that was suppressed by the imperialist as 'Sepoy Mutiny'. The British imperial power in order to fortify their position on the Indian soil and forestall any future threat to the empire, embarked upon a repressive policy. In spite of such massive repression, the revolutionary spirit was simmering underneath in Bengal where Swami Vivekananda was born. It was, thus, in a tense atmosphere in 1863 that Swami Vivekananda was born. As Prof. Hiren Mukerjee writes, "It was in this surcharged atmosphere and not in any kind of placid vacuum that young Vivekananda lived, moved and had his being."[4] So the air that Swami Vivekananda breathed, perhaps developed his flair for revolution against the agony of the British imperial power.

Fortunately this period of national history is synchronized by the cultural rebirth that goes by the title of Indian Renaissance. There emerged many reforming institutions prominent among them being Brahmo Samaj, Prarthana Samaj, Arya Samaj etc., patronized by the veteran apostles like Raja Ram Mohan Roy, Mohadeo Govind Ranade, Swami Dayananda Saraswati respectively. The organizations launched vigorous crusade to save Indian religion and culture from the barbaric onslaught of the West. This was the state of affairs when Swami Vivekananda was born and had his being.

(ii) Swami Vivekananda — His Horizon of Political Philosophy

Swami Vivekananda is acclaimed world over, as a metaphysician *par excellence* of Vedantic School. He was one of the great interpreters of Vedantic philosophy in modern times. He championed the cause of 'Sanatana Dharma' and made persistent effort to realize the dream of universalizing this religion and philosophy. He was never a political philosopher in the traditional sense of the term in which we regard Hobbes, Rousseau, or Hegel or Basanquet as system builders in the field of political thought. Politics was neither his concern nor his trait. As it is said, "He does not enter into the analytical study of the concepts of political philosophy nor does he probe into the dynamics of political process and behaviour."[5]

It is a fact that Swami Vivekananda was a great mystic of recent time. As a mystic spiritualism was the be all and end all of his life. Even the renascent spirit of the age could not influence him very much. He tilted towards spiritualism more and more. His soul craved for spiritual realization so much so that it caused severe turmoil and commotion in his heart. To satisfy the burning fire of his heart, he clung to meditation and study of the Vedas. However, under the guidance of his great spiritual preceptor — Sri Ramkrishna, the course of his life took a different turn. He realized that political liberation is the prelude to spiritual liberation. His thought that social emancipation is the basis of all spiritualism and it is a positive condition to spiritual realization, subsequently turned him to be a "great humanist, democrat, patriot and a distinguished leader of the spiritual culture of India,"[6] who inflamed the renascent spirit of 19th century. He turned out to be a great patriot with burning love for his motherland. He had a vision of the unity of the country against the British imperialism. He bent all his strength for regeneration of Hindu nationalism through revival of Vedantism. His teachings and personality had far-reaching influence on the nationalist movement of Bengal in particular and India in general. It changed the dimension of the polity of independent India. Dr. Karan Singh has aptly described him as "The spiritual progenitor of the radicals."[7]

Thus, though Swami Vivekananda did not propound any theory of nationalism like a political scientist, nationalism was his very creed. Love for his motherland was in his very blood, though he breathed the air of spiritualism. This led sister Nivedita to remark befittingly that, "Just as Ramkrishna in fact, without knowing any books had been a living epitome of the Vedanta so was Vivekananda of the National life. But of the theory of this he was unconscious."[8]

Underneath his spiritualism, there vibrates a strong current of nationalism that developed gradually and reached the high watermark when he returned triumphantly to India after his historic mission in the West and made a whirlwind tour through India.

(iii) Early Days

Swami Vivekananda of later days or Narendranath Datta, as he was called in his premonastic days, was born in Calcutta on 12 January 1863. Datta family was a rich and respectable family of wide repute, noted for charity, learning and strong passion for independence. His grandfather Durga Charan Datta, a Sanskrit and a Persian scholar, was well versed in laws. But after the birth of his son, Vishwanath Datta, he renounced the world and became a monk. Thus renunciation for realization of dharma formed the very blood of Datta family, which manifested at large in Vivekananda, the most illustrious son of the family.

Vishwanath, the father of Narendranath, was an attorney at Calcutta High Court. He was proficient in English and Persian and took great delight in reciting to his family the poems of great Persian poet — Hafiz. He also enjoyed the study of Bible and the Hindu scriptures in Sanskrit. Although he was a prosperous man, his charitable disposition was quite remarkable. He often spent beyond his means for bringing relief to the suffering humanity. As it has been observed, "While his earnings were large and Narendra was brought up in affluence, Vishwanath who was, known for his charity, liberal outlook and sympathy for the afflicted, spent his fortune recklessly without regard to the morrow or the financial future of the family."[9] Charitable and sympathetic to the poor and needy to an extravagant degree Vishwanath Datta was also very rationalistic and progressive in outlook in socio-religious matters.

Bhubaneswari Devi, mother of Narendranath, was a model of Indian womanhood with a regal bearing. She was profoundly religious and highly compassionate towards the poor beggars. It has been observed about her, "The poor and the hopeless were the special object of their solicitude."[10]

The nature and disposition of his parents left an indelible print upon the mind of little Narendranath. His mother influenced him more than his father. He himself has said, "I am indebted to my mother for whatever knowledge I have acquired."[11] Though restless and given much to fun and frolic during his early childhood, Narendranath had a special bent for spiritualism. He would play at worshipping or meditating on images of Ram, Sita, Siva, etc. The stories from the great epics, the Ramayana and the Mahabharat, which his mother told him left an unforgettable impression on his mind. As a result, traits, such as passion for freedom, courage for struggle, sympathy for the poor, compassion for the afflicted and devotion towards the wandering monks appeared spontaneously in him.[12] 'The growing plant reveals itself in the seedling' found its veracity in Narendranath.[13] Even in his childhood Narendranath put forth convincing argument for every proposition. With these vehement potentialities of head and heart, he grew into a vigorous youth.

(iv) At the Feet of Sri Ramkrishna

As a youth Narendranath's leonine beauty supplemented his courage. He had the build of an athlete, a resonant and a superb intellect. He distinguished himself in athletics, philosophy and music. Among all his colleagues he was the undisputed leader in every sphere. At college he studied and absorbed Western thoughts which implanted a spirit of critical inquiry in his mind. His inborn proclivity for religiocity and spiritualism, his great veneration and adoration for ancient Indian culture on the one hand and his argumentative nature coupled with sharp intellect on the other were now at war with each other.[14] He craved for solution of these problems for retaining his peace of mind. During this period he sought to find comfort in the Brahmo Samaj — a great socio-religious movement of the time, piloted by Raja Ram Mohan Roy, the doyen of Indian renaissance. Brahmo Samaj believed in formless God, deprecated the worship of idols and devoted itself only to various forms of socio-religious reforms. Inquisitive and restless Narendranath frantically met almost all the so-called veteran religious leaders, but could not get any convincing reply from them to his question about the existence of God. This only accentuated his spiritual restlessness.

Narendranath made hectic effort to quench his spiritual thirst. He dived deeply into the philosophy of Descartes, Hume, Kant, Fichte, Spinoza, Hegel, Comte, Darwin and Mill, but found no peace. The more he studied the Western philosophy the bigger became the mark of interrogation as regards the existence of God in his mental horizon. At this critical hour he remembered the words of his English Professor William Hasti, who had mentioned that a saint lived at Dakshineswar just outside Calcutta, who experienced ecstasy, described by Wordsworth in his poem "Excursion". His cousin Ramchandra Datta also influenced him to visit the saint. Thus, came about the historic meeting in 1881 of the two great souls — the greatest prophet of modern India and the greatest carrier of his message to the world. The weary traveller at last reached the shadowy oasis to take rest under and drink the ambrocia to his heart's content.

After meeting Ramkrishna Paramhansa Narendranath asked, 'Sir, have you seen God?' Sri Ramkrishna as a loving father answered, 'Yes, I have seen Him just as I see you here only more intensely.' At last he met here one who could assure him from his own experience that God exists. The gathering clouds of despair and misgiving were dispelled. The great mark of interrogation on the issue of providential existence vanished from his mind. While Ramkrishna tested him in so many ways, Narendranath on the other hand tested Sri Ramkrishna in order to ascertain the truth of his spiritual assertions.

With sad demise of his father terrible poverty and privation gripped Narendranath's rich and well-to-do family. Creditors were knocking at his door. Even some of his relatives threatened to turn away his family from his family home. Narendranath, the son of a rich man now became poorest of the poor in the college. Even shoe became a thing of luxury for him. His garments were of coarsest cloth and many time he went to his classes without food. Romain Rolland has observed, "There were six or seven mouths and swarm of creditors. From that day onwards Narendranath tasted misery, knew the vain search of employment and the denial of friends."[15] Of his hard days Swami Vivekananda has written, "I was dying of starvation. Barefooted I went from office to office and was refused everywhere. I learnt by experience what human compassion is. This was my first contact with the realities of life; and I discovered it...had no room for the weak, the poor, the deserted...."[16]

Such poverty, destitution, deprivation and unemployment for the first time in his life changed his view of life and philosophy. He clearly sensed the plight of the poor and the destitutes. Now he had the opportunity of contrasting his lot with those of the privileged class of people. He could experience what equality means and how inequality saps the energy and vigour of the people. However, poverty and privation did not dishearten Narendranath. He rather firmly stood the test of time. At the suggestion of his great Master he tried to pray to Mother Kali at Dakhineswar for the alleviation of family's distress. However, though his need was for wealth he could pray only for pure knowledge and devotion.

Narendranath surrendered himself to his Master *in toto*. Sri Ramkrishna in return with infinite patience calmed the rebellious spirit of the young disciple and led him forth from doubts to certainty and from anguish to spiritual bliss.[17] But more than Ramkrishna's spiritual guidance and support it was his great affection and love that conquered the heart of young Narendranath.

Gradually the spiritual fire which was lit in Narendranath sprang up high with formidable flame. He liked to satisfy it through various intense spiritual practices. One day Narendranath asked his Master to bless him with Nirvikalpa Samadhi — ordinarily regarded as the highest spiritual experience, the Master admonished him saying, 'Shame on you, I thought you would grow like a huge banyan-tree, sheltering thousands from the scorching miseries of the world. But now I see you seek your own liberation."[18] All the same Narendranath had the much coveted realisation after which the Master said that the key to this would thenceforth remain in his keeping and the door would not be opened till Narendranath had finished the task for which he was born. The great humanist Sri Ramkrishna hereafter entrusted Narendranath the great task of giving shelter to the suffering mankind and blessed him saying, "Oh' Naren today I have given you my all and have become a Fakir, a penniless beggar. By the force of power, transmitted by me, greatest things will be done by you; only after that you will go to whence you came."[19] Narendranath's drooping spirit awakened, which kindled a new passion in his heart. His view of life underwent a great change. The course of his life and thought took a different turn. He saw mighty task awaiting him and he felt to be saddled with enormous responsibility of providing shelter to mankind against the scorching miseries of the world. All the advice and admonition of his great Master knocked at the door of his heart all along.

At the feet of his Master, Narendranath realized the significance of Vedanta philosophy, the essence of non-dualism of the creator and the creation, the God and the Universe and the inseparability of each living being in the Universe. He realized under the impact of his Master that all the living beings are the embodiments of the 'Divine Self' or at least fragments of 'Divine Self' and the sparks of the Divine Flame. Hence, service to God can be rendered only by service to man.

One day some time in 1884, Sri Ramkrishna while discoursing on the essence of Vaishnava religion with his disciples, said, "This religion enjoins upon its followers the practice of three things — relish for the name of God, compassion for all living creatures and service to the Vaishnavas — the devotees of the Lord." Immediately thereafter he fell into Samadhi and regaining his consciousness he said, "Compassion for creature : Thou Fool : An insignificant worm crawling on earth, thou show compassion to others : who art thou to show compassion? No — it cannot be. It is not compassion for others but rather service to man recognizing him to be the veritable manifestation of God."

The Master's emphasis on 'Service to Man' had a very great impact on the disciple and that constituted the greatest message of the Master for Narendranath. That inspired him all the more to fulfil the great task, entrusted to him by the Master. The young unemployed Narendranath with the burden of a family to shoulder, now felt greatly relieved and saw the vision of service to the humanity at large rather than to a single family. After having realized the message of his Master he himself said, "What a strange light have I discovered in those words of the Master? How beautifully has he reconciled the ideal of Bhakti (devotion) with the knowledge of the Vedanta (Non-dualism). I have understood from these words of wisdom that the ideal of Vedanta lived by the recluse outside the pale of society can be practised even from the hearth and home and applied to all our schemes of life.

Whatever may be the vocation of a man, let him understand and realize that it is God alone who has manifested Himself as the world and created beings. He is both immanent and transcendent. It is He, who has become all diverse of creatures, objects of our love, yet is beyond all these — such realization of Divinity in humanity leaves no room for egotism. By realising it a man cannot have any jealousy or pity for any other being. Service of man knowing him to be the manifestation of God purified the heart, and in no time such an aspirant realises himself as part and parcel of God-Existence, knowledge and Bliss."[20]

The message of non-dualism of God and the Universe, the message that all are the manifestation of the 'Divine Self', was driven home to Narendranath by the Master. The disciple realized the inherent equality of all human beings. Hence, the principle of social inequality, division of society into privileged and unprivileged social groups, appeared irrational and unscientific to Narendranath. His philosophical outlook moved further in the direction of a free egalitarian society. In the context of his Master's message of non-dualism and divinity of human beings Narendranath later on said, "I shall make it the common property of all, the wise and the fool, the rich and the poor, the Brahmin and the pariah."[21]

At the feet of his Master, Narendranath also learnt the art of renunciation that became most essential ingredient of his concept of nationalism. Of course from his youth he had developed a flair for the life of renunciation. As he himself said, "From my youth up...every night just as I fell asleep two dreams take shape. In one I saw myself among the great ones of the earth; the possessor of riches, power and glory and I felt that the capacity to attain all these was in me. But the next instant I saw myself renouncing all worldly things, dressed in a simple loin cloth, living on alms, sleeping at the foot of a tree and I thought that I was also capable of living thus like the Rishis of old. Of these two pictures, the second took upper hand and I felt that only thus could a man attain supreme bliss.... And I fell asleep in the foretaste of that bliss.... And each night it was renewed."[22]

Narendranath's flair for renunciation that developed in him since his youth received unprecedented impetus from the message of his Master. It took deep-roots in him, who said, I was convinced that I was not born like humdrum people to earn money and maintain my family much less to strive for sense pleasure. I began secretly to prepare myself to renounce the world like my grandfather."[23]

Thus under the spell of his great Master, Narendranath not only renounced his desire of material pleasure and comfort but also renounced his desire for personal salvation — Nirvikalpa Samadhi, in the interest of social and spiritual emancipation of mankind.

After the death of his Master Sri Ramkrishna on 16 August, 1886, Narendranath took leadership of the Master's disciples in fulfilling the latter's vision of revolutionising the world by rendering service to the suffering humanity — the poor, the downtrodden. In an old dilapidated house at Baranagar, the disciples were organized into the Ramkrishna order. Thus the foundation of Ramkrishna botherhood was laid in the midst of a life of intense austerity and spiritual practices and it was on a Christmas Eve in 1886 at Antpur, sitting round a huge fire they took the vow of sannyasa. The sannyasis of the Ramkrishna order under Narendranath's leadership became crusaders of truth and children of light, ever learning, for whom the whole world became an open university. They discussed history and philosophy of different nations and examined thoroughly the thoughts of Plato, Aristotle, Kant, Hegel etc. along with that of

Buddha, Sankaracharya, Ramanuja, Chaitanya etc. Swami Nikhilananda writes, "Narendra did not want the brother disciples to be pain-hugging, cross-grained ascetics. They should broaden their outlook by assimilating the cross-currents of the world."[24]

However, for Narendranath — Swami Vivekananda of the future — there was a call from the unknown to know itself, to see itself more keenly, more intimately. If the master commanded that he must serve people his inner self commanded that he must first see these people in order to ascertain whether they actually need service and the nature of service that they need. So he decided to set out in his voyage of discovery of India alone as a wandering monk.

(v) The Wandering Monk

In 1888 Narendranath left the Baronagar monastery, the seat of Ramkrishna order and travelled alone as an unknown mendicant. He began to assume various names to conceal his identity in order to be swallowed up in the immensity of India. "Now it was that the natural desire of an Indian monk for a life of solitude gave way to prescience that he was to fulfil a great destiny; that his was not the life of an ordinary recluse, struggling for personal salvation."[25] Under the influence of his burning desire to know India better and the mute appeal rising all around him from oppressed India, he went to Vanarasi — one of the holiest cities of the Hindus. After Vanarasi he visited Lucknow, Agra, Brindaban, Hathras and Rishikesh and then he returned to Baranagar for a time. At Hathras he met Sarat Chandra Gupta who became his first disciple (Swami Saradnanda). He revealed to him the great mission — the mission of alleviating the miseries of the people around him, entrusted to him by his great Master — "I have a great mission to fulfil and I am at despair at the smallness of my capacity. I have an injuction from my guru to carry out his mission. This is nothing less than regeneration of my motherland."[26] Sarat Chandra, who was a Railway staff at Hathras resigned his post and followed his guru to help him in the fulfilment of his great mission. The plan of mission that Narendranath had embarked upon was Herculean in magnitude. Still, Narendranath did not lose his heart. He had abiding faith in his Master, who would help him to translate his plan into reality.

An important event in Narendranath's life took place in 1890, when he met Pavhari Baba of Gazipur, for whose saintliness he had the greatest admiration throughout his life. At this time he oscillated between two desires — to be absorbed in the eternal silence of the Absolute or to fulfil his great Master's mission. He hoped that Pavhari Baba would appease the remorse gnawing at his heart, which was due to the fact that the fervour for the highest absorption in the Divine drew him away from the work entrusted to him by his Master. For twenty days Narendranath was on the verge of yielding to this temptation, but the vision of Sri Ramkrishna always came to draw him back.

In July 1890 Narendranath took leave of Sri Sarada Devi, the spiritual consort of Sri Ramkrishna, who was the spiritual guide of the young monks after the great Master's passing away. He also took leave of his brother monks with the firm resolve to cut himself free from all ties and to go into the solitude of the Himalayas for he felt it was essential to remain all alone. As Romain Rolland has observed, "This was the great departure. Like a diver he plunged into the ocean of India and the ocean of India covered his tracks. Among its flotsam and jetsam, he was nothing more than one nameless Sannyasin in saffron robe among a thousand others. But the fire of genius burned in his eyes. He was a prince despite all his disguise."[27]

His wandering took him to various places of pilgrimage and historical interest in Uttar Pradesh, Rajasthan, Gujarat, Maharashtra, Mysore, Kerala, Madras, Hyderabad etc. Everywhere the glory of ancient India came vividly before his eyes — whether political, cultural or spiritual. In the midst of this rich heritage the abject misery of the Indian masses arrested his attention. It gave a shock to his heart and tears to his eyes. He moved from one princely state to another. Everywhere he explored the avenues of mitigating and ameliorating the lot of the poor and the downtrodden. He happened to meet many leading personalities and great rulers of the princely states. Among them Maharaja Ajit Singh of Khetri became his first friend and ardent disciple. At Poona he stayed with Balgangadhar

Tilak, a great nationalist leader of Maharashtra. At first Tilak talked with Swami Vivekananda somewhat ironically but later on his depth of learning and profundity of thought impressed him so much so that he invited Swami Vivekananda to stay with him. From there he toured to many places of India.

Wherever he went it was not the place but the people that moved him most. It was the terrible poverty and the misery of the masses that caused his soul to burn in agony and led him to moan, "The only God in whom I believe the sum total of all souls and above all my God — the afflicted, my God the poor of all races."[28] His love for the people of India reached the supreme height. As Dr. V.K.R.V. Rao has observed, "and his soul was caught up with an ecstasy of vision of the Narayana Himself — the supreme Lord of the Universe, whose love is boundless, whose pity knows no distinction between the high and the low, the pure and vile, the rich and the poor."[29]

He had travelled through the whole of India, often on foot for nearly three years, coming to know India at first hand. At the fag end of his journey he went to Kanya Kumari, the southern most tip of India and sat on a solitary rock. The vast panorama of his experience of his travel passed before his mind's eye. 'He meditated upon the greatness of India's past, her shattered present and the future of India, causes of her downfall and the ways of her resurrection.'[30] He discovered the supreme truth that as the life-force of India lies in spiritualism, nothing else but revival of spiritualism would resurrect India nationally. Spiritualism alone would reassure her national vitality against all evils of the foreign rule. Hence, he turned out to be a convinced nationalist and with firm conviction he took pledge to propagate the teachings and the messages of his great Master — Sri Ramkrishna, based on the spiritual philosophy of India. As it is said, "Here was a strong phenomena, Vivekananda, that nationalist has found in the teachings and practices of Sri Ramkrishna, based on the ancient Indian religion of Vedanta, a faith, which fully satisfied all the cravings of his intellect and completely quenched the thirst of his soul. They re-established his pride in the greatness of Indian tradition, which had been rudely shaken by Western thoughts."[31]

Narendranath's pilgrimage brought vividly home to him the wretchedness and squalor, both moral and mental in which India of his day was sunk. His heart bled to see the shocking state of his countrymen everywhere. He cried, "O' Lord, why do you create these miserable creatures? I cannot bear the sight of them. How long O' Lord, how long."[32]

The voice of his Master, 'Religion is not for empty bellies. The physical need of man must be fulfilled before aspiring for the intellectual and spiritual perfection' went deep into his heart. The responsibility that his Master had entrusted to him became crystal clear before his eyes and he could not think of the life of a recluse for him. He heard the piteous moans of hunger of teeming millions of Indians all-around. This made him take a momentous decision to go first to the West and seek help for the starving people of India to give a proper shape to his life's mission. He himself has said, "I travelled all over India and it was very painful to me to see the terrible poverty and lot of the masses. I cannot hold my tears. I am now firmly convinced that it is no use going on preaching a doctrine to the unfortunate people without mitigating their suffering and poverty. It is precisely for this, for the poor suffering people of India that I am going to America."[33]

With this decision he journeyed to Rameswaram and Madurai. He then went on to Madras. Madras found Narendranath a completely changed man. The city marked, above all, his tremendous nationalistic attitude and assertions. R. Ramkrishnan has written, "Madras saw in Swami not just an eminent person or a skilled savant, but a national phenomenon."[34]

In this city of the south Narendranath's desire for visiting the West was intensified when he came to know from the newspapers, about the Parliament of Religions, that was being convened at Chicago in America. He revealed to his Madras followers his intention of attending the Parliament of Religions. His strong nationalist passions made him further convince that "unless an energy comes from across the seas, it will not be possible to shake off the lethargy of the nation of Lotus-eaters, to rouse their dormant spirit and that the medium of the

Occident is necessary to infuse life and vigour into our fossilised constitution."[35] However, Narendranath would not leave the Indian shores unless there was Divine Will behind his plan. He was not yet certain that it was the Divine Mother's will that he should go to the West. At this juncture he had a sympathetic dream in which his great Master Sri Ramkrishna walked out into the sea and beckoned him to follow. This, coupled with the blessings and permission of Sri Sarada Devi, who also, in a dream, had received Sri Ramkrishna's consent, settled the question for him and his young friends set about collecting the necessary funds. Thereafter Narendranath called upon the Maharaja of Khetri and at his suggestion assumed the name Vivekananda. The Maharaja extended the best possible help and sent his personal secretary to see off Swami Vivekananda at Bombay. Swami Vivekananda's great journey to the West commenced on 31st May, 1893, which was really an expedition for Digvijaya (conquest of the quarters) on the part of an Indian spiritual nationalist like Swami Vivekananda.[36]

(vi) On the World Stage

Swami Vivekananda's voyage to America was an exhilarating experience. He travelled to America via China, Japan and Canada. He reached Chicago at the middle of July. At Canton he saw some Buddhist monasteries. He also found there many manuscripts in Sanskrit language and the Bengali alphabet. In Japan his heart overwhelmed with admiration for her tremendous industrial progress and calmness of the people. To quote Romain Rolland, "Everywhere both in China and Japan his attention was attracted by all that might confirm his hypothesis — his conviction — alike of the religious influence of ancient India over the empires of the Far-East and of the spiritual unity of Asia. At the same time the thought of the ills from which his country was suffering never left him and the sight of the progress achieved by Japan reopened the wound."[37]

Backwardness of India was his source of agony and anxiety. He conveyed his reactions to his Madras friends. It has been said, "His epistles were really fiery shafts from the quiver of his burning passion for the redemption of the motherland."[38] When he reached Chicago, dazzling with riches and affluence, side by side with Western inventive genius, he felt bewildered like a child. He was struck with awe to see the land with its uncommon grandeur of affluence. For twelve days he filled his eager eyes with this new world. He was overwhelmed to see the valour, vitality and drive of the Westerners to explore nature. He appreciated and extolled the achievement of the West more than Gandhi, Nehru and Tagore. Romain Rolland writes, "Being of a stronger vitality and more sensitive to the appeal of forces than Tagore and Gandhi who were oppressed by the frenzy of movement and noise and by the whole European mechanism, Vivekananda was at his ease in it, least at first he succumbed to its exciting intoxication and his first feeling was of juvenile acceptance, his admiration knew no bound."[39]

On knowing that the Parliament of Religions would not open till first week of September and that none could be a delegate to it without any credential, he felt utterly disappointed, but resigning himself to the will of the Providence, he did not abandon his hope altogether. He went to Boston which was less costly than Chicago. At Boston he was acquainted with Prof. John Wright of Harvard University, who having been eclipsed before the profundity of Swami Vivekananda's scholasticism asked him to attend the Parliament of Religions at Chicago and represent his nation there. Of the Professor Swami Vivekananda himself writers, "He urged upon me the necessity of going to the Parliament of Religions, which he thought would give me an introduction to the nation."[40]

On coming to know that Swami Vivekananda was not officially accredited and had no credentials to attend the Parliament of Religions, he said, "To ask you, Swami, for your credentials is like asking the sun to state its right of shine."[41] And thereafter, the professor wrote a letter of introduction for Swami Vivekananda to the chairman of the Parliament of Religions stating therein "Here is a man, who is more learned than all our learned professors put together."[42]

The Parliament of Religions opened on 11th September, 1893. The hero now entered the fort. But he was not hero-conscious. To himself he was an obedient messenger of his Master and his motherland. He would vindicate the cause of his motherland on the world platform. He would represent nothing — no creed, no sect, no community but India as a whole. Despite all her creeds and communities India is one nation which formed his subject matter and nationalism was his motto. That is why Romain Rolland has observed, 'The man represented nothing and everything — the man belonging to no sect but rather to India as a whole."[43]

Towards the afternoon, Swami Vivekananda's turn came. It was a momentous occasion for him. As he stood up on the dais and bowed to Saraswati, the goddess of learning, there came a new force into his body. He forgot his ownself. He was not Narendra or Vivekananda, he was somebody else or something else — "The Soul of India, the echo of the Rishis, the voice of Ramkrishna, the mouthpiece of the resurgent Time-spirit."[44]

Surveying the entire assemblage with his capitvating eyes, he addressed his auidence as 'Sisters and Brothers of America.' Hardly had he uttered these five simplest words "the solemnity of his voice, frankness of his expression, sincerity and candour of his heart spelled the entire environment. 'Seven thousand people rose to their feet as a tribute to something they knew not what."[45] There was thunderous applause from the vast audience, which lasted for full two minutes. Every heart was touched and thrilled to the core. The simple monk with a begging bowl had become the man of the hour.

Dr. Barrows, the president of the Parliament said, "India, the Mother of religions was represented by Swami Vivekananda, the Orange-monk who exercised the most wonderful influence over his auditors."[46]

The *New York Herald* remarked : "Vivekananda was undoubtedly the greatest figure in the Parliament of Religions; after hearing him we feel how foolish it is to send missionaries to this learned nation."[47]

The Press remarked : "Vivekananda's culture, eloquence, and his fascinating personality have given us a new idea of civilization."[48]

Another paper remarked : "One of the most interesting personages is Professor Swami Vivekananda, a Hindu theologian of great learning, who made an address which captured the Congress, so to speak. There were bishops, and ministers of every Christian Church present and they were all taken by storm. The eloquence of the man with intellect beaming from his yellow face, his splendid English in describing the beauties of his time-honoured faith, all conspired to make a deep impression on the audience."[49]

He was hailed as a cyclonic monk and as an orator of superb talent. Life-size pictures of Swami Vivekananda adorned the streets of Chicago. It has been observed, "The great Eastern Star had illumined the West and men were in rapture. It was an hour of glory and victory of the great Hindu Sanatana Dharma, the Eternal Soul-science of India."[50]

All his subsequent speeches at the Parliament were listened to with utmost devotion and sincere appreciation. All his speeches had one common theme — universality. While all the delegates to the Parliament spoke of their own religions, Swami Vivekananda spoke of a religion that was vast as the sea and deep as the ocean, sounding the death-knell of all religious persecution and fanaticism. He stressed on religious tolerance which is the cornerstone of Hindu religion. He vindicated India before the world. While glorifying Hinduism he asserted, "No religion on earth preaches the dignity of humanity in such a lofty strain as Hinduism."[51] He boldly declared that Hindu religion is the mother of all religions, based on the Vedantic principle of love, peace, tolerance and brotherhood. He held that Vedanta is the religion of all and stressed the need of spiritual ideal of India in the West. He concluded in his final speech on the platform of the Parliament of Religions that upon the banner of every religion would soon be written — 'Help not fight, assimilation and not destruction, harmony and peace and not dissension.' Really this declaration was made as if he were a true prophet of religion which impressed the Western bent of materialism by far. The people of America discerned a new light beyond the dark hedges of sects, creeds, communities, churches and dogmas. Romain Rolland writes, "Each of other orators had spoken of his God of the God of his sect. He — he alone — spoke of all their Gods and embraced them all in the Universal

Being. It was the breath of Ramkrishna, breaking down the barriers through the mouth of his great disciple."[52]

Swami Vivekananda made hectic tour of different parts of U.S.A., England and other continental countries. Everywhere he vindicated India, glorified Hinduism with its ancient sublime culture and captivated the minds of the millions of the people in the West. His tour to England was not less renowned. "His labours in England seemed to him to be even more successful than his labours in America. He plunged into work with his accustomed zeal holding classes and giving public lectures."[53] Since England was the ruling country and India was the subject nation Swami Vivekananda left no stone unturned to convince the British people in favour of India. India's political subjection had agonised him and his heart craved for emancipation. English people were deeply moved by his activities. The London press at different times worthily eulogized him "Since the days of Raja Ram Mohan Roy, with the single exception of Kesheb Chandra Sen, there has not appeared in the English platform a more interesting Indian figure...."[54] "Swami Vivekananda the popular Hindu monk whose physiognomy bore the most striking resemblance to the classic face of Buddha, denounced our commercial prosperity, our bloody wars and our religious intolerance...."[55] "Swami Vivekananda is a striking figure. His face lights up like that of a child. It is so simple, straightforward and honest."[56]

During his stay in England he had the opportunity of a talented lady — Miss Margaret Noble, to be drawn to him, who later on came to be known as Sister Nivedita — an ardent English disciple — a staunch Indophile. He had also the pleasure of meeting Max Muller, a great Vedic savant of the West.

His preachings were "unique combination of rationalism and ancient mysticism of the doctrines of Vedas and Upanishads and the knowledge of the scientific age of spiritual values and worldly realities. It breathed a spirit of Catholicism and tolerations. Vivekananda represented ancient divine wisdom, medieval devotion and modern rationalism. He placed Hinduism on a high pedestal, resisting the onslaught of Christianity and Islam. He inspired courage, confidence, devotion, faith and national pride."[57] In the words of V.P. Varma, "The triumphant marches of Swami Vivekananda — the Hindu Napoleon in the American continent and Europe — demonstrated to the people that Hinduism had grown once more vigorous and was intent upon making a spiritual, moral and cultural philosophical propaganda in the world. The new imperialism of America and Europe met with their counter-attack from Asia."[58]

Swami Vivekananda vindicated Hindu religion before the world and Hinduism regained its old vitality. "With his preachings of Vedantism, Hinduism stepped on to a new phase of evangelism and it was called aggressive Hinduism by Sister Nivedita."[59] His militant presentation of Hindu thought and his courageous proclamation that 'Vedanta is the religion for all' gave the Hindus a sense of pride in their religion. He was the first to interpret living Hinduism in all its aspects to the civilized world in a way which immediately brought recognition to its greatness. His bold proclamation before the world in support of the superiority of the sublime Hindu culture and civilization infused a refreshing boldness and consciousness of inherent strength among the Hindus, whose attitude was then characterized with a tone of apology and inferiority towards Western culture and civilization. He raised India to the eyes of the world and therefore is called, the 'Patriot saint of India'.

In fact Swami Vivekananda's appearance on the world scenario ushered in a new era in the history of evolution of Hindu culture. It marked the beginning of the waking up of India from the stupor and stagnation into which it had fallen for centuries together. The whole of India in the long run awoke to a mystical height and there came the consciousness of its superior identity and worth as a nation and its importance in the comity of nations. His success in the West as the exponent of the spiritual message of India was a surprising shock to the detractors of Indian cultural and a stimulating leaven to its enthusiastic protagonist. India, it was felt, was not certainly face to face with its cultural doom when a pure and authentic exponent of it could draw so much of acclamation at the hands of the races that dominated the world at a time. It resulted in the resuscitation of the national sense of self-respect.[60]

After a long period of strenuous campaign in the West Swami Vivekananda heard his beloved motherland calling him. India had always been the soul of Vivekananda's life, the queen of adoration as described by Sister Nivedita. When he left for India he was overwhelmed with the love for his motherland as a child feels on returning to the lap of its mother after a long separation. To a Western friend who asked him about his feelings in regard to India after his experience in the West, he said, "India I loved before as I came away (to the West). Now the very dust of India has become very holy to me. The very air is now to me very holy, it is now the holy land, the place of pilgrimage, the Tirtha."[61] Surely was Swami Vivekananda a paragon among the patriots, whose love for his motherland was extraordinary.

(vii) Triumphal Return — The Climax of the Evolution of His Nationalist Personality

When Swami Vivekananda came back India gave him the honour of an unprecedented magnitude. His roaring success in the West was matter of intense pride and gratification for every Indian. People throughout the country were afire with overwhelming enthusiasm. He was no more an unknown sannyasin. In every city, big or small, committees were formed to give him grand ovation. An Indian Newspaper reported, "Swami Vivekananda left India a pauper and returned a prince. We refer not to material resources but to popular esteem."[62]

As a matter of fact when he came back to India he was received with grand ovation. The welcome took almost the dimension of a mass movement. His glorious return after the great conquest of the West represented a national revival and heralded a new phase of nationalism. After the establishment of British power in India this was a major stirring of the spirit of nationalism, which sustained its tempo till India's independence in 1947. As Romain Rolland has observed, the Swami replied to the frenzied expectancy of the people by his message to India, a conch sounding the resurrection of the land of Ram, of Siva, of Karna and calling the heroic spirit, the immortal *atman* to march to war. He was a general, explaining his plan of campaign and calling his people to arise and *en masse*, "My India arise! Where is your vital force? In your immortal soul."[63]

It was after his heroic return from the West that Swami Vivekananda's spirit of nationalism reached the zenith of excellence. It assumed the shape of wild fire. It influenced the mass as magic spell. He gave a clarion call to the nation which had been debased to political serfdom and economic stagnation, that "suddenly realized that it had not to bend its head down in shame, inferiority and defeatism but that it could hold up its head in legitimate pride and absolute confidence."[64] He had wiped off from India's forehead every mark of despair and anguish. He kindled a new zeal and fervour for struggle for freedom in every corner of India.

Ceylon had the honour of first receiving the triumphant hero as the prophet of Indian nationalism on January 15, 1897. None but Swami Vivekananda knew better the beat of India's pulse. He knew that the Indian genius had its roots in spiritualism and he had the capacity to awake it. He had told to a friend in the West "India must listen to me. I shall shake India to her foundation. I shall send an electric thrill through her national veins. India will receive me in triumphs."[65]

Swami Vivekananda's idea of nationalism fully manifested itself in the lectures he delivered in reply to the addresses of welcome that were presented to him on his return to India, when he travelled from Colombo to Almora and Punjab to Kashmir. These lectures are the "perennial source of patriotic inspiration scintillating with the greatest spiritual ideal of the nation."[66] These lectures have been embodied in a volume — 'Lectures From Colombo at Almora'. These lectures are really unique in respect of the fact that they are only lectures, Swami Vivekananda delivered on Indian soil, while all the rest, dealing with various aspects of Vedanta, were delivered from world platforms in America and England. Therefore it is in these lectures that we come across Vivekananda's nationalistic fervour and realize the way in which his spiritual ideology shaped his nationalistic zeal. These lectures show how Swami Vivekananda was convinced that emancipation of the masses and the removal of their misery and suffering were impossible without the attainment of freedom and nationhood by India. Hence, his spiritual philosophy had a deeply nationalistic dimension.

In fact Swami Vivekananda's lectures from 'Colombo to Almora' was an encomium on nationalism, which will exhilarate the Indians for all times to come. It is a perennial source of inspiration to awake and arise and acquire national identity — its unity and solidarity. Hence, it is said, 'The lectures from Colombo to Almora is the Gita of the present day, meant to rouse millions of Tamosic Arjunas to hard work and pussiant vigour.'[67]

In the first speech at Colombo Swami Vivekananda's nationalistic persionality reached its apex. He attributed his grand success in the West to the cheers and goodwill of his motherland. He said that the idea that his motherland is a sacred place — a Punnya Bhumi — was a traditional belief in him, but having seen the world at large and the life of the people in other parts of the world, what was a mere belief in him had become a firm conviction.[68] Recalling the glory and spiritual nationalism of India he said, "If there is any land on this earth that lay claim to be the blessed Punnya Bhumi, to be the land to which souls on this earth must come to account for Karma, the land to which every soul that is wending its way Godward must come to attain its last home, the land where humanity has attained its highest towards gentleness, towards generosity, towards purity, towards calmness, above all, the land of introspection and of spirituality — it is India."[69] He stated that in the past from here had proceeded great ideas of religions and spirituality to all the surrounding countries and in future too, the waves that would spiritualise the materialistic civilization and quench the burning fire of the materialism in other parts of the world, was to originate in India.

To Swami Vivekananda, Indian nationalism is divine in inspiration and spirit although he talked of Hindu nationalism. In highlighting the divine aspect of our national-life he said, "...there is not one race on this earth to which the world owes so much as to the patient Hindu, the mild Hindu. 'The mild Hindu' sometimes is used as an expression of reproach but if ever a reproach concealed a wonderful truth, it is in the term 'the mild Hindu' who has always been the blessed child of God."[70] However, Swami Vivekananda meant by Hindu something different from what is normally meant by Hindu-people of a particular religious persuasion.

Ours is a multi-religious country. This diversity of religion has severely told upon the national solidarity, for which India has suffered a lot. To achieve unity among the people of various sects and faiths and to bridge the gulf of invidious communal distinction, Swami Vivekananda interpreted the word 'Hindu' in its original form and explained its original application. As he said, "The word 'Hindu' by which it is the fashion nowadays to style ourselves, has lost all its meaning, for this word merely meant, those who lived on the other side of the river 'Indus' (in Sanskrit the Sindhu). This name was murdered into 'Hindu' by the ancient Persians and all people living on the other side of the river Sindhu were called by them Hindus. Thus this word has come down to us and during the Mohammedan rule we took up the word ourselves. There may not be harm in using the word of course but as I have said it has lost its significance, for, you may mark that all the people who live on the other side of the Indus in modern times, do not follow the same religion as they did in ancient times. The word therefore covers not only Hindu proper, but Mohammedans, Christians, Jains and other people who live in India. I, therefore, would not use the word Hindu. What word we should use then? The other words which alone we can use are either Vaidikas — the followers of Vedas or better still Vedantists — the followers of Vedanta."[71]

Explaining the cause of India's survival in the world Swami Vivekananda said that great ideas have spread from several ancient people like the Greeks, the Romans, the Persians etc. as also from modern nations. But it was as a camp follower of their conquering armies that the ideas contributed by them had penetrated into different nations. But India had never been a conquering race, carrying fire and sword to helpless people, vanquished in war. Therefore India has survived as a nation in the world during these several millennia in spite of foreign conquest and subjections, while those nations, depending on military might had passed away long ago after a short period of meteoric existence of exultant and exhuberant dominance of a wicked national life.[72]

In his subsequent speeches Swami Vivekananda exhorted Indians to recollect their spiritual heritage and not to condemn their social and cultural past and not take to a life of imitation of the West. India has a glorious heritage. In religion and philosophy it had been the teacher of the world all through the ages. Even today India has retained her genius in this respect. Revival of spirituality has always been the prelude to the revival of culture and political life in India. For, "Spirituality is the soul of India. Its enhancement has always been the sure way to greatness and its erosion, the way to national suicide."[73]

Swami Vivekananda convinced the people that Hinduism had maintained its vitality through its capacity for absorption. It has been aggressive now and then, but its fundamental attitude was one of incorporation of the best elements of the system and forces it had to encounter. The secrets of its longevity lay in its catholic and constructive capacity for absorption. He said, "We must grow according to our nature. Vain is to attempt the lines of action that foreign societies have engrafted upon us, it is impossible, glory unto God that it is impossible, that we cannot be twisted and tortured in the shape of other nations. I do not condemn the institution of other races; they are good for them but not for us."[74]

From his study of the world history Swami Vivekananda expounded a theory regarding the survival of the nations and he applied it to explain the cause of India's survival in spite of all the disasters that threatened to destroy it. He said that human history shows that every nation has to make a contribution of its own in a chosen field for the general advancement of humanity and that when it ceases to do so it decays and dies. "Nature effaces it off to make way for more vigorous and younger races to take up the role. It is a natural practice to get rid of an atrophied part of an organism and let others to take up its function."[75] There had been great nations in the past — the Egyptians, the Babylonians, the Persians, the Greek and the Romans etc., whose civilization were contemporaneous with that of India but they have all disappeared from the face of the earth and the regions where they flourished are occupied by people whose culture and national history have no continuity with those of these ancient people. The reason for it, according to Swami Vivekananda is the fact that they ceased to fulfil their national purpose which were mostly political, social, military etc. After short periods of national life they lost their hold on the national theme which made them great and this led to their gradual decay and ultimate destruction at the hands of the more vigorous people.

India also had her national theme through the whole of its history, the beginning of which is beyond the capacity of man to know. That theme of India's specialization was spiritualism, which meant the adoption of a way of life that led to an immediate perception of the truth of the Atma and of God even in this embodied state. All through her history in spite of foreign invasions and subjections India had been producing man with spiritual insight and from this country had gone forth waves of movements that had brought spiritual light to the nations of the world.[76]

Swami Vivekananda stressed that even today India retains this capacity. It was during the early days of British occupation, when India was threatened with cultural effacement at the hands of the victorious West that a great spiritual personality was born in the person of Sri Ramkrishna. Thus in spite of political subjection and economic impoverishment India has all through the ages been keeping herself alive as a nation. The moment India abandoned its spiritual ideal — acceptance of spiritual essence in man and the world as the goal of human life — its national life was threatened with imminent extinction. "Therefore my friends," he said, "the way out is that first and foremost we must keep a firm hold on spirituality, that inestimable gift, handed down to us by our ancient forefathers.... Therefore whether you believe in spirituality or not, for the sake of national life you have to get a hold on spirituality and keep to it. Then stretch the other hand out and gain all you can from other races, but everything must be subordinated to that one ideal of life and out of that a wonderful glorious future India will come. I am sure it is coming — a great India than ever was."[77]

Swami Vivekananda's speeches had tremendous influence upon the mind of the people. It inculcated a Hindu feeling of nationalism among the people. 'His wonderful speeches as a divine orator and a defender of religion of his people,' wrote Bipin Chandra Pal, 'had an immediate warm response in India, inspiring the national consciousness, shaping in us and giving it new strength.'[78]

Swami Vivekananda warned the Indians to steer their nationalship very carefully between the two sources of dangers — the scylla of Western materialism and the charybdis of Eastern obscurantism. Spirituality is the cultivation of the great ideals taught in the Gita and Upanishads in such a way that they are reflected in our individual and national life. The practice of village customs, caste rules, don't-touchism, irrational usages in eating and drinking — these have nothing to do with spirituality. They do not represent the eternal values. Too much insistence on these externals to the detriment of real and eternal spiritual principles expounded in the Gita and the Upanishads had been the main baneful influence that had vitiated the life of the people. When Vivekananda exhorted the people to retain their hold on our spiritual ideals he did not ask them to relapse into this nightmare of social and religious obscurantism, but to be forward-looking and to go ahead without forgetting the great teachings of the Gita and Upanishads. To quote Sister Nivedita, "To his mind Hinduism was not to remain a stationary system, but to prove herself capable of embracing and welcoming the whole modern development."[79]

Swami Vivekananda said that we have to learn plenty of things from the West in the fields of organisation, science, politics and technology for the uplift of our social and economic conditions. Our deficiency in these respects was largely the result of the mania for exclusiveness and avoidance of contact with external world that crept into the soul of the nation sometimes back in its history. When the world marched forward with science and technology India remained smug in its own shell, glorifying itself in its don't-touchism, caste-obsession and kitchen religion. This kind of orthodoxy should go and India shall acquire the progressive spirit of the West without losing its moorings in the Gita and Upanishads. However, progressivism must be informed and directed by sensitiveness to spiritual values. Only then a wonderful glorious future India would come — an India greater than ever she was. As Dr. Radhakrishnan has said, "No religion can hope to survive if it does not satisfy the scientific temper of our age, sympathise with its social aspiration and faster the unity of the world."[80]

Swami Vivekananda was a great optimist. He waited for the day when the mighty minds would arise and go forth from India to the ends of the world to teach spirituality and renunciation — those ideas, which had come from the forests of India and belonged to the soil of India alone.

Swami Vivekananda criticized the Indian National Congress of those days because it did not make any positive and constructive efforts for the betterment of the lot of the masses. In an interview Ashwini Kumar Datta asked him, "But have you no faith in what Congress is doing?" Swami Vivekananda said, "No, I have not, but, of course, something is better than nothing, and it is good to push the sleeping nation from all sides to wake it up. Can you tell me what the Congress has been doing for the masses? Do you think merely passing a few resolutions will bring you freedom? I have no faith in that. The masses must be awakened first. Let them have full meals and they will work out their own salvation. If Congress does anything for them, it has my sympathy."[81]

Swami Vivekananda popularised the concept of freedom among the people. However, he identified political freedom, with spiritual freedom. He said that political freedom precedes spiritual freedom. He was a devout worhipper at the shrine of individual freedom. He decleared, "Liberty of thought and action is the only condition of life, growth and well being; where it does not exist the man, the race and the nation must go down; any clan or caste or nation or institution which bars the power of free thought and action of an individual, so long as it does not injure other, is devilish and must go down."[82] It has been observed, "Swami Vivekananda's heroic soul always yearned for freedom. Although primarily, he taught the concept of spiritual freedom, this gospel was bound to result in the popularization of other aspects of freedom, including the political freedom as well. Some of the terrorists and nationalists of Bengal learnt the value and sanctity of freedom from his poem — Songs of the Sannyasin."[83]

Along with individual freedom Swami Vivekananda also stressed the need of equality of all men. To him inequality stands as the greatest bar for the promotion of brotherhood among all men. So he voiced his great concern against all inequalities — social, political and economic, that shatter the unity of human society. Therefore Manomohan Ganguly writes, "Swami Vivekananda, always in thought and action strove hard to build the superstructure of India's salvation in which will reign for ever, Equality, Fraternity and Liberty."[84]

Emerson, a Western mystic voiced his doctrine of 'Shakti' when he said, "The world always to the energetic."[85] Like him Swami Vivekananda said, "What the world wants today is heroic men and women...."[86] Thus with the concept of liberty, equality and fraternity, Swami Vivekananda also propounded his theory of strength and fearlessness that received enormous support from all corners of the society. It appealed to them so much that the people accepted it as their creed without a least of hesitation. He stated that we have been degraded only because of the fact that we have lost our faith in ourselves. We have become very soft and weak. That is why a handful of foreigners had ruled over millions of us for centuries and we had succumbed to servitude and serfdom. They had commanded us only because they had tremendous faith in themselves. In the national minds of Europe there flows tremendous stream of man's faith in themselves. They had reduced us to the level of hewers of wood and drawers of water for centuries. But now we must awake and arise to resist it. We had a gigantic strength in ourselves. "What our country wants", said Swami Vivekananda, "are muscles of iron and nerves of steel, gigantic will which nothing can resist, which can penetrate into mysteries and secrets of the universe and will accomplish their purpose in any fashion even if it meant going down to bottom of the ocean and meeting death face to face."[87]

Swami Vivekananda asked his country men to be bold and fearless and not to yield to weakness of any sort. To him weakness is the bitterest enemy of man. This weakness can be overcome by the cultivation of strength and not by brooding over weakness. Since man is the son of God — spark of Absolute Brahma, the source of all strength and power, he can never be weak. It is only delusion that makes him weak. This false fear will vanish if we put our faith in the Upanishads. Vedanta is the source of all strength, the store-house of all power. "If there is one word that you find coming like a bomb from the Upanishads, bursting like a bombshell upon mass of ignorance, it is the word, fearlessness."[88] If a man shakes off his fear and awakes to his height he can come to know himself and his enormous strength. Weakness leads to misery. It is the cause of slavery and suffering. As he said, "Strength is life, weakness is death. Strength is felicity, life is eternal, immortal. Weakness is constant strain and misery, weakness is death."[89] He further said that unless every Indian puts up courage and fearlessness, India cannot achieve any success. Success comes to acting and daring man. Courage, confidence and will power is the only key to success and man has a world of success to achieve.

Swami Vivekananda also advocated his theory of struggle and resistance. Explaining this theory he said, "Life is the unfoldment and development of a being under circumstances, tending to press it down."[90] So to him, life is nothing but struggle — struggle against all adverse circumstances that puts an end to all miseries in life. This theory of struggle and resistance began to gain the ground among the Indian masses and provided an impetus to national struggle for freedom.

Swami Vivekananda encouraged the Indians in the midst of all national hazards and hurdles and asked them not to be disheartened. He infused new hopes and aspirations into the hearts of his country men by saying, "It is same India, which has withstood the shocks of centuries of hundreds of foreign invasions, of hundreds of upheavals of manners and customs. It is the same land which stands firmer than any rock in the world with its undying vigour, indestructible life. Its life is of the same nature as the soul without beginning and without end, immortal and we are the children of such a country."[91]

Swami Vivekananda said that the then prevailing predicament of India should not upset the people. It was not a curse rather a boon in disguise, which presaged the emergence of a new India with new life and hope. "A mighty tree produces a beautiful ripe fruit. That fruit falls on the ground. It decays and rots and out of that decay springs the root and the future tree perhaps mightier than the first one. This period of decay through which India have passed was all the more necessary. Out of this decay would emerge the new India of the future, it is sprouting, its first leaves are already out and a mighty gigantic tree, the Urdhamula, is here, already beginning to appear and it is about that that I am going to speak to you."[92]

The problems of our country according to Swami Vivekananda are more complicated than those of any other country. "Here there are people of diverse races, speaking different language, following manners and customs of utmost diversity. The only common ground that we have, according to Swami Vivekananda, is our sound traditions — our religion. There must be therefore, the recognition of one religion throughout the length and breadth of the country. People must be aware of those common grounds in the first place. All these diversity of race, religion and manners would melt away before the unifying power of religion. Unification of religion, therefore, is the initial step for the building up of future of Indian nation. In Europe political ideas form the basis of national unity. In Asia religious ideals form the basis of national unity. The unity in religion, therefore, is absolutely necessary as the first condition of the future of India."[93]

To Swami Vivekananda this unity of religion is not a very difficult job. It is rather very easy if the people would be made to understand the true end of religion. Whatever may be the religion, its ultimate end is to lead man to salvation. A man, to whichever religion he may belong, his ultimate aim is salvation or reunion with God. As he said, "The ultimate goal of all mankind, the aim and end of all religions, is but one — reunion with God, or, what amounts to the same, with the divinity, which is every man's nature."[94] As he further said, "The ideal of all religions, all sects, is the same — the attaining of liberty or salvation, the cessation of misery."[95]

For further conviction of the people Swami Vivekananda

held that religions may be different but same truth and same God reigns in the heart of all religions. As he said, "One Light shines in all; One Light comes through glasses of different colours; One Truth reigns in the heart of all religions; One Truth is expressed in different languages by different religions."[96]

The aim of Swami Vivekananda was to build up a new progressive India out of the debris of superstitions and ignorance that enveloped her. Unless the masses are free from the encircling gloom of ignorance they cannot discern the new light of life in the horizon. Education is the light that dispels the gloom far off and makes life conducive to novelty and newness of thought. It inculcates new strength of character among the people and induces one to be strong and self-reliant. "We want that education by which character is formed, strengthen of mind is increased, the intellect is expanded and by which one can stand on one's own feet."[97]

Swami Vivekananda said that the glory of India was ebbing away, culture decaying not because of her inferiority of intellect nor of dexterity. The chief cause of her extinction was hypnotism that had gripped her. "All that is needed is that she should dehypnotise herself and wake up from her age-long sleep to take her true rank in the hierarchy of nations.... The national ideals of India are renunciation and service. Intensify her in those channels and the rest will take care of itself."[98]

According to Swami Vivekananda the flame of our nationalism had not died down. It was still flickering in the tempestuous horizon. All the stresses and storms of our national life had not put down the flame. It had survived all the trials and tribulations. "Hidden under the ashes of apparent death, the fire of our national life is yet smouldering."[99] Swami Vivekananda's stirring speeches and writings set the minds of the common people ablaze with nationalistic feelings. They saw beyond the century-long dark clouds of lethargy and stagnation a great future beckoning them.

To Swami Vivekananda, India looked like a big dilapidated building and at first sight one would feel that there was no hope for India. But a nation would not be destroyed until the essential principle for which it had stood through the ages was destroyed.

It was just like a man, not ceasing to function even if his coat had been stolen away twenty times, because the coat was unessential. India had been invaded by several races and it had been despoiled of its wealth. But the soul of India had not yet been seriously affected. Its soul consisted in religion. There would be no more India if the people changed their religion and their institutions, because that was the vitality of that race.

Swami Vivekananda said, "In spite of poverty and loss of freedom India is holding fast to the idea that the real is God and everything else is but His shadow. She clings to this like a grim death."[100] So India was still living and like a patient who kept up his vitality amidst a crippling illness she had still hopes of a resurrection from her present state of downfall and degeneration.

The uplift of India was to be attempted through vitalizing her religious life which formed the soul of the nation. But there was no reason why India should necessarily be poverty-stricken. An ascetic ideal should not be imposed for the benefit of a few sages. That would be 'Tyranny of the sages'. This had to change. Along with spiritual administration steps were to be taken for improving the material condition of life as well.

Swami Vivekananda's nationalism aimed at all-round development of the nation. Spiritual progress is incomplete without material development. So he stressed the need of developing the resources of the country and utilizing them properly. For this purpose he said that Western scientific and technical method should be acquired. As Manomohan Ganguly has remarked, "We have often found the Swamiji to impress upon his countrymen the necessity of developing the resources of the country; he expressed the desire to give effect to it by sending youngmen to Japan and America for technical education."[101] He also put emphasis on the industrial development of the country. "Like Tilak and other Indian nationalist of the late 19th century and early 20th century, Swami Vivekananda saw that colonialism was retarding the economic and particularly industrial development of the country. Therefore visualizing real patriotism in tireless work on development of its industry, science and education,"[102] Swami Vivekananda wrote that 'one must not depend on any foreign help. Nation like individual, must help themselves. This is real patriotism. If a nation cannot do that its time has not yet come. It must wait...the new light must spread all over India. With this end...(we) must work."[103]

Thus, though Swami Vivekananda was a monk in yellow robe, he turned out to be a nationalist of high order. It is evident from his speeches and writings. Love for his country formed the very philosophy of his life. In all his speeches and writings, he espoused the cause of India, her religion, her culture, her civilization. In fact he was the champion of Indian spiritual nationalism. His speeches and writings had tremendous effect, "which apparently without his knowledge fell in so many cases like seed upon soil prepared for it and have sprung up already in widely distant parts of India into hearts and lives of devotion to the motherland."[104]

Swami Vivekananda did not openly advocate the cause of India's freedom. That was partly due to the fact that he was a sannyasin — a dedicated monk and he did not like to get himself entangled in political and legal controversies. Another reason was that Swami Vivekananda wanted to devote his whole time and energy to the cause of the emancipation and uplift of the poor and downtrodden. That is why he did not join the body politics of the country, whereby he would have been certainly arrested and put in prison by the British power.

Swami Vivekananda not only travelled abroad and delivered stirring speeches to make the Indian masses arise and awake to achieve the nationalistic goal, he also organized the Ramkrishna Mission, which could carry out his plan of action and uplift his country and help in the act of nation-building.[105] He first established two principal centres — one near Calcutta and another at Mayabati near Almora, where youngmen, who jointed the Ramkrishna Mission were trained as sannyasins (Renouncers of the worldly life) for religion and social welfare work. Thus an ancient and venerable institution came to be utilized for national service. The monks of the mission lived a life of dedication, engaging themselves in active service of the society and alleviating the suffering of the downtrodden. Besides, he started two papers — The Monthly, 'Prabudha Bharata' in

English and 'Udbodhana' a Bengali fortnightly. His treatises and lectures were published in several volumes. The result was the tremendous spread and progress of the Ramkrishna movement all over the country, contributing for the synthesis and harmony among the various faiths and cults, denouncing poverty and superstitions, encouraging mass education and inspiring the people for national emancipation. As R.C. Muzumdar writes, "He (Swami Vivekananda) wanted to carry into practice what he had so long preached by making the workers devote themselves an active life of service for the masses and thus to make the monastic organisation a potent instrument for social and national regeneration, by spreading education among the illiterate, helping them fight against poverty and disease, removing the social evils and inequities and raising them to a higher level of morality."[106] As Dr. V.K.R.V. Rao has also remarked, "Ramkrishna Mission is Vivekananda's greatest political contribution to the building up of 'New India'."[107]

REFERENCES

1. M.N. Das, *Indian National Congress Vs. The British*, Vol. I, p. vii.
2. *Ibid.*, p. xv.
3. B.N. Luniya, *Evolution of Indian Culture*, p. 483.
4. Prof. Hiren Mukerjee, *Vivekananda and Indian Freedom*, p. 10.
5. V.P. Varma, *Modern Indian Political Thought*, p. 10.
6. Described by I.P. Chelishev in the preface of *Swami Vivekananda — Studies in Soviet Union*, p. xiii.
7. Dr. Karan Singh, *The Prophet of Indian Nationalism*, p. 19.
8. Sister Nivedita, *The Master As I Saw Him*, p. 199.
9. V.K.R.V. Rao, *Swami Vivekananda*, p. 8.
10. *A Short Life of Swami Vivekananda*, Advaita Ashram, p. 11.
11. Swami Nikhilananda, *A Biography of Vivekananda*, p. 11.
12. Swami Budhananda, *Vivekananda — His Call to the Nation*, p. 2.
13. R. Ramkrishnan, *Swami Vivekananda, Awakener of Modern India*, p. 5.
14. Swami Budhananda, *Vivekananda — His Call to the Nation*, p. 3.
15. Romain Rolland, *Life of Ramkrishna*, p. 242.
16. Quoted in Romain Rolland, *Life of Ramkrishna*, pp. 241-42.

17. Swami Budhananda, *Vivekananda — His Call to the Nation*, p. 4.
18. Quoted in *Swami Vivekananda — His Call to the Nation* by Swami Budhananda, p. 5.
19. Quoted in V.K.R.V. Rao, *Swami Vivekananda*, p. 45.
20. *A Short Life of Swami Vivekananda*, Advaita Ashram, p. 25.
21. *Ibid.*, p. 25.
22. Romain Rolland, *The Life of Ramkrishna*, pp. 28-29.
23. Quoted in V.K.R.V. Rao, *Swami Vivekananda*, p. 37.
24. Swami Nikhilananda, *Biography of Swami Vivekananda*, p. 73.
25. Swami Budhananda, *Vivekananda — His Call to the Nation*, p. 7.
26. S.N. Dhaban, *Comprehensive Biography of Swami Vivekananda*, Part II, p. 287.
27. Quoted in Swami Budhananda, *Vivekananda — His Call to the Nation*, p. 8.
28. Romain Rolland, *Life of Swami Vivekananda and the Universal Gospel*, p. 26.
29. V.K.R.V. Rao, *Swami Vivekananda*, pp. 67-68.
30. Swami Budhananda, *Vivekananda — His Call to the Nation*, p. 10.
31. Dr. Tara Chand Mishra, *History of Freedom Movement in India*, Vol. II, p. 259.
32. Quoted in R. Ramkrishnan, *Vivekananda — Awakener of Modern India*, p. 50.
33. Quoted in 'Swami Vivekananda — Studies in Soviet Union', Article — *Ideals of Enlightenment*, p. 148.
34. R. Ramkrishnan, *Swami Vivekananda — Awakener of Modern India*, p. 50.
35. Manomohan Ganguly, *Swami Vivekananda — A Study*, p. 36.
36. R. Ramkrishnan, *Swami Vivekananda — Awakener of Modern India*, p. 52.
37. Romain Rolland, *Life of Swami Vivekananda*, p. 32.
38. R. Ramkrishnan, *Swami Vivekananda — Awakener of Modern India*, p. 54.
39. Romain Rolland, *Life of Swami Vivekananda*, p. 34.
40. Manomohan Ganguly, *Swami Vivekananda — A Study*, p. 39.
41. R. Ramkrishnan, *Swami Vivekananda, Awakener of Modern India*, p. 56.
42. Swami Budhananda, *Vivekananda — His Call to the Nation*, p. 12.

43. Romain Rolland, *The Life of Swami Vivekananda and the Universal Gospel*, p. 37.
44. R. Ramkrishnan, *Swami Vivekananda — Awakener of Modern India*, p. 57.
45. Swami Budhananda, *Vivekananda — His Call to the Nation*, p. 14.
46. Culled from Manomohan Gangualy, Swami Vivekananda — A Study, p. 40.
47. Culled from R. Ramkrishnan, *Swami Vivekananda — Awalener of Modern India*, p. 59.
48. Culled from Manomohan Ganguly, *Swami Vivekananda — A Study*, p. 40.
49. *Ibid.*, p. 40.
50. R. Ramkrishnan, *Swami Vivekananda -— Awakener of Modern India*, p. 60.
51. Romain Rolland, *The Life of Vivekananda and the Universal Gospel*, p. 70.
52. Collection of Essays, Edited by J.M. Mohanty, Cal., 1990, Topic : *A Great Journey to the West by Romain Rolland*, p. 58.
53. R. Ramkrishnan, *Swami Vivekananda — Awakener of Modern India*, p. 64.
54. Quoted in R. Ramkrishnan, *Swami Vivekananda — Awakener of Modern India*, p. 64.
55. *Ibid.*, 64-65.
56. *Ibid.*, p. 65.
57. B.N. Luniya, *Evolution of Indian Culture*, p. 494.
58. V.P. Varma, *Modern Indian Political Thought*, p. 617.
59. B.N. Luniya, *Evolution of Indian Culture*, p. 494.
60. Swami Tapasyananda, *Nationalistic and Religious Lectures of Swami Vivekananda*, p. vii.
61. Quoted in R. Ramkrishnan, *Swami Vivekananda — Awakener of Modern India*, p. 71.
62. *The Indian Nation, 1817*, Vivekananda in Indian Newspapers, p. 357.
63. Quoted in Swami Budhananda, *Vivekananda — His Call to the Nation*, p. 16.
64. R. Ramkrishnan, *Swami Vivekananda — Awakener of Modern India*, p. 72.
65. Quoted in R. Ramkrishnan, *Swami Vivekananda — Awakener of Modern India*, p. 73.

66. Swami Tapasyananda, *Nationalistic and Religious Lectures of Swami Vivekananda*, p. viii.
67. V.P. Varma, *Modern Indian Political Thought*, p. 642.
68. Swami Tapasyananda, *Nationalistic and Religious Lectures of Swami Vivekananda*, p. 12.
69. Swami Vivekananda, *Lectures From Colombo to Almora*, p. 3.
70. *Ibid.*, p. 3.
71. *Ibid.*, p. 17.
72. Swami Tapasyananda, *Nationalistic and Religious Lectures of Swami Vivekananda*, p. 12-13.
73. *Ibid.*, p. viii.
74. Swami Vivekananda, *India and Her Problems*, pp. 102-3.
75. Swami Tapasyananda, *Nationalistic and Religious Lectures of Swami Vivekananda*, p. viii.
76. *Ibid.*, p. ix.
77. Swami Vivekananda, *Lectures From Colombo to Almora*, p. 54.
78. B.C. Pal, *Memoirs of My Life and Time*, Vol. 2, pp. 274-75.
79. Sister Nivedita, *The Master as I Saw Him*, p. 199.
80. Dr. S. Radhakrishnan, *Recovery of Faith*, p. 15.
81. *Life of Swami Vivekananda*, Vol. II, Advaita Ashram, pp. 698-99.
82. Manomohan Ganguly, *Swami Vivekananda — A Study*, pp. 69-70.
83. V.P. Varma, *Modern Indian Political Throught*, p. 101.
84. Manomohan Ganguly, *Swami Vivekananda — A Study*, p. 72.
85. Quoted in T.L. Vaswani, *The Voice of Vivekananda*, p. 7.
86. *Ibid.*, pp. 7-8.
87. Swami Vivekananda, *Lectures From Colombo to Almora*, p. 92.
88. *Complete Works of Swami Vivekananda*, Vol. III, p. 267.
89. *Ibid.*, Vol. II, p. 3.
90. Quoted in Swami Gambhirananda, *A Short Life of Swami Vivekananda*, p. 119.
91. Swami Vivekananda, *Lectures From Colombo to Almora*, p. 194.
92. *Ibid.*, p. 95.
93. *Ibid.*, p. 196.
94. Quoted in Swami Gambhirananda, *A Short Life of Swami Vivekananda*, p. 116.
95. *Ibid.*

96. Quoted in T.L. Vaswani, *Voice of Vivekananda*, p. 60.
97. *Complete Works of Swami Vivekananda*, Vol. V, p. 342.
98. *Ibid.*, Vol. V, pp. 227-28.
99. *Ibid.*, p. 461.
100. *Complete Works of Swami Vivekananda*, Vol. VIII, p. 73.
101. Manomohan Ganguly, *Swami Vivekananda — A Study*, p. 64.
102. I.P. Chelishev, *Swami Vivekananda — Studies in Soviet Union*, Published on 150th British anniversary of Sri Ramkrishna, p. 53.
103. *Complete Works of Swami Vivekananda*, Vol. V, p. 83.
104. Sister Nivedita, *The Master as I Saw Him*, p. 199.
105. B.N. Luniya, *Evolution of Indian Culture*, p. 493.
106. R.C. Muzumdar, *Swami Vivekananda — A Historical Review*, p. 66.
107. V.K.R.V. Rao, *Swami Vivekananda — The Prophet of Vedantic Socialism*, p. 248.

2

Basis of Swami Vivekananda's Nationalism

History is replete with the phenomena of the rise and fall of the nations. Different nations came into existence and dazzled the world in soaring high like an eagle in the firmament of glory and prosperity, but in the twinkle of an eye they have burst like the bubbles in the ocean of events of history and passed into oblivion. History only records their meteoric rise and meteoric fall. In this process of rise and fall, the great Greek and Roman nations, whose civilization and culture once reached and highest pinnacle of glory, have been effaced from the surface of the earth. The most obvious reason of such effacement is that they failed to cope with the changing needs of the time.

Every nation, of course, has to wade through such ordeals of misfortune. But if it manages to pass through the ordeals successfully, it survives on the earth. Tagore the great nationalist poet has observed, "...difficulties have been different in different peoples of the earth, and in the manner of our overcoming them lies our distinction."[1] This distinction, is the distinctions of nationalism — the common sentiment or instinct that integrates the individuals into a coherent whole — a nation. Nationalism in order to achieve such distinction must conform to the canons of higher social life. So if nationalism fails to cope with those canons, it invites ruin. As it has been observed, "When this organisation of politics and commerce, whose other name is nation, becomes all powerful at the cost of the harmony of the higher social life, then it is a evil day for the humanity."[2] So nationalism in order to promote a higher social life among its people must have sound bases. A well-based nationalism is not to crumble. The mighty edifice of nationalism stands firm for all times in spite of severe quakes and tremors, if its bases are strong and concretised, gone deep into the national character. The events of recent past bears out the truth of this fact. The Fascist nationalism, which was based on the vain glory of military conquest and territorial aggrandisement, crumbled like a house of cards after an ephemeral existence, paving the path for the greatest catastrophe that has ever gripped the earth in the history of modern world.

Nationalism as a Western concept has developed on the background of materialism. It is based on common geographical background, common historical background, common culture, common race, common religion, common language, common political aspiration etc. But the theory of nationalism as chalked out by Swami Vivekananda, a great mystic and philanthropist, is based on values that are non-materialistic in nature. It visualises the basis which conforms to the canons of higher social life, that have permanent appeal and value for the whole mankind. Though it owes a lot to the Western basis of nationalism, unlike the Western concept of nationalism it directs the whole mankind towards effulgence and light of divine order. Such values shall sustain their appeal for the mankind to reach its goal till the sun continues to shine in the Eastern horizon and the moon in the West.

(i) Religious Basis

Swami Vivekananda was an advocate of a strongly built and homogeniously organised viable nation. However, not a politician by profession or connection he was not concerned with the political aspect of a nation and least of its political agitation. As he made it amply clear, "Nothing I say or write should be given any political interpretation; I do not wish to have anything to do with political follies, I do not believe in any politics."[3] But he called upon his country men to build up a strong, progressive and dynamic nation with religion as the keynote of the whole music of national life in India. Religion is the life-blood of every people of India. It is the most integral part of our life. It tingles in every drop of our blood that runs through our veins. It has become the nature and habit of the people of India. It is the trait of our national character. Our great nationalism lies in it. The Hindus can withstand all sorts of persecutions upon them but when it hits upon their religion, that constitutes their national sentiment, they become most formidable.

Bertrand Russell has observed, "National sentiment is a fact, and should be taken account of by institutions when it is ignored, it is intensified and becomes a source of strife."[4] History abounds in such phenomena. The Pathan rulers, according to Swami Vivekananda interfered with the religion of the native population of India. That is why no Pathan dynasty ruled for more than a few decades. The Moghuls knew it better and did not persecute their Hindu subjects and they would have ruled much longer, but for the principle of religious discrimination, introduced by Aurangzeb. For the first few decades after the Battle of Plassy the British rulers in India were busy in consolidating their power and did not touch the religious sentiment of their subjects. But as soon as they tampered a little with the religion of the native Hindus, the result was the great uprising — The Sepoy Mutiny of 1857. Though the awakening was crushed ruthlessly, in less than a century after the upheaval the British rulers had to quit India. The British, according to Swami Vivekananda should not have committed this blunder.[5]

For Swami Vivekananda, "India — our motherland, has religion and religion alone for its basis, for its backbone, for the bedrock upon which the whole building of its life has been based."[6] Politics and even intellect are secondary to the people of India. But what is primary, is religion. It is the language of our heart. As he said, "The Englishmen can understand religion through politics, the Americans through social reforms; but we understand even politics and sociology through religion...."[7] As he further said, "The voice of Asia has been the voice of religion. The voice of Europe is the voice of politics."[8] The Hindus, he felt will never accept politics without religion. He believes only in religion — the lifeforce. Therefore he appealed to all the reformers, "Before flooding India with socialistic or political ideas, first deluge the land with spiritual ideas."[9] The common populace never understand politics — an alien element, but they understand only religion. The Hindus can understand politics only when it is given through religion. Therefore Swami Vivekananda made religion the basis of his nationalistic doctrine. To him power and intellect are also insignificant as they are not consistent with our national tradition.

Swami Vivekananda asserted that since religion is the basis of our national unity, caution should be practised to effect reforms in social and political sphere with religion as the mooring. As he pointed out, "Political and social reforms must always be carried out in India, proceeding from her relgious life...."[10] The result of the reformation, if they fail to cope with the religious sentiment of the people will be disastrous. So, 'he addressed all people in the language of their own orthodoxy'.[11]

Swami Vivekananda saw that the eyes of the world were now turned towards this land — India, for spiritual solace. Westerners were striving to understand the spiritual ideas of the East. Religious search had discovered that there is not a country, that possesses a good ethical code, as we do have in our country and there is not even one religion in the world having correct ideas of the immortality of the soul as we do have in our religion.[12] We may be degraded or degenerated now, but however decadent and effete we may be, we can become great once again if only we begin to work in the lines of our national ideal, *i.e.*, religion.

Each nation according to Swami Vivekananda appears to have a particular ideal — a prominent ideal, running through its whole life and this ideal is the backbone of its national life. Politics, military-power, commercial supremacy, mechanical genius etc. are the fields of specialisation for different nations. But spiritualism has always become the way of life in India — her field of specialisation. If any country throws off its national vitality, the nation will die. So if we succeed in throwing off religion from India to take up another field of specialisation like politics or social refinement as the ideal of our national life, then extinction of the nation will be the obvious consequence. To prevent this we have to vitalise our religion first and subordinate everything-else to it. As he said, "That intense faith in another world, that intense hatred for this world, that intense power of renunciation, that intense faith in God, that intense faith in immortal soul is in you. How can you change your nature?"[13] So every improvement of India should be preceded by an upheaval in religion. The great truth, confined in Upanishads and the Puranas must be broadcast all over. Let the people hear it first and all who help in this process are practising the highest form of gift, namely the gift of the spiritual ideas. Dissemination of these spiritual ideas should not be confined to India alone but should spread to all parts of the world. This has been the mission of India since the pre-Buddhist time, the remnants of which are still found in China, Asia Minor and the heart of Malayan Archipelago.

This religion which is the prime concern in India is the secret of its strength. "To the other nations of the world religion is one of the many occupations of life...and among all these various occupations of life...there is perhaps a bit of religion. But here in India, religion is the one and the only occupations in life."[14]

To Swami Vivekananda, religion is the source of all vigour and vitality of our life. It is the chief unifying force of the nation. Hence this religion must always remain pure, immune to contagion. If it remains so, the vitality of body politic will be reassured.

Hence, religion which forms the very vitality of India is the basis of nationalism of Swami Vivekananda. He thought that if religion is interpreted in its correct sense and realised by everybody, much of our miseries, mental conflict and social evils would be automatically resolved. He considered religion to be the healthiest exercise that the human mind could have. He said, "Of all the forces that have worked and are still working to mould the destinies of human race, none, certainly is more potent than that, the manifestation of which we call religion."[15] Religion according to him has always worked as a great motive force.

In order to make religion an effective force in the field of national unity and emancipation of the masses, Swami Vivekananda firmly believed that Hinduism must broaden the scope of religion, associating it with the field of practical work and not of abstract judgments. He observed, "Religion is not words and not theory...its essence is not in listening and accepting, it is in being and becoming."[16]

Religion not only teaches man to refrain from evil but must insist on doing good to others. It awakes the spirit within man. As he said, "Religion is the idea which is raising the brute unto man and man unto God."[17] As he further said, "Take religion from human society and what will remain? Nothing but a forest of brutes."[18] Hence according to him, if religion is taken away from human society, the residue will be a mass of brutes. It constitutes man's very nature and unites him to his fellows. It gives vision and inspiration to man. It exerts tremendous influence on the life of man. Its significance is enormous and far-reaching. It is this religion that constitutes the basis of nationalism of Swami Vivekananda.

Admitting the apparent contradictions in different faiths and conflicting tenets, Swami Vivekananda taught love and mutual tolerance as the cardinal principles of religion. As he said, "Love and charity for the whole human race — that is the test of true religiousness."[19] He preached tolerance and religious universalism as the basis of his nationalism. If religion is true then all must be true. Hence, he insisted on harmony, peace, and goodwill and discarded fanaticism, rivalries and bloodshed in religion.

The aim of all religions, according to Swami Vivekananda, was the spiritual integration of India and of mankind as a whole. Unity of India — a land of diverse faiths and religions can be had only through spiritual integration. So this spiritual integration of the world is another feature of the nationalism of Swami Vivekananda. He said, "Our minds are like vessels and each of us tries to arrive at a realisation of God. And God is like the water that fills the vessels of different shape. In each vessel the vision of God takes a different form. Yet he is one; he is God in every case."[20] His aim of attending the Parliament of Religions at Chicago in 1893 was to show that the apparent contradictions in different faiths are not real. It was for this catholic approach that the won admiration of each delegate, attending the Parliament. After his address a man remarked, "Every delegate spoke of the God of his own religion. Swami Vivekananda alone spoke of the God of all." Pleading for the unity of faiths Swami Vivekananda said that the human society would have made far greater advances, had there been no sectarianism, fanaticism and violence in the name of religion. In a very painful tone he also said, "The earth was beautiful, but had, alas! been tormented by sectarianism, bigotry and fanaticism. They have destroyed the civilization. They have sent whole nations to despair."[21]

Religious harmony and tolerance, felt Swami Vivekananda is the only way leading to spiritual integration of mankind. There must be harmonious relations among the various faiths and religions of India and of mankind as a whole. As he said, "We believe not only in religious toleration, we also accept all religions are true."[22] For this harmony, toleration and co-ordination he suggested Vedanta to be the most suitable Philosophy. It alone could become the basis of universal religion of man. Manifesting the common ground among all religions of the world, it harmonises all the various aspirations of man. Therefore he said, "...it is Vedanta and Vedanta alone that can become the universal religion of man, and that no other is fitted for the role."[23]

In the context of Indian conditions, Swami Vivekananda was particularly concerned about good relations between the votaries of the two great religions *i.e.*, Hinduism and Islam. He considered the term 'Mlechchha' as a most unfortunate expression. He preached love for all, irrespective of the faith one professes. As he said, "Love makes no distinction between man and man, between Arya and Mlechchha, between Brahmin and Pariah nor even between man and woman. Love makes the whole universe as one's own home."[24] In the words of Romain Rolland, "Vivekananda wanted India to have an Islamic body and Vedantic heart."[25] This kind of compromise between Hindus and Muslims, he considered to be the only solution for all communal feelings in India.

In a letter to Mohammad Sarfaraz Hussain on June 10, 1898 Swami Vivekananda wrote "The truth is that Advaitism is the last word of religion and thought and the only position from which one can look upon all religions and sects with love. I believe, it is the religion of the future enlightened humanity."[26]

He wanted the two religions to form a synthesis for the promotion of national unity in India. In the same letter Swami Vivekananda wrote, "I am firmly persuaded that without help of practical Islam, theories of Vedantism however fine and wonderful they may be are entirely valueless to the vast mass of mankind. We want to lead the mankind to the place where there is neither Vedas nor the Bible nor the Koran."[27]

Karl Marx said about Luther — a great religious reformist of the West, 'Religion was for him the direct truth and so to say nature.'[28] But for Swami Vivekananda religion was mainly a means of coming together, a language understood alike by all sections of people and serves as a basis of Hindu nationalism as propounded by him.

(ii) Cultural Basis

The sublimity of Indian culture is as old as that of Indian religion. "The culture of India has been one of the great civilizing and humanising factors evolved by man."[29] For centuries together the general spiritual life of the larger part of the continent of Asia "meant mainly its response to the call of the eternal ideas, discovered systematised and humanised by the sages and saints of ancient India."[30] In other words culture of Asia has been a complex fabric of life, woven by several different strands of which India is most prominent. That is why Romain Rolland, a French philosopher observes, "If there is one place on the face of the earth, where all the dreams of living man have found home from the earliest days, when man began the dream of existence, it is India."[31]

Undoubtedly India was a great civilizing force for many backward countries of Asia. "India was the civilizer" from the beginning of the 1st millennium B.C. down to the closing centuries of the 1st millennium A.D. It was during this long period that there was the cultural unification of India and it went on simultaneously with the cultural expansion of India into overseas countries like Lanka, Burma, Siam, Indochina, Malaya, Indonesia and to a large extent into the countries of North-West like Afghanistan, Beluchistan, Turkistan in central Asia. The transformation of the Eastern countries like China,

Korea and Japan was achieved through their close contact with the spiritual forces from India. Thus, in the moulding of Asian culture Indian share has been very significant. As B.N. Luniya writes, "India or more precisely, the Hindu culture of India, was not merely a civilizing force, it brought to them intellectual awakening, social consciousness and material prosperity."[32]

With many backward races of Asia, the sense of social order and organisation, arts and crafts seem to have dawned for the first time with the advent of the merchants and the Brahman and Buddhist missionaries from India. It not only brought material uplift to these backward peoples but their dormant intellectual and other powers and talents were quickened to life and they were enabled to attain the fulfilment of those powers without any difficulty or hindrance. Indian culture thus, helped other peoples to make their own contributions to world civilization, while it absorbed them and participated in their deeper and wider life. Indian culture brought to other nations their own spiritual ideas and values. As it is said, "In the case of ancient and highly cultured people like the Chinese, contact with Indian thoughts gave the finishing touch in the formation and in the highest expression of their culture. Buddhism, which was carried to China by the Indians, brought home to the Chinese, the necessity of going into the fundamental questions of existence and endeavour."[33] Java, Siam, China, and Japan enjoyed richness of life and witnessed the astonishing efflorescence of their minds and spirit, manifesting itself in literature, fine arts, and religious ritual as a result of contact with Indian culture. Assimilation and unfoldment and not hindrance and suppression was the keynote of Indian cultural expansion. Indian philosophy and culture went abroad not to destroy and cause ruin but to awaken and fulfil. B.N. Luniya wrote, "It went there like the refreshing showers and life giving rain and not like the burning wind or the killing blight."[34]

It is when Islam came to India in the form of political conquest that there arose severe conflict between the two divergent cultures. But subsequently, in spite of fundamental difference and bitter strife between the Hindus and the Muslims, there began to flow a genial current of mutual harmony, tolerance and co-operation in different spheres of life and in course of time a beautiful synthesis of Hindu-Muslim culture was achieved. As Maulana Abul Kalam Azad said, "...many historical races and cultures and religions should flow to her, finding a home in her hospitable soil and that many caravans should rest here.... One of the last of these caravans, following the footsteps of its predecessors, was that of the followers of Islam.... This led to a meeting of the culture currents of two differents — the Hindus and the Muslims. Like the Ganges and the Jamuna, they flowed for a while through separate courses. But nature's immutable law brought them together and joined them in a 'Sangam'. The thousand years of our joint life have moulded us into a common nationability."[35]

Hindu culture absorbed most of the elements of Islamic culture and regained its vitality and force over Islamic culture. As Jawaharlal Nehru has observed, "On the one hand it encouraged the tendency of Hindu society to shrink still further within its shell; on the other, it brought a breath of fresh air and fresh ideals and thus had a certain rejuvenating influence."[36]

Wherever the Indian went settled they spread their own culture but at the same time were absorbing the native culture trends. Consequently they evolved a new culture, the key-note of which was Indian. Thus, they created culture in other Asiatic countries, the values of which were "awareness of the unity of life and love for the ultimate and universal in preference to the immediate and the particular."[37] As Nehru discribes it, "...it was ever searching for the ultimate and universal."[38] Hence its achievement unlike that of the Western culture, is more than that of a mere force of material civilization or civilized organisation.

But to our greatest misfortune, this unique and sublime culture, that forms an essential ingredient of our national life, althrough the history, dimmed with the advent of the British in the 18th century. With the establishment of political supremacy, "the British barred all the doors and stopped all the routes that connected us with our neighbours in Asia. They opened new routes across the sea to Europe and more particularly to England."[39] As a result, the storm of Western influence began to rage violently in the country. It darkened the most luminous firmament of Indian culture. As Professor Rapson has written, "This sudden isolation from the rest of Asia has been one of the most remarkable and unfortunate consequence of British rule in India."[40]

Western culture and civilization strongly affected the evolution of Indian culture. Supremacy of Western culture gave a rude shock to our effulgent Indian culture. Indian culture reached the lowest ebb. It lost all its evolutionary urge and creative power. Social evils like spiritual blindness, superstitions, and untouchability crept into Indian society, that gravely affected our socio-religious life. The vitality of Indian life collapsed. The economic life of the people received a terrible setback due to the British economic policy. The flourishing craft and industries were ruined. Poverty and starvation became the most glaring phenomena. The course of Indian economic life was clogged. This economic ruin adversely affected the social life of India. Life became dull and sluggish.

When this was the state of affairs, Swami Vivekananda resolved to awake India from the age-long morass and prostration by reviving India's decadent culture. He had strong conviction that "Culture is the totality of learned devices for problem-solving."[41] So referring to the wonderous beauties of the cultural heritage of our country he said, "Where stood the earliest cradle of ethics, arts, science and literature and the integrity of whose sons and the virtues of whose daughters have been sung by all the travellers."[42]

The sole aim of Swami Vivekananda was to revive Indian ancient culture and regenerate Indian nation on the basis of such cultural heritage. He made earnest appeal to his countrymen to look back upon our cultural past and revive the nation on that footing. He had tremendous faith in the pristine qualities of such cultural heritage and its capacity to rebuild the nation in wreckage. He believed that Indian nation could be made to awake only through the revival of her ancient culture. Her cultural heritage should constitute the most prominent force to tie together all divisive forces. Man is the product of his culture. Culture forms the sentiment or thought process of the people.

Cultural affinity is the greatest cementing force to hold all people together for national emancipation. It is the life-blood of the nation and the vitality of the race. So Indian nation shall have to be awakened through the vigour and vitality of our culture.

The Vedic culture of India, Swami Vivekananda felt, is the richest culture in the world. It is the mother of all cultures — the classic home of world culture. Vedas — the fountainhead of Indian culture, is the source of all knowledge, which can alone provide solutions to all the problems of India — social, political and economic. If this Vedic culture of the country is revived, other aspects of our national life will be reinvigorated. This led M.N. Roy to remark, "Vivekananda endeavours to utilise mass energy for the perpetuation or revival of that heritage of national culture...."[43]

It is knowledge that awakens the sense of dignity in man, impelling him to throw off the bondage of slavery. Knowledge makes man realise the integrity and the solidarity of his being and becoming. But knowledge without culture, according to Swami Vivekananda is only skin-deep.[44] All the knowledge imparted to man, must be based upon culture. So the culture of India should form the basis of nationalism. Hence Swami Vivekananda tried to rouse his people by harping on this supreme culture. As he said, "India is the ancient land where wisdom made its home before it went to any other country. Its rolling rivers, its towering mountains represent, as it were, its greatness on the material plane. Its soil has been trodden by the greatest sages that ever lived. The highest ideals of religions and philosophy have attained their culminating point here. From here the waves of spirituality have again and again rushed out and deluged the world. It is the land that withstood the shocks of hundreds of foreign invasions of hundreds of upheavals of manners and customs and yet stands firmer than ever with its undecaying vigour and indestructible life."

"I refer you to the past of India because its future is to take shape from that background. Out of the consciousness of our past greatness we must build an India yet greater than what she has been. Periods of decadence there have been, but out of these India emerged always as something greater, as a mighty tree from a decayed fruit."[45]

Thus Swami Vivekananda's concept of Indian nationalism was firmly planted on the culture of India that appealed to all the people and touched their sentiment. This cultural basis of his nationalism influenced almost all the subsequent leaders of the country. The view of D. Reincourt is that Ravindranath Tagore, Aurobindo Ghose and Mahatma Gandhi all acknowledge their debt to Ramkrishna and Swami Vivekananda.[46]

(iii) Concern for the Masses

The theory of Swami Vivekananda's nationalism is based on his deep concern for the masses. His concern for the masses was very great. As Dr. I.P. Chelishev points out, "The great merits of Vivekananda, in my opinion, is that he was one of the first in India to pay attention to the masses, to the suffering and misfortune of his compatriots; thereby he raised the paramount problem of India of his day."[47]

During his wandering days Swami Vivekananda came in direct contact with masses of India. Everywhere the grim misery and privation of the masses afflicted him. He failed to retain his patience. Once when he came to know from the newspaper, about a starvation death in Calcutta he sobbed and cried out in anguish "Oh my country! Oh my country." He beat his breast and interrogated himself, "What have we done, we so-called men of God, the sannyasis what have we done for the masses?"[48]

The misery of the masses that he witnessed, throughout the length and breadth of the country moved his heart so much so that it changed the course of his life and whipped up his nationalistic passions. The misery of the millions, their degradation and helplessness, according to Romain Rolland, "Pursued him like a tiger following in his prey from the north to south in his flight across India. It consumed him during sleepless night."[49]

Swami Vivekananda had not only a compassionate heart, he also had pragmatic head to discover the ways and means for the solution of these problems of poverty and degradation. He decided to bend all his strength to uplift the condition of the masses.

Apart from the poverty and degradation of the masses the unparalleled prosperity of the Americans and other continental countries, he came across, during his tour to U.S.A., gave a positive push to his nationalistic feeling and widened his sympathy for the masses. The main purpose of his visit to America was to collect funds for the amelioration of the lot of the downtrodden masses. He himself has confessed, "It is for this reason to find more means for the salvation of the poor of India that I am going to America."[50]

While residing in a luxurious lodge in U.S.A. the woeful panorama of poverty and starvation of the Indian masses in the face of unparalleled prosperity of the Western countries, did not let him sleep in peace. The bed became a bed of thorns for him. He rolled on an empty floor and in agony of his heart he cried, "Oh, mother, what do I care for, name and fame, when my motherland remains sunk in utmost poverty? Who will raise the masses of India? Who will give them bread? Show me, Oh Mother, how can I help them?"[51]

Having seen, all around, the miserable plight of the Indian masses, he appealed to his followers in India, "Gird up your lions, my boys, feel for the miserable and look up for help — it shall come. I have travelled twelve years with this load in my heart and this idea in my head. I have gone from door to door of the so-called rich and great. With a bleeding heart I have crossed half the world to this strange land seeking for help. I may perish of cold and hunger in this land, but I bequeath to you, young men, this sympathy, this struggle for the poor, the ignorant, the oppressed...go...down on your faces before Him and make a great sacrifice, the sacrifice of a whole life for them... these three hundred millions going down and down every day."[52]

Swami Vivekananda argued that ever since India ignored the great Vedantic principle of giving due consideration to the masses, there started the doomsday of India. For centuries, the vast masses — sudras had been treated loath-some and untouchable which was a great national sin. India was to undergo suffering and hardship for such sin. As he said, "I consider that the greatest national sin is the neglect of the masses and that is one of the causes of our downfall."[53] India would arise again and get her proper position in the comity of nations, if this vast mass of people would arise and get proper place in the society. The mass is the strength of the nation. It is the steel pillar of the nation. If the mass is neglected, ignored and underestimated the strength of the nation will give in. The whole nation will collapse.

In emphasising the strength of the masses he said that through the ages the source of all power in India has been the masses, who are sleeping Leviathan. Whenever those in power were alienated from the subject masses, they were over-thrown. The power of the Brahmins was over-thrown when they were alienated from the masses. The Kshatriyas came to power as they took their stand on the strength of masses. They also lost their power when they were alienated from the masses. The Vaisyas came to power because they took their stand on the strength of the masses. Swami Vivekananda declared that the Vaisyas would also lose their power because they were being alienated from the subject masses. He believed in the concept of popular sovereignty. His view was that the future of India was tied up with the future and the power of the Sudras of the country. As everybody belonged to that caste, that meant a state of castelessness and the masses as a whole will be supreme in future as against one group of people or the other. That's why he said, "A time will come when there will be rising of the Sudra class. They will gain absolute supremacy in the society."[54]

To Swami Vivekananda, the poor people in India sacrifice their stamina for our happiness. They make us live happily but we bother little about them. We hire their labour to make the society congenial to our living but in return we never pay them their legitimate due. On the other hand they are ignored and underestimated in every sphere of the society. 'They pay for our education, they build our temples, but in return they get kicks. They are practically our slaves. If we want to regenerate India we must work for them.'[55] Drawing the attention of the upper class people of India specially the educated elites he said, "So long as millions live in hunger and ignorance, hold every man a traitor who having been educated at their expense, pay not the least heed to them."[56] He argued that if India was to revive her vitality as a nation, the poor mass, the ignorant, the downtrodden illiterates must be made conscious of their lost individuality and manliness. There is leonine beauty of strength in them to constitute the vitality of the nation, but it has been ignored like anything.

Swami Vivekananda had tremendous faith in the masses of India. As it said, "He was able intuitively to arrive at the idea that the only working class which was just coming into being in India at that time, was the decisive force in social development."[57] When he saw the Bengali workers engaged in their tasks, his feelings of hopelessness about his compatriots vanished almost completely. He saw how they were gradually developing courage, becoming physically strong, fearless and energetic. Swami Vivekananda was convinced that only the people who became the masters of their destiny, could be the builders of the nation. He pointed out, "The only hope of India is from the masses. The upper classes are physically and morally dead."[58] That is why he held that it was the duty of all upright men of India to advance the cultural level of the people to sow the seeds of truth and knowledge in the hearts of the millions of men — the mass.

Swami Vivekananda not only expressed his sympathy and compassion for the well-being of the oppressed mass of India, as did at that time many liberal reformers, who through practical reforms in the way of life sought some how to ease the lot of their compatriots, he also criticised the crying inadequacy of such reforms and told those who thought it possible through half-hearted measures and the begging of favours from the colonialists to solve the cardinal social and political problems of the age : 'you talk of social reforms? But what do you do? all that you mean by your social reform is either widow remarriage or female emancipation or something of that sort.... Such a scheme of reform may do good to a few no doubt but of what avail is that to the whole nation.'[59]

Swami Vivekananda sought to put up in contrast to such half-hearted reforms affecting only narrow spheres of society's life, cardinal demands for a change in the condition of the working masses. 'The one problem you have is to give the masses right,'[60] he stressed. He called upon the reformers to go deep into life of the masses and ameliorate their lot. As he said, "Most of what you talk of social reform does not touch the poor masses."[61] "Go down to the basis of things, to the very roots. That is what I call radical reformation. Put the fire there and let it burn upwards and make an Indian nation."[62] He told the reformers that he himself was a big reformer than anyone of them. They wanted only partial, miserly reforms, while he called for radical reforms.

Swami Vivekananda was a spiritual man, who was supposed to be concerned with the spiritual aspect of life. But material backwardness of the Indian masses was a constant source of harrowing mental agony for him. He realised that spiritual progress is achieved only through material progress. A hungry man knows no religion nor spiritualism. He once asked himself, "What have we several millions of Sannyasins been doing for the masses? Teaching them metaphysics? It is all madness. It is mockery to offer religion to a starving man."[63] Hence he laid stress on the improvement of the condition of the Indian masses in all spheres of life to restore India's long-lost vitality and said, "India must rise, the masses and the poor are to be made happy."[64]

Swami Vivekananda, putting forward the ideal of service to the masses, placed in the centre of his spiritual system not God but man. He advised his disciples "Where have you to go, where to search for God?" he asked, "are these poor, the unfortunate, these weak people not really the Gods? Why not first pray to them? Why dig a well at the bank of the Ganges?"[65] Turning to his followers he appealed to them for working in the name of spiritual liberation and material progress of the masses. As he said, "Swear to devote all your lives to the work of saving these 300 millions, going lower and lower each day."[66]

Swami Vivekananda believed that service to mankind is service to God. He considered love for mankind to be the surest path leading to God. His love for man was so great that he made his religion and God subordinate to it : "I do not believe in a

God or religion which cannot wipe out the widow's tears or bring a piece of bread to the orphan's mouth.... I believe in helping the miserable, I believe even in going to hell to save others."[67]

Thus Swami Vivekananda's love for the poor and ignorant mass of India was so great that he drowned himself in ceaseless activity for the cause of their upliftment. His celebrated biographer Romain Rolland appropriately observed, "He dedicated his life to the unhappy masses."[68] Hence prosperity and happiness of the masses was one of the cornerstones of Swami Vivekananda's concept of nationalism.

(iv) Individual Freedom and Equality

Swami Vivekananda's nationalism is based upon the democratic concepts of freedom and equality of all men. His concept of freedom and equality of all men is a remarkable contribution to the doctrine of nationalism. He declared that freedom is the essence of the universe. It is the spirit — the life-force, with which the universe is created, sustained and forges ahead. It is the very go of the universe. As he said, "Freedom is the motive of the universe, freedom its goal."[69] As he further said, "In freedom it rises, in freedom it rests and into freedom it melts away."[70]

Everything and every being, according to Swami Vivekananda is manifestation of freedom and they feel an unremitting urge to be free. Freedom is the destination towards which everything moves. As he said, "Every thing that we perceive around us is struggling towards freedom from the atom to the man, from insentient lifeless particle of matter to the highest existence on earth, the human soul. The whole universe is, in fact, the result of this struggle for freedom."[71] Thus freedom is the ultimate goal of nature and consciously or unconsciously every sentient or insentient being or object is struggling for attainment of that goal.

What is true of each sentient and insentient beings or objects is more true of man. Man according to him is the final manifestation of passion for freedom. As he said, "The universal struggle for freedom attains its highest expression in man, in the conscious desire to be free."[72] Not only man is the highest expression of freedom and is moved by the consummate desire to be free; he aspires for complete freedom. Complete freedom is essential for the attainment of freedom. Accordingly Swami Vivekananda said, "To be more free is the goal of all our efforts for only in perfect freedom can there be perfection."[73] Believing in this grand concept of freedom of man he declared, "Freedom is the goal of all the noblest aspirations of mankind."[74] This aspiration for freedom is quite natural to man. It is his instinct, that forms a part of his innate nature. It is his birth right. As he said, "Freedom is its (human nature's) watchword. Freedom is its nature, its birth right."[75]

To Swami Vivekananda freedom is the divine endowment, bestowed upon man because of his divine descent. Hence this privilege for freedom is in the nature of divine rights. As he said, "Freedom is ours by divine rights."[76]

Swami Vivekananda as a spiritual man, not only stood for spiritual freedom, but also for material, social and political freedom. Freedom is the condition under which the individual develops his own self towards perfection. It provides the positive conditions for the unfoldment of various potentialities of life. As he said, "Freedom is the first condition of growth. What you do not make free will never grow."[77] In the ancient Vedic society there was complete freedom. There was no chain or clog of any sort that stunted the growth of evolution of the society. Society was altogether progressive and individual was all the more pioneering and enterprising. It was only when the freedom and equality of all men of the Indian society was put under restraints, the once progressive Indian society crumbled, yielding to untold misery of privation of all sorts. On the other hand the Western society that unfurled the banner of individual right and liberty along with equality of all men, made tremendous headway in every walk of life. That society is a well-knit, well-built and altogether progressive. He felt that to advance towards freedom — physical, mental and spiritual and help others to do so is the supreme prize of man. Those social rules which stand in the way of the unfoldment of this freedom are pernicious and steps should be taken to destroy them speedily. On the other, those institutions should be encouraged by which men advance in the path of freedom.'[78] Again "It is our natural right to be allowed to use our own body, intelligence or wealth according to our will without doing any harm to others and all the members of the society aught to have the same opportunity for obtaining wealth, education or knowledge."[79]

A mystic, Swami Vivekananda championed the cause of individual liberty — both material and spiritual. To him material freedom is the first condition of spiritual freedom. He advocated individual liberty and equality and strove to secure liberty through various channels. he asserted that liberty in thought and action is the only condition of life, growth and well-being, where it does not exist, the man, the race and the nation must go down.[80] In his plea for individual freedom he said, "In India, we have to take off the sackles from the society, there will come a wonderful growth and development of man."[81]

As a devout Vedantist, Swami Vivekananda upheld the doctrine of equality of all men irrespective of caste, creed, faith, birth and colour. In this sense he was true democrate. He said that no nation could gain physical freedom without physical equality. To him all men are alike. In 'Mother India' he said "Forget not that the lower classes, the ignorant, the poor, the illiterates, the cobbler, the sweeper are thy flesh and blood, the brothers."[82] He thought that social inequality is a curse upon mankind. It is the root of all miseries and degradations. It is the source of all bondage — physical, mental, and spiritual. Equality is essential not only in spiritual field but also in material fields. It is as important for the householder as it is for sannyasi. As he said, "This is the bane of human nature, the curse upon mankind, the root of all misery — this inequality. This is the source of all bondage — physical, mental or spiritual."[83]

Swami Vivekananda was dead against caste system, which in its wake brought feelings of class distinction of superiority, of untouchability and other social evils. He called upon his compatriots to discard all those customs which formed the basis of such unhappy differences among man. In a letter he wrote, "The conviction is daily gaining on my mind that the idea of caste is the greatest dividing factor and the root of Maya; all castes, either on the principle of birth or of merit is bondage."[84]

According to Swami Vivekananda caste-system exists in every society in some form or the other. In the West wealth and power have divided men into classes, while in India, the basis has been 'Varna' or caste. He was against this misuse and misinterpretation of this 'Varnashram' or caste system. 'Varnashram' is nothing but a social plan of division of labour but this has been misunderstood and misused in India, which has brought vengeance to Indian Hindu society. Varnashram provides equal opportunity to the people of all castes to rise higher and attain the best self. It is no more a barrier in the path of social progress. As he said, "Caste is good. That is the only natural way of solving life. Man must form themselves into groups and you cannot get rid of it. Wherever you go there will be caste."[85] Caste makes a man perform his duty efficiently in social life. In India caste distinction has become a barrier for social progress as it formed the basis of separation but not of unity in social life. He was much shocked to find that India, the land of the Vedas, where equality was the basis of society right from the dawn of human civilization, had been divided by the walls of casteism — the source of all inequalities. He considered this inequality as "fictitious and monstrous".[86] To him this attitude of inequality is the "Primal sin".[87] Although Swami Vivekananda was a spiritual personality, his view on society and social justice are more realistic and pragmatic than any other modern social thinkers. He considered society as a divine institution. He said, "That society is the greatest where the highest truths become practical. That is my opinion and if the society is not fit for the highest truths, make it so, and the sooner the better."[88]

Swami Vivekananda strongly pleaded for a democratic set up and social justice. He said, "Great liberty in social matters and so have a splendid social organisation."[89]

Integral freedom — physical, mental and spiritual, has been the watchwords of the Upanishads. As a staunch believer in Upanishads, Swami Vivekananda launched a vigorous campaign all along to make these watchwords more real and practical. To him, "The whole life of society is the assertion of that one principle of freedom."[90] He hoped that the freedom, which dawned in America on 04 July 1776 would become universal in the world. In the words of Dr. Y. Chelysev, "He flayed social injustice and dreamed a harmonious order in a society founded on the lofty ideals of freedom and equality."[91]

Swami Vivekananda presented a very ballanced view both for society and the individual. In a perfect society there must be proper harmony between man and man and the aim should be a synthesis between spiritualism and materialism. In the individual life there must be a balance between the higher and the lower nature of man, again a synthesis of the spirited body.

(v) Spiritual Integration of the World

Swami Vivekananda as a nationalist stood for spiritual integration of the entire world. Upanishads stand for the universal brotherhood and solidarity of the universe. Swami Vivekananda, inspired to the core by this Upanishadic message, gave a call to shed all ignorance that divides the world and makes people hate one another. He called upon his countrymen to give up such ignorance and work for the integration of the world and promotion of universal brotherhood through spiritualism. Advocating this cause of universal brotherhood and solidarity of the universe he said, "Why it is that all great men have preached the brotherhood of mankind and greatermen, the brotherhood of all lives? because whether they were conscious of it or not, behind all that, through all their irrational and personal superstitions, was peering forth the eternal light of the self, denying all manifoldness and asserting that the whole universe is but one."[92]

Spiritual integration of the world, that his master Sri Ramkrishna Paramahansa taught him was the core of Swami Vivekananda's spiritualism. He stood to unite the whole world into one family with the thread of spiritualism. He assumed the role of a world-teacher and tried to infuse into mankind the essence of absolute unity. For propagating this principle of universal unity he resorted to Advaita Vedanta or the philosophy of non-duality of God and the universe and non-duality of all individual entities. In explaining the Advaita philosophy he made the assertion of one man, one God, one religion and one universe, the centre of which is Brahma — the Absolute, source of all existence for both, living and non-living. He believed in such unity or oneness of the universe, as upheld by the Vedanta. This provided the clue to all ethical, moral and spiritual values. It is also the source of all morality, ethics and spirituality. As he said, "...there in lies the explanation of all ethics of all morality and all spirituality in the universe."[93]

Swami Vivekananda had not only profound faith in Advaita philosophy of universality and individuality of the absolute Atman; he also made it his life's mission to unravel this intricate doctrine and make it assessible to the whole mankind. As he declared, "We shall beat in all hearts, in all markets, at the height of hills and in the plains, the dream of Advaita."[94] Accordingly he carried the message of Advaita philosophy to the West — the citadel of materialism, the stronghold of non-believers. As Romain Rolland has observed, "He not only made himself the peripatetic salesman of the Advaita Vedanta philosophy in the Western world; he established Vedanta societies in U.S.A. to popularise the doctrine in the Western hemisphere."[95]

On the issue of spiritual integration of the world Swami Vivekananda said that several time in the past different conquering nations linked the different parts of the world by their military conquest, but it was shortlived. India, the land of ethics and spiritualism, does not believe in such military conquest. She believes only in spiritual conquest, which will provide a stable and permanent bond of unity among different nations of the world. As he said, "There have been great conquering races in the world. We also have been great conquerors. The story of our conquest has been described by that noble emperor of India, Ashoka, as the conquest of religion and of spirituality. Once more the world must be conquered by India.... The best work that you ever did for yourselves was when you worked for others, trying to disseminate your ideas in foreign languages beyond the seas.... This is the great ideal before us, and everyone must be ready for it. The conquest of the whole world by India — nothing less than that and we must all get ready for it, strain every nerve for it. Up, India and conquer the world with your spirituality."[96]

Referring to the flooding of the world with Indian spiritual philosophy that was silently taking place at the beginning of the century the great German philosopher Schopenhauer foretold, "The world is about to see a revolution in thought more extensive and more powerful than that which was witnessed by the Renaissance of Greek Literature."[97] Swami Vivekananda when saw the Western fascination growing more and more towards Indian thought and philosophy, said that the prediction of the German philosopher had come true.

Spiritual integration of the world through the Advaita philosophy of Vedanta, was the be all and end all of Swami Vivekananda's life. He dedicated his whole life to this cause. As he said to Mr. Erie Hammand in London in 1896 "It may be that I shall find it good to get out my body to cast it off like a worn-out garment. But I shall not cease to work. I shall inspire men every where, until the world shall know that it is one with God."[98]

Emerson, Thoreau and Whitman of the "Transcendentalist Movement" were the advocates of interlinking of the East and West. But their dreams remained unfulfilled because of civil war and hasty development of science and technology. Swami Vivekananda whipped up the interest of the nations and people of the world once again in this cosmopolitan, universalistic outlook and in the mitigation of national antagonism and racial prejudice and professed cultural, racial and linguistic synthesis. As Swami Vivekananda contended, "Now the time is ripe for the fulfilment of Thoreau's dream of marriage of East and West or a real synthesis of science and religion. And to bring this about no worthier person would have been found than Swami Vivekananda of India."[99]

Swami Vivekananda was against the tendency of isolationism and urged the Indians to assimilate the best that had been accumulated by the people of the Western world. "The mere material brilliance of the West could not dazzle him, nor could the emphasis on spirituality in India hide her social and economic drawbacks."[100] He tried to combine Indian spiritualism with the Western materialism in order to produce a wholesome culture and a balanced life for the people of the world.

Swami Vivekananda studied the life and philosophy both of the East and the West and said to Sister Nivedita, "Social life in the West is like a peal of laughter, but underneath, it is a wail. It ends in a sob.... Here in India, it is sad and gloomy on the surface but underneath are carelessness and merriments."[101] The West had tried to conquer external nature and the East had tried to conquer the internal nature. Now the East and the West must work hand in hand for the good of each other, without destroying the speciality of each. The future in fact, is to be shaped by a proper fusion of the two ideals. Then there will be neither West nor East but one humanity.

Criticising the Western materialistic civilization Swami Vivekananda said that mere material progress can never give peace and happiness to mankind. Unless the West accepts spiritualism as its prop, the entire scaffolding of the Western civilization is sure to crumble. The West has seen the life on its surface but has not gone deep into the sea of life. Matter is not enough. Matter with spirit completes the circle of life. The circle of life is incomplete without the arch of spiritualism. Spirit is inner self, but matter is the outer body. Only when matter and spirit are made to advance side by side, life becomes perfect. Wholesomeness and balance of life depends upon the proportional development of both spirit and matter. For this the West must accept spiritualism and the East materialism. As it is said, "Science of the West and philosophy of the East must meet at a point where humanity stood as an indivisible entity. Vivekananda visualised a new type of civilization and culture for the good of the humanity in which the difference between the East and the West would be eliminated."[102]

Swami Vivekananda asked the Indians to learn from the West their great concern for the masses and reverence and freedom for women. He also pointed out that the Indians lacked organisation and obedience to leadership. Organisation is key to the understanding of one's strength against all exploitation and oppression and people of India must learn it. Without imitating the Western culture India should learn from the West what is good in it and absorb it within the folds of her culture. Blind imitation of the West and forgetfulness of what is our own will bring ruin to the nation. As Jawaharlal Nehru has observed, "If our race forgets the Buddha, the Upanishad's and the great epics, what then will it be like! It would be uprooted and would lose the basic characteristics which have clung to it and given it distinction throughout these long ages. India would cease to be India."[103]

The interest of mankind always remains common. Therefore mutual accord and love are essential, which will yield immense benefit to both the cultures and to the humanity at large. He asked the people of the West to accept the Vedanta that preaches oneness of the universe as the religion because it alone can fulfil the life of the mankind. The immense reverence for all religions, which the Vedanta teaches, can overcome religious dissensions and racial prejudices and erase mutual hatred and conflict from our minds. The West should also accept the Vedantic concept of God — *i.e.,* every individual is a manifestation of divinity. They should have faith in Man-God, the highest embodiment of divinity. As he said, "It is impossible to find God outside of ourselves. Our own souls constitute all the divinity that is outside of us. We are the greatest temple."[104]

Thus the spiritual integration of the world and blending of the East and the West for promotion of world peace and goodwill, progress and happiness of mankind was Swami Vivekananda's prime concern and it formed the basis of his nationalism. His nationalism was not narrow nationalism, blind to the demands of larger humanity. His mission was not only to regenerate India but to regenerate the whole mankind and deliver to them the messages of peace and goodwill. Well-being of the whole humanity was his sole concern. He voiced his concern from the world scenario time and again and said that throughout the history, India has served as the forerunner of world peace and progress and now India will pickup her traditional role and become great again. As he said, "India will be raised not with the power of the flesh but with the power of the spirit, not with flag of destruction but with the flag of peace and love...."[105]

Swami Vivekananda's clarion call to humanity has tremendous appeal for all times. It has been observed, "Vivekananda's soul-stirring message will continue to inspire the millions of men and women for ages to come, to work for the unity of mankind and its happiness."[106]

In fact Swami Vivekananda's doctrine of nationalism gave a galvanising shock to the demoralised and denationalised Hindu race, that had been long derailed from her traditional path. As it has been observed, "This broad-minded and large-hearted Indian nationalist monk was the discoverer of India's long lost mission in the world."[107]

(vi) Non-Attachment, Non-Covetousness and Non-Possessiveness

Swami Vivekananda's concept of nationalism is also based on the great Vedantic doctrine of non-attachment, non-covetousness and non-possessiveness. To fulfil his mission of spiritualising the world, Swami Vivekananda wanted to popularise these Vedantic doctrines. He realised that unless man is selfless and non-covetous he cannot realise the essence of any religion. If a man, after giving up all his material comforts and pleasures concentrates all his thoughts and actions upon God, only will he have God — realisation. Without utmost sincerity, devotion and total-surrender, God-realisation is unattainable. As it has been said, "He (God) is to be worshipped as the one beloved, dearer than everything in this and next life."[108]

The world is too full of desires and temptations. We have to live amidst them all, but we should not be obsessed with all of them. For spiritual realisation we should develop a sense of dispassion and complete aversion towards all these material desires of life. If life is indulged in all these earthly temptations, there will be no liberation for man. Life must be detached from all these tendrils of passions that tend to pamper our senses and get supreme hold over our life, and deviate us from the path of God. Therefore, Swami Vivekananda has said, "Cut down the banyan tree of desire with the axe of non-attachment and it will vanish utterly. It is all illusions. He from whom blight and delusion have fallen, he who has conquered the evils of association, he alone is *azad* (free)."[109]

This Vedantic doctrine of nonattachment is fully developed in the Gita. Lord Krishna teaches, "He who works, having given up all attachment, resigning his actions to God, is not touched by sin even as a lotus leaf (is untouched) by water."[110] Hence man must live in this world like a lotus leaf, which though grows in water, does not get moistened by water. He must work without any attachment, which would finally bring him to supreme height of bliss and freedom. As Lord Krishna further teaches, "Therefore, without attachment, perform always the work, that has to be done, for man attains to the highest by doing work without attachment."[111]

Swami Vivekananda accordingly holds that man, though lives in the midst of all earthly desires he should not be obsessed with them. He should give up all his passions and desires that darkens his path from celestial light. As he said, "To work without motive is to work unattached that brings the highest bliss and freedom."[112] As he further said, "The less the sense enjoyment, the higher the life of man."[113]

For Swami Vivekananda, worldly attachment is opposed to God-realisation. Comforts and enjoyments, desires and passions cannot lead man to God. As he has said, "He who desires for a comfortable and a nice life and at same time wants to realise the self, is like a fool, who wanting to cross the river, caught hold of a crocodile, mistaking it for a log of wood."[114]

To Swami Vivekananda non-attachment is a means to an end, but not an end in itself. If God-realisation or moksha or salvation is the end of life, non-attachment is the means to it. As he said, "Vairagya (non-attachment) is the only way to freedom."[115]

Non-attachment according to Swami Vivekananda also implies love of God without expecting anything in return. God should not be loved with the expectation of some rewards, but for the sake of loving Him. Hence he presented the prayer, "Lord, I do not want wealth nor children nor learning. If it be Thy will, I shall go from birth to birth, but grant me this, that I may love Thee without the hope of reward-love unselfishly for love's sake."[116]

Swami Vivekananda said that if man lives according to the principle of non-attachment, — "with his heart to God and hands to work,"[117] success or failure does not overwhelm him. He feels, "I work for work's sake."[118] and derives infallible zeal and infinite patience for work. In such case whole world bubbles with actions and activities. As "non-attachment is complete self-abnegation,"[119] selfishness does not find any place in human mind. All men work in a spirit of sacrifice. As a result disturbance and disorder of all sorts vanish and peace and progress of high order come to prevail in human society. As he has observed, "When we come to that non-attachment, then we can understand the marvellous mystery of the universe; how it is intense activity and vibration and at the same time intensest peace and calm; how it is work every moment and rest every moment. That is the mystery of the universe."[120] Hence Swami Vivekananda appeals to his countrymen to practise this Vedantic principle of non-attachment in their private and national life and show the ideals of the principle to the world.

This Vedantic doctrine of non-attachment does not appeal to Western nations. They on the other hand, believe in sense enjoyment and comforts of life. They hold, "Enjoyment of senses, possessions and wealth to be the end of life. To them enjoyment is the goal of life but not God-realisation. As Swami Vivekananda has pointed out, "They worship God because God is the means to attain this end. The goal of life is enjoyment of sense objects and they come to know there is a Being who can give him a very long lease of these enjoyments and that is why they worship God."[121] Swami Vivekananda also has pointed out, "In the Western countries as a rule, people lay more stress on the body aspect of man; those philosophers who wrote on Bhakti in India, laid stress on spiritual side of man; this difference seems to be typical of the Oriental and Occidental nations."[122]

Though Swami Vivekananda highlights the great Vedantic principle of non-attachment as one of the basis of his nationalism, he dislikes poverty, wretchedness and squalor that debilitate the moral fibre of the nation and degrade its people to the level of slavery. To him non-attachment means non-covetous and non-possessive attitude in the midst of all wealth and affluence. As a matter of fact spiritualism cannot progress amidst poverty and starvation. Religion and spiritualism are meaningless to a man who cries out for a piece of bread with a parched throat. As he has said, "It is an insult to a starving man to teach him metaphysics."[123] But it does not mean material comforts or luxurious living. Dharma (righteousness), Artha (wealth), Kama (pleasure) and Moksha (liberation) have all been recognised by the Indian scriptures as values, relevant to human life, but the pursuit of them must be regulated in a way that they ultimately lead to Moksha. Hence, non-attachment is also an essential condition of material life of man. It is a secret to all morality. As he has said, "Only by practice of non-attachment can we conquer our mind."[124]

Besides, one should not have any greed for the wealth of others nor should he have any greed to possess more wealth than what one actually needs. As Ishopanishad reads,

> "Tena tyaktena bhunjitha
> Ma grudha kasyachit dhanam."[125]

To Swami Vivekananda, 'with the sense of possession comes selfishness'[126] and under its influence man never thinks for common good, that clears the path for starvation of others. Therefore, he condemned the possessive nature of the Western nations and criticised their government as "the tyranny of Shylocks"[127] and contemptuously branded their civilization as "Mercantile civilization with all pretension and humbug."[128] Pointing out the great evils of Western possessive nature Bertrand Russell has also observed, "Material possession, in fact or in desire, dominate our outlook, usually to the exclusion of all generous and creative impulses. Possessiveness — the passion to have and hold — is the ultimate source of war, and the foundation of all the ills from which the political world is suffering. Only by diminishing the strength of this passion and its hold upon our daily lives can new institutions bring permanent benefit to mankind."[129]

This possessive nature of the Western nations has given rise to capitalistic system of economy with its evils of exploitation and injustice to the backward peoples of the globe. The miserable wage system of capitalism, which is the prime cause of poverty and starvation in other backward nations, has been subject to scathing criticism all over the world. As it has been pointed out, "Capitalism and the wage system must be abolished; they are twin monsters which are eating up the life of the world. In place of them we need a system which will hold in check man's predatory impulses and will diminish the economic injustice that allows some to be rich in idleness while others are poor in spite of unremitting labour."[130]

Swami Vivekananda hated the wretchedness, poverty and privation that confronts the dignity of the individual and stunts his growth, finally leading to the moral death of the nation. Both the individual and the nation, thereby lose their moorings paving the path for serfdom and servility. The grim poverty and squalor of India of his time was the prime cause of India's servitude and suffering. So before doing anything else Swami Vivekananda embarked upon the plan of socialism, which is the panacea for all socio-economic ills, to awake India from the anguish of poverty and improve the standard of living of the masses. He felt it to be the foremost need of the hour. As he has said, "It is my firm conviction that it is futile to preach religion amongst them without first trying to remove their poverty and their suffering.[131]

Thus, Swami Vivekananda's nationalism that seeks to satisfy the material needs and spiritual salvation of man, is based upon the lofty Vedantic ideal of non-attachment, non-covetousness and non-possessiveness.

(vii) Reliance on Karmayoga

Swami Vivekananda, although a sannyasin, was a firm believer in Karmayoga and expected that Indian nationalism should be based upon Karmayoga. This Karmayoga which has been elaborately dealt with in the Second and Third Chapter of the *Bhagvad Gita* is a special attraction. Therefore Bal Gangadhar Tilak aptly observed, "The principal subject-matter of the Gita, is the exposition of the Karmayoga."[132]

Karma or action is considered the supreme need of life. Life cannot be conceived of without action. Explaining this Karmayoga, Dr. Radhakrishnan says, "So long as we lead embodied lives, we cannot escape from action. Without work life cannot be sustained."[133] By the very nature of things one cannot remain actionless even for a moment. It is the very innate nature of man. As the *Bhagvad Gita* says, "No one can remain even for a moment without doing work; Every one is made to act helplessly by the impulses born of nature."[134] Accordingly Swami Vivekananda has said, "Intense activity is necessary; we must always work. We cannot live a minue without work."[135] Even saints and sannyasins are not exempted from the obligation of work. Even God, who is the source of the universe, from whom the entire creation proceeds is not free from such obligation. As Lord Krishna says to Arjuna,

"Look at me!
Thou son of Pritha in the three wide worlds,
I am not bound to any toil, no height
Awaits to scale, no gift remains to gain,
Yet, I act here."[136]

Besides, God by His incessant activity and action also preserves the world and prevents it from being ruined.[137] As Lord Krishna again says to Arjuna, "If I should cease to work, these worlds would fall in ruin and I should be the creator of disordered life and destroy these people."[138] Hence, to Swami Vivekananda, Karma or action is the root of all existence — from individual to universe.

Life is a 'Karma Bhumi'. Karma or action is the religion of man. It is the only way to reach the goal of life *i.e.*, freedom. As Swami Vivekananda said, "Our goal is freedom...and that goal is to be reached through works."[139] But Karmayoga provides the clues to such works. It lays down the process, the way, the mode, and the manner of performing the works, that lead to freedom. As it has been observed, "It is the secret of work, the method of work the organising power of work. A vast mass of energy may be spent in vain if we do not know how to utilise it. Karmayoga makes a science of work; we learn by it how best to utilise all the workings of the world."[140] Hence, to Swami Vivekananda, "Karmayoga is a system of ethics and religion intended to attain freedom through unselfishness and through good works."[141]

Karmayoga, according to Swami Vivekananda, is not only to be practised in individual life, it is to be sincerely practised at national level also. As he has said, "In whatever you do, for a particular person, a city, or a state, assure the same attitude — expect nothing in return."[142] Therefore, Swami Vivekananda's mission was to enlighten and inspire the people of India and the mankind as a whole, with the ideals of Karmayoga, that provides a cogent basis to his theory of nationalism.

Explaining Karmayoga, Swami Vivekananda said that every man is the architect of his own destiny. Others cannot make him happy unless he tries to make himself so. It has been said, "As long as we require someone else to make us happy, we are slaves."[143] So dependence on others is nothing but a sort of slavery. By dint of karma one makes himself happy and prosperous. Without karma life is bound to suffer. It is only out of ignorance that we blame others or our fate for such suffering. As said Swami Vivekananda, "We reap what we sow. We are the makers of our own fate. None else has the blame, none has praise. The wind is blowing; those vessels, whose sails are unfurled catch it and go forward on their way, but those which have their sails furled, do not catch the wind. Is that the fault of the wind?"[144]

Swami Vivekananda, whose love for the starved and the down-trodden was very great, tried with all sincerity to arouse the spirit of unremitting toil or activity or karma among man. To him karma is the only passport to human happiness. It alone can mitigate our misery and sufferings. He exhorted his countrymen, "...stand up, be bold be strong. Take the whole responsibility on your own shoulders and know that you are the creator of your own destiny. All the strength and succour you want is within yourselves."[145] Again, he exhorted, "This world is a great gymnasium, where we come to make ourselves strong."[146]

To Swami Vivekananda, 'Work is worship', 'Duty is God'. Duty of any kind is not to be slighted. It has been pointed out, "The man who does what is considered a lower work, is not, for that reason alone, a lower man than he who does what is considered a higher work."[147] It has been further pointed out, "Even the lowest form of work is not to be despised."[148] Hence, a man is not to be judged by the nature of his duties but by the manner is which he does them or the purpose for which he does them — whether they conform to the ideals of Karmayoga or not. But every duty is holy and devotion to duty is the highest form of worship to God. It is certainly a source of great help in enlightening and emancipating the deluded and ignorance-encumbered souls, the bound ones.

It is sincerity and devotion to duty that brings success in life. There must be co-ordination and consistency between word and action of every man. Man should not be platform-hero, he must be a hero of action. He must have leonine vigour in the practical field. As it is said, "The great leaders of mankind belong to higher fields than the fields of platform works."[149]

There are two types of works — good works and bad works. Man should abstain from bad works though he feels tempted to perform it. Since he is the manifestation of divinity, he should involve himself only in those works which will provide a positive push to his soul for higher development. Such works, though initially discouraging should be taken up with a strong conviction that God is there to help. As said Swami Vivekananda, "...you must always remember that each word, thought and deed lays upon a store for you and that as the bad thought and bad works are ready to spring upon you like tigers, so also there is inspiring hope that the good thoughts and good deeds are ready with the power of a hundred thousand angels to defend you always and for ever."[150]

Non-attachment, which has been described in the previous section, is the essential hallmark of 'Karmayoga'. It implies that every man should work for work's sake. He should not be deluded by any attachment to work. This attachment comes from expectation of a reward or fruit. As Swami Vivekananda has said, "Attachment comes only where we expect a return."[151] This expectation of reward that begets attachment, encumbers the soul. Swami Vivekananda realised the truth of the version of the Gita, "Man has right to work but not to aspire for any result." In the light of this version he held that man should leave all result to God, but he should do his work with utmost sincerity and devotion. As he said, "Work unceasingly but refuse to have any attachment to work."[152] As he further said, "The only true duty is to be unattached and to work as free beings, to give up all work unto God. All duties are His."[153]

To Swami Vivekananda, "Non-attachment is perfect self-abnegation and utter unselfishness."[154] Works must be performed with a spirit of sacrifice or service for the community. The *Bhagvad Gita* says that those who enjoy the fruits of action without sacrifice or service to the community are thieves.[155] They commit violence against the Divine and their acts become the acts, tainted in sin.[156] Hence, the *Bhagvad Gita* emphasises on the actions for the service of God or for the welfare of His creation, but not actions with the ultimate objective of self-aggrandisement. That is why Annie Besant in the Preface of her *Gita* has remarked, "Teachings of the Gita lift man from lower level to the loftier heights, where desires are dead; it can be a practical guide to action.[157]

Swami Vivekananda says that one of the special characteristics of the *Bhagvad Gita* is its emphasis on "Niskama-karma" or "Work without desire or attachment."[158] He understood the message of the Gita, "Work constantly; work but be not attached; be not caught. Reserve unto yourself the power of detaching yourself from everything, however beloved, however much the soul might yearn for it, however great the pang of misery you feel, if you are going to leave it; still, reserve the power of leaving it whenever you want."[159] But Swami Vivekananda, a great believer in Man-God, thought the poors, the down-trodden to be the real living Gods. As he said, "The only God who exists, the only God in whom I believe...my God, are the unfortunates, the poor of all nations."[160] Therefore, he went further to say that the essence of this "Niskamakarma" or work without attachment is love, sympathy, and service to the whole world. As he said, "The true "Niskamakarma" is neither to be like a brute nor to be inert nor heartless.... His heart is so full of love and sympathy that he can embrace the whole world with his love. The world at large cannot generally comprehend his all embracing love and sympathy."[161] Hence, according to Swami Vivekananda Karmayoga provides tremendous impetus to universalism and cosmopolitanism. Sincere pursuit of

Karmayoga at national and international level will accelerate the process of achieving the goal of universal brotherhood, peace and progress of perennial nature.

Man lives through action. Action prepares his path for Moksha or salvation. But all sorts of work cannot lead man to Moksha or salvation. Only the Niskamakarma or work without attachment entitles him to salvation. The Gita gives the most lucid interpretation of the doctrine of Niskamakarma and lays down that man should not be guided by any motive — motive for money, power or reputation. Swami Vivekananda also said, "He works best who works without any motive neither for money, nor for fame, nor for anything else; and when a man can do that, he will be a Buddha, and out of him will come the power to work in such a manner as will transform the world."[162]

Most of the people nowadays think that working without any motive means not to be affected by any pleasure or pain but this is not true. As said Swami Vivekananda, "If that were its real meaning then heartless brutes and the walls would be the best exponents of the performance of the 'Niskamakarma'. It will make man stony-hearted and the worst criminals will have to be considered saints."[163]

What the *Gita* has taught us is work with the intention of attainment of higherself and forgetfulness of lowerself. This is the meaning of working through yoga. There are many functions of the body that we perform subconsciously and many other consciously. So also there can be work with the mind, immersed in samadhi, eliminating the smaller ego. This is what happens to some extent when a painter or an artist performs his best. His lower ego is kept in obeyance. So while explaining Karmayoga Swami Vivekananda said, "Let your soul remain free.... Do not bring egotism into it, I...My....."[164] The *Gita* further teaches that he who is one with the Lord through yoga performs all his works immersed in concentration and not looking for any personal self or personal benefit. Such works really brings good to the world. The whole mankind is benefited by it. Personal interest is not sought. Common interest or common good is the basis of such work. Individual interest is identified with common interest. As it has been said, "It is only work that is done as a free will offering to humanity and Nature that does not bring with it any binding attachment."[165]

The *Bhagvad Gita,* according to Swami Vivekananda teaches that we must do those works only which will exalt and ennoble us in accordance with the ideals and activities of the society in which we are born. But we must remember that same ideals and activities do not prevail in all societies and nations. There are different societies and different nations. They have different customs and different activities. So we should not judge others on the basis of our own and conceive any prejudice against others. In most cases, according to Swami Vivekananda, this ignorance is the main cause of much of the hatred of one nation towards another. As he has said, "An American thinks that whatever an American does in accordance with the custom of his country, is the best thing to do, and that whoever does not follow his custom must be a very wicked man. A Hindu thinks that his customs are the only right ones and are the best in the world and that whosoever does not obey them must be the most wicked man living. This is quite a natural mistake, which all of us are apt to make. But it is very harmful.... Much of the oppression of powerful nations on weaker ones is caused by this prejudice. It dries up their fellow-feeling for fellowmen."[166]

Therefore we aught to always remember that we should always try to see the duty of others through their own eyes and never judge the customs of other peoples by our own standard. We, each should know that we are not the standard of the universe. We have to accommodate ourselves to the world and not the world to us. We must also know that environment changes the nature of duty in different societies and nations.[167] Besides, we must judge others not by the nature of their work but by the manner and spirit in which they perform — whether in an unselfish manner and in a spirit of sacrifice or not. As Swami Vivekananda has observed, "Man is not to be judged by the mere nature of his duties but all should be judged by the manner and the spirit in which they perform them"[168] Hence according to Swami Vivekananda Karmayoga provides an international ethics for a sound international behaviour and relation.

Swami Vivekananda says that all works are covered by some evils always like fire by smoke. We should therefore do such work as brings the largest amount of good and the smallest measure of evil to the people. To explain his point he said, "Arjuna had to kill Bhisma, Drona and Karna etc. in the battle-field of Kurukshetra. If he had not done that the country would have been usurped by a body of proud and unrighteous kings to the greatest misfortune of the mankind."[169] Hence, those who do not work for their personal interest, are not affected by any evil, for they work for the good of the world. This motiveless works bring the highest bliss and freedom to the individual, to the nation and to the mankind as a whole.

(viii) Veneration for Woman

Swami Vivekananda's concept of nationalism was based on the veneration for woman, which is the keystone of the whole system of Indian religion, philosophy, culture and civilization. Woman in every sphere of Hindu society is held in high esteem because the Hindus treat woman as the symbol of 'Divine Mother'. From his childhood Hindus learn to adore their motherhood. As Swami Vivekananda said, "...the ideal woman in India is mother, the mother first and the mother last. The word woman calls up to the mind of the Hindu, motherhood; and God is called Mother."[170]

The mother is the ideal of Indian womanhood. The idea that every woman is an embodiment of Divine Mother, runs through our national veins. It has assumed the form of our national ideal. Whenever this ideal of veneration for woman has been disgraced in our land or when tear is caused in the eyes of a woman — the mother, great national catastrophe has overtaken the nation. The two great wars of the Ramayana and the Mahabharata, which were fought against the disgracing of woman — Sita and Droupadi, respectively bear ample testimony to it. Besides Hindus identify nationhood with divine motherhood and considers mother and motherland holier to Heaven, which finds its expression in the great Vedas.

In the West woman is essentially a wife — an instrument of procreation. In the West it is the wife that rules the homes, but in India it is the mother that rules. In the concept of mother woman stands above all carnality. As said Swami Vivekananda, "No, No! woman! thou shall not be coupled with anything connected with the flesh. The name has been called holy once and forever, for what name is there which no lust can ever approach, no carnality ever come near than the one word mother? That is the ideal in India."[171] In a Hindu home the mother walks at the front, the wife only follows. The mother is the mistress of the family. A son places his children under the governance of his mother but not under his wife. A son does not like to see his wife over-riding his mother. A Hindu family is identified with mother — the centre of all attachment. As Swami Vivekananda has said, "But the mother is the ideal of love, she rules the family, she possesses the family."[172]

Mother is the source of infinite love in this mortal world. In this earthly existence mother's love is the nearest approach to God's love. Father takes his wicked son to task. There is abundant evidence of it. But in the entire Indian religious literature and philosophy we do not find a mother punishing her wicked son seriously. As the great saint Ramprasad has said, "Mother, O'mother, be merciful; I am wicked! Many children have been wicked, but there never was a wicked mother."[173] Mother shields her child against all evils. She is the most selfless in her affection to her child. She embraces all miseries and hardship gladly for the up keep of her child. To Swami Vivekananda, "Woman as mother is marvellous, unselfish, all suffering and ever forgiving."[174]

To be the mother of a child is a sacred task of an Indian woman. How to produce a god child, who will build up the nation is the sole concern of the Indian woman. For this purpose she picks up a very conspicuous role. She keeps her body and mind always pure and prays to God to bless her with a good child. A child must be born in prayer but not in a lust. The great Hindu lawgiver Manu says, "He is Aryan, who is born through prayer."[175] A child born otherwise is illegitimate according to Manu. This attitude of sanctity with which the Hindu mind regards motherhood, springs from the conviction that it is the pre-natal influence that gives the impetus to the child to be good or evil. Education and all the rest are secondary. As Swami

Vivekananda said, "...our books teach that it is the pre-natal influence that gives the impetus to the child for good or evil. Go to hundred thousand colleges, read a million books, associate with all the learned men of the world — better off you are when born with the right stamp. You are born for good or evil. The child is a born good or a born demon; that is what the books say. Education and all these things come afterwards — are a mere bagatelle."[176] The mother has to maintain a strict rule of morality and ethics, chastity and purity of body and mind, if she is to conceive a noble son. Commenting on the purity of woman in India Lepel Griffin in the introduction of the book — *Famous Women of India* — remarked, "The women of the East are not so much an evidence as those of Europe, but their influence within the legitimate circle of their domestic relations is quite as great, their manners are as good and their morality is as high."[177] The woman invokes the blessing of God with top sincerity and devotion so that a divine soul will land on her womb. Slightest aberrations might frustrate her hope. So the responsibility for a good child is solely on the mother. As Swami Vivekananda said, "For that which brings forth the child is the holiest symbol of God himself. It is the greatest prayer between man and wife, the prayer that is going to bring in to the world a soul fraught with tremendous power for good or for evil."[178]

Napoleon Bonaparte realised the role of a good mother in building up a good nation. As he said, "Give me a good mother I shall give you a good nation."

Another stage of woman's life that appears to be very miserable to the surface is widowhood. To the ordinary mind widowhood is a curse. But to Swami Vivekananda it is a boon in disguise. All miseries and hardships of widowhood are preparation for spiritual elevation. A true widow never curses herself for her miseries and misfortune. As it has been said, "She (widow) lives a life of asceticism and devotion, thus elevating her life to higher levels of perfections."[179] Thus while widowhood is a hardship to many it is a doorway to higher spiritual perfection to many others.

Further Swami Vivekananda was of the opinion that woman as a daughter in her father's family does a very noble work *i.e.*, a purely motherly work. The Sanskrit word for daughter is 'Duhita'. The word 'Duhita' comes from the root verb 'Duh' which means to milk the cow and supply nutrition to the members of the family, which is purely a motherly function.

Thus in all phases of life a woman in India renders her divine, selfless service to the society without expecting anything in return. This ideal of womanhood in India has become an example for the whole world. It has attracted the world attention that led J.J. Pool to remark "...Woman in Eastern land also, notwithstanding the fact that she is immured in a zenana and is invincible to the eyes of the world, exerts a powerful influence, not only over her friends at home, but a society at large."[180]

But Swami Vivekananda was much shocked to see the terrible degeneration of women in India. Their low, inferior and miserable position in the orthodox Hindu society became a constant source of anxiety for him. He repeatedly called upon his countrymen to recognise women as the symbol of Divine Mother and not to treat her as a door-mat or an instrument of procreation. For regenerating Indian women, he once disclosed his plan of establishing a Woman's Math, for providing appropriate training to unmarried girls and widows. It was his conviction that no nation could progress which trampled on women, neglected them, and kept them in bondage and perpetual backwardness. He said, "We are horrible sinners and our degeneration is due to our calling women despicable worms, gateway to hell and so forth."[181] Though he was not very enthusiastic about the reforms such as abolition of early marriage, remarriage of widows etc. he realised in the words of Annie Besant, "Indian greatness will not return until Indian woman obtains a large, a freer and a fuller life, for largely in the hands of Indian women must lie the redemption of India."[182] He wanted the ancient Indian condition to be resorted under which women were treated with great veneration and played a very significant role. As he said, "Oh, India! Forget not that the ideal of thy womanhood is Sita, Savitri, Damayanti; forget not that the God thou worshipest is the great Ascetic of ascetics, the all renouncing Sankara, the Lord of Uma,...; forget not that thy social order is but the reflex of the Infinite Universal Motherhood...."[183]

Later on Gandhiji also emphasised on the reival of this ancient Indian tradition of woman in his national programme and said, "India's salvation depends on the sacrifice and enlightenment of her women.... Women used to be honoured and their work and worth were regarded as of special value. Let us continue the tradition in letter and spirit."[184]

Thus veneration for woman constitutes the basis of Swami Vivekananda's nationalism, which aims at reviving the old Indian traditions.

To sum up Swami Vivekananda's nationalism rests on an octagonal foundation. As far as the octagonal foundation is concerned religion constitutes one of the sides of this foundation. Religion constitutes the very bedrock of Indian life, both private and public. Swami Vivekananda, a Hindu saint, felt that the Indian nation survives in the strength of religion. Religion is the only source of her national vitality and vigour.

The second side of the octagonal foundation of Swami Vivekananda's nationalism has been provided by the cultural heritage of India. India with a very ancient and rich culture stands out as the unique land, whose culture has outlived all other ancient cultures that were contemporaneous with it. This is so because of its inherent vitality to absorb and assimilate various influences. This assimilative and synthetic aspect of Indian culture according to Swami Vivekananda should constitute an essential arm of the octagonal foundation.

The third side of the octagonal foundation of Swami Vivekananda's nationalism is furnished by his passionate love and concern for the masses. The sight of poverty, hunger, destitution and deprivation of millions struck a vital chord of Swami Vivekananda's saintly personality. He wanted that such disabilities of the Indians should be removed and for the sake of the same India must be constituted into a mighty nation. Hence his concern for the masses provides another arm of Swami Vivekananda's nationalism.

Swami Vivekananda, a Vedantic saint, witnessed Atman all

along. He considered the entire universe as manifestation of the freedom loving Atman. Hence he considered freedom to be the very essential hallmark of the universe. This spirit of freedom should not only animate all organisms including human beings; it should also enliven all group and communitarian life. Hence this freedom should manifest itself in form of national freedom. Accordingly this consciousness of freedom provides another arm of Swami Vivekananda's concept of nationalism.

Swami Vivekananda a Vedantist was also a universalist. He was opposed to all sorts of narrowness and sectarianism. He was opposed to religious, linguistic, racial and cultural isolationism. Hence, while advocating national resurgence, he also emphasised on spiritual integration of the entire world. Hence, spiritual integration of the universe constitutes another arm of Swami Vivekananda nationalism.

Swami Vivekananda, a saint of the Ramkrishan's order was by nature and commitment a real sannyasin who not only renounced the world but also desired for earthly possessions and worldly reputations. Renunciation, non-possession and non-covetousness constituted his philosophy of life. He also found that culturally speaking India consisted of people who were non-possessive and non-covetous in nature. Hence, he advocated that non-possessiveness and non-covetousness should constitute one of the essential hallmarks of Indian nationalism. Thus, non-possessiveness and non-covetousness shall constitute another arm of the octagonal foundation of Swami Vivekananda's nationalism.

Although Swami Vivekananda is a sannyasin, he believed in the doctrine of 'Karmayoga' as preached in the Bhagvad Gita. He was a saint to be contented with meditation in mountain caves, seeking his own salvation. Instead he was a saint of different type, who shall have his hand in the society with his heart in salvation. He wanted to rebuild the society by individual and collective effort. Hence, he was a passionate advocate not of passivity but of action and activity. Hence a nation for him shall bubble with activity. In other words 'Karmayoga' constituted another arm of the octagonal foundation of Swami Vivekananda's nationalism.

Above all Swami Vivekananda was a disciple of Ramkrishna Paramahansa, who was an adorer of female deity of Prakriti or divinity expressed through the medium of mother deity. Hence although a sannyasin, Swami Vivekananda realised the significance of woman in the creation. Accordingly he worshipped not only his motherland, which he wanted to be welded to a mighty nation; he also wanted that woman should play a significant role in building up the nation. Hence veneration for woman constitutes the eighth and the final arm of the octagonal foundation of Swami Vivekananda's nationalism.

REFERENCES

1. R.N. Tagore, *Nationalism*, p. 1.
2. *Ibid.*, p. 7.
3. Quoted from Romain Rolland, *Life of Swami Vivekananda*, p. 275.
4. Bertrand Russell, *Political Ideals*, p. 79.
5. S.C. Sengupta, *Swami Vivekananda and Indian Nationalism*, p. 58.
6. *Complete Works of Swami Vivekananda*, Vol. III, p. 177.
7. Quoted in V.S. Narvane, *Modern Indian Thought*, p. 97.
8. Quoted in Swami Ganbhirananda, *A Short Life of Swami Vivekananda*, p. 114.
9. Swami Vivekananda, *Lectures from Colombo to Almora*, p. 125.
10. Quoted in Romain Rolland, pp. 278-79.
11. *Life of Swami Vivekananda*, Advaita Ashram, p. 533.
12. *Complete Works of Swami Vivekananda*, Vol. III, p. 138.
13. Swami Vivekananda, *Lectures from Colombo to Almora*, p. 126.
14. *Complete Works of Swami Vivekananda*, Vol. III, p. 107.
15. *Ibid.*, Vol. V, p. 409.
16. Quoted from *Swami Vivekananda — Studies in Soviet Union*, p. 294.
17. *Complete Works of Swami Vivekananda*, Vol. V, p. 409.
18. Quoted in Swami Gambhirananda, *A Short Life of Swami Vivekananda*, p. 116.
19. *Complete Works of Swami Vivekananda*, Vol. III, p. 325.
20. Swami Vivekananda, *Idea of Universal Religion* (Selected Works), p. 180.
21. Quoted in T.L. Vaswani, *The Voice of Vivekananda*, p. 59.
22. *Ibid.*, p. 59.

23. *Complete Works of Swami Vivekananda*, Vol. III, p. 182.
24. *Ibid.*, Vol. V, p. 79.
25. Romain Rolland, *Life of Swami Vivekananda and the Universal Gospel*, p. 155.
26. *Complete Works of Swami Vivekananda*, Vol. VI, p. 415.
27. *Ibid.*, p. 415.
28. Karl Marx and Engels, Vol. I, p. 28.
29. *Cultural Heritage of India*, Published by R.K. Mission, Vol. III, p. 87.
30. *Ibid.*, pp. 87-88.
31. Jawaharlal Nehru, *Discovery of India*, pp. 77-78.
32. B.N. Luniya, *Evolution of Indian Culture*, p. 231.
33. *The Cultural Heritage of India*, Vol. III, p. 90 (Published by R.K. Mission).
34. B.N. Luniya, *Evolution of Indian Culture*, p. 232.
35. Quoted in Lanka Sundaram, *A Secular State for India*, p. 27.
36. Jawaharlal Nehru, *India Today and Tomorrow*, p. 11.
37. *The Cultural Heritage of India*, Vol. III, p. 93 (Published by R.K. Mission).
38. Jawaharlal Nehru, *India Today and Tomorrow*, p. 4.
39. Jawaharlal Nehru, *Discovery of India*, pp. 46-47.
40. E.G. Rapson, *The Cambridge History of India*, Vol. I, p. 52.
41. F.L. Schuman, *International Politics*, p. 7.
42. *Complete Works of Swami Vivekananda*, Vol. II, p. 510.
43. *Selected Works of M.N. Roy*, Vol. I, p. 345.
44. Swami Vivekananda, *Lectures from Colombo to Almora*, p. 200.
45. *Complete works of Swami Vivekananda*, Vol. III, p. 285.
46. Amaury De Reincourt, *The Soul of India*, p. 151.
47. *Swami Vivekananda — Studies in Soviet Union*, Published on 150th Birth Anniversary of Sri Ramkrishna, p. 209.
48. Quoted in Romain Rolland, *The Life of Swami Vivekananda*, p. 26.
49. *Ibid.*, p. 26.
50. Quoted in V.K.R.V. Rao, *Swami Vivekananda*, pp. 67-68.
51. Quoted in Romain Rolland, *The Life of Vivekananda*, p. 31.
52. *Ibid.*, pp. 70-71.
53. *Complete Works of Swami Vivekananda*, Vol. V, Third edition, p. 152.

54. *Ibid.*, Vol. V, pp. 468-69.
55. *Ibid.*, Vol. V, p. 152.
56. Romain Rolland, *The Life of Vivekananda and the Universal Gospel*, p. 72.
57. Swami Vivekananda, *Studies in Soviet Union*, p. 212.
58. *Complete Works of Swami Vivekananda*, Vol. V, p. 106.
59. *Ibid.*, Vol. V, p. 249 (Third Edition).
60. *Ibid.*, Vol. V, p. 153.
61. *Ibid.*, Vol. V, pp. 333-34.
62. *Lectures from Colombo to Almora*, p. 121.
63. *Life of Swami Viveknanda by His Western and Eastern Disciples*, Vol. 6, p. 177.
64. Swami Vivekananda, *Studies in Soviet Union*, p. 394.
65. *Ibid.*, p. 400.
66. *Ibid.*, pp. 400-09.
67. Quoted in V.K.R.V. Rao, *The Life of Swami Vivekananda*, p. 169.
68. Romain Rolland, *The Life of Swami Vivekananda*, p. 27.
69. *Complete Works of Swami Vivekananda*, Vol. V, p. 434.
70. *Ibid.*, Vol. II, p. 125.
71. *Ibid.*, Vol. I, p. 108.
72. *Ibid.*, Vol. I, p. 434.
73. *Ibid.*, Vol. I, p. 333.
74. *Ibid.*, Vol. II, p. 97.
75. *Ibid.*, Vol. II, p. 323.
76. *Ibid.*, Vol. II, p. 283.
77. *Ibid.*, Vol. II, p. 115.
78. *Ibid.*, Vol. II, pp. 115-16.
79. *Ibid.*, Vol. III, p. 521.
80. Manomohan Ganguly, *Swami Vivekananda — A Study*, p. 69.
81. *Complete Works of Swami Vivekananda*, Vol. II, p. 115.
82. *Ibid.*, Vol. IV, p. 480.
83. *Ibid.*, Vol. VI, p. 329.
84. *Ibid.*, Vol. IV, p. 392.
85. *Ibid.*, Vol. III, p. 245.
86. *Ibid.*, Vol. IV, p. 358.

87. *Ibid.*, Vol. VIII, p. 18.
88. *Ibid.*, Vol. II, p. 85.
89. *Ibid.*, Vol. II, p. 115.
90. *Ibid.*, Vol. II, p. 126.
91. Swami Vivekananda, *A Centinary Vol.*, 1963, p. 150.
92. *Complete Works of Swami Vivekananda*, Vol. II, p. 252.
93. *Ibid.*, Vol. II, p. 252.
94. Quoted in *Swami Vivekananda — Studies in Soviet Union*, p. 198.
95. Romain Rolland, *The Life of Swami Vivekananda*, p. 157.
96. *Complete Works of Swami Vivekananda*, Vol. III, pp. 276-77.
97. *Ibid.*, Vol. III, p. 109.
98. Quoted in Swami Budhananda, *Swami Vivekananda, His Call to the Nation*, p. 25.
99. Swami Nikhilananda, *Swami Vivekananda – A Biography*, p. 134.
100. Swami Budhananda, *Swami Vivekananda, His Call to the Nation*, p. 21.
101. *Complete Works of Swami Vivekananda*, Vol. III, pp. 261-62.
102. Dr. D.R. Bali, *Modern Indian Thought*, p. 40.
103. Jawaharlal Nehru, *India Today and Tomorrow*, p. 14.
104. *Complete Works of Swami Vivekananda*, Vol. VII, p. 59.
105. Swami Tapasyananda, *Nationalistic and Religious Lectures of Swami Vivekananda*, p. 96.
106. Dr. D.R. Bali, *Modern Indian Thought*, p. 144.
107. *The Life of Swami Vivekananda by His Western and Eastern Disciples*, Vol. IV, p. 193.
108. *Complete Works of Swami Vivekananda*, Vol. I, p. 11.
109. *Ibid.*, Vol. VII, p. 66.
110. S. Radhakrishnan, *The Bhagvad Gita*, p. 179.
111. *Ibid.*, p. 138.
112. *Nationalistic and Religious Lectures of Swami Vivekanand*, p. 193.
113. *Complete Works of Swami Vivekananda*, Vol. IV, p. 13.
114. *Nationalistic and Religious Lectures of Swami Vivekanand*, p. 194.
115. *Complete Works of Swami Vivekananda*, Vol. 1, p. 209.
116. *Ibid.*, Vol. 1, p. 13.
117. *Ibid.*, Vol. 1, p. 12.
118. *Nationalistic and Religious Lectures of Swami Vivekanand*, p. 190.

119. *Complete Works of Swami Vivekananda,* Vol. 1, p. 81.
120. *Ibid.*, Vol. 1, p. 442.
121. *Ibid.*, Vol. IV, pp. 12-13.
122. *Ibid.*, Vol. IV, p. 12.
123. *Ibid.*, Vol. 1, p. 20.
124. *Ibid.*, Vol. VII, p. 64.
125. *Ishopanishad,* Mantra — 1.
126. *Complete Works of Swami Vivekananda,* Vol. 1, p. 100.
127. *Ibid.*, Vol. III, p. 158.
128. *Ibid.*, Vol. VI, p. 44.
129. Bertrand Russell, *Political Ideals,* p. 24.
130. *Ibid.*, p. 25.
131. Quoted in Tejesananda, *A Short Life of Swami Vivekananda,* p. 39.
132. B.G. Tilak, *Gita Rahasya or the Science of Karmayoga,* p. 909.
133. S. Radhakrishnan, *The Bhagvad Gita,* p. 133.
134. *Ibid.*, p. 133.
135. *Complete Works of Swami Vivekananda,* Vol. 1, p. 34.
136. Arnold Edwin, *The Song Celestial,* p. 16.
137. *Complete Works of Swami Vivekananda,* Vol. 1, p. 58.
138. S. Radhakrishnan, *The Bhagvad Gita,* p. 141.
139. *Complete Works of Swami Vivekananda,* Vol. 1, p. 115.
140. *Ibid.*, Vol. 1, p. 99.
141. *Ibid.*, Vol. 1, p. 111.
142. *Ibid.*, Vol. 1, p. 59.
143. *Nationalistic Religious Lectures of Swami Vivekananda,* p. 190.
144. *Complete Works of Swami Vivekananda,* Vol. II, p. 224.
145. *Ibid.*, Vol. II, p. 225.
146. *Ibid.*, Vol. V, p. 410.
147. *Nationalistic and Religious Lectures of Swami Vivekananda,* p. 190.
148. *Complete Works of Swami Vivekananda,* Vol. 1, p. 33.
149. *Nationalistic and Religious Lectures of Swami Vivekananda,* p. 190.
150. *Complete Works of Swami Vivekananda,* Vol. II, p. 225.
151. *Ibid.*, Vol. 1, p. 59.
152. Romain Rolland, *Universal Gospel of Vivekananda,* p. 22.

153. Quoted in Swami Gambhirananda, *A Short Life of Swami Vivekananda*, p. 118.
154. *Complete Works of Swami Vivekananda*, Vol. 1, p. 93.
155. S. Radhakrishnan, *The Bhagvad Gita*, p. 136.
156. *Ibid.*, p. 136.
157. Annie Besant, *The Bhagvad Gita*, pp. 11-12.
158. *Complete Works of Swami Vivekananda*, Vol. IV, p. 7.
159. *Ibid.*, Vol. II, pp. 3-4.
160. Romain Rolland, *Universal Gospel of Vivekananda*, p. 86.
161. *Complete Works of Swami Vivekananda*, Vol. IV, p. 107.
162. *Ibid.*, Vol. I, pp. 117-18.
163. *Ibid.*, Vol. IV, p. 107.
164. Romain Rolland, *Universal Gospel of Vivekananda*, p. 22.
165. *Nationalistic and Religious Lectures of Swami Vivekananda*, p. 90.
166. *Complete Works of Swami Vivekananda*, Vol. I, p. 65.
167. *Ibid.*, Vol. I, p. 66.
168. *Ibid.*, Vol. I, p. 66.
169. *Nationalistic and Religious Lectures of Swami Vivekananda*, p. 193.
170. *Complete Works of Swami Vivekananda*, Vol. VIII, p. 57.
171. *Ibid.*, Vol. VIII, p. 58.
172. *Ibid.*, Vol. VIII, p. 58.
173. *Ibid.*, Vol. VIII, p. 59.
174. *Religious and Nationalistic Lectures of Swami Vivekananda*, p. 104.
175. *Complete Works of Swami Vivekananda*, Vol. VIII, p. 59.
176. *Ibid.*, Vol. VIII, p. 60.
177. John J. Pool, *Famous Women of India* (Preface).
178. *Complete Works of Swami Vivekananda*, Vol. VIII, p. 61.
179. *Nationalistic and Religious Lectures of Swami Vivekananda*, p. 106.
180. John J. Pool, *Famous Women of India* (Preface).
181. Quoted in Dr. D.R. Bali, Modern Indian Thought, p. 43.
182. Annie Besant, *The Education of Indian Girls*, p. 10.
183. *Complete Works of Swami Vivekananda*, Vol. IV, pp. 479-80.
184. Mahatma Gandhi, *Harijan*, December 27, 1936.

3

NATURE OF SWAMI VIVEKANANDA'S NATIONALISM

Nationalism is not a doctrine that provides an invariable standard. It is not a doctrine that is constantly fixed, unchangeable at all times and in all places irrespective of the prevailing condition in the country and the nature of the people who advocate it. Instead, the doctrine changes its nature and character depending on the social, religious, political and economic condition of the country from which it emanates, the nature and character of the leadership that motivates the people, and the attitude of the authority in possession of the political power against which it is enkindled. Hence, while describing the nature of nationalism H.J. Laski has remarked, "Nationalism is broadly speaking, hardly older than first partition of Poland and it differs from all previous form and character into which its ideology has been cast...."[1] Even the nationalism of the same country, for the attainment of the same goal of nationalhood differs in its nature at different phases of national struggle. In India the moderate nature of its nationalism changed when the militant nationalists dominated the scene of Indian polity during the freedom struggle. The great nationalists of India like Dadabhai Naoroji, Ferozshah Mehta, Gopal Krishna Gokhale, M.G. Ranade, W.C. Banarjee, Surendra Nath Banarjee etc. not only took the British rule in India for granted but they considered it as divine dispensation for India's progress and prosperity. They had profound faith in the British sense of justice and fair-play, their inherent goodness. M.G. Ranade observed, "The aegis of British protection is an acknowledged necessity."[2] W.C. Banarjee in the same tone remarked, "It is to England that we must turn, if our political aspirations are ever to be realized."[3] Thus the moderates believed in the potency of technique of appeal, persuasion, resolution etc. But with the advent of the extremist nationalists like Lala Lajpat Rai, Bal Gangadhar Tilak, Bipin Chandra Pal, Aurobindo Ghose etc. the nature of Indian nationalism assumed a militant nature. They argued that a colonial and imperial power, accustomed to the privileges of governing a country and exploiting its economy cannot be persuaded to renounce its privileges. They believed that the imperial power will never concede to the request of the governed for self-government. So they scornfully branded the nationalism of the moderate nationalists as "Political mendicancy". Lala Lajpat Rai observed, "The line of least resistance of empty resolutions, on a paper, of simple resolutions, memorials and not petitions, backed up by anything which would place our earnestness beyond the shadow of doubt, is a line of action more worthy of women than of men."[4] So the extremist leaders advocated extreme measures for reaching the goal of nationhood and Indian nationalism assumed a different nature under their leadership. The moderate nationalism of India was transformed into militant or extreme form of nationalism.

(i) Spiritualism

Though nationalism of the West emerged as a secular doctrine, in India the country with a profoundly religious and spiritual background, nationalism could not but assume spiritualistic tone. As Rabindranath Tagore has observed, "In fact our history has not been of the rise and fall of kingdoms, of fights for political supremacy. In our country records of these days have been despised and forgotten, for they in no way represent the true history of our people. Our history is that of our social life and the attainment of spiritual ideals."[5] Swami Vivekananda — a mystic of the modern world, had a thorough study of the ancient history of India, from which he gathered that in all ages, spiritualism has become the secret of all strength of national life of India. It is the bedrock upon which the edifice of our national unity has been built up. It is the vital force that determines our national character. It is the source of all power that kindles confidence, courage and faith in us. It has upheld the existence of our nation in the history of the world. Politics or anything else as in case of the Western nations did not constitute the vitality of our race. He was firmly convinced that "India is immortal if she persists in her search for God,"[6] "If she holds to her treasure — house of religion and spirituality."[7] So the theory of nationalism that Swami Vivekananda sought to propound is primarily spiritual in nature. Spirituality forms the soul of his nationalistic doctrine. It is the unique norm, nature and the character of nationalism that Swami Vivekananda intended to diffuse among his countrymen to galvanize the drooping spirit against the British yoke.

According to Swami Vivekananda, "...there is a certain point where the life of a nation centres, where lies the nationality of the nation and until that point is touched, the nation cannot die."[8] It is just like certain serpents as we hear in our childhood stories that cannot be killed unless the jewel in their heads is not destroyed. Again some giants and ogresses, as we hear in our grandmother's tale, keep their soul living with some birds, hidden under the hallow of a mighty trunk of a tree, who can never be killed by any power on earth, unless that bird is killed. Similarly our national life, the soul of which lies in spiritualism can never receive any setback of any sort so long that spiritual core of our nationalism is retained. As long as we keep our soul of nationalism, living with spiritualism, no power on earth can destroy it. That according to Swami Vivekananda is the reason why the Hindus have still survived as a nation in spite of numerous calamities and catastrophes of foreign invasion in the past. As Swami Vivekananda has said, "Wave after wave of barbarian conquest has rolled over this devoted land of ours. "Allah Ho Akbar" has rent the skies for hundred of years and no Hindu knew what moment would be his last. This is the most suffering and the most subjugated of all the historic lands of the world. Yet we still stand practically the same race."[9]

Swami Vivekananda felt that our ancestors in the past, finding that the quest for the secret of Nature through external investigation is useless, turned their attention inward. They focused their attention on this inward quest, which is grander and infinitely higher, infinitely more blissful till it has become the national characteristic, till it has become our sacred nature. Thus spiritualism and Hindu life have become one. This is our national characteristic — the source of all vitality of our race. As long as we hold on to this grandest of all our inheritances, namely spirituality, said Swami Vivekananda no external force can destroy us. Spirituality is the greatest immunity of our national body. So he said, "Bearing this in our mind we shall be in better position to understand why for our national welfare, we must seek out all the spiritual forces of the race. National Union in India must be gathering up of its scattered spiritual forces — a union of those whose hearts beat to the same spiritual tune."[10]

Swami Vivekananda believed that nationalism in India is the concomitant of spiritualism. There can be no regeneration of India unless India sticks to her century-long tradition of spiritual goal. He said, "Each nation has a destiny to fulfil, each nation has a message to deliver, each nation has a mission to accomplish. Therefore we must have to understand the mission of our own race, the destiny it has to fulfil, the place it has to occupy in the march of nations, the role of which it has to contribute to the harmony of races."[11] Revival of spiritualism is not only efficacious for India but upon it depends the welfare of the whole world. Nation after nation has risen and based its greatness upon materialism, declaring man is all matter. All such civilizations as based upon the sandy foundations of materialism, have disappeared from the face of the world. One after another after a short period of meteoric appearance. But the civilization of India lives even up to the present day and there are signs of its revival. Its life is like that of a phoenix, a thousand times destroyed, but ready to spring up again more glorious. But a materialistic culture once dashed down can never come up again.

(ii) Didactic in Nature

Swami Vivekananda's nationalism is didactic in nature. It is highly educative, with a deep moral tone. He realized that moral power is the highest power of the individual and a nation that serves this power all along must reach its goal. So he decided to strengthen the moral fibre of the people by insisting on character building, discipline and strength of mind. To him character is destiny. Hence in almost all of his lectures and writings that aimed at promoting nationalism, he laid stress on strong moral character of the people, which he considered to be the keynote of all success. To him morality is the essence of all religions. As he said, "No religion for you, my children, but morality."[12]

A man with strong moral fibre is perfect and he has complete control over his mind. He does no bad things. He does no harm to others but makes peaceful co-existence with others imperative. As a result society becomes progressive both spiritually and materially. As he said, "Perfect morality is the all in all of complete control over mind. The man who is perfectly moral, cannot possibly hurt anything or any body."[13]

The sole aim of Swami Vivekananda was thus man making. Therefore he very often laid stress on honesty and sincerity as the key to success. As he said, "Every successful man must have behind him somewhere tremendous integrity, tremendous sincerity and that is the cause of his signal success in life."[14]

Truth, purity and unselfishness, according to Swami Vivekananda should be the special traits with all individuals, constituting the nation. As they keep strength of mind intact that finally brings success to all individuals against all adversities. Therefore Swami Vivekananda observed, "Truth, purity and unselfishness — wherever these are present, there is no power below or above the sun to crush the possessor thereof. Equipped with these one individual is able to face the whole universe in opposition."[15]

Swami Vivekananda was of the opinion that man is the maker of his own fortune. But unfortunately he blames his fortune or star for the failure in his life. As he said, "This is tale" — so says Sanskrit proverb. But it is the strong man who stands up and says, 'I will make my fate.' It is the people who are getting old who talk of fate. Young men generally do not come to astrology."[16]

Swami Vivekananda believed in slow and steady progress of

the society and nation. Therefore he advised his compatriots not to be in haste and have fully patience and perseverance. Sincerity, accompanied by patience brings success to all men. It has no failure. Therefore he has said, "Purity, patience and perseverance are the three essentials to success and above all love."[17] Everything will come right if people are sincere and hardworking. Such people, according to Swami Vivekananda will herald a new era of life and truth for whole mankind.

Swami Vivekananda let loose his passionate anger at the weakness, cowardice and lethargy among the people of his country. He inspired all his countrymen against all these chronic maladies of national life and said, 'Above all be strong and manly.' He admonished his countrymen and said, "Anything that makes you weak physically, mentally and spiritually, reject as poison, there is no life in it. It cannot be true. Truth is strength. Truth is purity. This Truth is all knowledge."[18]

His recognition of divinity in all men and worship of man-God, opened a new chapter in the history of nationalism of the world. It changed the concept of worship of both East and West. As he said, "This is the gist of all worship — to be pure and good to others. He who sees Siva in the poor, in the weak and in the diseased, really worships Siva and if he sees Siva only in the image, his worship is only preliminary."[19] His call to the world for worship of man-God unfolded the inner chamber of consciousness of the great diplomats and statesmen of the world for universal organisation for service of the mankind. As a result world organisation like W.H.O., U.N.E.S.C.O. evolved into fulfledged institution.

Swami Vivekananda's concept of unity in the midst of diversity — the great Vedantic truth, changed his world outlook. He established the great Vadantic truth of non-duality *i.e.*, man is one, religion is one and the whole universe is one — All are subject to one Absolute Soul — the Brahma. It is only in ignorance that we see the difference. As it has been observed, "There is nothing else, for Brahma is all! There is nothing else but Brahma. He is all and the Universe is in Him. Its manifestation is only a manifestation of Himself."[20] His preachings of the Vedantic concept of unity in the midst of diversity led him to spread the most cardinal democratic principle of equality, fraternity, and fellowship. Since all are manifestation of the same Brahma, have the same origin, they are all equal. Hence he advocated that all prejudices of caste, colour, rank, sex etc., should disappear from the mind of the people of the world. The whole mankind should realises the Vedantic truth of divine unity of all men.

Swami Vivekananda preached that neither by acquisition of property or wealth or knowledge nor propagation of the race, man attains the best self that he is capable of attaining. On the other hand the surest path to salvation consists in self-sacrifice and renunciation. As the Upanished says, "Not by progeny, nor by wealth, but by renunciation, alone immortality is reached."[21] This appeal for renunciation and sacrifice had tremendous effect upon the imperial capitalistic policy of the West and paved the path for materialization of the socialistic doctrines of distribution of wealth among all.

Through his living touch and fiery speeches, the mental, emotional and inborn lethargy of Indians shaken and they arouse from the inertia to the fully developed, active, sincere, zealous nationalists. His insistence on the true end of life — Dharma, Artha, Kama, Moksha — brought about a psychological ferment, that stirred the individual to the very depth and endowed them with a new bent of mind that inflamed our nationalism. Divinity of nation, revelation of national ideal, glorification of human life, realization of God as the prime goal of life — all these constitute the norms and natures of Swami Vivekananda's nationalism that make it highly didactic and moral.

(iii) Socialistic in Nature

The most unique aspect of Swami Vivekananda's nationalism is that it combines both materialism and spiritualism — the two sides of human life. So though Swami Vivekananda invariably insists on the spiritual ideal of the nation it does not mean that his nationalism does not provide any scope for upgradation of the material condition of life of man. In his scheme of nationalism, there is abundant place for eradication of poverty and improvement of man's material condition of life. He was of the view that religion will have little hold on hungry man. As he said to his disciples, "For want of food and clothing, and plunged in anxiety for it, the country has come to ruin. Throw aside your scriptures in the Ganga and teach the people first the means of procuring their food and clothing and then you will find time to read to them scriptures. If their material wants are not removed, none will listen to words of spirituality."[22] He also recalled the words of his great Master, "It is no good preaching spiritual doctrines to hungry stomachs."[23] Spiritual message would melt in the air before the wrath of hunger, penury and sad spectacle of the poor, demoralized the degenerated mass of people, devoured by senseless credulity and fetishism. So according to Swami Vivekananda's scheme of nationalism man has to be above poverty line and possess sound physical health if he is to undergo spiritual discipline. With his compassion for the poor and the down-trodden he appealed, "My boy, if you have any respect for my words, the first thing I will advice you to do is to throw open all the doors and windows of your room. In your quarter there are lot of poor people sunk in degradation and misery — you will have to go to them and serve them with your zeal and enthusiasm. Arrange to distribute medicines to those who are sick and nurse them with all care, supply food to him, who is starving, teach with as much as lies in you the ignorants; and if you begin to serve your brethren in this wise, I tell you my child, you will surely get peace and consolation."[24] What right have we to preach any religion, metaphysical idea or high moral principle to poor millions if we fail in our primary task to give a morsel of food to hungry stomach and elevate them from dark, dingy hovels to bring sunshine and glimmering surface of life?

Swami Vivekananda branded him a traitor, who having received education accumulates wealth at the cost of the blood of the toilers, and does not bother about them. As he said, "I call him a traitor, who having been educated, nursed in luxury by the heart's blood of the down-trodden millions of toiling poor, never even takes a thought for them."[25]

Swami Vivekananda was conscious of the fact that India through the ages adores poverty; but it is not the wretchedness, poverty, want and privation but non-covetous and non-possessive attitude of the ancient sages, rich in the wealth of spirit. Hence his concept of spiritual upliftment did not neglect the upliftment of the material condition of life in India. So in all his lectures and writing we find powerful exhortations by Swami Vivekananda for the improvement of the standard of the people of India; at the same time he warned too against the material comforts and luxurious way of life of the West. Dharma (morality), Artha (wealth), Kama (pleasure) and Moksha (liberation) have all been recognised by the Indian philosophy as values relevant for human life. But the pursuit of them must be regulated in a way so that the fulfilment they offer, ultimately lead to Moksha. Spiritual value is most vital. Material values are desirable to the extent they subserve the development of the former. However, they should not be treated as end in themselves. He condemned the Western view of nationalism that 'revived and developed the theory of Colbertism and made each nation by means of the Tariff and Free-Trade, a complete economic unit.'[26]

Subash Chandra Bose has clearly stated that socialism in India owes its origin to Swami Vivekananda and only its later development are due to Karl Marx.[27] Gandhiji's movement for the uplift of the scheduled caste and scheduled tribe got tremendous inspiration from Swami Vivekananda concept of Vedic equality that impressed Gandhiji very much.

Swami Vivekananda, who declared, "I am a socialist not because I think it is a perfect system but because half a loaf is better than no bread,"[28] derived his socialism from the spiritual heritage of India. His socialism is not a product of mere emotional upsurge or expression of human compassion. It is based on the solid philosophy of man and his infinite possibilities — the philosophy of Advaita, which proclaims the divinity and solidarity of all human beings. As he said, "You are the veritable Gods of the universe, nay, there are not two, there are but one. It is the mistake to say 'you and I'...."[29] He thus connects the modern political and social democratic demand for freedom and equality with India's ancient Vedic spirituality.

Swami Vivekananda's view of society was just like that of

C.E.M. Joad, who said, "...society is an association of human beings formed with the object of giving all its members equal opportunity to satisfy their desire for spiritual freedom and the good of life."[30] That is why according to Swami Vivekananda there is no place for any special privileges for any group or class of people in the society. He was the first spiritual personality of modern India who dealt with the socio-economic problems of man along with his religious cravings and aspirations. His socio-economic thoughts are based upon the 'philosophy of Advaita, which he and also his great Master Sri Ramkrishna upheld — a unifying philosophy, oriented to action in the world so as to change it and not merely to contemplate on Reality.'[31] Advocating the cause of abolition of the social privileges he said, "Wherever you go there will be caste. But that does not mean that there should be these privileges.... If you teach Vedanta to the fisherman he will say 'I am as good a man as you, I am fisherman, you are a philosopher but I have the same God in me as you have in you. And that is what we want, no privilege for any one, equal chances for all'."[32] Again he said, "The work of the Advita therefore, is to break down all these privileges."[33]

According to Swami Vivekananda this privilege that one enjoys over another has become the source of all discontent and resentment in all societies, leading to all revolutions. This is a global problem. So without elimination of privilege human society cannot progress. As he said, "What can be attained is the elimination of privileges. This is really the work before the whole world. In all social lives there has been that one fight in every race and in every society."[34]

Swami Vivekananda has deep aversion for bourgeoisie society and capitalistic system of economy, which according to him degenerates man to low level. As he said, "The Western society is governed by a handful of shylocks. All the things that you hear about constitutional government, freedom, liberty, and parliaments are but jocks."[35] He foresaw that socialist system shall emerge in countries like Russia and China and declared, "The next great upheaval which was to bring about a new epoch would come from Russia or China."[36]

As his ear was keenly attuned to the voice of the epoch, Swami Vivekananda discerned in these countries indistinct grumbling of the toiling masses, rising to fight for their rights. As he said, "The lower classes are gradually awakening to this fact and making a united front against this, determined to exert their legitimate dues."[37] Pointing out that the workers of Europe and America were already fighting for their legitimate rights, Swami Vivekananda wrote, "Signs of this awakening have shown themselves in India, too, as is evident from the number of strikes among the lower classes nowaday."[38]

(iv) Reformative in Nature

Though Swami Vivekananda exhorted his countrymen to retain their hold on the spiritual ideal as the ideal of their nationalism he is not asking them to relapse in to the nightmare of social and religious superstitions, but to be progressive and forward looking. The practice of village customs, caste rules, don't-touchism, irrational practices in eating and drinking according to him have nothing to do with spiritualism. Too much insistence on them is rather detrimental to the real progress of spiritualism, that has vitiated the socio-religious life of India.[39]

Albert Eine-stein, the great scientist said, "Religion without science is blind and science without religion is lame." Hence religion should base upon science. Religion or spiritualism is barren if they deviate from the path of science. This is what had happened in India, said Swami Vivekananda. He pointed out that when the whole world marched forward with science and technology India remained smug in its own shell, glorifying itself in its don't touchism, caste obsession and kitchen religion. As Swami Vivekananda has said, "There is danger of our religion getting into our kitchen. We are neither Vedantist nor Puranics nor Tantrics, we are just 'Don't touchists.' Our religion is the kitchen, our God is in the cooking pot and our religion is 'Don't touch me', I am holy."[40] This kind of orthodoxy and dogmatism, Swami Vivekananda felt should be done away with and progressive spirit of the West be captured without losing our moorings in spiritualism.

Swami Vivekananda held that religion for a long time had become static in India. It must be made dynamic.[41] Social traditions should change according to the changing needs of the society so that the society will be more progressive. If some social customs are to be changed we should not think that we are going to lose our religion. Customs must change in order to meet the need and suit the time, and society thereby becomes more progressive. So he said, "As time rolls on, new Smritis will come, sages will come and they will direct the society through better channels according to the need of the age."[42]

But progressivism according to Swami Vivekananda also does not mean forgetting the origin. It means all progress must be made on the basis of Hinduism. In other words we must be progressive but with all sincerity and devotion to our Hindu traditions. As he said, "Let us be progressive and at the same time be as faithful and conservative towards our traditions as Hindus."[43]

Swami Vivekananda explained that we have to learn many things from the West in the field of organisation, science, politics, and technology for the improvement of our socio-economic conditions of life. Our deficiency in these respect is largely due to our ignorance and illiteracy. So he said, "We have to find our way between the Scylla of old superstitions and orthodoxy and the charybdis of materialism of Europeanism of soullessness of the so-called reforms, which has penetrated to the foundation of Western progress. These two have been taken care of."[44]

According to Swami Vivekananda reformation does not mean the blind imitation of the West. It is the sincere study of the West and assimilation of what is scientific and real for our life and growth. Blind imitation is very dangerous. It paves the path for being ridiculed, leading finally to national degeneration. As he said, "...imitation is not civilization. I may deck myself out in a Raja's dress, but will it make me a Raja? An ass in a lion's skin, never makes a lion. Imitation, cowardly imitation, never makes for progress. It is verily the sign of aweful degradation in a man."[45]

Many reformers emerged for about a century and they voiced their concern against the socio-religious degeneration of the society. But according to Swami Vivekananda they achieved nothing except creating a body of vituperative literature. Therefore he suggested that for effecting social changes revolutionary and disruptive methods are of little use. Public opinion or mind is to be educated first. A few intellectuals, trying to solve the problems of reforms by condemning fanaticism and orthodoxy, said Swami Vivekananda, is not reformation. The reformers, on the other hand, are to touch the very life of the masses what our great ancient masters like Sankara and Ramanuja did. They knew that changes cannot be accomplished overnight. The only way left for them was slowly to bring the masses up to the highest ideal, held forth by the existing religion.

Hence Swami Vivekananda believed in the policy of gradualism in the sphere of social change. Hence it is said, "Vivekananda, like Aristotle was a believer in moderation with regard to social change. Social customs are the results of the arrangements of society for self-preservation. But if these regulations are perpetuated, society may suffer decadence. But the way to do away with social regulations is not to destroy them violently but gradually to remove the forces which had necessitated the incorporation of those customs. Thus the particular social custom will wither-away. Mere denunciation and condemnation create unnecessary social tension and antagonism and are not of much avail."[46]

Thus the aim of Swami Vivekananda was fixed on socio-religious reformation for the cause of national regeneration. Socio-religious evils, he thought, would weaken the foundation of the nation. So to build up a strong moral nation he fought tooth and nail to root out these evils first. As it is rightly said, '...Swamiji's personality was unique in its comprehensiveness and deep sensitiveness to the evils, prevalent in the socio-religious and moral structure of the country.'[47]

His scheme of reformation for national reconstruction greatly influenced the leaders of India during the subsequent period of national history like Jawaharlal Nehru. As the latter writes, "Science today challenges the old concept of religion. But if religion deals not with dogmas and ceremonials but rather with higher things of life, there should be no conflict with science or *inter se* between religions. It might be the high privilege of India to help in bringing about this synthesis."[48]

(v) Expansionist in Nature

Expansionism is one of the unique features of Swami Vivekananda's nationalism. The nation according to him shall spread, grow, develop, and expand. However according to him expansion does not mean military conquest or territorial expansion but expansion of the spiritual culture of India to the four corners of the world. As he said, "By conquest of the world I mean the conquest by religion and spirituality and not conquest by armies."[49] Besides by expansion he also meant that the nation should expand itself intellectually and spiritually by absorbing that are best in other nations. As he felt, "No individual or nation can live by holding itself apart from the community of others and whenever such an attempt has been made under false idea of greatness, policy or holiness — the results has always been disastrous to the secluding one. To my mind the most important cause of the downfall and the degeneration of India was the building of a wall of custom, whose foundation was hatred of others round the nation and the real aim of which was to prevent the Hindu from coming into contact with surrounding Buddhist nations...."[50]

Reciprocation has characterized Indian nationalism in all ages of history. This is the law of existence for our nationality and whenever there has been violation of this law it has brought about the degeneration of India. As he said, "...give and take is the law and if India wants to raise herself once more it is absolutely necessary that she brings out her treasures and throws them broadcast among the nations of the earth and in return be ready to receive what others have to give her. Expansion is life, contraction is death.... Love is life and hatred is death."[51]

According to Swami Vivekananda thoughts like merchandise require channels and roads for their expansion. Whenever in the world history conquering races have established communications with India, Indian thoughts also moved along those lines and influenced the life of the people. Thus even long before Buddhism, Vedanta had penerated into China, Persia, Islands of Eastern Archipelago etc. When Greek conquest established the link between East and West Indian thoughts penetrated into those regions and Christianity with its boasted civilization is but a collection of little bits of Indian thoughts. The Greek ambassador Megasthenes, sent by Syrian king to the royal court of Chandragupta Maurya, is said to have admitted this fact in his accounts of travel (written in form of a book) to India. As Prof. Henry Rowlinson writes, "The accounts written by Megasthenes, supplimenting as it did the earlier works of Alexander's companions, gave the Greek world a vived impression of the Greek and opulent civilization of contemporary India."[52] Greek world was surprised to see the similarity between Indian and Western philosophy. To Swami Vivekananda Hinduism is pretty older to Christianity and so Christianity is undoubtedly an imitation of old Hinduism. As it has been said, "Ours is a religion of which Buddhism is a rebel child and of which Christianity is a very patchy imitation."[53]

For last two generations India has remained aloof from the world at large and narrowed herself into a shell of misery and downfall. So he made fervent appeal to his countrymen to embark upon the plan of spiritual conquest and flood the world with Indian spiritualism. As he said, "Let foreigners come and flood the land with their armies, never mind. Up, India and conquer the world with your spirituality."[54]

According to Swami Vivekananda this narrow wall of Indian exclusiveness and isolatedness has begun to break down from the time of Raja Ram Mohan Roy. India has got something very precious for all times, which the world at large wants very much — the greater spiritual ideals that are enshrined in her scriptures. Whole world is awaiting that treasure. Little do we know how much of hunger and thirst there is outside of India for these wonderful treasures of our forefathers. Swami Vivekananda said, "Therefore you must go out and exchange our spirituality for anything they have to give us. From the marvels of the region of the spirit we will exchange the marvels of the region of matter."[55]

India has to fulfil its age-long mission by allowing its thoughts to flow out to all parts of the world and enlighten the whole mankind with the ultimate goal of the humanizing the whole world. So Swami Vivekananda called upon his countrymen to conquer the world and fulfil the traditional mission and bring glory to the country. As he said, "It is not only that we want to revive our own country, that is a small matter. I am an imaginative man and my idea is the conquest of the whole world by Hindu race."[56]

This programme of world conquest influenced very much the young Indians. It aroused a new hope and spirit in their minds for implementing the task. As M.N. Roy has remarked, "This romantic vision of conquering the world by spiritual superiority, electrified the young intellectuals...."[57] However conquest of the world did not mean for Swami Vivekanands, conquest by armies, but conquest by religion and spirituality — the true conquest, as described by the story of the great Hindu conqueror Ashok.

(vi) Smooth, Silent and Tacit Nature

India is the fountain head of spiritualism and the whole world awaits with greedy look, the ambrocia of Indian spiritualism as an antidote against the utter dissatisfaction, arising out of gross materialism of the West. Through the ages India has assumed the role of spiritual guide to the whole world by diffusing her spiritual message all over. It has become our customery rule — a part of Hindu national tradition. But the *modus-operandi* of this customery rule is quite unique. India has accomplished this role without indulging in high sounding, ear-rending publicity. She has never held any banner or flag nor has she blown any trumpet or beaten any drum to announce to the world, the operation of her mission. She has never led any procession or slogan as she believes in action rather than vociferous propaganda. Though silent and tacit the result of her plan of action has always been very tremendous. Describing the mode of operation of India's plan for spiritualizing the world Swami Vivekananda has observed, "Gifts of political knowledge can be made with the blast of trumpets and march of cohorts. Gifts of secular knowledge and social knowledge can be made with fire and sword, but spiritual knowledge can only be given in silence like the dew that falls unseen and unheard, yet bringing to bloom masses of roses."[58]

Whenever a conquering race brings the nations of the world together making roads and transit possible, immediately India has contributed her quota of spiritual power to the sumtotal of world progress and culture. This happened ages before Buddha was born, the remnants of which are still found in China, in Asia Minor and in the heart of Malayan Archipelago.[59] When the Greek conqueror united the four corners of the world India rushed out with her spiritualism to the West and the boasted civilization of the West is but the remnant of that deluge.

According to Swami Vivekananda, the same opportunity is available once again. The British nation has linked the world together as was never done before. English roads and channels of communication rush from one end of the world to the other. The trade centres have sprag up such as had never been before in the history of mankind. So immediately India should pick up her traditional role to pour forth her gifts of spirituality placidly over the world like the gentle dew drops to cool down the tension of the day of grim materialism. But the deluge must be very smooth, slow, silent and unperceived. It should be free from bloodshed or brutality or violence of any sort, that have stained the pages of history of Islam and Christianity. As Swami Vivekananda has observed, "The one characteristic of Indian thought is its silence, its calmness. At the same time the tremendous power that is behind it, is never expressed by violence. It is always the silent mesmerism of Indian thought."[60]

Swami Vivekananda further held that a foreigner feels disgusted with our literature at the first study as he does not find any thrill or the stir of the European literature that rouses him instantly. European tragedies are full of actions that rouses him forthwith. But the moment it is over, there comes the reaction and everything is gone — washed off from the brain. Indian tragedies, on the other hand, are like the mesmerist's power-quiet, silent. But as we go on studying them they fascinate us, we cannot move; we are spell-bound and whoever has dared to touch our literature has felt the spell and is there bound forever. Like the gentle dew there has been the contribution of

India to the thoughts of the world. As said Swami Vivekananda, "Silent and unperceived yet omnipotent in its effect, it has revolutionised the thoughts of the world, yet no body knows when it did so."[61]

Thus Swami Vivekananda's spiritual nationalism is smooth, silent and tacit that abhors brutality, bloodshed or violence of any sort.

(vii) Liberalism

Swami Vivekananda, the nationalist was also a great liberal. A nation free from external bondage must provide liberty or freedom to its members. Liberty or freedom he considered to be the very core of his nationalism. To him freedom is the life-spirit of the universe. It is the ultimate goal, the destiny and the destination towards which the whole universe moves. As he said, "Freedom is the goal of the universe. Nor love nor hate, nor pleasure nor pain, nor death nor life, nor religion nor irreligion, not this, not this."[62] Everything animate or inanimate and every being of the universe are activated by the passion for freedom. To quote him, "We see that the whole universe is working. For what? For salvation, for liberty; from the atom to the highest being working for the one end; liberty for the mind, for the body, for the spirit. All things are always trying to get freedom, flying away from bondages."[63]

Thus the passion for breaking to pieces the bondages of all sorts and emerging to the realm of freedom is very common to inanimate and animate objects, from the minutest atoms to the mightest planetary bodies. This passion is the propelling force that set things in their respective places and make them operate as per the law of the Nature. As Swami Vivekananda has said, "All human life, all nature is struggling to attain freedom. The sun is moving towards the goal, so is the earth circling round the sun, so is the moon circling round the earth."[64]

Besides, Swami Vivekananda argues on the basis of the history of human civilization that all social, economic and political institutions also aim at this goal and aspire to reach the destination of freedom. As he said, "What is it we all seek? Freedom. All the efforts and struggles of life is for freedom. It is the march of Universal of races of the worlds and of systems."[65]

Above everything freedom is the most distinguishing characteristic of man. Passion for freedom is his special trait. It is more discernible in man than in others : "Whereas men are capable of visualing freedom and pursuing it others are incapable of the same." Hence he said, "This freedom that distinguishes us from mere machines, is what we are striving for."[66] Love for freedom, he believed to be the characteristic feature of more developed and evolved in the process of evolution. As he said, "Freedom is the test of the higher being."[67]

Swami Vivekananda believed that the urge for freedom in man is irrepressible and illimitable. There is an eternal call from within and a dictate of the supra self-urging each of us persistently for assertion of the right of freedom. Hence he said, "Within ourselves is the eternal voice, speaking of eternal freedom."[68]

Swami Vivekananda believed that freedom is indispensable for spiritual realization of man and it is also equally indispensable for him for the realization of his personality in social, economic and political spheres. He therefore wanted to make freedom the natural possession of all citizens of a nation. He expected that every individual should cultivate his body, mind and the spirit to the utmost extent. As he said, "Liberty does not certainly mean the absence of obstacle in the path of misappropriation of wealth etc. by you and me, but it is our natural right to be allowed to use our own body, intelligence or wealth according to our will without doing any harm to others."[69]

Passion for liberty is the urge for the unhindered expression of our personality. It is the liberty that provides necessary condition under which the individual develops his various potentialities of life. In the words of H.J. Laski, "Freedom are the opportunities, which the history has shown to be essential to the development of personality."[70] It is natural with man to enjoy liberty and flourish in the society. Liberty makes man happy and society progressive. So according to J.S. Mill, "Freedom is one of the principal ingredients of human happiness and quite the chief ingredient of individual and social progresses."[71] Vindicating the same cause, Swami Vivekananda also said that liberty in thought and action is the only condition of life, growth and well-being, where it does not exist, the man, the race and the nation must go down.[72] Explaining his attitude towards freedom he further said, "Freedom is the watchword. Be free! A free boy, a free mind and a free soul! That is what I have felt all my life. I would rather be doing evil freely than be doing good under bondage."[73]

According to Swami Vivekananda the individual perfects himself by acting freely and the perfect individual, in turn, perfects the society, the nation. The strength and vitality of the nation depends on the individual's initiative and freedom. When individual's growth is obstructed state or nation ceases to flourish. Hence the individual must be made free and not be hindered in his quest for freedom. The state, he felt is only a social agency and it should not encroach upon the domain of individual's liberty and freedom with multiplicity of laws, rules and regulations. Too much of rules and regulations is a positive danger to the individual initiative and growth. Hence he said, "This life is a tremendous assertion of freedom.... Too many laws are sure sign of death. Wherever in the society there are too many laws, it is a sure sign that the society will soon die."[74]

Swami Vivekananda's belief in individual freedom led him to advocate equal rights of men in the society. Liberty is meaningless without equality of man. His faith in the inherent individual freedom is the basis of his defence of equal rights and opportunities for all individuals for their growth. Hence he emphasized on the abolition of all privileges in the society and upheld the right of each individual to equality. Like H.J. Laski by equality he meant the "absence of special privilege"[75] and "adequade opportunities, laid open to all equally."[76] So he condemned existence of privileges as baneful and tyrannical. As he said, "The idea of privilege is bane of human life.... And whenever privilege is broken down, more and more light and progress come to a race."[77]

Swami Vivekananda's concept of individual freedom and equality of rights is based upon the democratic principles — 'To live and let other live.' The individual will enjoy all his freedom and rights in such a way that he will not hinder the interest of others. He will live freely and allow others to live so. As he pointed out, "No one deserves liberty who is not ready to give liberty."[78] He suggested that for proper progress of the society people must cultivate an assimilative outlook and identify themselves with others by which social freedom shall be furthered. In other words by social liberty Swami Vivekananda meant growth-oriented social life, based on individual freedom and equality. As he said, "The whole life of society is the assertion of that principle of freedom."[79]

Thus Swami Vivekananda advocated the cause of liberty and equality very ardently and inspired his countrymen to grow and prosper luxuriantly in an atmosphere of liberty and equality without being rotten under the bondage of British rule. Nehru therefore has befittingly remarked, "Again and again Swami Vivekananda laid stress on the necessity for liberty and equality and raising of the masses."[80] His very insistence on liberty and equality gave a severe jolt to the authoritarian outlook of the British. It also kindled a new spirit among the degenerated mass. Millions of people came forward to claim their freedom, liberty and equality by over-throwing the fetters of the British regime.

(viii) Organic Nature of the Nation

In Swami Vivekananda's theory of nationalism we find an organic nature of the nation. This organic nature of the nation refers to nationalism as a living organism. To Swami Vivekananda each nation is like an individual that has one special theme in its life. This theme is the principal note and all other notes come to identify themselves with this principal note to produce the national harmony. As he said, "I see that each nation, like each individual has one theme in this life, which is its centre, the principal note round which every other note comes to form the harmony."[81] As in case with individuals so also in case with nations, the individual speciality differs. In one nation it may be political power as is the case in England, in another artistic excellence in case with Rome and philosophic uniqueness as with Greece. However in case of India religion forms the centre, the key-note of the whole music of national life. The individual if abandons his speciality, that he has attained since his birth, sinks to ruination. Same is the case with a nation, if it violates its theme or speciality. As Swami Vivekananda said, "If any nation attempts to throw off its national vitality — the direction, which has become its own through the transmission of centuries — that nation dies, if it succeeds in the attempt."[82] If India throws off her religion — her life-force overboard and picks up politics or social refinement as the centre of her national life, then she will pave the path for her own extinction. In order to prevent this, India has to vitalize her religion first and subordinate everything to it. Therefore he said, "That intense faith in another world, that intense hatred for this world, that intense power of renunciation, that intense faith in God, that intense faith in immortal soul is in you...how can you change your nature?"[83]

Further according to Swami Vivekananda, India's life blood is spirituality. If it courses pure, strong and vigorous everything will get right. If the disease-carrying germ is thrown out of our body, then the vitality of our body is reassured. We become strong, stout and immune to ailment. In the same way when national body is weakened all sorts of disease-carrying germs creep into the social, educational and economic fields and paralyse the whole national organism. Various organs of the national organism become weak. The spirit of nationalism becomes dim. The ship of the nation faces storms and shivers. As he said, "When the life blood is strong and pure, no disease germ can live in that body. Our life-blood is spirituality. If it flows clear, if it flows strong and pure and vigorous, everything is right; political, social, any other material defects, even the poverty of the land, will be cured if that blood is pure."[84] So we must guard the vitality of our national life with full vigil to keep the spirit of our nationalism immune from attack against disease-carrying germs that seek to crowd into the social system and paralyse our national backbone.

Although spiritualism and religiosity are the key-notes of our nationalism other aspects of national life — social, political etc., should not be neglected. Yet spiritualism and religiosity are primary whereas other aspects are secondary. As he said, 'if religion the prime factor of our national life, is strengthened all other aspects of our life, too will be invigorated.'[85]

(ix) Religion as a Unifying Factor

After having studied world history thoroughly well Swami Vivekananda arrived at the conclusion that religion is the most cardinal ingredient for the integration of human society. It is as a matter of fact is the most important unifying force of a nation. As Dr. Radhakrishnan has observed, "Religion is a social cement, a way in which men express their aspirations...."[86] A nation is strong if it has no ethnic problem and people have a common religious sentiment. Misunderstanding and misinterpretation of religion is the cause of all nefarious upheaval. Swami Vivekananda was much shocked to see how humanity is broken up into a number of separate worlds, each with its particular religious tradition. Hence he felt that religion should form the unifying factor of a nation. He felt that when religion is estranged from this spiritual urges towards oneness, it is degenerated into dry formalism or dry mechanized drilling, a routine affairs of life that causes untold misery to human society in the long run. True religion according to him should lift us out of our ruts.

Swami Vivekananda realized that in a multi-religious country like India unity and concord at national level cannot be expected unless people are made to understand the true essence of religion. So he tried to solve all religious conflicts and dissention and gather all the scattered spiritual forces of India to concentrate themselves into one focus. As he said, "National union in India must be a gathering up of its scattered spiritual forces. A nation in India must be a union of those whose heart beat to the same spiritual tune."[87]

Swami Vivekananda felt that 'Variety is the very nature of man' and as philosophy of life differs, various sects and creeds are obvious in human society. But there should not be for this reason, sectarian quarrels and conflicts that rend the sky and the air. There should be co-ordination, harmony among the various faiths, creeds and sects of people as religion is one, the end of which is 'to uphold human existence'. Therefore he said, "Sects..., as a matter of fact must exist here. But what need not exist is sectarian quarrel. Sects must be, but sectarianism need not."[88]

To bring the people of various creeds and faiths home to the oneness of Godhead and religion, Swami Vivekananda referred to the most ancient book of the Hindus — the Vedas, that declare, "That which exist is one, but sages call Him by various names."[89]

Unification of religions to lead mankind to one path and one goal was the most fundamental principle of Swami Vivekananda, which he inherited as a genuine successor from his great Master Sri Ramkrishna, about whom he said, "To proclaim and make clear the fundamental unity underlying all religions, was the mission of my Master.... He felt every religion undisturbed because he had realized that in reality they are all part and parcel of the one eternal religion."[90]

For unification of all these religious sects, faiths and creeds of India and elimination of the meaningless diversities that hinder the great national unity, Swami Vivekananda visualized that there are certain principles that are common to all sects, who call themselves as Hindu. Of all these principles the first is that all sects believe the Vedas to be the eternal teaching of Hinduism. People of all faith believe that this holy literature, without beginning and without end, coeval with nature, is the source of all spiritual solace. Before this all our sectarian quarrel and conflicts melt into oneness of belief. As he said, "We all believe that this holy literature is without beginning and without end, coeval with nature...and that all our religious differences all our religious struggles must end when we stand in the presence of that holy book; we are all agreed that this is the last court of appeal in all our spiritual differences."[91]

The second point of agreement among various faiths he felt is that all faiths believe themselves to be different paths leading to the same goal *i.e.*, realisation of God. This conviction, enshrined in the Hindu scriptures, appeals to people of all faiths. Swami Vivekananda was much impressed by his great Master on this point who said, "I have practised all religions — Hinduism, Islam, Christianity and I have also followed the paths of different Hindu sects. I have found that it is the same God, towards whom all are directing their steps though a long different paths. You must try all beliefs and traverse all the different ways once. Wherever I look I see man quarreling in the name of religion — Hindus, Mohammedans, Brahmos, Vaishnavas and the rest but they never reflect that He who is called Krishna is also called Siva and bears the name of primitive Energy. Jesus and Allah as well — the same Ram with thousand names."[92] The very declaration that all faiths have but one goal and one destination mesmerized the people of all faiths who forgot their ideological differences and merged in the ocean of Hinduism that served as a boost to Hindu national unity.

The third principle on the basis of which Swami Vivekananda sought to unify all sects of people is the belief of all in God — the creating and preserving power of the whole universe. The conception of God of different sects may be different; still they believe in God. As he said, "We may differ as to our conception of God. One may believe in a God, who is entirely personal, another may believe in a God, who is personal and yet not human and yet another may believe in a God, who is entirely impersonal.... Still are all believers in God.... Man, who does not believe in a most marvellous infinite power from which everything has come, in which everything lives and to which everything must in the end return, cannot be called a Hindu."[93]

The fourth common point of agreement among the various faiths is the theory of Samsara and the eternity of soul. Nature and man were not created at one point of time. There is a cyclic movement of time and of the universe. For certain period of time the gross material universe is in manifested form and then it dissolves into its primeval elemental nature to come out once again after an equally long period of abeyance. Man is involved in this cyclic process, living and dying and again getting a new body until he evolves into his highest possibility and is released from the cyclic process of Samsara. He is not only a gross material body, not only even a finer body constituted of mind but basically the Atman, which has neither a beginning nor an end and knows not what death is. There will be differences in the conception of soul as in that of God, but we are all one in the basic belief that the soul was never created, that it will never die and that it will evolve passing through various bodies till it attains perfection through the human form.

But contrary to it, according to Swami Vivekananda, other races of the world hold a different view. They believe that this world was created only so many thousand years ago and is going to be destroyed eternally on a certain day. They also believe that the human soul has been created along with this Universe just out of nothing.[94]

Another common point that according to Swami Vivekananda marked all Hindu sects — a point in respect of which we differ from the Western religion, is the acceptance of the idea that the soul in its essential nature is spirit, pure and perfect, infinite and blissful. As he said, "It is this that we hold whether we are Shaktas, Sauras or Vaishnavas even whether we are Buddhists or Jainas, we all hold in India that the soul is by its nature pure and perfect, infinite in power and blessed."[95] Therefore we close our eyes and look within when we try to find God, whereas in other religions they look outwards for their God, who is dangerous. As George Bernard Shaw remarked, "Be aware of him, whose God is in the sky." The Hindus therefore do not suffer from self-depreciation. They are conscious of their divinity within. This faith in oneself, according to Swami Vivekananda, made us great at one time and its loss has brought us to degeneration. We have been reduced to slavery under the foreign rule and Hindu nationalism has suffered.

Last but not the least is the idea which is special to all sects of Hindu religion, the idea that religion means realisation. It is not a theory or some doctrine, enshrined in the holy books only. Mere believing in certain theory or doctrines won't bring any realization of the soul to any individual. Knowledge of soul is to be acquired only through realisation that prepares the path for salvation. As Swami Vivekananda said, "Religion is to be realised, not only heard; it is not only learning some doctrine like a parrot.... And there is no salvation for man until he seeks God, realises his own soul."[96] Further as he said, "Religion is not speculation, not argumentation, but realization, and he is truly spiritual who lives and moves and has his being in the vision of One in all."[97]

Thus Swami Vivekananda sought to unify all the Hindu sects of India by pointing out their common bases, which are rooted in old Hindu religion. He declared that Hinduism is the main religion and these sects are its offshoots. If they are estranged from the main stream, they will lose their way. Therefore he asked the Indians to forget all their sectarian bickerings and fightings and merge with the main stream to save the great religion and their great nationality. As he said, "Therefore make way for the life-current of the nation. Take away the blocks that bar the way to the progress of this mighty river, clear its path, clear the channel and out it will rush by its own natural impulse and the nation will go on careering and progressing."[98]

(x) Secular in Nature

It is true that Swami Vivekananda was deeply devoted to religion and spirituality. Yet he is also described as the 'Father in Hindu Secularism.'

The secular philosophy of Swami Vivekananda, was greatly influenced by the philosophy of his great Master Sri Ramkrishna, who took to the religious practices of various creeds like Tantrism, Vaishnavism, Advaitism, Buddhism, Islam, and Christianity and realised God through all of them. To him "The worthiest object of life is the realisation of God as the highest human ideal attainable only by development of high spiritual life and turning all actions and thoughts towards God. It is the essence of religion to a man, who has realised; and all religions are the paths that lead to the same goal."[99] He deprecated all metaphysical subtleties and philosophical discussions. The one thing that is essential for realisation of God, according to him, is the intensity of yearning for God and love for God. This is the only way to reach God.

Like his great Master Swami Vivekananda believed that religion is a means to an end but not an end in itself. All religions are alike, leading to that one end *i.e.*, realisation of God. He thought that races and religions like Hindu, Christian, Islam etc. are the greatest bars to fraternal feelings between man and man, and it shatters the very fabric of human society. As Dr. Radha Krishnan said, "Racial discrimination is opposed to the teachings of world brotherhood."[100] Swami Vivekananda therefore asked the people of break down these barriers as they had no significance in promoting the spiritual attitude of men. Instead it had some baneful impact on human mind, turning human beings into satans and demons. His attitude towards other religions is best expressed in his own words, "I accept all religions that were in the past and worship God with everyone of them in whatever form they worship him. I shall go to the mosque of Mohammedan; I shall enter the Christian church and kneel before the Crucifix; I shall enter the Buddhistic temple where I shall take refuge in Buddha and in his law. I shall go into the forest and sit down in meditation with the Hindu, who is trying to see the light which enlightens the heart of everyone."[101]

Hence as one who had profound faith in secularism, Swami Vivekananda emphasized on religious toleration and the sameness of truth in all religions. He took pride in declaring that "India is the only country that believes in religious toleration and accepts all religions are true."[102] He criticised the Western countries for their religious persecution and once again felt proud of his nation "which has sheltered the persecuted and the refugees of all religions and all nations of the earth."[103] However his secularism went much beyond mere religious toleration. The secular constitution of Indian Republic owes a lot to Swami Vivekananda.

Swami Vivekananda is said to have observed that what India needed was not more of spirituality as she needed bread too. The material demands of the poor is as important as their spiritual demands. He stood for a complete separation between religion and social laws. As he said, "Social laws are created by economic conditions under the sanctions of religion. The terrible mistake of religion was to interfere in social matters. What we want is that religion should not be a social reformer but we insist at the same time that society has no right to become a religious law-giver. Hands off! keep yourself to your own bounds and everything would come rights."[104]

According to Swami Vivekananda what we want is not so much of spirituality as the bringing down of Advaita into the material world. Bread must be taken care of first and then religion. We stuff them with too much of religion when the poor fellows have been starving. As he said, "Man is guided by stomach. He walks and the stomach goes first and the head afterwards."[105] Hence for the eradication of the poverty of the people of India Swami Vivekananda advocated a secular policy. Swami Vivekananda had really felt the pulse of India. He realised that religious discrimination touches the very sentiment of the people. So he sought to place, in his plan of national reconstruction, all sects and faiths on equal footing, after having eradicated all parochialism of religious outlook of the people of different faiths. He held that the human society would have made far greater advancement had there been no sectarianism, fanaticism and violence in the name of religion.[106] So in a multi religious country like India secularism is the only panacea to solve the socio-religious problems and pave the path for national integration and build up the edifice of a viable and powerful Indian nation. This was really the true mission of Swami Vivekananda.

(xi) Cultural Revivalism

Swami Vivekananda after his study of the history of India was surprised to discover its glorious heritage and culture. The eternal values of her religion and philosophy struck him with awe. The unending glorious panorama of her heritage flashed in his mind's eye. As an illustrious and worthy son of the land, he could hardly withstand the cultural extinction of his mother country under the influence of the West. He was upset to see the predicament of his country. He took firm decision to revive India's past heritage and rejuvenate India on the basis of her scriptures like the Vedas, the Upanishads, the Gita and the Puranas.

It has been said, "This sentiment of revivalism was generated as a reaction against the great challenge thrown by an alien aggressive and arrogant civilization, politically dominant and economically powerful."[107] Even Jawaharlal Nehru a thoroughly westernized man, vindicating the cause of revivalism in the regeneration of India said, "The future has to be build on the foundation laid in the past.... To deny the past and break with it completely is to uproot ourselves and sapless, dry-up.[108] Swami Vivekananda tried to awake Indians by presenting to them the glorious picture of India's past, her customs and traditions, and not by imitating the West. He was of the view that blind imitation paves the path for further extinction. However, he had abiding faith in Indian customs and traditions and he wanted to revive them for national awakening. As he said, "Our ancestors were great. We must first recall that we must learn the elements of our being, the blood that courses in our veins; we must have faith in that blood and what it did in the past; and out of that faith and consciousness of the past greatness, we must build an India yet greater than what she was."[109] He appealed to all the reformers of the country to make the countrymen understand the past as the past he felt is the source of all aspirations to rebuild the future of the nation. As he said, "The more therefore the Hindus study the past, the more glorious will be their future and whoever tries to bring the past to the door of every one, is a great benefactor to his nation."[110]

Swami Vivekananda's aim was to stimulate the pride of the Indians in their own customs, civilization and way of life. He projected the Indian religious culture and civilization even in the world scenario. In India he travelled to every nook and corner and presented before his countrymen the glorious picture of their hoary past and established its superiority over the West. Swami Gambhirananda has observed, "He (Vivekananda) was never tired of showing to his countrymen the value and significance of the culture they had inherited from their ancestors — a culture in comparison with which any other civilization, past or present, paled into insignificance — till their hearts throbbed at the very name of India.[111]

Swami Vivekananda tried to convince his people that indiscriminate imitation of the West is pernicious to national integrity. He deplored the growing despiritualisation and denationalization of the Indians under the influence of the West. So emphasizing on the revival of India's way of life he said, "We must grow according to our nature. Vain is to attempt the lines of action that foreign societies have engrafted upon us : it is impossible. Glory unto God that it is impossible, that we cannot be twisted and tortured into the shape of other nations. I do not condemn the institution of other races; they are good for them, but not for us. With other sciences, other institutions and other traditions behind them they have got their present system. We, with our traditions, with thousands of years of karma behind us naturally can only follow our own bent, run in our own grooves and that we shall have to do."[112]

According to Swami Vivekananda Indians cannot be Westerners. Therefore imitating the West is very dangerous. If we try to copy the West, we will die, we will have no more life in us. In support of his argument he said, "A stream is taking its rise away beyond where time began, flowing through millions of ages of human history; do you mean to get hold of that stream and push it back to its source to a Himalayan glacier? Even if that were practicable, it would not be possible for you to be Europeanised. If you find it is impossible for the European to throw off the few centuries of culture, which there is in the West, do you think it is possible for you to throw off the culture of shining scores of centuries? It cannot be."[113] Therefore according to Swami Vivekananda to Europeanise India is an impossible and foolish task.

Though the whole theory of Swami Vivekananda's nationalism aimed at reviving the old valuable culture of India, it is not repugnant to assimilate any new things to suit the need of the time and make Indian nationalism more dynamic and resourceful. So the assimilative nature of Swami Vivekananda's nationalism is very noteworthy. It is evident from his own statement : "In the remote past our country made gigantic advances in spiritual ideas. Let us today bring before our mind's eye that ancient history. But the one great danger in meditating over the long past greatness is that we cease to exert ourselves for new things and content ourselves with vegetating upon that by gone ancestral glory and priding ourselves upon it. We should guard against that."[114]

Thus both revivalism and careful assimilation characterize Swami Vivekananda's nationalism, that inspired all the great leaders of the country like Tagore, Aurobindo and Gandhi. Indian freedom movement received tremendous impetus from it. Jawaharlal Nehru in his famous essay — 'Synthesis is our Tradition' writes, "Vivekananda brought-back some thing of the vigour of old Indian thought and dressed it in a modern garb.

Political and cultural movements grew up and culminated in Gandhi and Tagore."[115]

(xii) Universalistic Nationalism

Swami Vivekananda's nationalism is universalistic in nature. Unlike the exclusive and racial nature of German nationalism, it is of universal nature. It has wide and universal application and importance. His concern for the poor and downtrodden of India is his concern for the poor downtrodden of all nations. His vigorous drive against social injustice, communal discord and caste prejudices in India benefits the whole human society. It is a solution for similar problems of all nations. His clarion call for general fraternity and unity of India's people to rise against the alien oppression is a great lesson for other countries, rotting under foreign domination. His synthesis of the two divergent ideals — spiritualism and materialism, bridged the age-long gulf between East and West and ushered in an era of international peace, goodwill and fellow feelings. Hence his nationalism is not narrow nationalism, meant for India only; it is wide open for the whole world to share and enjoy through India as a stage. As I.P. Chelishev has observed, "Vivekananda's impassioned call to the general fraternity and unity of India's people to the abolition of religious and communal discord and of caste prejudices, were combined with an appeal for peace and friendship among all nations of the world, which is the corner-stone of the Indian tradition, the main content of the Indian national character."[116]

Swami Vivekananda's nationalism is frought with cosmopolitan view that upholds the doctrine of solidarity of all human beings and of all nations, irrespective of race, religion and culture. It seeks to solve the problems of the world — of all nations, East and West — whether Hindu or Muslim or Christian. As he said, "To become broad, to go out to amalgamate to universalize is the end of our aims."[117] His nationalism is a move against all sorts of racialism, sectarianism, linguism or regionalism. It treats the whole world to be one family, where the whole mankind is its member. It envisages the idea of "Oneness of all, the infinite, the idea of the impersonal, the wonderful idea of the eternal soul of man, of the unbroken continuity in the march of being and the infinity of the Universie."[118] This is what the Vedanta teaches to the world.

Though Swami Vivekananda some times talks of Hindu nationalism yet his concept of nationalism is universalistic in nature. As he said, "I know my mission in life and...; I belong as much to India as to the world."[119]

After a thorough study of the world history, Swami Vivekananda expounded the theory of survival of all nations of the world. He said that from human history we come to know that every nation has to give a quota of its own in the field, its specialisation for the general advancement of humanity and when it is forgotten the nation decays and dies. Nature replaces it by more vigorous and younger races to pick up the role. For it is the nature's law to get rid of an atrophid part of an organism and let some others take up its function. Thus there emerged the great nations in the past — Egypt, Babylon, Persia, Greece and Rome etc., whose civilizations were very rich and flourishing. But they all went out of the scene and are occupied by nations whose culture and national history have nothing to do with these ancient nations. The reason for it, said Swami Vivekananda is that they failed to accomplish their national purpose or ideal, which were either political, social or military etc. After a short period of meteoric appearance they lost their moorings in their national theme or ideal that led to their extinction and the emergence of new power in their place. As he said, "...each race and each nation appears to me to have a particular ideal — a prominent ideal, running through its whole life and this ideal is the back-bone[120] of the national life. He further said, "...no nation can rise, can be come great, can work at all, without enthusiastically coming under the banner of one of those great ideals in life."[121]

Swami Vivekananda's concern for the mankind is best expressed in his concept of individual liberty, right and equality — that he considered to be the greatest contribution for healthy progress of human society. He asserted that 'Liberty, Right and Equality are the noblest aspirations of man-kind that unfolds human personality towards all-round development — both material and spiritual.' These are the divine possessions, endowed with divinity for the happiness of the mankind. Liberty, Right and Equality are the birth right of every individual. It reminds us of the words of Jefferson in the 'Declaration of Independence' "...that all men are created equal, that are endowed by their creator with certain unalienable Rights that among these are Life, Liberty and the pursuit of happiness."[122]

Swami Vivekananda's epoch-making and unprecedented call for strength and fearlessness is no less renowned. It is his fiery message to the mankind to fight the dark forces of evils that chain him to the dungeon of suffering. The nefarious imperialistic design of the West met with a fatal blow at his call. I.P. Cheleshev has observed, "Urging people to be fearless and bold to fight the dark forces for their happiness and better future, Vivekananda at the same time declared that it was hopeless and useless to try and rule the world by force of arms."[123]

Thus Swami Vivekananda's nationalism is not narrow and selfish nationalism of India, blind to the interest of mankind. It provides a positive milieu for peaceful coexistence of all nations of the world. His whole theory is based on love for man-God. So we can regard Swami Vivekananda in the words of I.P. Chelishev as "one of the initiators in India of the most human movement of our time — the peace movement."[124]

To sum up Swami Vivekananda nationalism is spiritualistic in nature. Himself a spiritualistic personality, he considered spiritualism to be a secret of national life and the cementing factor for bringing about national unity and national integration. His nationalism is also didactic in nature. He has preached the secret doctrine of making a nation strong, united and prosperous. He has called upon his countrymen to be truthful, pure and unselfish to build up a mighty nation. Himself a saint who not only renounced the world but also worldly desires wanted to remove all poverty of the people and establishment of socio-economic equality in the nation. A universalist by faith and profession, he believed in spiritual expansionism of the nation. A saint who moved round the East and West to preach the philosophy of Vedanta, himself believed that India as a nation should make its presence felt round the globe not by shouting high sounding slogans but by smooth and silent work of service and sacrifice. He was an advocate of liberalism and desired that such liberalism should constitute the core of his nationalism and Indian nationalism. He believed in the organic nature of the nation and felt the utility of religion as an integrating factor of the nation. Although a saint under a religious teacher, he believed that the nation and the Indian nation should be a secular one, accommodating and assimilating within its bounds of people of different faiths and religious persuasion. For the sake of building of a mighty nation he felt the need of cultural revivalism in India. Above all Swami Vivekananda, although a nationalist, believed in universalism. His nationalism was not exclusive, arrogant and jingoistic nationalism.

REFERENCES

1. H.J. Laski, *A Grammar of Politics*, p. 218.
2. P.R. Jagindar, *M.G. Ranade*, p. 133.
3. *Bangalee*, 22 March, 1896.
4. *Modern Review*, 1907, p. 288.
5. R.N. Tagore, *Nationalism*, p. 3.
6. Swami Gambhirananda, *A Short Life of Swami Vivekananda*, p. 114.
7. *Complete Works of Swami Vivekananda*, Vol. III, p. 148.
8. *Ibid.*, Vol. III, p. 369.
9. Swami Vivekananda, *Lectures from Colombo to Almora*, p. 285.
10. *Complete Works of Swami Vivekananda*, Vol. III, p. 371.
11. *Ibid.*, Vol. III, p. 369.
12. *Ibid.*, Vol. V, p. 1.
13. *Ibid.*, Vol. VI, p. 126.
14. *Ibid.*, Vol. V, p. 240.
15. *Ibid.*, Vol. IV, p. 279.
16. *Ibid.*, Vol. VIII, p. 184.
17. *Ibid.*, Vol. VI, p. 281.
18. Romain Rolland, *Life of Swami Vivekananda and Universal Gospel*, p. 112.
19. *Complete Works of Swami Vivekananda*, Vol. III, pp. 241-42.
20. Annie Besant, *The Wisdom of Upanishads*, p. 5.
21. *Complete Works of Swami Vivekananda*, Vol. IV, p. 314.

22. *Complete Works of Swami Vivekananda*, Vol. VII, p. 183.
23. *Nationalistic and Religious Lectures of Swami Vivekananda*, p. X.
24. *Reminiscence of Swami Vivekananda*, p. 330.
25. *Complete Works of Swami Vivekananda*, Vol. VIII, pp. 329-30.
26. H.J. Laski, *A Grammar of Politics*, p. 218.
27. Swami Vivekananda, *Proletariat! Win Equal Rights*, p. VIII.
28. *Complete Works of Swami Vivekananda*, Vol. VI, p. 381.
29. *Ibid.*, Vol. VI, p. 381.
30. C.E.M., Joad, *Introduction to Modern Political Theory*, p. 53.
31. Swami Vivekananda, *Proletariat! Win Equal Rights*, p. VIII.
32. *Complete Works of Swami Vivekananda*, Vol. III, pp. 245-46.
33. *Ibid.*, Vol. I, pp. 423-24.
34. *Ibid.*, Vol. I, p. 435.
35. *Lectures From Colombo to Almora*, p. 59.
36. Swami Vivekananda, *Proletariate! Win Equal Rights*, p. V.
37. *Complete Works of Swami Vivekananda*, Vol. VII, p. 149.
38. *Ibid.*, Vol. VII, p. 149.
39. *Nationalistic and Religious Lectures of Swami Vivekananda*, p. XI.
40. *Complete Works of Swami Vivekananda*, Vol. III, p. 167.
41. *Ibid.*, Vol. III, p. 383.
42. *Nationalistic and Religious Lectures of Swami Vivekananda*, p. 35.
43. *Ibid.*, p. 35.
44. *Complete Works of Swami Vivekananda*, Vol. III, p. 172.
45. *Ibid.*, Vol. III, p. 381.
46. V.P. Varma, *Modern Indian Political Thoughts*, p. 108.
47. *Ibid.*, p. 636.
48. Jawaharlal Nehru, *India Today and Tomorrow*, p. 44.
49. *Nationalistic and Religious Lectures of Swami Vivekananda*, p. 56.
50. *Complete Works of Swami Vivekananda*, Vol. IV, p. 365.
51. *Ibid.*, p. 365.
52. Prof. H. Rowlinson, *Contact between India and the West.*
53. *Complete Works of Swami Vivekananda*, Vol. III, p. 275.
54. *Ibid.*, Vol. III, p. 277.
55. *Ibid.*, Vol. III, p. 317.
56. *Ibid.*, Vol. III, p. 276.
57. M.N. Roy, *India in Transition*, p. 169.

58. *Complete Works of Swami Vivekananda,* Vol. III, p. 222.
59. *Ibid.*, Vol. III, p. 223.
60. *Ibid.*, Vol. III, p. 274.
61. *Ibid.*, Vol. III, p. 274.
62. *Ibid.*, Vol. VIII, p. 344.
63. *Ibid.*, Vol. I, p. 99.
64. *Ibid.*, Vol. II, p. 126.
65. *Ibid.*, Vol. VIII, p. 401.
66. *Ibid.*, Vol. I, p. 333.
67. *Ibid.*, Vol. VIII, p. 40.
68. *Ibid.*, Vol. II, p. 325.
69. *Ibid.*, Vol. V, p. 145.
70. H.J. Laski, *A Grammar of Politics,* p. 44.
71. Quoted in C.E.M. Joad, *Introduction to Modern Political Theory,* p. 28.
72. Monmohan Ganguly, *Swami Vivekananda — A Study,* p. 60.
73. *Complete Works of Swami Vivekananda,* Vol. III, pp. 515-16.
74. *Ibid.*, Vol. V, p. 287.
75. H.J. Laski, *A Grammar of Politics,* p. 152.
76. *Ibid.*, p. 154.
77. *Complete Works of Swami Vivekananda,* Vol. I, pp. 423-24.
78. *Ibid.*, Vol. IV, p. 368.
79. *Ibid.*, Vol. II, p. 115.
80. Jawaharlal Nehru, *Discovery of India,* p. 315.
81. Swami Vivekananda, *Lectures From Colombo to Almora,* p. 125.
82. *Ibid.*, p. 125.
83. *Complete Works of Swami Vivekananda,* Vol. III, p. 221.
84. *Lectures From Colombo to Almora,* p. 197.
85. *Nationalistic and Religious Lectures of Swami Vivekananda,* p. 61.
86. Dr. Radhakrishnan, *Recovery of Faith,* p. 27.
87. Swami Vivekananda, *Lectures From Colombo to Almora,* pp. 286-87.
88. *Ibid.*, p. 287.
89. *Complete Works of Swami Vivekananda,* Vol. III, p. 372.
90. *Ibid.*, Vol. IV, p. 187.
91. Swami Vivekananda, *Lectures From Colombo to Almora,* p. 288.
92. Romain Rolland, *The Life of Ram Krishna,* pp. 84-85.
93. Swami Vivekananda, *Lectures From Colombo to Almora,* pp. 288-89.

94. Swami Vivekananda, *Lectures From Colombo to Almora*, p. 289.
95. *Ibid.*, pp. 290-91.
96. *Ibid.*, pp. 293-94.
97. T.L. Vaswani, *The Voice of Vivekananda*, p. 60.
98. *Complete Works of Swami Vivekananda*, Vol. III, p. 382.
99. B.N. Luniya, *Evolution of Indian Culture*, pp. 492-93.
100. Dr. Radhakrishnan, *Recovery of Faith*, p. 29.
101. *Complete Works of Swami Vivekananda*, Vol. II, p. 372.
102. T.L. Vaswani, *The Voice of Vivekananda*, p. 59.
103. *Ibid.*, p. 59.
104. *Complete Works of Swami Vivekananda*, Vol. IV, p. 358.
105. Swami Vivekananda, *Proletariat ! Win Equal Rights*, p. 57.
106. D.R. Bali, *Modern Indian Thought*, p. 36.
107. V.P. Varma, *Modern Indian Political Thought*, p. 618.
108. Jawaharlal Nehru, *India Today and Tomorrow*, p. 8.
109. *Complete Works of Swami Vivekananda*, Vol. III, p. 286.
110. *Ibid.*, Vol. IV, p. 324.
111. Swami Gambhirananda, *A Short Life of Swami Vivekananda*, p. 92.
112. *Complete Works of Swami Vivekananda*, Vol. III, p. 219.
113. *Ibid.*, Vol. III, p. 172.
114. *Ibid.*, Vol. III, p. 454.
115. Jawaharlal Nehru, *Synthesis is Our Tradition, Living English Prose*, Edited by J. Mohanty, Calcutta, 1990, p. 95.
116. *Swami Vivekananda — Studies in Soviet Union*, Published on 150th Birth Anniversary of Sri Ramkrishna, p. 217.
117. *Complete Works of Swami Vivekananda*, Vol. III, p. 271.
118. *Ibid.*, Vol. III, p. 454.
119. *Ibid.*, Vol. V, pp. 95-96.
120. *Ibid.*, Vol. III, p. 137.
121. *Ibid.*, Vol. III, p. 315.
122. Dr. Radhakrishnan, *Recovery of Faith*, p. 28.
123. *Swami Vivekananda — Studies in Soviet Union*, Published on 150th Birth Anniversary of Sri Ramkrishna, p. 217.
124. *Ibid.*, p. 217.

4

Special Features of Swami Vivekananda's Nationalism

Bertrand Russell has observed, "What constitute a nation is a sentiment and an instinct, a sentiment of similarity and an instinct of belonging to the same group or herd."[1] But the sentiment and instinct or the sentiment of similarity and the instinct of belonging to the same group or herd differ from people to people in respect of their nature and intensity, character and commitment to values. Hence although all nations have some characteristic in common, still they differ in respect of other features. This is why Eastern nations differ from Western nations and both Eastern and Western nations differ from one another. Such differences are not unhealthy or unwelcome from the stand point of humanity or the universe; rather such differences make the civilization richer. Hence Russell has once again pointed out, "It is not necessary or even desirable to obliterate the differences of manners and customs and traditions between different nations. These differences enable each nation to make its distinctive contribution to the sum-total of the world civilization."[2] In this relation R.N. Tagore has also said, "It (cultural variety) is best for the commerce of the spirit that people differently situated should bring their different products into market of humanity each of which is complementary and necessary to the other."[3]

Hence Indian nationalism differs from other nationalism in various respects. Although it possesses some features that are common to all nations and their nationalism still Indian nationalism has some special features. Particularly the Indian nationalism as conceived by Swami Vivekananda has the following special features.

(i) Its Spiritual Nature

Dr. Radhakrishnan has said, "Sensitive and informed minds believe that the fundamental need of the world, far deeper than any social, political or economic readjustment, is a spiritual reawakening, a recovery of faith."[4] Swami Vivekananda realised it much earlier. He felt that all social, political and economic evils in India would be remedied only through recovery of faith or spiritual awakening. To Swami Vivekananda, "The Hindu man drinks religiously, sleeps religiously, walks religiously, marries religiously, robs religiously...."[5] So religiosity or spiritualism is the way of life in India, the root of all types development. It is the special feature of India over other nations. In fact different political scientists or nationalists have propounded different theories of nationalism, but Swami Vivekananda's nationalism is most unique in respect of the fact that the whole theory of his nationalism is characterised by religiosity or spiritualism. This spiritualism is the most striking feature of Swami Vivekananda's nationalism, that places him on a high pedestal of universal approbation.

It is of course true that M.N. Roy holds a contrary view. Not enamoured of Indian spiritual heritage, of which Swami Vivekananda was proud, he considered it as, 'The romantic vision of conquering the world by spiritual superiority.'[6] He further considered it as a reaction against the prevailing social order. As he said, "The young followers in their religiousness and wild spiritual imperialism embodied the reactionary social forces...."[7]

Roy is of the opinion that spiritual progress cannot bring any benefit to human society. It fails to provide any impetus to any movement for material progress of man. This is why India is much legging behind the progressive nations of the world. As he said, "It was narcotic effects of much vaunted spiritual civilization, which kept Indian masses apathetic to any movement for material progress.[8] According to him spiritual civilization of India would not satisfy the needs of modern nations. So the benefit of the soul-less Western civilization is necessary.[9]

Roy clearly stated that spiritual force have never brought any progress to human society. In all ages, it is the material forces that have actually brought progress to mankind. As he said, "Human progress, however have not been actuated, by any eternal, abstract idea, nor by any inspiration of a soul being. It has been done, is being done by material forces."[10]

Hence Swami Vivekananda's spiritual nationalism did not appeal to Roy. He branded Swami Vivekananda's nationalism as spiritual imperialism. However, a deep study of Swami Vivekananda's nationalism reveals that the very idea of spiritual imperialism is a contradiction in terms. What Swami Vivekananda pleaded for was not imperialism, but nationalism founded on the rock of spiritualism. Hence, Swami Vivekananda is aptly acclaimed as the 'Father of Spiritual Nationalism' in India. That is why he is called 'The Patriot Saint of India'.

According to Swami Vivekananda, "Race, religion, government, all these together make the nation. The one common ground that we have is, our sacred tradition, our religion. This is the only common ground and upon that we shall have to build. In Europe political ideas formed the national unity. The unity in religion, therefore, is absolutely necessary as the first condition of the future of India."[11] However, to Swami Vivekananda religion does not mean denominational religion like Christianity or Buddhism. He maintained that in Hindu religion there are certain common grounds and Hindu religion also admits variations. What he meant by religion is that certain fundamentals which are common to all religions, would be accepted throughout India. He emphasised on the importance of unification of all religious principles. As he said, "We see how in Asia, and specially in India, race difficulties, linguistic difficulties, social difficulties, national difficulties, all melt away before this unifying power of religion.... In the case of India it is the only possible means of work; work in any other line, without first strengthening this, would be disastrous. Therefore, that first plank is the making of a future India, the first step that is to be hewn out of that rock of ages, is this unification of all religions."[12]

Swami Vivekananda had a deep study of the cultural history of India that led him to form a firm conviction that spiritualism should be the soul of Indian nationalism. It should be the bed-rock upon which the entire edifice of Indian nationalism should stand. Explaining its significance he said, "This is the motherland of philosophy of spirituality and ethics of sweetness, gentleness, and love. These still exist and my experience of the world leads me to stand on a firm ground and make the bold statement that India is till the first and foremost of all nations of the world in these respects."[13]

Swami Vivekananda viewed that every nation has its peculiar soul and its own method of growth. The special bent of India is spiritualism, and its method of growth is nothing but spiritual. He explained that the Western people believe in social and political movement. But people of India never understand this. They believe only in their religion and spirituality. However, ordinary a ploughman might be, he definitely has some knowledge about his God and religion although he has no idea about the socio-economic movement.[14] This is so because of the fact that religion and spirituality have been assimilated into the very flesh and blood of Indian people. Their life-blood is religion and philosophy. Their life-current is spiritualism. Their hearts beat to the tune of spiritualism.

Like Hegel Swami Vivekananda believed that a dominating principle manifests itself in the life of each nation. As he writes, "In each nation as in music, there is a main note, a central theme upon which all others truth. Each nations has a theme, everything else is secondary. India's theme is religion. Social reform and everything else are secondary."[15]

To Swami Vivekananda, spiritual strength is the highest strength. It makes man fearless. It heightens one's will-power. It makes one bold and brave. In the words of Dr. Radhakrishnan, "We can swim against the current and even change its direction."[16] Aurobindo, who also believed in spiritual strength, like Swami Vivekananda declared, "It is the spirit alone that saves and only by becoming great and free in heart that we can become politically great and free."[17] So according to Swami Vivekananda we must have, first and foremost, faith in religion and spiritualism. As we have forgotten our religion, we have succumbed to weakness and fear. That is why only forty million of Englishmen have been able to rule the three hundred million Indians. So we must accumulate our will-power with spiritualism as the basis. Then there will be no power on earth that can subdue us as we will be very strong and powerful as in the past and there will be an end to our hardship and misery. Therefore, he appealed to his countrymen : "This...is the vitality of our race and so long as that remains, there is no power under the sun that can kill the race. All the tortures and miseries of the world will pass over without hurting us and we shall come out of the flames like Prahalada, so long as we hold us to this grandest of all our inheritance — spirituality."[18]

Thus spirituality as the keynote of Indian nationalism, is the most striking speciality of Swami Vivekananda's nationalism.

(ii) Universalism

Modern age is the age of nightmares. It is an age of fear and tension. We are aware of our insufficiencies and helplessness. Our materialistic craze has paved the path for it. We have left religion much behind us and have forgotten the goal of our life. Emphasising the need of religion in the life of modern man Dr. Radhakrishnan has said, "Though our age has largely ceased to understand the meaning of religion it is still in desperate need of that which religion alone can give. The recognition of a transcendent supreme, the freedom of the human individual as a manifestation of the supreme and the unity of mankind as the goal of history are the foundations of the major religions."[19] Swami Vivekananda, the earliest of all the makers of modern India realised the truth of this statement. He realised that religion is the only panacea for all our social evils. It is religion alone that can make our life worthliving and society free from all ills. He was a vigorous thinker and a staunch believer in the supremacy of Hindu religion and culture. Every where he spoke of the greatness of his motherland and the universality of his religion and challenged the Western society. All along his life he stood for the cause of Hinduism and Hindu culture before the world.

Swami Vivekananda breathed the spirit of India's universality and broadmindedness that captivated the hearts of millions of people of the world. In the Parliament of Religions held at Chicago in 1893 he remarked that Hindu religion is the mother of all religions. It is the ultimate source of all peace, universal brotherhood, and religious tolerance. The Western people saw a new light beyond the dark hedges of sects, creeds, communities, churches and dogmas. There he proved Hinduism to be most universal of all religions. It is infinite like the God. It preaches that it "will not be Brahmanic or Buddhistic, Christian or Mohammedan but the sum total of all these and still have infinite scope for development."[20] In its catholicity it embraces with its infinite arms and provides a place for every human being within its embrace — from the grovelling savage to the man of spiritual enlightenment. It has no place for persecution and intolerance in its polity. On the contrary it extends hope to all the humanity and recognises divinity in every man and women and aids all to realise its own true divine nature.[21]

Swami Vivekananda maintained that Hinduism teaches the world both tolerance and universal acceptance. It believes that just as all the rivers having different sources mingle in the sea, so all religions in spite of their differences and methods of worship, lead to the same God. As he said, "Every religion is only evolving a God out of the material man and the same God is the inspirer of all of them."[22] He further said that if they contradict one another in some respects "the contradictions come from the same truth adopting itself to the varying circumstances of different nations."[23] It is same light projected through glasses of different hues. The consequence of his universalism of the Hindu outlook is that "throughout the whole system of Sanskrit philosophy there is no such expression as that the Hindu alone will be saved not others."[24] Swami Vivekananda's approach to Hinduism was so catholic that he won the admiration of every delegate, attending the parliament of religions. Pleading for the unity and progress of mankind Swami Vivekananda remarked that human society would have made a greater development, had there been no sectarianism, fanaticism and violence in the name of religion. Emphasising on the need of universal tolerance Jawaharlal Nehru said, "The only course open is for us to accept the world as it is and develop toleration for each other. It should be open to each country to develop in its own way, learning from others and not being imposed on by them."[25]

Swami Vivekananda's teachings and lectures were published in several volumes. The result was the rapid spread of influence and popularity of Hindu faith all over the world. It brought about a synthesis or harmony among various faiths and creeds of the world.

Swami Vivekananda through his speeches exhibited unique combination of modern rationalism and ancient mysticism of the Vedas and Upanishads, the knowledge of the scientific age and spiritual values and worldly realities. It breathed the spirit of catholicism and tolerance. He represented ancient divine wisdom, medieval devotion and modern rationalism. Thereby he gave Hinduism a new touch, by which the religion came to suit the need of the modern world. Islam and Christianity lost their lustre before Hinduism and became dim.

Swami Vivekananda preached Vedanta abroad. In America, while emphasising on Hinduism he asserted, "No religion on earth preaches the dignity of humanity in such a lofty strain as Hinduism."[26] Hinduism stepped on to a new phase of evangelism, in which people found a new view of life that appealed to all the people of the world. It fascinated people of various faiths and creeds. His bold proclamation : "Vedanta is the religion for all" drew the attention of people all over the world. This militant declaration shattered the false vanity of all religious sects of the world and upon it established the universality of old Hindu religion. Emphasising on the universality of Hindu religion, Nehru like Swami Vivekananda pointed out, "In Europe there had been a fierce conflict between science and traditional religion, and the cosmology of Christianity did not fit in at all with scientific theories. Science did not produce that sense of conflict in India and Indian philosophy could easily accept it without doing any vital injury to its basic conceptions."[27]

Swami Vivekananda was the first to interpret the living Hinduism in all its aspects to the civilized world in a way that immediately brought recognition of its greatness. There opened a glorious phase in the history of Hindu civilization and culture that made Hindu religion, a religion for the whole mankind.

It would not be out of place to quote the remarks of Prof. Louis Renou, "The troubles of present age, which are rightly or wrongly attributed to Western materialism, has helped to increase the prestige of Hinduism. Some people see it as the authentic survival of a tradition, or rather, of the one tradition, and make it the basis of their philosophia perennis. Others try to incorporate it in a universal religious syncretism.... The fact remains that Hinduism provides an incomparable field of study for the historian of religion : its aberrations are many, but there is in it, a great stream of mystical power; it manifests all the conceptions of religion and its speculation is continually revealing them in a new light.... In Bhakti and still more in Yoga, it has perfected unrivalled techniques of mystical initiation, that contrast strongly with the frequently haphazard methods of spiritual training in the West. Above all, in the interpretation of religion and dharma in general and the reciprocal stimulus of abstract thought and religious experiment, there is an underlying principle that, given favourable conditions may well lead to a new integration of human personality."[28]

Swami Vivekananda's interpretation of the universality of Hindu religion infused a sense of pride in the mind of the Hindus, that acted as a tremendous inspiration for the development of Indian nationalism. The old Hindu nationalism revived its vitality and vigour that acted as a stimulus to the rise of Indian nationalism against the foreign domination. As Nehru writes, "He (Swami Vivekananda) came as a tonic to the depressed and demoralised Hindu mind and gave it self-reliance and some roots in the past."[29]

(iii) Assimilative and Synthetic Character

Power of assimilation and synthesis has characterised Indian culture throughout the ages. It forms a trait of our national life. No other culture of the world has such enormous assimilative potentialities as the ancient Indian culture possesses. In this respect Indian culture enjoys precedence over other cultures of the world, which have almost ephimeral existence. Various cultures have flourished and dazzled the pages of history, but after a short stay, they have disappeared from the surface of the earth. In this connection Swami Vivekananda has observed, "There was a time when Roman eagle floated over everything worth having in this world; every where Rome's power was felt and pressed on the head of humanity; the earth trembled at the name of Rome. But the Capitoline Hill is a mass of ruins, the spider weaves its web where the Caesars ruled. There have been other nations equally glorious that have come and gone living a few hours of exultant and exuberant dominance and of a wicked national life and then vanishing like ripples on the face of waters."[30]

But we have still lived. No force or power has ever eclipsed our subtle Indian culture. India has withstood the buffets of a thousand years of hurricane and still stands with the unimpaired vigour of eternal youth. This is because of its tremendous power of assimilation and synthesis. As it is said, "So immense was the assimilative potentiality of old Hindu culture and civilization that the earlier invaders of India like the Greeks, the Sakyas, the Huns etc. were easily absorbed within the fold of her population and in due course they completely lost their identity."[31] So vast and so deep is the ocean of Indian culture that it has absorbed all external influences in all ages of history. Different cultures that came in contact with India, mingled as the streams mingle in the mighty ocean and lose their entity. The Greeks, the Scythians, the Mongolians, the Parthians etc. had been completely Hinduised in name, speech, manner, religion, dress and ideas, just a few generations after their settlement in India, and joined our national life.

The assimilative force worked not only in religious thoughts and social institutions of ancient India but also manifested itself in the persistent efforts at the conciliation of conflicting tendencies during the medieval period, when the influence of the Turko-Afghan culture became very prominent in Indian society. At the initial stage the assimilative force of Indian culture received a tremendous setback. As it is said, "In the wake of Muslim invasion, new divergent and definite social and religious ideas were brought into India and it was not possible to achieve a perfect absorption of these conceptions. Simple, clearcut and aggressive Islam had nothing in common with the elaborate ritualistic and absorptive Hinduism. Its well-defined social system, philosophy, laws and strong monotheistic outlook made its absorption in Hinduism impossible."[32] Islam being a fiercely monotheistic religion and a different culture did not allow any compromise with polytheism or admit a plurality of deities. Its followers tried to live as a separate community from the ancient Hindu community and hold a special identity. In the words of Sir Jadu Nath Sarkar, "The Indian Muslims throughout the succeeding centuries turned towards a spot in Mecca, had their new law-code, their own administrative system, their own language, literature, shrines and saints."[33] They never restricted themselves to India as is the case with the Hindus. They sought models from Arabia, Syria, Iran, Egypt. Moreover they were frequently engaged in "oppressing and persecuting the majority of the country with which they had cast their lot."[34] The Hindus, on the contrary in their zeal to absorb the Muslims went so far as to make an 'Avatar' of the emperor Akbar in the Allopanishad.[35] But the Muslims did not yield on the cardinal points of their faith and culture.

However, "in spite of the fundamental difference and bitter strife between the Hindus and the Muslims, beneath the ruffled surface of storm and stress there began to flow a genial current of mutual harmony, co-operation, and tolerance in different spheres of our life in course of time." Consequently not only Hindu art, Hindu religion, Hindu literature and science assimilated the Muslim elements and influenced the Muslim culture; the Hindu culture instead of being influenced by Islam deeply influenced Islam and its followers. Titus in his book, 'Indian Islam' stated that "...when all is said there seems to be little doubt that Hinduism has wrought a far greater change in Islam than Islam has wrought in Hinduism, which still continues to pursue even tenure of its way with a complacency and confidence that are amazing."[36] In spite of the political subjection in the Medieval Age India was culturally so much alive that it served like a tree that provides shade to the person who cuts off its branches. E.B. Havell has remarked, "Islam seized her political capitals, controlled her military forces and appropriated her revenues, but India retained what she cherished most, her intellectual empire and her soul was never subdued."[37]

In matters of production and industrial organisation, Islam did not compare favourably with what had been achieved in India. Prior to its advent Indian traditions faith, and beliefs were still strong to resist the influence of Islam and its followers. The political triumph of Islam did not lead to intellectual, moral, or religious conquest. Whatever India lost in the battle-fields was regained by her spiritual and cultural forces. Admitting the truth of the fact Pandit Nehru has observed, "The mughals were outsiders and strangers to India and yet they fitted into the Indian structure with remarkable speed.... The Afghan rulers and those who had come with them merged into India. Their dynasties became completely Indianised with their roots in India, looking upon India as their homeland, and the rest of the world as foreign."[38]

Although Medieval India by dint of her power of assimilation, and synthesis, sustained her cultural integrity and superiority in the teeth of great onslaught of foreign invaders, her assimilative force began to decline with the advent of the British in 19th century. By the end of 18th century the foundation of the British rule was firmly laid in India. Together with the establishment of political supremacy, the storm of Western culture and civilization began to rage violently in the country. The expansion of the British Raj and the advent of the Western ideas in India, gave a very rude shock to our ancient religion and social organisations. At this time we had reached the lowest ebb of our cultural decadence and lost all revolutionary urge and creative powers. All social, religious, economic and political institutions began to crumble. The very roots of our national life were violently shaken. Indian nationalism was altogether disappearing. Indiscriminate imitation and adoption of the Western ways of life and habit assumed a vigorous shape. The vision of the people underwent a tremendous change. It was felt as if a new

Europe was to emerge out of the ruins of Indian nation. Fortunately however, the progress of westernisation of Indian life and society received a vehement setback by the forces of Indian Renaissance. Among the veterans of the Renaissance Movement of 19th century, Swami Vivekananda, was an outstanding personality, who achieved signal success in fighting and resisting the Western influence and saving Indian religion and culture to stimulate our pride of nationalism. He advocated assimilation of Western culture in India.

In the Parliament of Religions Swami Vivekananda laid stress on the assimilative power of Sanatan Dharma. Sanatan Dharma withstood all persecution and oppression and survived in the teeth of great threats of foreign invasions. He explained that a religion becomes great by assimilating the good points of other religions but not by persecuting and destroying other religions. As he said, "The Christian is not to become Hindu, or a Buddhist, nor a Hindu or a Buddhist to become Christian, but each must assimilate the spirit of others and yet preserve his individuality and grow according to this own law of growth."[39] Assimilation, thus, is the most essential quality that any religion must possess. This bold declaration in the Parliament of Religions gave a galvanising shock to our national tradition.

Swami Vivekananda said that India had to learn many things from the West but it should not be by blind imitation but thoughtful absorption. For this, first of all India must be conscious about the worth of the essential values of their own religion and culture. When the people will realise the proper values of their own culture they will stop to run after the culture of others. But blind aping of other cultures will cause bruises and bleeding in the national life leading to death. He said, "By imitation, others ideals and ideas, never become one's own — nothing unless earned, is one's own. Does the ass in the lion's skin become a lion?"[40]

Swami Vivekananda advised his countrymen not to imitate the West under the impression that everything of the West is good and their way form a panacea for all our ills. He held that Western civilization looks very fascinating to the surface, but underneath it there is a curse of agony. "All the fun and frivolity are on the surface, really it is full of tragic intensity."[41]

Swami Vivekananda further said that a nation that thinks that it has nothing to learn from others, is on the brink of disintegration. This self-complacency paves the path for ultimate ruin and devastation. A nation with vitality will keep itself open to outside influence and learn valuable lessons from whatsoever sources they may come, but will absorb and express those lessons in its own way and not imitate the way of others.

Swami Vivekananda explained that there are three religions from the pre-historic times — Hinduism, Zoroastrianism, and Judaism. Of these, Judaism has been ousted from its own place of birth by its all conquering daughter Christianity. As for Zoroastrianism, it has been wiped out of existence but for the handful of Parsis, who had taken refuge in India. But "Hinudism, however, has survived the shock of numerous invasions and in course of time has succeeded in absorbing and assimilating most of the cultures that threatened its existence."[42] In this way Swami Vivekananda made fervent appeal to all his countrymen to absorb and assimilate the Western elements, that are best in their culture and civilization. Jawaharlal Nehru, following the foot-prints of Swami Vivekananda also emphasised on the assimilative and synthetic nature of our culture and national life and said, "It might be high privilege of India to help in bringing about this synthesis."[43]

This call for assimilation and absorption of Swami Vivekananda even appealed to Western minds. They realised that by living in isolation and hostility to other religions, they had lost a great opportunity to enrich their own religion and culture more. W.R. Inge regretted much for having ignored Indian religion and philosophy for a long time without absorbing them to enrich their own religion and culture. As he said, "It is a reproach to us that with our unique opportunities of entering into sympathetic relation with Indian thoughts, we have made few attempt to do so.... I am not suggesting that we should become Buddhist or Hindus, but I believe that we have almost as much to learn from them as they from us."[44] Whitehead also in his "Religions in the Making" wrote, "The self-sufficient pedantry of learning and the confidence of ignorant zealots have combined to shut up each religion in its own forms of thought. Instead of looking to each other for deeper meanings, they have remained self-satisfied and unfertilised."[45]

Stressing the need of assimilation, absorption and synthesis of Western and Indian philosophy in the interest of mankind Dr. Albert Schweitzer also said, "Western and Indian philosophies must not contend in the spirit that aims at the one proving itself right in opposition to the other. Both must be moving towards a way of thinking which shall...eventually be shared in common by all mankind."[46]

Thus the spirit of assimilation and synthesis that have characterised Indian nationalism in all ages of history also characterises Swami Vivekananda's concept of nationalism. It appeals most to the Indians and to the Western people as well.

(iv) Religious Harmony and Toleration

Religious harmony and toleration is another special feature of Swami Vivekananda's nationalism. To him India is a unique land based on the principle of religious co-operation, harmony and toleration. While explaining it, he referred to the history of the ancient Babylonians and the Jews, who were divided into tribes, each having its tribal gods, known often under the generic name Merodac among the Babylonians and Moloch among the Semetic Jews. As the tribes fought, the victorious party destroyed the gods of the vanquished and installed their own gods in their place. This religious conflict entailed a long period of bloodshed. Moloch Yahveh of the Jews finally displaced all other gods. Thus supremacy of religion was established by battles.[47]

According to Swami Vivekananda it is just the opposite in our country. There are many gods worshipped in India. In place of fighting for supremacy of one over the other it is declared by a wise Vedic sage, "He who exists is one, the sages call him variously."[48] This idea gained strength in India with the progress of life and civilization. It became the bedrock of the great Indian ideal of universal acceptance in contrast with Western ideas of religious intolerance. In the light of the great Vedic tradition of our country, it is the same god that different cults worship under different names and forms. As Swami Vivekananda said, "It is not that Siva is superior to Vishnu nor is it that Vishnu is everything and Siva is nothing, but it is always the same — one whom you call either Siva or Vishnu or by a hundred other names. The names are different but God is the same one."[49]

Such religious toleration is one of the basic features of Hindu religion and Hindu nationalism. This concept of sameness of god is the source of religious harmony and tolerance in India. As a consequence of this concept of divinity, there is no persecution in our country like in the West, where hostility to other religions and even other sects of the same religion is profound. The history of the West is replete with religious wars. Even now there is very little religious toleration in the West. Westerners may talk of it, but the orientation of their religion makes it impossible for them to practise it. To quote Swami Vivekananda, "There is tremendous religious persecution yet in every country to which I have been and the same old objection are raised against learning anything new. The little toleration, that is in the world, the little sympathy that is yet in the world for religious thought is practically, in the land of Aryas and nowhere else."[50]

According to Swami Vivekananda the great lesson that the world wants most, that the world has yet to learn from India is the idea not only of religious toleration but of oneness of the goal of all religions. To preach this sameness of the goal of all religions Swami Vivekananda referred to Mohimnah Stotra that describes, "As different rivers, taking their start from different mountains, running straight or crooked, at last come into the ocean, so, O Siva, the different paths which men take through different tendencies, various though they appear, crooked or straight, all lead into thee."[51] This means that we must understand and accept that all worship is given to one God, whatever be the name or the form; that all knees bending towards the Caba or kneeling in the Christian Church or in a Buddhist temple, are kneeling to Him, whether they know it or not. Hence, there is no difference among the various holy books of Hindus, Christians and Muslims. They are one and identical in philosophy bearing different names only. Their purpose is one, their goal is one, but the methods or the paths pursued are only different. Hence Swami Vivekananda said, "We want to lead the mankind to the place where there is neither the Vedas nor the Bible, nor the Quoran yet this has to be done by harmonizing the Vedas, the Bible and the Koran."[52] This expression also helps one in understanding Swami Vivekananda's conception of universal religion. He wanted complete freedom for each individual to choose whatever religion he considers best.

Of course differentiation is the law of life and religious differences are bound to persist. But it does not mean that we should hate each other. This hatred is sure to mar the life of man and clog the progress of human society as a whole in the long run. Hence Jawaharlal Nehru said, "I want the narrow conflicts of today in the name of religion or caste, language or province, to cease and a classless and casteless society to be built up where every individual has full opportunity to grow according to his worth and ability."[53]

This grand idea of religious toleration is the very backbone of our national existence. According to Swami Vivekananda this spirit of religious toleration will give rise to universal toleration, a grand idea, the whole world is waiting for. This idea of universal toleration will be a great asset to our civilization. No civilization can attempt to survive without religious toleration. As Swami Vivekananda said, "Nay, no civilization can long exist unless this idea enters into it. No civilization can grow unless fanaticism, bloodshed and brutality stop. No civilization can begin to lift up its head until we look charitably upon one another."[54] Not that we should only be charitable, we should be helpful at the same time also to each other, however different our religious ideas and conviction may be. This is what we are doing exactly in India. It is in India that we Hindus have built Churches for the Christians and Mosques for the Mohammedans. In spite of their brutality and persecution cruelty and their virile language we continue to build Churches and Mosques for Christians and Mohammedans. So according to Swami Vivekananda the religion, we believe in, is based upon love, sympathy and mutual co-operation. Love is the most essential ingredient of India. As he said, "Until we conquer through love, until we have demonstrated to the world that love alone is the fittest thing to survive and not hatred, that it is gentleness that has the strength to live on and to fructify, and not mere brutality and physical force."[55]

It is worthwhile to quote Dr. Radhakrishnan in the light of Swami Vivekananda's idea of religious harmony and tolerance, which is one of the special features of Indian nationalism. As he said, "The unity of different religions cannot be achieved at the external level. It has to be realised in an inward and spiritual way without prejudice to any particular forms. The Hindu seer has no contempt for other religions. He looks upon them as aids to our knowledge of God as channels of divine revelation. He does not believe that salvation is to be had only through any one particular religion. God does not refuse his truth, his love and his grace to any who in sincerity, seek him, wherever they may be and whatever creed they may profess."[56]

Thus as a highly spiritual man Swami Vivekananda tried to eliminate the difference between one sect and the other and promote a sense of religious harmony, tolerance and fellowfeelings, among people of different faiths and religions, following in India for the progress of Indian nationalism.

Emperor Ashok also subscribed to this doctrine of religious toleration and practised it in his life. His 12th edict bears eloquent testimony to this fact. It proclaimed, "...He who does reverence to his own sect while disparaging the sects of others, wholly from attachment to his own, with intent to enhance the glory of his own sect, in reality, by such conduct, inflicts the severest injury on his own sect. Concord therefore is meritorious, to wit, hearkening and hearkening willingly to the Law of Piety, as accepted by other people."[57]

When Swami Vivekananda preached the doctrine of religious toleration and equality of all religions, it lifted the veil of ignorance from the Western minds. They thought in terms of religious co-operation and harmony instead of intoleration and apathy. That is why, perhaps, C.F. Andrews remarked, "If Christianity is to succeed, it must not come forward as an antagonist and a rival to the great religious strivings of the past.

It must come as a helper and a fulfiller, a peacemaker and a friend. There must no longer be the desire to capture converts from Hinduism but to come to her aid in the needful time of trouble and to help her in the fulfilment of duties...."[58] William Law, seeking to bridge the external differences among various religions and promote a healthy spiritual toleration, also said, "There is but one possible way for man to attain this salvation of life of God in the soul. There is not one for the Jews, another for Christian and third for the heathens. No, God is one, human nature is one, salvation is one and the way to it is one...."[59]

Thus religious toleration and harmony that appealed to both East and West, forms a special feature of Swami Vivekananda's concept of nationalism.

(v) Spirit of Renunciation

Nationalism, as propounded by Swami Vivekananda is founded on the Vedantic ideal of renunciation and sacrifice. This as a matter of fact is the most unique aspect of Swami Vivekananda's nationalism. This has immortalised the Indian nation in all ages of history. As he said, "Race after race have taken the challenge up and tried their utmost to solve the world riddle on the plane of desires. They have all failed..., we have solved our problems ages ago.... Our solution is unworldliness — renunciation."[60]

Swami Vivekananda had realised how influence of Hegelianism distorted our Hindu philosophy of renunciation. He asked his compatriots to guard themselves against Hegelianism and its baneful influence. He said, "Hegel's one idea is that the absolute is only chaos and that the one, the absolute is only chaos and that the individualised form is the greater."[61] In one word Hegel makes Samsara greater than salvation. The more one plunges into Samsara the more his soul is covered with the working of life and the better he is for the same. On the other hand our philosophers have from the very first declared that every manifestation what one calls evolution is a vain, a vain attempt of the unmanifested to manifest itself. When this is recognised the soul of man beats a retreat to the place from where it has come. This is vairagya or renunciation on which all religions should be based. This is the conviction of all Indian philosophers that without renunciation there cannot be any true religion. As Swami Vivekananda said, "The first ideal of this attempt to realise religion is that of renunciation."[62] Besides through renunciation alone immortality is to be reached. Immortality cannot be dreamt of without renunciation. As Swami Vivekananda said, "Neither through wealth nor through progeny but by giving up alone that immortality is to be reached."[63] Renunciation is the alpha and omega of immortality. It is the power, the greatest power that cares not even for the universe. Swami Vivekananda said, "The whole universe becomes like a hollow, made by a cow's feet."[64]

Emphasising on renunciation as the special trait of our national character and cultural heritage, Swami Vivekananda held, "Renunciation, that is the flag, the banner of India, floating over the world, the one undying thought, which India sends again and again as a warning to the dying races, as a warning to all tyranny, as a warning to wickedness in the world."[65] To Swami Vivekananda this banner is exclusively the belonging of the Hindus. It is the most valuable asset of the Hindu race. The Hindu should not lose it come what may. The Hindu should not grumble that he is too weak to hold it aloft.

According to Swami Vivekananda, renunciation conquered India in the days of yore. It has still to conquer India. Still it stands as the greatest and highest of Indian ideals. He held that ours is the land of Buddha, Ramanuja, Ramkrishna Paramahansa, the land of renunciation, the land wherefrom the days of yore Karma Kanda was preached and even today there are hundreds who have given up everything and become jivanmuktas.

Explaining the doctrine of renunciation Swami Vivekananda said that renunciation is the only secret to achieve success in life. All the greatmen of the world have realised it, and they have sacrificed their everything for the good of the people and society. As he said, "...greatmen are those who build highways for others with their heart's blood. This has been taking place through eternity, that one builds a bridge by laying down his own body and thousands of others cross the river through its help."[66] Emphasising on the extent of sacrifice Swami Vivekananda said that desire of any kind is bad. Even desire for salvation should not be cherished by man. This desire for salvation is to be abandoned for the interest of others. As he said, "Throughout the history of the world, you find great men make great sacrifices and the mass of mankind enjoy the benefit. If you want to give up everything for your own salvation it is nothing. Do you want to forgo even your own salvation for the good of the world? You are God, think of that."[67] Hence, an Indian should never seek salvation for himself. He believed in renunciation for others which will ultimately bring salvation for oneself. As he said, "When you would be able to sacrifice all desire for happiness for the sake of society, then you would be the Buddha, then you would be free."[68]

According to Swami Vivekananda man cannot think of doing good to others if he is not free from his personal pleasure and comforts. Without the spirit of sacrifice one cannot think of the good of the society. Only selfless and unattached people do good for the society. As he said, "The history of the world is the history of persons like Buddha and Jesus. The passionless and unattached do most for the world."[69]

Swami Vivekananda was afraid of Indians succumbing to the luxury of the West and drinking deep into enjoyments rather than leading a life of renunciation and sacrifice. He was, however, optimistic that at least there will be some people, if not all, in his holy motherland, to whom religion will ever be a reality and who will ever be ready to give up and hold to this lofty ideal of Hindu nationalism."[70]

To Swami Vivekananda, man lives in sacrifice but not in enjoyments. Human life is very short, but he, who lives for others, only lives long. Time cannot kill him, nor can history forget him. So he appeals to all men not to be indulged in vain enjoyments of life, which are short-lived. He has said, "This life is short, the vanities of the world are transient, but they alone live, who live for others, the rest are more dead than alive."[71]

Swami Vivekananda pointed out how the Western intellectuals failed to understand Jesus in the light of his own preachings. To many Western intellectuals Jesus was a great politician, a great leader, a great patriotic jew, but they did not discover the most sublime aspect of his life and philosophy *i.e.*, absolute renunciation and sacrifice. This aspect of Jesus did not draw the attention of the materialist West. But Swami Vivekananda interpreted Jesus in terms of perfect renunciation and describe him as one of the prophets of renunciation of the world. As Jesus said, "The foxes have holes, the birds of the air have nests but the son of Man hath nowhere to lay his head."[72] Swami Vivekananda found that Jesus stood for absolute renunciation. He had no idea of property, money or wealth. He had no family ties, no sex ideas. He was a soul, nothing but the soul, just working a body for the good of the humanity. That was all his relation with the body. He was a disembodied soul, a life of complete renunciation. Swami Vivekananda said, "The disembodied soul has no relationship to the animal no relationship to the body. The ideal will be far away beyond us. But never mind, keep to the ideal. Let us confess that it is our ideal but we cannot approach it well."[73]

To Swami Vivekananda renunciation should be the very motto of our national life, without which Indians cannot grow up. The vitality of our race lies in renunciation. It is the strength and stamina of our race. All enjoyments and pleasures come from renunciation. All powers all glories come from sacrifice. Our Vedas say that one who cannot sacrifice cannot enjoy. The real enjoyment come from sacrifice. The real power comes from renunciation. He called upon his people, "India will be raised not with the power of flesh but with the power of spirit, not with the flag of destruction but with the flag of peace and love — the garb of sannyasin, not by the power of wealth but by the power of begging bowl.... Sitting in the luxurious homes, surrounded with all the comforts of life, and doling out a little amature religion may be good for other lands but India has a truer instinct.... You must give up. Be great. No great work can be done without sacrifice.... Lay down your comforts, your pleasures, your name, fame or positions, nay, even your lives and make a bridge of human chains over which millions will cross the ocean of life...."[74]

Thus renunciation is one of the special features of Swami Vivekananda's nationalism.

(vi) National Building through True Education

Bertrand Russell has observed, "What constitutes a nation is a sentiment, an instinct, a sentiment of similarity and an instinct of belonging to the same group or herd."[75] The concept of nation grows out of the feelings of oneness among the people. It is the feeling of oneness among the people that gives rise to a state or nation. This feeling is the feeling of solidarity or exclusiveness. Some times this feeling remain dormant or suppressed among the people. As a result they become subject to untold misery and suffering under the foreign domination, society degrades and life degenerates. This feeling of oneness or similar sentiment can be aroused among the people through mass-education. Education makes the inner self of man active. It makes man realise his right to life, liberty, etc. In short man regains his consciousness by undergoing the process of education. As Professor H.J. Laski said, "Nor must we fail to notice the way in which the solidarity and therefore the exclusiveness of a nation may be consciously fostered. That may be done by education. In America, very notably, emphasis upon national tradition has welded the most diverse elements into a proudly self-conscious unity."[76]

Education fastens unity and solidarity among the people. People become more and more nationally conscious. Besides, education makes man realise what life ought to be, in which society, life can flourish better towards greater happiness. Education promotes man to discern light in the dark horizon of dogmas, superstitions, injustice and oppression. Ignorance disappears and man attains reason. Man feels enlightened in every sphere of life — social, political and economic. In short, man realises his value of life in the society through education.

Swami Vivekananda realised the very importance of education in the work of nation-building. He realised that true education makes a true nation. So in his scheme of nationalism he laid great stress on education. As he said, "Education is the manifestation of perfection already in man."[77] In Plato's metaphor it is the education that trains our inward eye towards light. It shapes human nature and habit. It forms our character and conduct. It strengthens our will power — the key to all success in life. To Swami Vivekananda "It is the training by which the current and expression of will are brought under control and become fruitful."[78] It keeps the society free from all taints and corruptions. All sorts of evils and ignorance can be remedied only through education. Education is the light of man.

But according to Swami Vivekananda the education that we are now getting may have some good points but its defects outweigh its merits. It is entirely negative in nature. It teaches that all our ancients were worthless men and that our past is blank, devoid of all values. Therefore, Swami Vivekananda said, "Give up the awful disease that is creeping into our national blood that idea of ridiculing everything.... Give up. Be strong and have this Sradha."[79]

The present system of education, according to Swami Vivekananda, is barren and has not produced therefore any original man from the day of its inception. So this system of education has to be replaced forthwith by a system of man-making education. As he said, "Education is not the amount of information that is put into your brain to remain there undigested all your life. We must have a life building, man-making, character-making assimilation of ideas."[80] If we assimilate five ideas and allow them to enter and mould our life and character we will have more education than any man, who has got by heart a whole library.

The ass carrying its load of sandal wood, knows only the weight and not the value of the sandal wood. So according to Swami Vivekananda if education is identified with information the librarians are the greatest sages in the world, and the encyclopaedias are the Rishis. The ideal therefore is that we must have the whole education of our country — spiritual and secular in our own hands and it must be on national lines, through national methods are far as practicable. If the education does not make us appreciate the value of our own culture, it is of no use. This national system of education, based on our own culture is the only solution to all the evils that beset our national life.

Education, according to Swami Vivekananda must help man in his struggle for life. It should teach patience and perseverance to man. It shall also promote strength of character, that brings every success to life. He said, "The education which does not help the common mass of people to equip themselves for the struggle for life, which does not bring out strength of character, a spirit of philosophy and courage of a lion, is worth of the name? Real education is that which enables one to stand in his own legs."[81]

Our foremost duty, according to Swami Vivekananda, is to educate the lower and backward class of people in order to awaken them to a higher state of consciousness, to make them understand their real worth of life. He said, "The only service to be done for our lower class is to give them education to develop their lost individuality. ...Give them ideas — that is the only help, they require and then the rest must follow as the effect. Ours is to put the chemical together, the crystalisation comes in the law of nature.... Now if the mountain does not come to Mohammed, Mohammed must go to the mountain. If the poor boy cannot come to education, education must go to them."[82]

Education makes man strong and self-reliant. It makes man stand on his own feet. It inculcates strength of mind. India as a nation must have that type of education. Hence Swami Vivekananda said, "We want that education by which character is formed, strength of mind is increased, the intellect is expanded and by which one can stand on one's own feet."[83]

To build up a sturdy nation, Swami Vivekananda felt that knowledge of Sanskrit should be cultivated and education should be imparted through one's mother tongue. As he said, "Sanskrit must be popularised among the people. Education must be given to the people in their own language, and at the same time Sanskrit education must go along with it, because the very sound of Sanskrit words gives a prestige and power and strength to the race."[84] No other language, he felt, has played so dominant a role as Sanskrit in uniting India in spite of her diversities. In all ages Sanskrit has become the cementing force for the people of India. As Jawaharlal Nehru has observed, "Hardly any language in the world has probably played that vital part in the history of a race which Sanskrit has. It was not only the vehicle of highest thought and some of the finest literature, but it became the uniting bond for India in spite of its political division."[85]

Lord Buddha used Pali instead of Sanskrit in propagating his religion as Pali was the language of the common man. It was easily assessable to all. But Swami Vivekananda did not like such omission of Sanskrit. He said, "Even the great Buddha made one false step when he stopped Sanskrit language from being studied by the masses. He wanted rapid and immediate results, and translated and preached in the language of the day, Pali. That was grand; he spoke in the language of the people and the people understood him. That was great; it spread the idea quickly and made them reach far and wide. But along with that Sanskrit ought to have spread. Knowledge came but prestige was not there, culture was not there. It is culture that withstands shocks, not simple mass of knowledge.... There must come culture into the blood. Knowledge is only skin-deep."[86]

According to Swami Vivekananda to build up a mighty nation the educational system must be based upon the culture of the country. Education without culture is only skin-deep. Culture is deep-rooted in the mind of the people as man is the product of his culture. As culture is deep-rooted in man, culture-based education touches the very heart of the people, which cannot be erased from mind so easily. So culture-based education is essential for the building of a mighty nation. A nation is great if its people are true to its culture. India has been great in all ages of history because of her great culture. So Swami Vivekananda said, "Teach the masses in the vernaculars, give them ideas; they will get information but some more is necessary, give them culture."[87] Culture forms the vitality of the nation. So culture should be taught to the people that fastens unity and integrity of the nation among its people. Annie Besant also felt the need of a culture-based education in India and said, "The needs of India are, among others, the development of a national spirit and an education founded on Indian ideals and enriched, not dominated by the thought and culture of the West."[88]

The whole aim of Swami Vivekananda was to build up a mighty Indian nation on the solid foundation of her culture.

Unless the mass of people are free from the encircling gloom of ignorance, caused by the advent of Western culture they cannot discern the new light of life in the horizon. Education based on Indian culture is the only light that will dispel the gloom far off and makes life conducive to novelty of thought in the direction of national progress. So education based on Indian culture constitutes one of the special features of Swami Vivekananda's nationalism.

(vii) Spiritual Oneness of the Universe

Swami Vivekananda was born in India but he was not meant for India alone. Whole universe was his chief concern. As he himself said, "I know my mission in life,....; I belong as much to India as to the world."[89] Bearing the load of misery and the afflictions of the world on his back, he thought for the redemption of the whole mankind. His great Master Sri Ramkrishna, admitting it, once said, "Narendra is not a twig that sinks even if a bird alights upon it. Rather he is a great tree-trunk, carrying men, beasts and merchandise upon its chests."[90] In fact he was a huge banayan tree to shelter the whole mankind in its shade from the scorching miseries of the world. His love for the mankind was so great that he looked upon the universe as one family. His heart bled to see the fragmented world. Although the old lines of demarcation and differentiation of creeds, dogmas and nationalities are fast vanishing, people are not profoundly influenced by it. Swami Vivekananda thought that the Veda with its doctrine of non-duality of soul or unity of existence is the only unifying force that can bring about the integration of the whole universe. The Veda alone can eliminate all the differences and discriminations in human society and bring about the spiritual integration of the mankind. Therefore, he asked the people to accept and preach this Advaitic doctrine to all and said, "I am doing so not in a sectarian sense but upon universal and widely acceptable ground."[91] Elaborating the doctrine of nonduality of soul he said that the universe emanates from the all-pervasive Atma and is enveloped by such Atma. This Atma or Brahma is both within and outside the entire universe and all animate and inanimate objects. As Dr. Annie Besant has interpreted it, "There is only one consciousness and that is God-consciousness. All is God consciousness for there is none other. And as consciousness unfolds from the grain of sand to the man, from the man to the Deva, it is only God unfolding."[92] Swami Vivekananda said that there is nothing, as Brahma is all. It is supreme — the Absolute Brahma to which the whole universe is confirmed.

To Swami Vivekananda this spiritual oneness or solidarity of the whole universe on the basis of non-duality of soul is the grand new idea that the world is yet to know. It is completely a new idea, enshrined in the Vedas and unknown to the whole world. India has to disseminate this knowledge throughout the universe. As he said, "The....great idea that the world wants from us today, the thinking part of Europe, nay, the whole world — more, perhaps, the lower classes than the higher, more the masses than the cultured, more the ignorant than the educated, more the weak, than the strong — is that eternal grand idea of the spiritual oneness of the whole universe."[93]

Swami Vivekananda held that oneness or solidarity of the whole universe is the cry of the day. International organisation and international laws are coming out for this purpose. In politics and sociology it is increasingly found that problems of each nation are international and cannot be solved at purely national level. Electricity and steam power are placing the different parts of the world in intercommunication with each other and as a result different spralling parts of the world are linked together.[94] So oneness of the world is becoming more and more possible. The scientists have also established the solidarity of the whole universe. They demonstrate "the sun, the moon, the stars and all men are but little waves or wavelets in the midst of an infinite ocean of matter."[95] The Indian psychology also long ago demonstrated that "the same is the case with mind. Both body and mind are mere names, composed of same matter."[96] All these are parallel to the Vedantic idea of "one unchangeable unbroken, homogeneous Atma."[97] The Vedanta shows that there is but one soul throughout the whole universe, the real and eternal soul. All is but one existence *i.e.*, Absolute.

Swami Vivekananda said that "this great principle of oneness of the universe is even now unconsciously forming the basis of all the latest political and social aspirations that are coming up in England, Germany, France and in America. In all literature, voicing man's struggle for freedom, universal freedom, Indian Vedantic ideals are coming out prominently again and again. In some cases the writers do not know the source of this inspiration, but there are few who are bold and grateful enough to mention the source and acknowledge their indebtedness to our Vedanta, the ultimate, and eternal source of all power and strength."[98]

This infinite oneness of soul is the eternal sanction for all morality which never gives way under any circumstance. Fear of death cannot frighten it. It is the source of all strength, the infinite power. This oneness of soul is also the source of brotherhood for all. This spiritual affinity among the living beings is the bond of this brotherhood, which is unbroken and long lived. Besides, this understanding that we are part and parcel of one divine spirit the ultimate source of all strength, generates faith in oneself. Lack of this faith, according to Swami Vivekananda is the cause of all degeneration of character in India. As he said," "...it is the one great life-giving idea, which the world wants from us today and which the masses of India want for their uplifting, for none can regenerate this land of ours without the practical application and effective operation of this ideal of the oneness of things."[99]

According to Swami Vivekananda the people in the Western countries believe themselves to be strong though their religion teaches them to be the sinners, and that is why they dominate the world politics. It is pointed out, "...the Englishman believes that he is born lord of the world. He believes that he is the great and can do anything in the world. If he wants to go to the sun or moon he believes that that he can and that makes him great."[100] That is not only the characteristic of the English people, but the characteristic of all the Europeans and that is why the Europeans are dominating the world.

But in spite of the great ideas, contained in the Upanishads we think ourselves to be very weak. It is the strength that we want, which will bring us freedom from the British bondages, and save us from all injustice and oppression. Therefore Swami Vivekananda said, "...the first step in getting strength is to uphold the Upanishads and believe I am the soul — me, the sword cannot cut, nor weapon pierce, me the fire cannot burn, the air cannot dry. I am the omnipotent and I am the omnicient."[101] But at present according to Swami Vivekananda, "We cannot rise to that high level of Upanishads. The feelings of courage, morality and faith will not come to us, simply because our blood is only like water, physical weakness is the cause and nothing-else."[102]

However, according to Swami Vivekananda, still there is time for us. We can revitalise ourselves. We can regain our past strength. The only way to regain our vitality is to follow the doctrines of the Upanishads sincerely. We can overcome all our weakness only by our sincere adherence to Upanishads. As he said, "We have lost faith in ourselves. Therefore to preach Advaita aspect of Vedanta is necessary to rouse up the hearts of man, to show them the glory of their souls."[103]

Thus by preaching the Advaita aspect of Vedanta Swami Vivekananda tried to arouse strength, fearlessness and courage in the mind of Indians against the British oppression and injustice. By instilling in their mind this self-confidence he thought of teaching them the technique of resistance of foreign rule.

According to Swami Vivekananda, the only way for effecting the oneness of the universe is to broadcast this great ideal of the Upanishads. He condemned therefore the world dictators who sought to integrate the whole world by force and power. To him world solidarity can only be achieved through the Vedantic philosophy that preaches that we are all the parts and parcels of the same divine soul. This spiritual affinity is the source of perennial brotherhood that binds mankind with the universal bond of brotherhood. Hence love and service is the only force to hold the entire mankind together. As he has observed, "Look upon every man and woman and everyone as God. You cannot help any one. You can only serve, serve the children of the Lord. Serve the Lord himself, if you have that privilege. If the Lord grants that you can serve everyone of his children, blessed you are; do not think for much yourselves...do it only as worship."[104] According to him the poor and the miserables help in our salvation. So we must serve the Lord coming in the shape of diseased, lunatics, lepers and sinners.

This idea of salvation through forging universal unity is unknown to the whole world. So this idea should be diffused by Indian nation all over the universe. Hence he appealed to the people of his country, "Bring light to the poor; and bring more light to the rich for they require more than the poor. Bring light to the ignorant and more light to the educated for the vanities of the education of our time are tremendous."[105]

Thus one of the specialities of Swami Vivekananda's nationalism is the call for the propagation of this Vedantic ideal of oneness by Indian nation all over the world. When the ideal will reach the entire mankind, and the entire mankind will discern the light, Indian's mission as a nation shall be fulfilled. Then all the divisions and differences will vanish. There will be one world — one family — one mankind — one soul — the absolute integration, and Indian nation shall fulfil itself.

(viii) Unity in the Midst of Diversity

India is a vast subcontinent. The size of the country is quite enormous. It is as large as the whole Europe excluding Russia and is nearly twenty times as big as Great Britain. But more remarkable than the geographical vastness and wide area of the country is the bewildering diversity of its race, language, religion, culture etc. So India is known as 'the land of varieties.' It is described as 'the epitome of the world.'

India presents a great variety of racial types through her teeming millions. V.A. Smith rightly calls India as "ethnological museum."[106] As early as 5th century B.C. Herodotus observed, "Of all the nations that we know, it is India which has the largest population."[107] Really the total number of inhabitants in India amount to about 1/7th of the whole population of the world. This huge assemblage of human beings is made up of diverse race, the jungle tribe (like Kols, Bhils, Gonds, Santals), the Greeks, the Sakas, the Kushanas, the Huns, the Mongolians, the Arabs, the Turks, the Afghans etc. Today India has the primitive tribesmen as well as the polished and cultured inhabitants.

There is in India as many as 15 separate recognised

languages. Each community has its own language and literature. Besides more than 200 different dialects and languages are spoken in this vast subcontinent.[108]

There is also to be found a variety of religions. All the major world religions are found here — Hinduism, Buddhism, Jainism, Islam and Christianity. All have their sects and subdivisions. The Hindu religion itself is split up into countless creeds — the Vedic, the Pauranic Hinduism, the Sanatans, the Brahmo Samaj, the Arya Samaj etc. The primitive tribes have their own peculiar cults.

These people differ considerably in their social habits. Culture of the people varies from state to state. So Jawaharlal Nehru has said, "The diversity of India is tremendous; it is obvious; ...It concern itself with physical appearances as well as with certain mental habits and traits."[109] Financially also speaking, we find man with an income of barely a few paise a day and others who rank among the richest of the world.

Thus India is made up of a complex diversity. There is no wonder if "India is a museum of cults and customs, creeds and cultures, faiths and tongues, racial type and social system."[110] The vastness of the country, the extreme diversity of its physical features, endless variety of its race, and magnitude of its population, divided into countless cults, professing numerous creeds, speaking a variety of languages and dialects — all these have made it difficult to establish a stable and permanent cohesion. As a result India has been a hunting ground for quite a good many foreign invaders like the Greeks, the Sakyas, the Huns, the Yabanas etc. Lastly, the European nations — the Dutch, the French and the British made India their happy hunting ground. The British defeated all in the long run and established their paramount hegemony over India. India suffered from age-long slavery under the heels of the British. Poverty and starvation became the glaring phenomena of the day. In the words of Swami Vivekananda, "The people of India were compelled to be merely hewers of wood and drawers of water for centuries, so much so that they are made to be believe that they are born as slaves, born as hewers of wood and drawers of water."[111]

When this was the state of affairs, Swami Vivekananda realised that welding national unity of India is an impossible task. In the midst of such complex diversity, political unity is very difficult to achieve. As he said, "...political unity is not the normal characteristics of ancient and medieval history. There was no political cohesion. In all the past ages India was divided into many principalities. They were from time to time brought under subjection and integrated into an extensive empire by powerful rulers like Chandra Gupta Maurya, Ashoka.... But when internal weakness and disorder or foreign invasions, or both, shattered their empires, India relapsed once again into political disunity."[112] In fact India had never enjoyed political unity till 19th century. Politically a popular national feeling was almost absent. Politics did not control Indian minds and found no great appeal among the masses. To the Indian life politics remained a separate feature, absolutely external, having no relation to day-to-day life. This absence of political unity retarded seriously the political progress of the country and hindered India from becoming a nation.

Swami Vivekananda tried to discover the way of unifying the Indian nation with a common thread. He realised that in spite of its bewildering diversity in respect of geographical feature, race, religion, language, etc. there existed a deep underlying fundamental unity that has upheld the country in all ages of history in the midst of all national vicissitude. He succeeded to find out "the one in the many, the individual in the aggregate, the simple in the composite."[113] That is, the underlying unity of life from Himalayas to Cape Comorin. His deep-penetrating vision into the cultural history of India led him to realise the fact that India is primarily a land of religion and there is an undercurrent of religious unity among the people. There may be various religious sects in the country, but the Vedas, the Gita, the Ramayana, the Mahabharata, the Puranas and other scriptures are respected equally throughout the length and breadth of the country. The ancient religion of the Vedas and Puranas have been the source of eternal solace to the simple hearted Hindus. They have faith in unseen reality and sense of sacredness of life, charity and tolerance. Religious rites and rituals have almost the same uniformity throughout the vast land. A permanent and characteristically Indian expression of this religious unity is the network of shrines, and sacred places with which the country has been covered. The most sacred places of Hindu pilgrimages such as Badrinarayana in the North, Dwaraka in the West, Rameswaram in the South, and Lord Jagannathpuri in the East embrace the whole of the country and they speak of India being one land. Hence the concept of spiritual unity in India is very old. Sir Herbert Risley has observed, "Beneath the manifold diversity of physical and social type, language, custom, and religion which strikes the observer in India, there can still be discerned a certain underlying uniformity of life from Himalaya to Cape Comorin."[114]

All these led Swami Vivekananda to arrive at the conclusion that unity form the very backbone of Indian national life. Spirit of unity is the most fundamental feature of the people of India in spite of their diversity. Hence Rabindra Nath Tagore has observed, "In spite of our great difficulty, however, India has done something. She has tried to make an adjustment of races to acknowledge the real differences between them where these exist and yet seeks for some basis of unity. This basis has come through our saints like Nanak, Kabir, Chaitanya and others, preaching one God to all races of India."[115] Thus the spirit of unity is the foundation upon which the total edifice of our nationality is built up. It is the life-current of our nationhood. As Swami Tapasyananda points out, "Our ancestors in the past finding that the quest for the secret nature through external investigation, is useless, turned their attention on this inward quest, which is grander, infinitely higher, infinitely more blissful, till it has become the national characteristic, till it has become our second nature."[116] Thus according to Swami Vivekananda, spirit of unity in the midst of manifold diversities, is our national characteristic, the vitality of our race. As long as we hold on to this grandest of all our heritage namely Unity, no external force can destroy us. Before this spirit of unity all other disruptive forces will melt away, all diversities will vanish.

However, Swami Vivekananda felt that this sense of unity is a product of deep religious faith of the Indians. Hence the unity of the nation has to be forged once again. It shall have to be done with the help of religion — the Vedantic religion. As R.N. Tagore has pointed out, "...The Indian devoid of all politics... whose one ambition has been to know this world as of soul, to live here every moment of her life in the meek spirit of adoration, in the glad consciousness of an eternal and personal relationship with it."[117] So Swami Vivekananda found that national unity in India is to be achieved through kindling the religious spirit of Indians. The people of India understand politics if it is given through religion to them. As he said, "But the Hindus can understand politics if it is given through religion; sociology must come through religion, everything must come through religion."[118] This is the very peculiarity of Indian mind. Their mind is so much obsessed with spiritualism that it is not ready to accept anything other than religion. So Swami Vivekananda said, "The one common ground that we have, is our sacred tradition, our religion. That is the only common ground and upon that we shall have to build."[119]

Thus forging national unity by stimulating religious and spiritual instinct in the midst of all diversity of India as mentioned above, is one of the special features of Swami Vivekananda's nationalism.

(ix) Emphasis on Humanism

The lofty ideal of humanism, the finest flower of Indian culture occupies an important place in the theory Swami Vivekananda's nationalism. Humanism is a system of thought concerned with human affairs in general. It is an attitude that attaches primary importance to man and his faculties, affairs and aspirations. It upholds the truth that man after all is supreme. These ideas emanate from the philosophy of the Upanishads. As I.P. Chelishev has observed, "Since the ancient times, lofty life asserting humanistic ideas formed the foundation of India's world outlook. These ideas have been expressed in religious, philosophical form which as they developed, paved their way in constant struggle against the scholastic, ascetic and passive contemplation, of the world."[120] Swami Vivekananda accepted and modified this idea of humanism as the condition of a new life. His voice at the end of the last century echoed loudly in the enslaved, brutally exploited mankind, where human dignity and right was trampled under the heels of the colonialists of the West. This ideal of Swami Vivekananda's humanism influenced other succeeding writers of India like Tagore, Aurobindo, Gandhi etc.

In fact Swami Vivekananda's humanism has nothing in common with the Christian ideology which dooms man to passivity and begging God for favours. He tried to place religious ideology at the service of national interest and the interest of mankind at large. He loudly declared that the colonialists were building one church after another in India while the Eastern countries needed bread and not religion. This shows his great love for human beings. As Swami Ranganathananda said, "Vivekananda made Indian philosophy concern itself with the problems of the common man. He brings down the Vedanta to fertilise the fields of common life."[121]

To evaluate man Swami Vivekananda identifies him with God. As he said, "The only God to worship is the human soul in the human body. Of course all animals are temples too, but man is the highest, the Taj Mohal of temple."[122] In his desire to elevate man he put forward the idea that the highest divine substance Brahman is personified in millions of ordinary living people and therefore the worship of God is tantamount to serving man. As he said, "If you want any God to come, just throw your ceremonials over board and worship the living God — the Man-God, every being that wears the human form. God in his universal as well as individual aspect."[123] He called it perfect lunacy to place edibles before the image of God and also rebuked the zealots for spending crores of rupees on building temples, while the common man died of hunger.

Swami Vivekananda realised that man is the perfect image of God. He said, "If you want to find God, serve man."[124] He expressed his desire to be born again and suffer thousands of miseries so that he can worship the only God, the sum total of all souls. This is not only the highest expression of religions but the clearest statement of humanism. He laid emphasis on practical religion. He asked people to worship and offer the poor what they offer to the image of God in the temple. He had such compassion for the poor that once he burst into tears when a disciple of Ramkrishna narrated to him the poverty of the poor in general. His disciples had strict instructions to avoid the paraphernalia of worship, and work for the poor Daridra-Narayana. How often he said to Sister Nivedita, "You do not yet understand India! We Indians are man-worshippers after all. Our God is man!"[125] He looked upon every man as God. He wanted to make it a cult in Hindu religion and philosophy. He emphatically said, "Serve the living God! God comes to you in the blind, in the halt, in the poor, in the weak, in the diabolical. What a glorious chance for you to worship."[126]

Swami Vivekananda advocated all-round development of human personality, assertion of the rights of man and the sense of his own dignity. In the words of V.S. Kostyuchenko, "...It poses many features of active humanism manifested above all in a fervent desire to elevate man, to instill in him a sense of his own dignity, sense of responsibility for his own destiny and the destiny of all people to make him strive for the ideals of good, truth and justice, to foster in man abhorence for any suffering."[127]

Swami Vivekananda reminded his disciples of the vows of the Sannyasins, that is, giving up everything and doing good to others. As he said, "It is only by doing good to others that one attains to one's own good and it is by leading others to Bhakti and Mukti that one attains them oneself."[128] He wanted his disciples to move from village to village and help the poor. To him altruistic service is the only religion and all other ceremonial practices are sheer madness.

The whole force of Swami Vivekananda's argument is to bring home to mankind that religion, consisting of service, and renunciation is service of and renunciation for man. Once he said to Sister Nivedita, "This idea of man-worship exists in nucleus in India, but it has never been expanded. You must develop it. Make poetry, make art of it. Establish the worship of the feet of beggars as you had it in Medieval Europe. Make man-worshippers."[129]

Swami Vivekananda's aim was to strengthen the humanistic trend of religion that exalts man as the true abode of divinity against the orthodox religion that portrays man as miserable sinners or a weak or helpless being completely at the mercy of God. His unqualified emphasis on love and service reminds us of the Buddha, who asked his disciples to wander for the welfare of many. He bent all his strength, and dedicated his whole life for the service of human beings. Romain Rolland has observed, "There was no single hour of his life when he was not brought into contact with the sorrows, the desires, the abuses, the misery and the feverishness of living man, rich and the poor, in the town and field."[130] Swami Vivekananda's aim in emphasising on the Vedantic identification of man and God was to raise the dignity of man in the world. He declared, "This human body is the greatest body in the universe and a human being is the greatest being. Man is higher than all animals, than all angels; none is greater than man."[131]

Swami Vivekananda was not a pessimist and refused to call man a sinner in spite of all his follies. The world in which we live, is the best of the world and therefore he never advised one to abandon it. He rather prescribed that men should enjoy both material and spiritual pleasures of the world that make life most enjoyable. In this context he once said, "I do not believe in God, who will give me undying bliss in heaven, but who cannot give me bread in this world."[132] It is in this world and through enjoyment of the material objects of life that man can attain perfection.

Swami Vivekananda was really a prophet of the poor. He dedicated his whole life for the cause of the poor and the downtrodden. His sympathy, his love for the poor and miserable was very uncommon. He said, "Forget not that the lower class, the ignorant, the poor, the illiterate, the cobbler, the sweeper, are thy flesh and blood, the brothers."[133] It was because of his desires and will to work for the cause of the downtrodden of India that Swami Vivekananda left his family in most pitiable condition. His renunciation for the cause of the poor amounts to that of Buddha, who renounced his royal estate, wife, son etc. for the redemption of mankind. Swami Vivekananda himself wrote about it in one of his letters : "On the one hand my vision of the future of Indian religion and that of the whole world, my love for the millions of beings sinking down and down for ages, with nobody to help them; on the other hand making those who are nearest and dearest to me miserable, I choose the former."[134] He wanted to organise the youths of India and send them like waves all over India and world, bringing comfort, morality, religion and education to the doors of the meanest and the most downtrodden.

Ordinarily humanism implies love for man but not necessarily belief in man. Swami Vivekananda considered man as God himself and on that ground had abiding faith in man. Speaking to the students of Lahore College, he urged them to have faith in man as the preparation for faith in God. He urged them to work for the good of the society without any idea of sectarianism. In the words of Romain Rolland, "He tried to remedy social injustices by preaching intermarriage between castes and sub-divisions of castes so that they might draw near to each other, by ameliorating the condition of the outcastes by occupying himself with the fate of unmarried woman and Hindu widows, by fighting sectarianism wherever it was to be found and vain formalism, the don't touchism as he called them."[135]

Swami Vivekananda's love for mankind was so great that he thought the whole universe as one family and strove his utmost for the redemption of the whole mankind. He was not an abstract philosopher, but a devoted humanist not merely concerned with a spiritual but also material well-being of the whole humanity. He was not only concerned with India's regeneration but with the regeneration of mankind at large. His nationalism is not narrow nationalism, blind to the demands of larger humanity. His nationalism is rather universalism that holds great faith and love in man in its sacred fold. So he is rightly called, "The discoverer of India's long lost mission in the world."[136]

Swami Vivekananda's humanism is based on his tremendous faith in the powers of man as enshrined in the Vedas. He tried to direct his religious philosophy to the service of India and the mankind for their spiritual uplift and total emancipation from injustice, fear and evil. So it is rightly said, "Everything that Vivekananda proclaimed in India for the first time at the last century, facilitated the development of the equalitatively new humanism which played an important part in the general upsurge of national consciousness and struggle for Indian people for Independence."[137]

To sum up Swami Vivekananda's nationalism is spiritual in nature. He had firm conviction that spiritualism should be the soul of Indian nationalism. Besides Swami Vivekananda's nationalism breathes the spirit of universalism. That apart, based on the assimilative and synthetic character of Indian cultural heritage, Swami Vivekananda's nationalism is also assimilative and synthetic in character.

Swami Vivekananda's nationalism also preaches the lofty ideals of inter-religious harmony and toleration. Based on the Indian spirit of and particularly the Vedantic spirit of renunciation, Swami Vivekananda's nationalism also admits the flavour of renunciation and self-sacrifice. That apart, he advocated nation-building by imparting true education, that shall promote the qualities of patience, perseverance and strength of character. His nationalism preaches the doctrine of spiritual oneness of the universe. He even advocated that man's salvation is possible by forging universal unity. Besides, inspite of religious, racial and linguistic diversities, he advocated unity of the Indian nation. He considered unity in the midst of diversity to be the very backbone of Indian national life. Above all, Swami Vivekananda's nationalism is based on humanism that appeals most to the people world over.

REFERENCES

1. Bertrand Russell, *Political Ideals*, p. 78.
2. *Ibid.*, p. 89.
3. R.N. Tagore, *Sadhana*, p. 12.
4. Dr. Radhakrishnan, *Recovery of Faith*, p. 7.
5. *Complete Works of Swami Vivekananda*, Vol. VIII, p. 74.
6. *Selected Works of M.N. Roy*, Vol. I, p. 333.
7. *Ibid.*, Vol. I, p. 333.
8. *Ibid.*, Vol. I, p. 345.
9. *Ibid.*, Vol. I, p. 338.
10. *Ibid.*, Vol. II, p. 168.

11. *Complete Works of Swami Vivekananda,* Vol. III, p. 286.
12. *Ibid.,* Vol. III, p. 287.
13. *Ibid.,* Vol. III, p. 147.
14. *Ibid.,* Vol. III, p. 108.
15. *Ibid.,* Mayavati Memorial Edition, 1936, Part I, p. 40.
16. Dr. Radhakrishnan, *Recovery of Faith,* p. 10.
17. Sri Aurobindo, *Essay in Karmayogin.*
18. *Complete Works of Swami Vivekananda,* Vol. III, p. 371.
19. Dr. Radhakrishnan, *Recovery of Faith,* p. 186.
20. *Complete Works of Swami Vivekananda,* Vol. I, p. 19.
21. *Nationalistic and Religious Lectures of Swami Vivekananda,* p. 10.
22. *Complete Works of Swami Vivekananda,* Vol. I, p. 18.
23. *Ibid.,* Vol. I, p. 18.
24. *Ibid.,* Vol. I, p. 18.
25. Jawaharlal Nehru, *India Today and Tomorrow,* pp. 26-27.
26. Romain Rolland, *The Life of Vivekananda and the Universal Gospel,* p. 70.
27. Jawaharlal Nehru, *India Today and Tomorrow,* p. 13.
28. Louis Renou, *Religions of Ancient India,* p. 110.
29. Jawaharlal Nehru, *Discovery of India,* p. 338.
30. *Complete Works of Swami Vivekananda,* Vol. III, p. 106.
31. B.N. Luniya, *Evolution of Indian Culture,* p. 320.
32. *Ibid.,* p. 320.
33. J.N. Sarkar, *India Through the Ages,* p. 41.
34. B.N. Luniya, *Evolution of Indian Culture,* p. 311.
35. Stated in B.N. Luniya, *Evolution of Indian Culture,* p. 311.
36. *Ibid.,* p. 314.
37. *Ibid.,* p. 314.
38. Jawaharlal Nehru, *Discovery of India,* p. 219.
39. *Complete Works of Swami Vivekananda,* Vol. I, p. 24.
40. *Ibid.,* Vol. IV, p. 477.
41. *Ibid.,* Vol. VIII, pp. 261-62.
42. *Nationalistic and Religious Lectures of Swami Vivekananda,* p. 2.
43. Jawaharlal Nehru, *India Today and Tomorrow,* p. 44.
44. W.R. Inge, *Mysticism in Religion,* p. 8.

45. Whitehead, *Religions in the Making*, p. 146.
46. George Seaver, *Albert Schweitzer*, p. 276.
47. *Nationalistic and Religious Lectures of Swami Vivekananda*, p. 16.
48. Rig Veda, Mandala — I, Sukta — 164, Mantra — 46 (Quoted in *Swami Vivekananda's Complete Works*, Vol. III, p. 186.)
49. *Complete Works of Swami Vivekananda*, Vol. III, p. 113.
50. *Ibid.*, Vol. III, p. 114
51. *Ibid.*, Vol. III, p. 114.
52. *Ibid.*, Vol. VI, p. 145.
53. Jawaharlal Nehru, *India Today and Tomorrow*, pp. 43-44.
54. *Complete Works of Swami Vivekananda*, Vol. III, p. 87.
55. *Ibid.*, Vol. III, p. 188.
56. Dr. Radhakrishnan, *Recovery of Faith*, p. 172.
57. *Ibid.*, p. 181.
58. *Ibid.*, p. 183.
59. *Works of William Law*, Vol. VII, p. 46.
60. *Complete Works of Swami Vivekananda*, Vol. IV, pp. 314-15.
61. *Ibid.*, Vol. III, p. 342.
62. *Ibid.*, Vol. IV, p. 180.
63. *Ibid.*, Vol. III, p. 343.
64. *Ibid.*, Vol. III, p. 344.
65. *Ibid.*, Vol. III, p. 344.
66. *Ibid.*, Vol. VI, pp. 273-74.
67. *Ibid.*, Vol. VI, p. 280.
68. *Ibid.*, Vol. IV, p. 491.
69. *Ibid.*, Vol. VIII, p. 226.
70. *Nationalistic and Religious Lectures of Swami Vivekananda*, p. 82.
71. Manomohan Ganguly, *Swami Vivekananda — A Study*, p. 69.
72. *Complete Works of Swami Vivekananda*, Vol. IV, p. 145.
73. *Ibid.*, Vol. IV, p. 145.
74. *Ibid.*, Vol. IV, p. 352.
75. Bertrand Russell, *Political Ideals*, p. 78.
76. Professor H.J. Laski, *Grammar of Politics*, p. 221.
77. *Complete Works of Swami Vivekananda*, Vol. IV, p. 358.
78. *Ibid.*, Vol. IV, p. 490.

79. *Complete Works of Swami Vivekananda,* Vol. III, p. 320.
80. *Lectures from Colombo to Almora,* p. 212.
81. *Complete Works of Swami Vivekananda,* Vol. VII, pp. 147-48.
82. *Ibid.*, Vol. IV, pp. 362-63.
83. *Ibid.*, Vol. V, p. 342.
84. *Ibid.*, Vol. III, p. 290.
85. Jawaharlal Nehru, *India Today and Tomorrow,* p. 4.
86. *Complete Works of Swami Vivekananda,* Vol. III, p. 291.
87. *Ibid.*, Vol. III, p. 291.
88. *Auto Biography of Annie Besant,* p. 508.
89. Swami Budhananda, *Swami Vivekananda — His Call to the Nation,* p. 101.
90. *Gospel of Sri Ramkrishna,* p. 793.
91. *Nationalistic and Religious Lectures of Swami Vivekananda,* p. 39.
92. Annie Besant, *The Wisdom of the Upanishad,* p. 5.
93. *Complete Works of Swami Vivekananda,* Vol. III, p. 188.
94. *Ibid.*, Vol. III, p. 240.
95. *Nationalistic and Religious Lectures of Swami Vivekananda,* p. 39.
96. *Complete Works of Swami Vivekananda,* Vol. III, p. 188.
97. *Ibid.*, Vol. III, p. 241.
98. *Ibid.*, Vol. III, pp. 189-90.
99. *Ibid.*, Vol. III, p. 189.
100. *Ibid.*, Vol. III, p. 243.
101. *Ibid.*, Vol. III, p. 244.
102. *Ibid.*, Vol. III, p. 191.
103. *Ibid.*, Vol. III, p. 246.
104. *Ibid.*, Vol. III, p. 246.
105. *Ibid.*, Vol. III, p. 247.
106. V.A. Smith, *The Early History of India,* p. 16.
107. Quoted in B.N. Luniya, *Evolution of Indian Culture,* p. 11.
108. 15 languages are provided by the constitution. They are : Assamese, Bengali, Gujarati, Hindi, Kannada, Kashmiri, Malayalam, Marathi, Oriya, Punjabi, Sanskrit, Sindhi, Tamil, Telugu, and Urdu.
109. Jawaharlal Nehru, *Discovery of India,* p. 44.
110. Radhakumud Mukherjee, *The Fundamental Unity of India,* p. 11.
111. *Lectures From Colombo to Almora,* pp. 94-95.

112. B.N. Luniya, *Evolution of Indian Culture*, p. 12.
113. Radhakumud Mukherjee, *The Fundamental Unity of India*, p. 11.
114. Sir Herbert Risley, *People of India*, p. 299.
115. R.N. Tagore, *Nationalism*, p. 59.
116. *Nationalistic and Religious Lectures of Swami Vivekananda*, p. 85.
117. R.N. Tagore, *Nationalism*, pp. 3-4.
118. *Complete Works of Swami Vivekananda*, Vol. III, p. 314.
119. *Ibid.*, Vol. III, p. 286.
120. *Swami Vivekananda — Studies in Soviet Union*, Published on 150th Birth Anniversary of Sri Ramkrishna p. 207.
121. Swami Ranganathananda, *Essential Values for Changing Society*, pp. 111-15.
122. *Thus Spake Vivekananda*, p. 24.
123. *Complete Works of Swami Vivekananda*, Vol. VI, p. 269.
124. Quoted by Romain Rolland, *The Life of Vivekananda and the Universal Gospel*, p. 11.
125. Sister Nivedita, *The Master As I Saw Him*, p. 260.
126. *Complete Works of Swami Vivekananda*, Vol. I, p. 442.
127. *Swami Vivekananda — Studies in Soviet Union*, Published on 150th Birth Anniversary of Sri Ramkrishna, p. 209.
128. *Complete Works of Swami Vivekananda*, Vol. VI, pp. 265-66.
129. Sister Nivedita, *The Master As I Saw Him*, p. 261.
130. Romain Rolland, *The Life of Vivekananda*, p. 21.
131. *Complete Works of Swami Vivekananda*, Vol. I, p. 142.
132. V.S. Naravane, *Modern Indian Thought*, p. 103.
133. *Complete Works of Swami Vivekananda*, Vol. IV, p. 480.
134. Letter written by Vivekananda to Diwan Hari Das Dasai, *Complete Works of Swami Vivekananda*, Vol. VIII, p. 200.
135. Romain Rolland, *Life of Vivekananda and the Universal Gospel*, p. 157.
136. *Life of Swami Vivekananda by His Eastern and Western Disciples*, Vol. IV, p. 193.
137. *Swami Vivekananda — Studies in Soviet Union*, Published on 150th Birth Anniversary of Sri Ramkrishna, p. 209.

5

Swami Vivekananda's Nationalism and National Freedom

Swami Vivekananda was far off from the arena of politics. He had little faith in politics. As he said, "I do not believe in any politics. God and Truth are the only politics in the world, everything else is trash."[1] He was a great mystic. He spent most of his time in deep study of Indian culture, spiritual literature and meditation. Yet he caught the imagination of the Indian masses. So immense was his inspiring personality that on his return to India from America he was asked by some young man to enter into the sphere of politics and inspire the people for freedom of the country. But his reply was, "I can get you freedom tomorrow, but will you be able to keep it? Where are the men? First create men and freedom will come automatically."[2]

Swami Vivekananda had a very strong conviction that Acts of Parliament cannot create proper men. It is religion alone that can do so. He thought man-making to be his first and foremost task to reach the goal of freedom of the country. 'First man and then freedom', was his conviction. If man is trained properly freedom will come automatically. As Sister Nivedita has observed, "He neither used the word 'nationality' nor proclaimed an era of 'nation-making' man-making was his primary task. But he was born a lover and the queen of his adoration was his motherland."[3]

Swami Vivekananda did not like to entangle himself in the practical politics of the country because, he thought that politics would not influence the mass as religion, which is the most vital force of our national life. As a true prophet of Hindu nationalism, he realised that the road to Indian nationalism lies through spiritualism. So he wanted to spiritualise the life of the people of India and foster nationalism thereby. Hence he had no connection with politics. As he wrote in September 1894, "I am no politician or a political agitator, I care only for spirit.... So you must warn the Calcutta people that no political significance be ever attached falsely to any of my writings or saying.... I have said a few harsh words in honest criticism of Christian government in general, but that does not mean that I care for or have any connection with politics."[4]

However, having assumed the garb of a Sannyasin, Swami Vivekananda championed the cause of freedom movement of the country. As Jawaharlal Nehru remarked, "He (Swami Vivekananda) kept away from politics and disapproved of his politician, but again and again he laid stress on freedom...and the raising of the masses."[5] Prof. Hiren Mukerjee also observed, "...in his own unique way, Vivekananda could, if any one person did, give a vibrant unequivocal, people oriented colour to subject India's nationalism and will ever be remembered as one of the supreme figures in the annals of our freedom struggle."[6]

(i) Religion as the basis of National Freedom

Swami Vivekananda felt that if religion is understood by every body in its true perspective and its essence properly grasped, much of our miseries, mutual conflicts and social evils would be automatically resolved. He stressed on the necessity of religion specially in an age when the world is moving very fast in the fields of science and technology. He held that religion is the healthiest exercise that human mind can have. As he said, "Of all the forces that have worked and are still working to mould the destinies of all human race, none certainly, is more potent than that, the manifestation of which, we call religion."[7] Religion is a great cementing factor yet unfortunately it has often become the cause of conflicts and dissensions among the people. However to integrate the vivisected Indian society and create a unified and viable nation, Swami Vivekananda sought to take advantage of religion. It has been pointed out, "He strove to interpret the religious tenets and dogmas of Hinduism in such a way as to place religion at the defence of India's national interests to unite the people to fight for independence."[8]

Swami Vivekananda held that religion may be different but the goal of all religions is the same. The paths only differ but they lead to the same destination. The contradictions posed by different faiths are not real but only apparent. These contradictions are like the different shapes of vessels that contain the same honey. To fortify his argument he has referred to verse of Chapter IV of the *Bhagavad Gita* that reads, "...In that way in which they worship Me, I give them fruit accordingly. O' Partha! whichever path is followed, a man ultimately comes and joins into my path."[9]

Swami Vivekananda says that the same truth can be found in every religion and that good and noble souls have been produced by every creed. He further maintained that every religion consists of three parts — its philosophy and details, its mythology and its rituals. The last two vary from one religion to the other. But there is essential identity in regard to the first. It is the ritualistic part of religions that becomes the point of conflict. Hence he laid stress on the need for the unity of all religions in India. Variation in religious belief, he said, is the sign of life, the essential trait of mankind, yet unity of religion is the strength that our nation needed most.

Swami Vivekananda in emphasising on the unity of all religions stressed on the fact that the soul is one although the individuals differ. As he said, "There is but one soul throughout the universe, all is but one existence."[10] The soul or spirit is absolute which is manifested in everything in the universe and every being specially man. The same soul exists in men, to whichever creed or faith they may belong.

Bertrand Russell has written, "Diversities of manners and customs and traditions are on the whole a good thing, since they enable different nations to produce different types of excellence."[11] In the same way Swami Vivekananda emphasised on the diversities of faith, beliefs, customs, practices and rituals of different individuals, professing different faith or religion. Such variety makes the society richer. Variety he felt to be the spice of life. Such variety need not be eliminated from the society. Sometimes some fanatics have attempted to eliminate this variety. But the result has always been disastrous. As it is said, "Rousseau preached the doctrine of political equality which Robespierre took literally and result was the Reign of Terror which ultimately led to the emergence of Napoleon, who swallowed the republic and declared himself emperor. Marx's doctrine of classless society, somewhat loosely phrased, was taken seriously by Lenin, who while trying to put it into practice, made the breath-taking statement that he had no objection to extermination of the three-fourths of the world's population provided the remaining one-fourth were converted to marxism."[12] So variety is to be retained and unity has to be sought amidst them. Unity is to be so achieved that variety would not be affected thereby.

Hence, Swami Vivekananda while seeking national unity also sought unity in the midst of variety. This principle touched the Indian minds most and without losing their racial, religious or cultural identity they rallied round him like a swarm of bees. As a result deep sense of fellow feelings, co-operation among the people of various sects and creeds, caste and race developed. This recognition of variety, as laid down by Swami Vivekananda, became a source of attraction for all and national unity became inevitable.

Swami Vivekananda explained his mind regarding the usefulness of imageworship. Other reforming institutions like Brahmo Samaj, Arya Samaj, etc., vehemently opposed the cult of image-worship. But Swami Vivekananda upheld it boldly and said that it is a means to an end although not an end in itself. Although he considered that worship of image cannot lead a man directly to Mukti, he did not disregard its utility. He considered it necessary for a common man to prepare his mind for the realization of God. He realized its utility at the initial stage of spiritual progress. As he said, "...it is a lowest stage; struggling to rise high, mental prayer is the next stage...."[13]

Image worship according to Swami Vivekananda is as necessary for realization of God as infancy and childhood are essential for the maturity and wisdom of an old age. Idolatry can be wrong only if childhood and youth is a sin.[14]

Swami Vivekananda was of course conscious of the fact that the mystery-mongering cult, the so-called Yogism or magic had crept into the soil of India for long. Besides idolatry had also penetrated into the mind of the Hindus. Reformers and reforming organisations had sprang up in the country to rid Hinduism of such nuisances, yet he openly came out to justify idol-worship if not idolatry.

Swami Vivekananda studied the religious background of India and found that Hindu-Muslim unity is most essential for the sake of national freedom movement. Hence, he fervently strove to bridge the gulf between the followers of the two major religions of the country, Hinduism and Islam. He tried to achieve this end by preaching the great Vedic concept of Advaitism or non-duality of soul or unity of universal existence. In 1898 he wrote to Mohammed Sarfaraj Hussain, "Advaitism is the religion of the future enlightened humanity. The Hindu may get the credit for arriving at it, earlier than other races.... Yet practical Advaitism, which looks upon and behaves to all mankind as one's own soul was never developed among the Hindus universally...my experience is that if any religion approaches to this equality, it is Islam alone."[15] Thus by highlighting the genuine merit of Islamic faith, he wanted to draw the attention of the people of either sect and sought to eliminate the deep-seated distrust between the Hindus and the Muslims in India.

Swami Vivekananda further said in the same letter, "We want to lead mankind to the place where there is neither the Vedas nor the Bible nor the Koran, yet this has been done by harmonizing the Vedas, the Bible and the Koran. Mankind aught to be taugh that religions are but the varied expressions of the religion, which is Oneness, so that each may choose the path that suits him best."[16]

The whole aim of Swami Vivekananda was to make our motherland a junction of the two great systems — Hinduism and Islam — Vedantic brain and Islamic body.[17] He hoped that in future-India there would be no conflict and bloodshed of the two faiths if they are so reconciled.

Swami Vivekananda's plan of Hindu-Muslim unity closely approximated to that of Mahatma Gandhi — the Father of

Indian Nation, who believed, "Without Hindu-Muslim unity there would be no progress for India."[18] For national unity and independence he also sought to eliminate mutual distrust and doubts between the Hindus and the Muslims. As he said, "If the Hindus and the Muslims rid themselves of mutual distrust and fear there is no power that can stop their freedom. We are the makers of our own slavery."[19] Therefore, he appealed to all Indians to accept Hindu-Muslim unity as a "creed for all times and under all circumstances."[20]

Swami Vivekananda's emphasis on religion for national reconstruction left tangible impact on the thought process of many freedom fighters. Although he was a Hindu monk, preaching certain form of Vedanta, it is so catholic that men of all faiths including atheists and agnostics, drew inspiration from his writings. His religion did not recognize any heaven beyond the earth, and lost the sight of temporal forces — racial or ethnic and joined the main-stream of spiritualism, that was purely Indian in character. This amply contributed to the growth of Indian spiritual nationalism. Hence, it has been rightly pointed out, "Vivekananda's nationalism is so catholic that it is acceptable to men, professing different faiths, inhabiting different regions and speaking different languages and yet it is distinctively Indian, it is as thoroughly Indian as the Ganga and Narmada."[21] This Indianism of Swami Vivekananda became very prominent in the blood of the people and this Indianism sought to bring about a sort of cohesion among the people of different faiths, that paved the path for national emancipation in the long run.

(ii) Culture as the basis of National Freedom

Swami Vivekananda explained that the word 'Hindu' is not a religious term. It really means the people who live on this side of the rive 'Sindhu'. The Persian pronounced 'S' as 'H' and the Greeks 'H' as 'I'. So Hindu means the people, living on this side of the 'Indus', whatever may be their faith or creed or religious conviction. Hence, India embraces in her infinite arms all the people of various faiths and cults with all greatness and glories in all ages of her history. But when India came under the British yoke the people forgot their own glory and were dazzled by the splendour of the West. As it is said, "Not to speak the dumb millions who were awestruck by the all conquering prowess of the white races or of the English educated Indians, who were lured by Western culture, even men, versed in English learning like Raja Ram Mohan Roy, and Iswar Chandra Vidyasagar, spoke of the barrenness of Sanskrit grammar and Naya, Vedanta and Sankhya philosophies. There was a reaction against this tide of westernization, but no one held aloft the torch of Indian culture with greater vigour than Swami Vivekananda, who carried the war into the enemy's camp."[22]

Swami Vivekananda refuted the allegation that Indians are too much absorbed in their past by pointing out how they are too forgetful of their rich tradition. He also showed that though Indians have much to learn from the West, they have more to give to the Westerners. The successive waves of immigration into India have always been a turning point in the history of the nations that made incursions into this land from abroad. He said, "This is the one great truth, India has to teach to the world, because it is nowhere else. This is spirituality, the science of soul."[23] The Western nations are no doubt more wealthy than India, yet that do not mean that they are superior to her in the matter of intellect or spiritual refinement. Ignorance and poverty are no doubt curses that are to be eradicated, yet hoarding of material wealth is often accompanied by intellectual arrogance and spiritual degradation.

Swami Vivekananda reinforced his aforesaid conclusions by delving deep into the remote past and attempting a comparison between the West and East, and particularly Indian and the West. He said, "The whole of Asian civilization was first evolved on the plains near large rivers and on fertile soils, on the banks of Ganga, the Yangtseking and the Euphrates. The original foundation of all these civilization is agriculture and in all of them the *Daivi* nature (God-like) predominates. Most of the European civilization on the other hand originated either in the hilly countries or on the sea coast. Piracy and robbery formed the basis of this civilization; there the Asuri (Demoniac) nature is preponderant."[24] Indeed when Europeans developed a rich culture, in Greece, the Helenic heritage would have lost but for the Arabs, who preserved it. Swami Vivekananda goes further and says that it was as a result of the crusade that Europe began to be civilized by coming in contact with Asian culture, specially Indian. In this way the Knight Templars learnt Advaita Vedanta and the Moors, a Mohammedan tribe, established a civilized kingdom in Spain. Even amongst the Asiatics, Indians could claim distinction for their peaceful, tolerant attitude to life. Johavah, Hebrew God was an ugly deity, whom man had to propitiate in order to escape punishment. But the Aryans worshipped a God who was 'not only a supreme Being but...the Father in heaven. This is the beginning of love.'[25] This Aryan concept reached Palestine, where Jesus, who was rejected by the Jews, preached the doctrine of love saying that he and his father in the heaven are one.

Swami Vivekananda's writings and speeches, emphasizing on the inborn superiority of Hindus, filled the Indian mind with pride and a sense of greatness of their old culture. The inferiority complex of the Hindus were removed. They were no longer ready to admit the vain superiority of the West. It steeled their determination to rise against the British and assert their independence. As Jawaharlal Nehru has pointed out, "He (Vivekananda) came as a tonic to the depressed and demoralized Hindus and give it self-reliance and some roots in the past."[26] Bipin Chandra Pal has also written, "Influence of Swami Vivekananda was quite tremendous. It quickened our self-consciousness far more."[27]

By establishing superiority of Indian culture over the West Swami Vivekananda tried to check the spread of Western influence in India. Blind imitation of Western way of living led to the spread of Western civilization very fast in India. Swami Vivekananda realized that without counteracting the Western inflence and reviving the ancient Indian culture, reconstruction of India is not possible. So he voiced his concern against this blind imitation and appealed to the people of India that imitation is not civilization, it is weakness; it is an act of cowardice — a positive curse to nation-hood. As he repeatedly said, "...imitation, cowardly imitation never makes for progress."[28] He held that man, seeking freedom and progress, never imitates, but revives what is his own, that has made the Chinese, the

Japanese very great. As he said, "...Japan and China even live to the present days, and there are signs even of revival among them. Their lives are like that of the phoenix, a thousand times destroyed but ready to spring up again more glorious."[29]

So as the worthy heir of India, said Swami Vivekananda, we must revive our own glorious culture of the past and build a new India upon it. Imitation can never make us great. A Raja's dress (King's dress) cannot make us Raja nor can an ass become a lion in lion's dress.[30] In his article 'Modern India' contributed to 'Udbodhana', March 1899, he wrote, "O' India! With this mere echoing of others, with this base imitation of others, with this dependence on others, this slavish weakness..., wouldst thou...scale the highest pinnacle of civilized greatness. Wouldst thou attain by means of thy disgraceful cowardice that freedom deserved only by the brave and heroic."[31]

To make the people ashamed of their mean habit of imitating the West, which is contrary to their national character, Swami Vivekananda reminded them of their noble tradition of doing the most distinguished work of diffusing spiritual knowledge world over. He held that India was the only fountain-head of spiritualism and source of such knowledge. His countrymen should not forget such century-long tradition and their contribution to the world progress. As he said, "Great works are to be done, wonderful powers have to be worked out, we have to teach other nations many things."[32]

Thus Swami Vivekananda's appeal, warnings and admonitions against the base imitation of the West made people of India feel ashamed of such mean habit, and they began to think in the direction of their own national heritage and the national or the freedom movement got a concrete shape out of it.

(iii) Spirit of Freedom

Swami Vivekananda's heroic soul always craved for freedom. Freedom was the key-note of his spiritual philosophy. Though he stood for spiritual freedom, interpreting freedom like J.S. Mill "he rose to the conception of liberty as free play for the spiritual originality with all its results in individual vigour and manifold diversity which alone can constitute a rich balanced and developed society."[33] Though he primarily propagated spiritual freedom, the gospel resulted in the galvanization of the passion for struggle for freedom of the nation in the long run.

Swami Vivekananda declared that freedom is the goal of all — from individual to universe. Everything and every being of the universe aspires for freedom. Therefore, struggle for freedom is a universal phenomenon. As he said, "Freedom is the goal of the nature, sentient or insentient and consciously or unconsciously everything is struggling towards that goal."[34] All men and the entire nature is struggling to attain freedom. Even the whole planetary bodies are making movement and the wind is blowing to achieve the same goal *i.e.,* freedom. As he said, "All human life, all nature, therefore, is struggling to attain freedom.... To that goal the planet is moving and the air is blowing. Every thing is struggling towards that."[35]

According to Swami Vivekananda the whole universe is but the manifestation of freedom. It is the result of the struggle for freedom.[36] Freedom is life as without freedom there would be death. As he said, "There cannot be life even in the plant without the idea of freedom."[37] So the nature of life is to make a search for freedom. This search is the religion or dharma of life. As he said, "Wherever there is life there is search for freedom. That freedom is same as God."[38] Freedom is the sign of life. Without freedom there would be no life on earth. So he said, "The idea of freedom you cannot relinquish. Your action, your life will be lost without it."[39]

To Swami Vivekananda freedom is the way to perfection. The whole world in order to attain perfection needs freedom. A man who is free has enormous power to perfect the world, but a man, in bondage of any sort is not expected to make the world perfect. As he said, "If we are not free how can we make the world good and perfect?"[40] Hence according to Swami Vivekananda freedom that perfects the individual also perfects the universe and individual freedom is the basis of universal freedom.

Swami Vivekananda felt that freedom is the watch-word of Hindu philosophy. The entire Hindu philosophy is based on freedom. All faiths and sects of India propagate the same principle of freedom — freedom in all respects. He said, "The word freedom which is the watch-word of our religion really means freedom physically, mentally and spiritually."[41] The great Upanishads — the source of Hindu philosophy and religions — stands for freedom. As he said, "Freedom, physical freedom, mental freedom, and spiritual freedom are the watch-words of Upanishads."[42]

To Swami Vivekananda, love for freedom is the trait with each man. It is his inborn quality. It is his divine possession. A sort of divine force is always in operation within man to inspire him to be free. As he said, "Within ourselves this eternal voice is speaking for eternal freedom."[43] But as we have been illusioned or hypnotised we fail to hear such voice within us and never feel our own nature. It exists only in our memory. As he said, "Freedom in man now a memory...."[44] We have been altogether indifferent to it. But the first and foremost duty of each Indian is to free himself from illusion or dehypnotise himself to realise his own nature. As he said, "Every body is hypnotised already. The work of attaining freedom of realising one's own nature, consists in dehypnotisation."[45] This illusion or hypnotisation is the root of all bondages that cause all misery. As long as we do not try to break off these fetters there is no light for us. We are to sink in misery. As he said, "Dependence is misery. Independence is happiness."[46]

Swami Vivekananda declared that liberty is the first condition of growth and it is the condition in which the individual attains his best self — his all-round development. As he said, "Liberty is the first condition of growth."[47] He advocated all-round freedom — freedom in every sphere of life and championed the cause of perfect freedom. As he said, "Just as man must have liberty to think and speak so he must have liberty in food, dress, and marriage and in every other things...."[48]

Swami Vivekananda believed that freedom is beneficial both to the individual and the society. It is liberty that makes the individual and society progressive. Like J.S. Mill, he believed that "Intellectual and political freedom are in general beneficial both to society that permits them and to the individual that enjoys them...it produces and gives scope for a high type of moral character."[49]

But Swami Vivekananda felt agrieved to find that freedom which is the natural possession of men was beyond the reach of the people of India. Indians had been subject to slavery. Misery and hardship had beset the people, causing vital injury to their national life. He wanted to awaken the Indian masses so that they enjoy their legitimate right. As he said, "We have been slaves forever *i.e.,* we have never been given to the masses of India to express their inner light which is their inheritance."[50]

Swami Vivekananda urged the people of India to rise in revolt since freedom is our birth right, the very goal of a human being. He held that it is our legitimate right or congenital claim to revolt against all bondages. As he said, "We are born rebel against this, we rebel and cry out.... The first inkling of life on its higher level is in seeing this struggle within us to break the bond of nature and to be free. 'Freedom O' Freedom! Freedom O' Freedom!' is the very song of the soul."[51] He further said, "The fundamental principle is that there is eternal freedom for every one. Every one must come to it. We have to struggle, impelled by our desire to be free."[52]

Explaining the method for the attainment of freedom by Indians Swami Vivekananda emphasised on "Karma-Yoga that lays down selflessness and sacrifice as the only way for achieving freedom. As he said, "Karma-Yoga...intend to attain freedom through unselfishness and by good works."[53] This explanation inflamed the zeal of the people of India to sacrifice their life for freedom of the country.

Like Rousseau who said, "Man is born free but every where he is in chains,"[54] Swami Vivekananda declared, "Stand up and say I am the Master, the master of all, we forge the chain, we alone can break it."[55] He also declared, "Be free and know once for all there is no chain for you."[56] Like Rousseau who set the whole French society ablaze with his fiery speeches and statements, Swami Vivekananda inflamed the mind of the people of India by fiery speeches for revolution against all injustices — social, political and economic.

Swami Vivekananda felt that freedom is our destination and we are born to reach that destination. In reaching this destination of life, we must lay down all our pleasures and comforts. Struggle for freedom is the most pious duty of man and each man must realise this duty. As he said, "What are we here for? We are here for freedom, for knowledge. We want to know in order to make ourselves free. That is our life: one universal cry for freedom.... the plant grows from the seed overturning the ground and raising itself up to the skies? What is the offering for the earth from the sun? What is your life? The same struggle for freedom.... The struggle with nature is going on. Many things will be crushed and broken in this struggle for freedom."[57]

Swami Vivekananda further felt that we should devote all our time and energy whole-heartedly in our struggle for freedom. Failure in the struggle should not deter us from the struggle. We should dedicate our all — body and mind for achieving freedom. As he said, "How some people give all their energies, time, brain, body and every thing to become rich! They have no time for breakfast! Early in the morning they are out and at work! They die in attempt — ninety per cent of them — and the rest when they make money cannot enjoy it.... One can have the same amount of energy and struggle for freedom as one has for money. We know we have to give up money and all things when we die and yet see the amount of energy we can put forth for them. But...should we not put forth a thousand fold more strength and energy to acquire that which never fades, but which (freedom) remains to us forever?"[58]

Swami Vivekananda not only advocated individual freedom; he also warned his countrymen against all evil forces that invariably endeavour to snatch away freedom from them and enslave them. Man should remain alert all along. They must pay the price of eternal vigilance for the procurement and protection of their freedom. As he said, "Be aware of everything that takes away your freedom. Know that it is dangerous and avoid it by all the means in your power."[59]

Swami Vivekananda further said that strong moral character is a permanent guarantee against loss of true freedom. All weakness in our character like passions and desires are positive danger to freedom. Such weakness in character will endanger freedom and turn men into a miserable slave. So he said, "One may gain political freedom and social independence but if one is a slave to his passions and desires one cannot feel the pure joy of real freedom."[60]

Swami Vivekananda not only emphasised on the freedom of man; he also emphasised on the equality of all men irrespective of caste, creed and religion. He held the view that freedom of man is impossible without equality of all men. As he said, "Above all, follow this great doctrine of sameness in all things, through all being, seing the same God in all. This is the way to freedom; inequality, the way to bondage. No man, no nation can attempt to gain physical freedom without physical equality.... Ignorance, inequality and desire are the three causes of human misery."[61]

Swami Vivekananda's concept of equality is based upon the idea of basic sameness of the spirit and abolition of all differences on the ground of caste, colour, creed etc., that are sure enemies to human progress and "stiffles our soul, regiments our thoughts and trims our creative adventures into narrow groups of slavish minds."[62]

Swami Vivekananda's concept of equality is very practical. It envisages a society of equals, where there is freedom of thought and action. As he said, "We preach neither social equality nor inequality but that every being has the same right and insist upon freedom of thought and action in every way."[63]

Swami Vivekananda's interpretation of freedom of thought and equality widened the political outlook of the Indians. Every Indian thought in terms of freedom and sameness of all beings irrespective of their external diversity, that led to the promotion of national unity and emancipation. It gained popularity among the masses enormously and culminated in the outbreak of the revolution against the British rule. As A.D. Litman pointed out, "His social political and specially enlightening ideas objectively helped in the awakening of the wide masses of India, and prepared them for the subsequent growth of national liberation movement, which, as a result of the heroic efforts of the Indian people, culminated in the heroic victory in the creation of the independent Republic of India."[64]

(iv) Galvanised the National Spirit

Swami Vivekananda wanted to demoralise the British people so that the freedom movement gains strength in India. In attempting to demoralise the British he showed how the British had been the Blood-suckers of the people of India and how they had exploited other nations to make itself prosperous. He said, "We see England the most prosperous Christian nation in the world with her foot on the neck of 250,000,000 Asiatics. We look back into history and see that the prosperity of Christian Europe began with Spain. Spain's prosperity began with the invasion of Mexico. Christianity wins its prosperity by cutting the throats of its fellowmen. At such a price the Hindu will not have prosperity."[65] To fortify his argument, Swami Vivekananda referred to the history of India and said that the British adopted the most barbaric policy towards the Indians for which history will never excuse. Comparing the Mohammedans with the British he said, "The Mohammedans came upon them, slaughtering and killing : slaughtering and killing.... India has been conquered again and again for years and last and worst of all came the English men. You look about India what has the Hindu left? Wonderful temples, every where. What has the Mohammedans left? Beautiful palaces. What has the English men left? Nothing but mounds of broken brandy bottles!"[66]

The British all along pursued the policy of profiteering in complete disregard of the interest of India. As it is said, "Its whole aim was to flush out all Indian resources to enrich their own country."[67] Mohammedan invaders on the other hand were very considerate in this respect. They conquered India and plundered it. They also held a very tyrannical policy, destroying Hindu temples and shrines. But when they settled down in India they brought back all their booty to enrich the country they had ravaged and established a stable government in India. They thought India to be their motherland. But the British were worse than the Muslim invaders. By establishing a firm administration in India they only wanted to make it easier and seemingly more legal for them to take away India's wealth to England.

Swami Vivekananda said that in the name of civilizing our country they exploited our country making us poorer day by day. There were perpetual famine and starvation in India. But the British had always been callous to it. Had they been sympathetic a little, millions of Indians would not have died like flies and insects. He criticised the British that they pretend love but in their heart there is terrible blood-thirst. As he said, "The love of man is on their lips, in their heart there is nothing but evil and every violence. 'I love you my brothers, I love you' and all the while they cut his throat. Their hands are red with blood...but the judgment of God will fall upon them...."[68]

Thus Swami Vivekananda wanted to demoralise the British and popularise the nationalist movement among the people. He wanted to boost an upheaval that was to sweep over the country and create a new India out of it. People who suffered from injustice and oppression for centuries would breathe in peace and live happily. As he said, "Let new India arise out of the peasant's cottage grasping the plough; out of the hearts of the fisherman, the cobbler and the sweeper. Let her spring from grocer's shop, from beside the oven of the fritter-seller. Let her emanate from the factory, from the marts and from the markets. Let her emerge from the groves and forests from the hills and mountains."[69] He wanted to spread the fire of revolution to every nook and corner of the country and make it a concern of the masses. As he said, "Have fire and spread all over, work, work...we shall succeed, may be slowly, but surely. Work as if on each of you depend the whole work. Fifty centuries are looking on you. The future of India depends on you. Work on."[70]

Swami Vivekananda insisted that life is nothing but struggle. Struggle is the *sine qua non* of life. Inertia and indulgence are the sources of all misery that darkens our life. So if death occurs in course of such struggle, we should not step back as it will bring glory to us. As he said, "...Stand up and fight! Not one step back.... Fight it out, whatever comes. Let the stars move from the sphere! Let the whole world stand against us! Death means only a change of garment. What of it? Thus fight. You gain nothing by becoming cowards...taking a step backward you do not avoid any misfortune."[71]

Swami Vivekananda glorified struggle as religion of life. Man should not abstain from such struggle even if the whole world stands against him. As he appealed, "If the whole world stands against you sword in hand, would you still dare to do what you think is right? If your wife and children are against you, if all your money goes, your name dies, your wealth vanishes would you still stick to it? Would you still pursue it and go steadily towards your own goal?"[72] He exhorted repeatedly that struggle to break off the fetters of miseries, to reach the goal of freedom is the very call of our Vedas, as the Vedas declare "Awake, arise and stop not till the goal is achieved."

To Swami Vivekananda nothing is impossible in the world since soul-power is infinite. Man has tremendous power to move the world. Man is the source of all power and strength. To think any thing to be impossible is a sin. Man thinks impossibility because of his weakness. This weakness comes from fear that brings failure. As he said, "Never say, 'No'. Never say I cannot, for you are infinite. Even time and space are as nothing, compared with your nature. You can do any thing and everything, you are almighty."[73] He further said, "Come up O' lion and shake off the delusions that you are a sheep. You are souls immortal, spirits free, best and eternal."[74]

Citing the example of Nachiketa — an embodiment of sacrifice from the epics, Swami Vivekananda said that we must have sradha in us for sacrifice. Like him we all should think, "I am superior to many, I am inferior to few, but nowhere I am the least. I can also do something."[75] This lack of sradha has brought about our downfall. We have become weak. Ever since India forgot the cult of her sacrifice, she has been subject to untold misery under the foreign rule. Therefore, he appealed to the people, "...forget not that thy marriage, thy wealth, thy life are not for sense pleasure, are not for thy individual, personal happiness; forget not that thou art born as a sacrifice to the Mother's altar...."[76]

Swami Vivekananda's writings and speeches were very heart-touching. It not only roused fire and fury in the mind of the people; it also enkindled love for the motherland. In course of a lecture at Lahore he said, "And slaves become the great masters! So give up being slaves. For the next fifty years this alone shall be our key-note — this our great Mother India. Let all other vain Gods disappear for the time from our minds. This is the only God that is awake, our own race — every where his hands, every where his feet, every where his ears, he covers everything. All our gods are sleeping. What vain gods shall we go after and yet cannot worship the God that we see all-around us, the Virat? When we have worshipped this we shall be able to worship all other gods."[77] What mother wants is strength and fearlessness from her children, who will be able to fight for her, if they realise that they are the 'one spirit that animates the universe'.

Swami Vivekananda's words were like magic sparks that impressed the people forthwith. He convinced the people that there is intellect in India and there is money, but there is no enthusiasm for strength and fearlessness. So he wanted to arouse the sense of strength and fearlessness among the people of India to resist the evils of British rule. He was convinced that fear and weakness were at the root of the sufferings of Indians. Unless they know how to resist the evils that deprived them of their happiness they cannot enjoy any pleasures of life. Hence he said, "Arise, awake and stop not till the desired end is reached. Young men...arise, awake for the time is propitious. Already everything is opening out before us. Be bold and fear not.... We have to become...fearless and our task will be done."[78] He further said, "This is the great fact! Strength is life, weakness is death. Strength is felicity, life eternal, immortal, weakness is constant strain and misery, weakness is death."[79]

Swami Vivekananda's speeches and writings inflamed the courage and confidence of the people. They agitated their mind against the British imperialism. Young men full of self-confidence, were determined to give up all their fears and doubts and face all eventualities against their opponents. As it is rightly observed, "To people, muzzled by military defeat and enervated by ceaseless propaganda about the inborn superiority of the white races, Vivekananda's message of courage and hope, sustained by logic and scholarship was like milk and honey; and old nation seemed to be born anew."[80]

Swami Vivekananda had no qualms — philosophical or practical — about the use of violence. He was opposed to the policy of non-violence, because once you adopt such a policy you give a long rope to the wicked to revel in harassing others. He knew that a man has to kill millions of microbes if he has to breathe and several worms if he has to walk and also millions of insects if he has to read the Gita by candle light. He once exhorted, "First of all our young man must be strong. Religion will come afterwards. Be strong, my young friends, that is my advice to you. You will be nearer to heaven through football than through the study of the Gita.... You will understand the Gita better with your biceps, your muscles, a little stronger. You will understand the mighty genius and mighty strength of Krishna better with a little strong blood in you. You will understand the Upanishads better and the glory of Atma when your body stands firm upon your feet and you feel yourself as a man. Thus we have to apply these to our needs."[81]

Swami Vivekananda was a great adorer of strength and tenacity rather than weakness. He paid high tribute to Rani of Jhansi, who courted death instead of surrendering to her enemy. She fought for the cause of her own freedom and the freedom of her people. To Swami Vivekananda such sacrifice of life for a noble cause is worth-emulating. As he said, "Death is better than a vegetating ignorant life; it is better to die on the battlefield than to live a life of death."[82]

Swami Vivekananda's exhortations were direct and forthright. He wanted to revive kshatriya spirit among the people of India. He extolled Ravana as more and not less civilized than Rama because the demon king was more spirited than his righteous victor. In advocating the cult of violence he said, "It is constant struggle against nature that constitutes human progress, not conformity with it."[83]

He further declared "Good and evil are not separate existence. They are inextricably intertwined."[84] Such teachings were heartening to the Indian youths, who became determined to challenge the imperialistic laws and pave the way for national freedom. They drew inspiration from Swami Vivekananda's message : "We must die that is certain, let us die for a good cause.... The true man is he who is as strong as strength itself and possesses a woman's heart."[85]

Swami Vivekananda was a source of inspiration for the Indian minds. He tangibly changed the course of life of the people. The pre-independent Indian polity took a new turn, that became marked by exhibition of strength and fearlessness. As it has been observed, "A lion among men, he roared and thundered forth rousing the leviathan of the sleeping nation from century-old slumber and mental stupor, to rise on its feet and march on freely. He wanted in us the sleeping divinity to awaken that austere elevation of spirit, which rouses heroism.... It was due to his message of courage and fearlessness that he was described as tamer of soul."[86]

As a matter of fact very few nationalist leader exercised as much influence on the youth of 20th century as did this Hindu monk — Swami Vivekananda. At a time when nation was seized with apathy, inertia and despair Swami Vivekananda preached the gospel of strength and fearlessness. Strength was the political testament of Swami Vivekananda to the Indian nation. With his speeches and writings a new India seemed to be born. Of course as a mystic he stood for the practice of 'Karma Yoga', but this gospel underwent the process of political metamorphosis and the people of India accepted selfless social and political service for the motherland as an example of Karma Yoga.[87]

Swami Vivekananda's march from Colombo to Almora was a triumphal progress in 1897. The whole of India was thrilled to a mystical height by his speeches and writings. It prepared the ground for national emancipation through a religious ferment. It was about this time in 1899 a new Viceroy came to India, who felt the impact of the monk's personality and tried to counter his influence. This viceroy and governor general was Lord Curzon — a true successor to Wellesly and Dalhousie in ability and discretion. He came to India with an imperious will to give effect to his imperial visions. But within a few months of his arrival, he found something disheartening and disconcerting and thus wrote, "...there is no doubt that a sort of quasi metaphysical ferment is going on in India; strongly conservative and even reactionary in general tendency.... What is to come out of this superstitions, transcendentalism, mental exaltation and intellectual obscurity — with European ideas thrown as an outside ingredient into the crucible — who can say."[88] It is evident from the above statement that Swami Vivekananda's influence was gaining ground enormously and the British authority was alarmed by it.

Subsequently, Ramkrishna Mission came to be regarded as the refuge of revolutionaries by the British Indian government. A research brochure in Bengali by Ladi Mohan Roy Chaudhury on the 'Ramkrishna Mission in the Eyes of the Police 1897 — 1917' (Calcutta, 1983) brings out how the Mission was very much in the bad books of the administration. The then police commissioner Mr. Charles Tegart, in his confidential report said, "Not to speak of Vivekananda's followers, Vivekananda's own writings are pregnant with seditions."[89]

Rawlatt Committee Report (1918) also affirmed that Swami Vivekananda had an important influence on those who created a big pro-freedom tumult in the first decade of this century.[90] This shows that Swami Vivekananda's contribution for national freedom was quite remarkable and the British attitude towards him was also suspicious. It was perhaps with a view to escaping from the eyes of the British that Swami Vivekananda laid down, "One belonging to the Order can have no connection with politics."[91]

Swami Vivekananda some times apprehended that the British government would shot him. But as he was quite aware of his influence on his people, he believed that such action on the part of the imperial power will unleash a spate of violence in the country. As he said, "It would be the first nail to their coffin and my death would run through the land like fire."[92]

(v) Impetus to Extremist Movement

The Indian National Congress was eight years old, when in 1893 Swami Vivekananda went out on his historic mission. Eight years after, when the congress met in Calcutta in 1901 he was a dying but also a world famous man to whom the leading delegates went to pay their veneration at Belur Math. He was glad that the Congress had tried to take all Indians within its fold, but he did not like the westernised way of the leaders and their sole gift of 'Shouting' at public meetings and had no patience for their "politics of mendicancy, their begging the foreign government for crumbs of favour."[93]

Among the Congress men there was one exception and that was Bal Gangadhar Tilak, whose patriotism was marked by 'sacrifice, scholastic fervour and militancy.'[94] Tilak a great scholar, was also a fearless patriot, who wanted to meet the challenge of British imperialism with passive resistance and boycott of British goods. This programme came to the forefront in 1905-7, some years after the death of Swami Vivekananda. It would be useless to speculate what Swamiji would have said about this programme, if he had been living during the Swadeshi agitation, but we know that Tilak had been much impressed by Swami Vivekananda's gospel of strength and fearlessness and his cult of violence, as he had given publicity to Swami Vivekananda's works abroad and wrote eloquently about him after his death in 1902. He wrote, "Vivekananda's contribution to the awakening of India raised him to the status of Sankaracharya."[95]

Tilak stood for three principles at this time — national education, Swadeshi and Boycott. It was on these principles that Tilak split the Congress at Surat and went into wilderness with his followers, known as extremists. The principal figures among the extremists were Aurobindo Ghose, Bipin Chandra Pal and Lala Lajpat Rai.

Tilak left the scene of Indian politics in 1908 when he was sentenced to transportation for six years on a charge of sedition. Of his chief lieutenants, Aurobindo Ghose quietly left the British Indian territory in 1910 and settled at Pondicherry to devote himself to spiritualism. Bipin Chandra Pal went on an European tour and was very soon out of agitational politics. Lala Lajpat Rai also went out on a foreign mission and when he came back he shuttled between the extremists and moderates, so much so that he was seriously considered for the presidentship of the Congress in 1914, when the extremists had no place in it.

Tilak's biographer — Ram Gopal writes, "Thus ended the extremist party, so sedulously built up by Tilak."[96] M.N. Roy also writes, "Tilak who was sentenced to six years hard labour in 1908 broke down the extremist party."[97] This however is far from true. The extremist party was not built up by Tilak, who was at one time a foremost leader; neither did it end with Tilak's incarceration in 1908. It is a matter of history that the extremists were out of the Congress till 1916, but they had to be received back in 1917 when their representative Mrs Annie Besant was elected president in preference to Raja of Mahmudabad, the nominee of moderates. Annie Besant, the theosophist came nearer than Aurobindo to the secret of Swami Vivekananda's influence. In her presidential address at Calcutta Congress 1917, she analysed the forces that led to the national awakening and gave pride of place to Swami Vivekananda's influence. She often referred to Swami Vivekananda's speeches and writings.

B.C. Pal also endorsed the influence of Swami Vivekananda in his book — Spirit of Indian Nationalism. He wrote, "Under the influence of Neo-Vedantism, associated to a large extent with the name of Late Swami Vivekananda, there has been at work a slow and silent process of liberalisation of old social ideas."[98] Extremism as Aurobindo preferred to call it, stands for that motto and methods of that school of politics, which aimed at complete independence of India, to be attained by non-violent means if possible and by violent means if necessary. Actually this movement for wresting freedom obviously by violence had started much earlier and Basudeo Phadke, who might have inspired Bankim Chandra, was its first Martyr. Great publicity was achieved by the Chapekar brothers who killed the two oppressive officials — Rand and Ayerst in 1897 at Pune. These gallant deeds were not the achievements of isolated individuals in Maharashtra and elsewhere. As far as it is known, the extremist party was formed in Bengal in the early years of 20th century and it owed its inspiration primarily to the writings and speeches of Swami Vivekananda. As Rabindra Nath Tagore has observed, "Swamiji's speeches inspired the daring deeds of youths of Bengal and awakened in them the spirit of dedication and service to the nation."[99]

Swami Vivekananda wanted Indians to awake from hypnotism of fear and cowardice and acquire strength — physical, mental and moral. It is only with strong biceps that man can have self-confidence, the root of all success. He also advocated violent technique to achieve the goal if circumstances so demanded.

Swami Vivekananda died in 1902 and within a few years after his death, concerted efforts were made to wrest freedom by violence. Hence it is very much natural to believe that the extremists derived their inspiration from his speeches and writings. Though he was not a participant in the revolutionary movement, it is seen that his influence continued to extend from Bengal to other parts of India even beyond the shores of India. Prof. Hiren Mukerjee has befittingly observed, "His (Vivekananda's) words of fire had reached everywhere in India and the revolutionaries owed much to him as they moved into action that in the late nineties of the last century put fear in the alien rulers. Even more direct was his impact on Bengal revolutionaries...of Chittagong Armoury Raid (1930). They all have avowed their debt to the cyclonic monk."[100]

All the patriots irrespective of their political affiliation, had to dodge the law; they had to procure arms by surreptitious means from abroad or make explosives in secret hideouts at home. Even when Bagha Jatin (Jatin Mukherjee) met the British military police in an open encounter, he and his men had to fight with stolen military Pistols. Other rebels put on disguises, and assumed false names in order to elude official agents and collected money through secret donations or open robberies. Of the leading politicians of India, Tilak alone recognised their selfless patriotism, but he did so in an indirect way by resuscitating Sivaji-Afzalkhan affair or by referring to Krishna's teaching that no blame attaches to any person, who is not activated by any selfish motive or does not derive any personal profit from his actions. He went a little further when he said that Khudiram and Prafulla Chaki were inspired by a desire to mend the administration by a murderous assault when they found that the British would not do it themselves. He would not defend the use of bombs but said that the rulers by their persistence in their ruthless ways had invited such reprisals.

Now a question crops up wherefrom did the young men who had jumped into the struggle, get the inspiration that quickened their spirit and gave strength to their arms? Whatever their personal affiliations or learning, as soldiers of freedom, they recognised only one God — Mother India and they believed in one cult — the cult of shakti worship. They saw not the mother that had suckled them but the mother that would send them to fight the common enemy. They would read and re-read the new message, "Buddha ruined us and so did Christ ruin Greece and Rome,"[101] obviously with their lessons in Ahimsa (non-violence) *i.e.* "Have no enemy, bless them that curse you, whosoever shall smite thee on thy right cheek, turn to him the other also; stop all your work and be ready for next world...."[102] They synthesised the Indian needs for 'the worship of Shakti, not in mere thoughts, not in imagination but in actual visible form....'[103]

It was Swami Vivekananda, who introduced the cult of Shakti worship and violence, which was inherited by a galaxy of brilliant men, the first two being Aurobindo Ghose and Barindra Ghose, who might be called the joint authors of Bhavani Mandir. They were firm believers in the dictum of the Gita : "Always work with greater enthusiasm, destroy your enemies and enjoy the world."[104] This sort of conviction guided the course of Indian nationalism all along. Though the advent of Gandhi in the scene of Indian politics in 1921 eclipsed the influence of Swami Vivekananda to some extent, his soul stirring message continued underneath to inspire millions of men and women of India to sacrifice their life at the altar of 'Mother India' till the end of Indian independence movement in 1947. Hence it is some times said that Swami Vivekananda sowed the seeds of revolution against the British, but Gandhi and Nehru reaped the harvest.

Thus the contribution of Swami Vivekananda to Indian Freedom Movement is very great. His name may be recorded in the history of Indian Freedom Movement in indelible terms. Hence it is said, "This preacher of religious harmony and toleration, who was Sankara in wisdom, Buddha in love and sympathy to all beings, Christ in humanity, Mahavir in faith and loyalty to his Lord, Narada in Bhakti, Arjuna in courage and Karma Yoga, Vysa in the knowledge of shastras, Suka in purity,"[105] still shines almost alone as a star of inspiration in the horizon of this nation. From East to West his name is still honoured.

REFERENCES

1. *Completed Works of Swami Vivekananda*, Vol. V, pp. 95-96.
2. Quoted in *Swami Vireswarananda, Our Duty Towards Motherland*, p. 39.
3. Sister Nivedita, *The Master As I Saw Him*, p. 69.
4. Quoted in V.P. Varma, *Modern Indian Political Thought*, p. 111.
5. Jawaharlal Nehru, *Discovery of India*, p. 315.
6. Professor Hiren Mukerjee, *Vivekananda and Indian Freedom*, pp. 4-5.
7. *Complete Works of Swami Vivekananda*, Vol. V, p. 409.
8. *Swami Vivekananda — Studies in Soviet Union*, Published on 150th Birth Anniversary of Sri Ramkrishna, p. 213.
9. *The Gita*, Chapter IV, Shloka 11.
10. *Complete Works of Swami Vivekananda*, Vol. III, p. 188.
11. Bertrand Russell, *Political Ideals*, p. 68.
12. S.C. Sengupta, *Swami Vivekananda and Indian Nationalism*, p. 59.
13. *Complete Works of Swami Vivekananda*, Vol. I, p. 16.
14. *Ibid.*, Vol. I, p. 17.
15. *Ibid.*, Vol. VI, p. 415.
16. *Ibid.*, Vol. VI, p. 415.
17. *Ibid.*, Vol. VI, p. 416.
18. Mahatma Gandhi, *Young India*, July 28, 1921.
19. *Ibid.*, January, 27, 1927.
20. *Ibid.*, February, 25, 1930.
21. S.C. Sengupta, *Swami Vivekananda and Indian Nationalism*, p. 62.
22. *Ibid.*, p. 62.
23. *Complete Works of Swami Vivekananda*, Vol. III, p. 160.
24. *Ibid.*, Vol. V, p. 526.
25. Quoted in S.C. Sengupta, *Swami Vivekananda and Indian Nationalism*, pp. 62-63.
26. Jawaharlal Nehru, *Discovery of India*, p. 338.

27. Bipin Chandra Pal, *Indian Nationalism*, p. 44.
28. *Lectures from Colombo to Almora*, p. 297.
29. *Ibid.*, p. 296.
30. *Ibid.*, pp. 296-97.
31. *Complete Works of Swami Vivekananda*, Vol. IV, p. 479.
32. *Lectures from Colombo to Almora*, p. 47.
33. Barker, *Political Thought in England from 1849 to 1914*, p. 10.
34. *Complete Works of Swami Vivekananda*, Vol. I, p. 109.
35. *Ibid.*, Vol. II, p. 127.
36. *Ibid.*, Vol. I, p. 108.
37. *Ibid.*, Vol. I, p. 336.
38. *Ibid.*, Vol. I, p. 337.
39. *Ibid.*, Vol. II, p. 125.
40. *Ibid.*, Vol. I, p. 109.
41. *Ibid.*, Vol. V, p. 216.
42. *Ibid.*, Vol. III, p. 238.
43. *Ibid.*, Vol. II, p. 325.
44. *Ibid.*, Vol. VII, p. 48.
45. *Ibid.*, Vol. VI, p. 126.
46. *Ibid.*, Vol. V, p. 436.
47. *Ibid.*, Vol. IV, p. 367.
48. *Ibid.*, Vol. IV, p. 368.
49. G.H. Sabine, *A History of Political Theory*, p. 708-09.
50. *Complete Works of Swami Vivekananda*, Vol. IV, p. 440.
51. *Ibid.*, Vol. I, p. 335.
52. *Ibid.*, Vol. V, p. 282.
53. *Ibid.*, Vol. I, p. 111.
54. Rousseau, *Social Contract* (Opening sentence).
55. *Complete Works of Swami Vivekananda*, Vol. VI, p. 54.
56. *Ibid.*, Vol. VI, p. 4.
57. *Ibid.*, Vol. IV, pp. 239-40.
58. *Ibid.*, Vol. V, p. 252.
59. *Ibid.*, Vol. I, p. 173.
60. *Ibid.*, Vol. V, p. 419.
61. *Complete Works of Swami Vivekananda*, Vol. IV, p. 328.

62. R.C. Gupta, *Great Political Thinkers*, p. 85.
63. *Complete Works of Swami Vivekananda*, Vol. IV, p. 356.
64. *Swami Vivekananda — Studies in Soviet Union*, Published on 150th Birth Anniversary of Sri Ramkrishna, p. 157.
65. Swami Vivekananda, *Proletariat! Win Equal Rights*, p. 18.
66. *Ibid.*, p. 18.
67. S.C. Sengupta, *Swami Vivekananda and Indian Nationalism*, p. 66.
68. *Complete Works of Swami Vivekananda*, Vol. VII, pp. 278-79.
69. *Ibid.*, Vol. VII, p. 327.
70. *Ibid.*, Vol. IV, pp. 369-70.
71. *Ibid.*, Vol. I, p. 461.
72. *Ibid.*, Vol. III, p. 226.
73. *Ibid.*, Vol. II, p. 300.
74. *Ibid.*, Vol. I, p. 11.
75. *Ibid.*, Vol. III, p. 319.
76. *Nationalistic and Religious Lectures of Swami Vivekananda*, p. 118.
77. *Complete Works of Swami Vivekananda*, Vol. III, p. 300.
78. *Ibid.*, Vol. III, p. 318.
79. *Ibid.*, Vol. II, p. 3.
80. S.C. Sengupta, *Swami Vivekananda and Indian Nationalism*, p. 63.
81. *Complete Works of Swami Vivekananda*, Vol. III, p. 242.
82. *Ibid.*, Vol. II, p. 124.
83. Quoted in S.C. Sengupta, *Swami Vivekananda and Indian Nationalism*, p. 72.
84. *Ibid.*, p. 72.
85. *Ibid.*, p. 72.
86. R.C. Gupta, *Great Political Thinkers*, p. 79.
87. V.P. Varma, *Modern Indian Political Thought*, p. 102.
88. Quoted in Amales Tripathy, *The Extremist Challenge*, p. 125.
89. S.C. Sengupta, *Swami Vivekananda and Indian Nationalism*, p. 65.
90. Prof. Hiren Mukerjee, *Vivekananda and Indian Freedom*, p. 15.
91. Sankari Prasad Bosu, *Letters of Sister Nivedita*, Vol. I, pp. 38-39.
92. Marie Louis Burke, *Swami Vivekananda — A New Discovery.*
93. S.C. Sengupta, *Swami Vivekananda and Indian Nationalism*, p. 67.
94. *Ibid.*, p. 68.

95. Mentioned in introduction to *Proletariat! Win Equal Right* by Swami Vivekananda.
96. Ram Gopal, *Life of Bal Gangadhar Tilak*, p. 203.
97. *Selected Works of M.N. Roy*, Vol. I, p. 338.
98. B.C. Pal, *The Spirit of Indian Nationalism*, p. 40.
99. Mentioned in introduction, *Proletariat! Win Equal Right*, by Swami Vivekananda.
100. Prof. Hiren Mukherjee, *Vivekananda and Indian Freedom*, p. 21.
101. *Complete Works of Swami Vivekananda*, Vol. V, p. 454.
102. *Ibid.*, Vol. V, p. 453.
103. *Ibid.*, Vol. V, p. 506.
104. *Ibid.*, Vol. V, p. 453.
105. *The Life of Swami Vivekananda by his Western and Eastern Disciple*, Vol. IV, p. 104.

6

SWAMI VIVEKANANDA'S NATIONALISM *VIS-A-VIS* WESTERN NATIONALISM

(i) Introduction

Nationalism is one of the most dominant forces of the modern world. So immense is the persuasive force of nationalism that it has dominated almost all spheres of thought and action of the people world over. Without any second thought modern men indulge in so much of its adulation that it has assumed the status of universally accepted faith. Charlton J.H. Hayes has therefore rightly observed, "So much is nationalism a common place in the modes of thoughts and actions of the civilized population of the contemporary world that most men take nationalism for granted. Without serious reflection they imagine it to be the most natural thing in the universe and assume it that it must always have existed."[1]

Nationalism, as a philosophy, appeals so much to the modern mind that the contemporary man almost accepts it as a new religion and expresses its unqualified allegiance and uncompromising adherence to it so much so that it far surpasses its adherence to any other religion. Hence Dr. Radhakrishnan has observed, "Nationalism is a political religion which stirs the hearts and wills of men and rouses them to service and self-sacrifice in a way that no purely religious movements have done in recent time."[2] It is further pointed out, "Nationalism has become a kind of secular religion along side other religious faiths, but in our day it has sometimes actually replaced super natural religion."[3] Arnold Toynbee has characterised it as "the real if unavowed religion of post-modern Western society."[4]

(ii) Back-drop

Nationalism as a political concept evolved in the west on a vexed and complicated backdrop. It has evolved through different periods and different phases and the course of its evolution has been sometimes zigzag and sometimes contradictory. As William Ebenstein writes "Complex in its origin, it has developed along many and often contradictory lines."[5]

During the medieval period people were not conscious of anything like nationalism or nation-state. Society was altogether feudalistic and hierarchical. This feudal system of society hindered the development of centralised system of government. At that time human loyalties did not go beyond the frontiers of locality — the village or city. Sabine in support of the fact writes, "Medieval society in its effective political organisation was almost wholly local."[6]

With the erosion of the authority of the feudal lords or the kings, the Christian Church emerged as another symbol of authority. However the Pope who assumed the role of the head of the Holy Roman Empire, exercised his authority so arbitrarily that it hindered the growth of nationalism. As Prof. Dunning has observed, "The Holy Roman Empire and the universal church exercised authority over the European state and acted as a stumbling block to the rise of Nation-states."[7]

Yet the Renaissance, the Reformation and geographical discoveries, which marked the end of medieval period as much as the supremacy of the Church, were responsible for the establishment of the strong national monarchies. Renaissance taught the people not to accept anything blindly. The Protestant Reformation Movement freed the European states from the control of arbitrary Papal authority. Strong national monarchies were established in Europe and this gave rise to the spirit of national unity. The feudal order of the society and authority collapsed making way for a new order of national society. Strong monarchies were established first in England and then in France. Industrial development, spread of trade and commerce and growth of a large middle class in big territorial states were also responsible for the growth of nationalism. As it is said, "A prosperous and articulate middle class, whose commercial and intellectual element combined in the development of nationalist ideology, encouraged the development of nationalism in order to maintain their power and influence."[8]

In these European states with strong monarchies, vernaculars developed and Latin lost the pride of place. Different languages of different peoples came into existence that promoted a sense of affinity among the people, who spoke it. Common language served as an important unifying force. In the words of Ramsay Muir "...in very many cases unity of language and the community of ideas which it brings, have proved the main binding force in a nation."[9] Prof. Dunning has also observed, "A more acceptable criterion of identity as a nation was found in language. On the basis of sameness of speech...nations were distinguishable as nature itself has divided them, quite without reference to the will of men."[10]

Gradually the racial characteristics of the European people became very prominent that gave a positive push to the rise of nationalism. People, living in a particular physical boundary developed certain racial characteristics which differentiated them from other groups of people that helped in the growth of nationalism. To quote Hayes, "...an imaginary belief in blood relationship, that is, in race has been effective force in building and cementing nationalism."[11] Prof. Dunning has also pointed out, "All through the history of political theory we have seen distinctions of race presented as the causes and sufficient explanations and distinctions in institutions and power. The Greeks, the Romans, the Teutons all left copious records of their conviction that their national unity was due to the qualities inherent in a peculiarly gifted blood."[12]

Side by side with language and race, religion also came to play its role in the growth of nationalism in Europe. Though during the medieval period, the Catholic Church and catholicism prevented the growth and development of nationalism, in later ages, when protestantism emerged and Reformation overtook Christianity, religion become one of the most adhesive forces to hold its followers together and instill in them the sense of nationality. Emphasising on the force of religion in the formation of a nation, Schleicher has rightly pointed out, "the unity of nation is weakened or strengthened by the religious similarities or differences among its people."[13]

Geographical factor also helped in the growth and development of nationalism. Geographical situation united a particular group and kept it separate from the other groups. Geographical homogeneity that developed similarity of interest and outlook among the people of a particular geographical boundary, promoted a sense of nationalism among them. Justifying the influence of geography in the formation of a nation Ramsay Muir has pointed out, "Undoubtedly the most clearly marked nations have enjoyed a geographical unity and have owned their nationhood in part to this fact."[14] Prof. Dunning has further pointed out, "The course of theory on the relation between nation and geography is clearly analogous to that of the relation of nation to race. Through Bodin and Montesquieu as we have seen, the determination of nationhood by geographical situs was made an important feature of scientific politics."[15]

Thus different factors like language, race, religion and geography in course of time came to help the growth of nationalism in Europe. R.G. Gettell has, therefore, significantly observed, "As population became stationary and common interest developed, it became increasingly evident that new states would in general follow geographic and ethnic lines. Bonds of nationality and language strengthened by national boundaries, grouped the feudal fragments into more and more permanent combinations : the France, Spain, England, Switzerland, the Netherland, Russia and later Germany and Italy arose."[16]

The French Revolution of 1789 is the greatest landmark in the history of development of nationalism. It not only sounded the death-knell of feudalism; it also established a strong national government in France. It provided a fillip to the development of nationalism in Europe with democratic concept of liberty and equality of man. Prof. Schuman has rightly observed, "It is not without significance that nationalism has flowered most luxuriantly in the period since the French Revolution...."[17] Arnold Toynbee has also remarked, "From about French revolution we have been in the period of nationalistic internecine."[18] It is also pointed out, "French Revolution was particularly fruitful for the evolution of nationalism."[19] William Ebenstein has also observed, "Since the French Revolution, nationalism has been one of the driving forces of domestic, imperial and international politics."[20]

Rise of Napoleon in the European politics, further galvanised the feeling of nationalism among the European states. All European peoples thought in terms of unity of the country as a defense against Napoleon that led to the promotion of nationalism. So it has been pointed out, "Out of the gigantic efflorescence of patriotism in Napoleonic France, out of the military impact of Napoleonic France upon Europe, was born a nationalistic awakening."[21] It is also remarked, "....Napoleonic war was particularly fruitful for the evolution of nationalism."[22]

The Congress of Vienna in 1815 was another milestone in the history of development of Western nationalism. Different states, whose nationalist sentiment was wounded by the settlement, branded it 'unjust' and rebelled against it. They upheld the cause of 'one nation one state'. Prof. Dunning in this connection has observed, "In the negotiation at Vienna the doctrine that nationality should be the basis of independent statehood came strongly to the front in providing for the future of Poland, Italy and Germany."[23] Since then the theory of 'one nation one state' dominated the European politics that gave further impetus to the movement of nationalism in Europe. As Hans J. Morgenthau has pointed out, "The nation needs a state. 'One nation one state' is thus the political postulate of nationalism...."[24]

The tide of nationalism drew further inspiration from the writings of John Stuart Mill and Fitche. Slowly but steadily with democratic consciousness growing among the people, monarchies declined and democracy gained ground. With the spread of democracy, the spirit of nationalism got further momentum and in 19th century democracy and nationalism became almost the two inseparable concepts. Consequently this century witnessed many national movements, culminating in the unification of Germany and Italy. Hence Prof. Dunning has befittingly pointed out, "These movements (Nationalist

Movements) were the concomitant of the steady growth of democratic ideas in all phases of social and political life."[25] Subsequently the principle of 'one nationality one state' assumed a terrible dimension after the first world war and the 'principle of self-determination' came to the forefront of European politics. It was argued that each nationality had the birth right to have a separate independent state of its own. Prof. Dunning has pointed out, "The doctrine that nationality and political independence were inseparable, was basic in all the revolutionary agitation of the time."[26] This 'principle of self-determination' was nothing but an outcome of oneness among the people of each nationality. As a result different new states emerged in Europe. It has been rightly observed, "A tremendous explosion of nationalism in 1918 and 1919 led to the political fragmentation of Central Europe in the name of self-determination."[27]

Thus evolved through different phases and ages, nationalism that has become by far the greatest dynamic force in the history of the world to shape the course of human destiny in 20th century. Though it has brought about two world wars, causing wide massacre and untold devastation world over, still people of the world have tremendous cravings for nationalism. John H. Randall has therefore rightly remarked, "Nationalism is still almost the one idea for which masses of man will still die."[28]

(iii) Indian Nationalism

The political rottenness of India enabled the British to establish their foothold in this land and subsequently they made India their stronghold. If we analyse British Indian history, we find that the establishment of British rule in India on a systematic basis began with Anglo-French Wars (1740-1763) in South India, the Battle of Plassy and Buxer and the grant of Diwani rights by Shah Alam. The introduction of military force of British imperialism, harnessed with all the powers of diplomacy, state-craft and advanced military apparatus, appeared like a cataclysmic element in Indian polity and gradually the major portions of India came under the territorial possession of the East India Company.

India in the long run became a happy hunting ground for British, the profit seekers. As India was yoked to British plough for the development of the British, the socio-political and economic life of India reached the lowest ebb. Interests of India were made subservient to the British interest at all levels. As it is said, "Indian economy and social development were completely subordinated to British economy and social development.... When British was developing into the leading developed capitalist country of the world, India was being underdeveloped into becoming the leading backward colonial country of the world. In fact the two processes were interdependent in terms of cause and effect."[29]

The grand Indian civilization and culture that dazzled the Eastern horizon for centuries, lost their lustre and India succumbed to British imperialism by the cruel joke of her fate. Such political dominance of the British over the country and their economic preponderance, coupled with their so-called notion of superiority of Western civilization and culture, enabled them to give a rude shock to the old Indian order, that was crumbling fast all over the country.

It was indeed a dark age, considered from all angles and nothing of great importance was produced at that time. All indigenous arts and crafts declined. There was no place for reason in religion, which was flooded by meaningless ceremonies and rites. Superstitions and dogmas were all powerful. People were pessimistic and found no hope in the future. They became fatalists. Their vision became narrow. There was complete prostration in socio-political and economic life of India. As H.G. Rawlinson writes, "General condition of India in 18th century was perhaps the unhappiest in the chequered history of the country."[30] Aurobindo himself has pointed out, "The 18th and early 19th centuries in India were periods of political decline, defeat and anarchy, which practically killed the creative spirit in religion and art. India began to imitate Europe and forgot her own achievements."[31] Agriculture, Industry and trade were utterly ruined under the British imperial policy. Politically it was an age of decay and dissolution. Economically it was a period of ruination. Culturally it was a time of stagnation. Poverty and starvation were the common phenomena in the society. The imperial power invested huge capital in India and made enormous profit. The British looked upon India as a place where capital could hope to maintain a heaven. But paradoxically enough, the Indian masses were rotting in poverty and starvation. Thus a great predicament, surrounded India in 18th and early 19th century.

However, after age-long hardship and suffering there came a signal for change in Indian history in 19th century. There occurred great mental ferment in India, leading to a great Renaissance in Indian thought. The mind searched for inner meaning of Indian culture and the lost values of Aryan religion. It too felt enamoured of the values and utilities of the science of the West. A galaxy of leaders of men, social workers and reformers appeared on the scene to reach the avowed goal of renaissance. There also started a series of socio-religious reform movement to renovate the society and religion. The vision of a new India emerged out of such movement, the vision of a united, free, liberated nation.

All sorts of lethargy and stagnation began to disappear. India became vibrant with tremendous energy. Throughout India, nationalism became the dominating urge and demand for national identity became too vibrant to be subdued. It is said, "The intellectual life of Indian people began to undergo revolutionary changes, influenced by such ideas as democracy and sovereignty of the people, rationalism and humanism. These new ideas helped Indians not only to take a critical look at their own society, economy and government but also to understand the true nature of British imperialism in India."[32]

Such nationalistic urge knit the people together and led to the emergence of a common national outlook. It served to awaken among the Indians a keen desire for national freedom. As F.L. Schuman writes "...slowly and painfully the literati imbibed the western ideas of nationalism and put forward demands for Swaraj (Self-rule) with increasing urgency and frequency."[33]

Of the greatest forces in making India renascent Ramkrishna Movement, led by Swami Vivekananda, a foremost leader, who gave India spiritual leadership, stands out as the most dominant. With his charming personality, unlimited physical energy, tremendous mental capacity, deep spiritual vision and boundless sense of duty, Swami Vivekananda appeared on the Indian scene as the messiah of new age. He was the symbol of renascent spirit and sources of strength for India's avowed goal. He undertook a lot of cultural and humanitarian work in Bengal, whose impact was subsequently felt all over India. By his fiery speeches and writings in India he awakened Indian spirit in the realms of philosophy, religion and culture and political consciousness came as an inevitable consequence.[34]

Swami Vivekananda, a product of both Eastern and Western culture, was as much a product of such Indian renaissance as one of its architects. As a consequence, his nationalistic ideas or nationalism exhibit certain traits that are identical with that of Western concept of nationalism.

(iv) Resemblance

A close study of nationalism in the West and the concept of Swami Vivekananda's nationalism, reveals some resemblances between the two. Western nationalism during its early stage emanated from emphasis on certain values and movements that determined too the nationalistic fervour and nationalistic ideology of Swami Vivekananda. These values and movements that are common to Western concepts of nationalism and Swami Vivekananda's nationalism are (1) Indebtedness to Renaissance (2) Emphasis on the spirit of self-determination.

(1) Indebtedness to Renaissance

"Renaissance" it is said, "is the rebirth or revival of classical learning...to dispel some of the misconceptions long prevalent about the period."[35] It is a movement that sought to "Understand the ancient to 'breathe fresh life' and to emulate the ancient masters."[36] It fostered in man a scientific spirit to question the prevailing superstitions and dogmas of the medieval period.

"Medieval period was obviously dark; disorderly, confused and choatic; unsatisfactory and dirty, primarily ecclesiastical and superstitious."[37] But Renaissance held at a discount blind faith, unsupported by scientific inquiry and investigation. It brought about a general transformation of mind from medievalism to modern. It was an intellectual awakening, dawn of a neo-consciousness. As it is said, "Renaissance was reaction against medieval ignorance and it was a pointer to a newer vision. It was a spirit of enquiry, which opened unlimited vistas of newness in the realm of thought and action."[38]

Renaissance thus revolutionised the whole system of human thought. Art, literature, architecture, politics — everything underwent a spectacular change. Above all changes, political change was most remarkable that affected the whole of European society. As Prof. Sabine has written, "Thus changes of political thought and practice reflected changes in the whole fabric of European society, which were everywhere similar."[39] With the growth of political consciousness, people became much aware of their rights and liberty. It is said, "...individualism emerged in renewed strength, rights of the individual became the essential feature of the new era."[40] Out of political consciousness and consciousness of individual right, there emerged a sense of nationalism among the people that inspired them for national unity.

Thus Renaissance led not only to revival of interest in classical culture and breathed a fresh life in the heart of the people and instilled in them a sense of pride for the past glory and greatness of the people of the ancient world; it fostered in them a sense of national identity. Hence nationalism emerged as a direct and necessary concomitant of Renaissance. Accordingly Western nationalism may be considered as a byproduct of Renaissance.

Renaissance prepared the ground for Religious Reformation in Europe. With the new spirit of enquiry, engendered by Renaissance, there arose a burning desire for religious reforms. No more, were the people ready to tolerate undesirable and unwarranted supremacy of the priests, who exploited the society in many ways and lived the life of worldly comforts.

The corruption and scandal of the bishops and clergies, and financial abuses of the Church became matters of deep concern even for the people, all over Europe. In the words of Ramsay Muir, "A great part of Europe was full of explosives only waiting for a spark. The spark came from Martin Luther, a friar Professor of Wittenberg in Saxony of Germany."[41] The spirit of reformation did not confine itself to Germany. Soon it spread to other parts of Europe like wild fire which ultimately put an end to an epoch of Papal supremacy that existed in Medieval Europe. Thus Renaissance that led to Religious Reformation also put an end to medieval feudalistic order and Papal supremacy giving rise to a new creative spirit of the age.

As Papal authority was set aside, and feudal order of the society crumbled, a sense of nationalism which was unknown to medieval people cropped up in Europe. On the fertile ashes of feudalism the plant of nationalism took a luxuriant growth and different conducive factors like ethnic, linguistic, religious and territorial bonds, that gave people a sense of unity, also stimulated their sense of nationalism. It was natural under such situation, on the part of the European peoples to cling to a national government. Since they also desired peace and security of life, immediately they looked upon their kings as the symbol of national spirit. The kings also captured the nationalistic aspirations of the people and extended their royal support and sympathy to them. Prof. Dunning writes, "The throttling grip of ecclesiastical authority on the intellectual life was relaxed. In every way the princes and monarches gave sympathy and support to the intelligent and progressive middle class against the stagnating clergy and nobility."[42] It is also written, "Politically the tendency to form a large homogenous states with a strong central government was overcoming the tendency to disintegration, inherent in feudalism."[43]

As a result strong national monarchies were established in Europe. Several nation-states like England, France, Spain, Portugal and Switzerland emerged before the end of 15th century. Use of gun power, rise of national taxation and setting up of standing armies strengthened these nation-states. Industry, trade and commerce developed in Europe, which ultimately gave rise to rivalry, competition and jealousy among the nation-states. As Ramsay Muir writes, "It (16th century) was a period of profound and rapid change. It saw the break up of the religious unity of Latin Christiandom. It saw the emergence of powerful nation-states and the beginning of acute rivalries between them :

it saw...and an extension of European rivalries and of European civilization into these new fields."[44]

Thus Renaissance and Reformation freed the European people from Papal Supremacy and laid the foundation of nationalism in the fifteenth and sixteenth century. Hence Western nationalism emerged as a by-product of Renaissance and religious Reformation.

India, a land and a people with a hoary past and rich culture, the land of the Vedas, Vedantas and the Upanishads, as indicated earlier in this chapter, relapsed into obscurity and oblivion and particularly so with the advent of the British. Becoming an appendage of the British empire, it not only lost its political identity but also its traditional vitality, its urge for growth and development, faith in its pristine values of its own culture and heritage, and started imitating the West and took solace in, identifying itself as the jewel in the crown of the British empire. However in the 19th century and particularly with the advent of intellectual giants, like Raja Ram Mohan Roy and Dayananda Saraswati in the Indian scene, was set in motion a movement for the revival of interest in India's ancient culture and heritage and an attempt to rebuild India on its own image and bestow on it a sense of national identity and project it in the world as a force to be reckoned with. Thus started a new phase in national history with a passion for national revival or rebirth, what the Westerners call 'Renaissance'.

As the Renaissance and Reformation ushered in a new era — an era of nationalism in the West so also Indian Renaissance and Religious Reformation movement of 19th century inaugurated the age of nationalism in India. V.P. Varma has written, "As the Italian Renaissance and German reformation provided intellectual foundation of European nationalism so also the teaching of various reformers and religious leaders in India, gave rise to the desire for an autonomous and self-determinate political existence in the country."[45] Indian Renaissance stirred the Indian soul to its very depth. It brought about striking changes in the realism of religion, society and culture with a demand for national regeneration. There arose a sense of self-consciousness among the people of India. The soul of India began to unfold itself and break the shackles of the dead past. It can be said without any exaggeration that modern India owes everything to Indian Renaissance. The spirit of Renaissance gathered new strength and affected almost all aspects of life — social, political, economic and religious. As in the West so also in India it whipped up nationalistic sentiment. It has been befittingly observed, "...the life-breath of nation moved as a subordinate undercurrent in the religious movement of Bengal and Punjab, in the political aspiration of Maharashtra and the literary activity of Bengal."[46]

It is an acknowledged fact that this Indian Renaissance is an outcome of Western influence. Though it is difficult to decide when exactly did India come in contact with the West and came under its sway, it is but a foregone conclusion that ever since Vasco da Gama came to Asian shores in 1498, there began a new Epoch in Asian History, that K.M. Panikkar significantly termed as "The Vasco da Gama Epoch in Asian History (1498-1945)."[47] Since then some ports of India were opened to Western traders, colonialists and invaders, the agents of Western influence. Hence it is clear that in 16th century India witnessed the emergence of some new forces of Western character to influence Indian society.

However, it was only in 18th and early 19th century that India came in direct contact with the advanced phases of Western rationalistic and scientific thought currents. Contact with West widened the mental outlook of the Indians to a considerable extent. They began to assimilate the Western ideas and values in every sphere of their life and enrich them. Regarding the Western influence on Indian minds Hans Kohn writes, "The rising generations assimilated European teachings with astounding receptivity. They quickly became nationalists, democrats and socialists. Cavour, Mazzini and Mill became their teachers and heroes. A more intimate acquaintance with European culture had been attained and it was no longer accepted uncritically.... Ruskin, Carlyle, Tolstoy and others played their part."[48] That apart, the untiring efforts of the well-known educationists like David Hare, dedicated missionaries like Carey and able administrator like Macaulay brought about radical change in the political, social and religious outlook of Indians. The contact with Europe, U.S.A. and Japan revealed to Indians, a panorama of immense possibilities in every walk of life and roused the Indian intelligentsia to a creative spirit. With the introduction of Western learning in India, a new spirit of intellectual quest was generated and it applied itself to religious, social, economic and political problems, paving the path for a greater intellectual renaissance in 19th century.

Yet the Indian Renaissance in the land of Sanatana Dharma commenced with religious reformers. Hence the leadership of Indian Renaissance was taken over by religious and spiritual leaders of the soil like Raja Ram Mohan Roy, Dayananda Saraswati, Ramkrishna Paramahansa, Swami Vivekananda and later on Aurobindo Ghose. Raja Ram Mohan Roy who is acclaimed as the father of Indian Renaissance, was a religious reformer as well as the harbringer of Renaissance on Indian soil. He commenced his mission of national revival of rebirth by an appeal to the spiritual gems contained in the Upanishads and Vedantas. Whether as a religious reformer or as a social reformer or an advocate of Western system of education in India, Raja Ram Mohan Roy was not only a pioneer in the sphere of Indian Renaissance in the sense of cultural revival of India; he was a pioneer too, in the sense of also national revival. As it is rightly said, "Ram Mohan was longing to see his country in the same position of eminence and efficiency in the family of nations as European had achieved."[49] Hence he laid the foundation of Indian nationalism and unity of the nation. A.R. Desai has rightly observed, "Raja Ram Mohan Roy inaugurated a new era for the Indian people by proclaiming the principles of individual freedom, national unity, solidarity and collaboration and the democratisation of all social institutions and social relations."[50] It is further said about Raja Ram Mohan Roy, "His attempt was to establish our people on the full consciousness of their own cultural personality to make them comprehend the reality of all that was unique...in their civilization and simultaneously make them approach other civilization in the spirit of sympathetic co-operation."[51]

Dayananda Saraswati another stalwart of Indian Renaissance

was of course primarily a religious and spiritual leader. He wanted to revitalise the nation by purging Hinduism of all its ugly accretions and aberrations. He felt a burning passion at the core of his heart to project India, as a land of great people and rich culture. His harping on the wisdom of the Vedas was not a mere sign of Hindu revivalism. On the basis of such pride Indian may regenerate itself and assume the status as a great nation in future. Appreciating the role of Dayananda in the national regeneration Romain Rolland has rightly said, "...how great an uplifter of the people! He was in fact the most vigorous force of the immediate and present action in India at the moment of the rebirth and the re-awakening of the national consciousness. He was one of the most ardent prophets of reconstruction and of national organisation."[52]

Thus, Dayananda Saraswati's primary purpose was not only to infuse among the Hindus a sense of pride about her own religion but also to instill in them a sense of pride for their heritage and thereby enthuse them to think in terms of national unity of the country.

Among all the spiritual leaders, who sought to quicken the forces of Indian Renaissance, Swami Vivekananda was very prominent. Ramkrishna Paramahansa, the great theologian of the then Bengal was his spiritual preceptor. He is acknowledged as a man of profound spiritual realisation and deep religious vision. He had tremendous influence on the spiritual and moral regeneration of Bengal. Swami Vivekananda was much influenced by him. Apart from it, he derived much of his inspiration from Indian Renaissance, that shaped his mind to a great extent. Right since the early teens, of Swami Vivekananda the country was in a ferment, brought about by the aforesaid spiritual leaders and their reforming societies. The pulse of the nation had begun to beat quickly in unison with the new ideas, engendered by the Renaissance. In the domain of spirituality, religion, politics and literature, there were great upheavals that influenced and inspired him to the core. Hence it is said, "Although Swamiji was a true genious, yet his mind was being shaped to a great extent by the inspiration which he was drawing unconsciously from this Renaissance."[53]

As a product of Indian Renaissance Swami Vivekananda's heart and mind bubbled with tremendous zeal and enthusiasm to precipitate the renascent spirit of India further. He was a great intellectual and an orator of high order. He had deep penetration both in Vedantic scriptures and European philosophy. With such prolific mind, he employed his intellect and energy to bring about national regeneration of India. As it is said, "He was a pilgrim of the city of God and warrior to the cause of the suppressed."[54]

Swami Vivekananda's historic role at the Parliament of Religions at Chicago in 1893, prepared the ground for propagation of Hinduism and popularisation of Hindu philosophy in Western hemisphere that stimulated the pride of Indian people and instilled in them a sense of nationalism. The great savant Sri Aurobindo has observed, "The going forth of Vivekananda, marked by the Master as the heroic soul destined to take the world between his two hands and change it, was the first visible sign to the world that India was awake not only to survive but to conquer the world...."[55] B.C. Pal also writes that the effect of Vivekananda's American Mission was more visible and wide in India than in Europe or America. It quickened the self-consciousness of Indian people far more than it was able to establish any real and abiding intellectual and moral relations between India and the Christiandom.[56]

After his historic return from the West, Swami Vivekananda's whirlwind tour from Colombo to Almora and his fiery speeches at various places, quickened the force of Renaissance and nationalism on Indian soil. The whole aim of his tour and speeches was to stimulate the pride of Indians in their own religion, culture and civilization that promoted a sense of nationalism among them. He deplored the decadence of the mighty Indian culture under the influence of the West and stood for the radical reforms in the socio-religious and economic life of India.

Swami Vivekananda deplored that in spite of India's superior intellect and dexterity she has become a backward nation in the world. All other Aryan nations, in spite of their national vices, were more advanced than India. But India he felt will rise again, and occupy her right position in the hierarchy of nations if she abandons her age-long sleep and awakes to life. Lethargy, stagnation or indolence are the only cause of her national downfall. As he said, "Can you aduce any reason why India should lie in the ebb-tide of Aryan nations? Is she inferior in intellect? Is she inferior in dexterity? Can you look at her art, at her mathematics, at her philosophy and answer yes? All that is needed is that she should dehypnotise herself and wake up from her age-long sleep to take her true rank in the hierarchy of nations...."[57]

Swami Vivekananda wanted to raise the individual from the abyss of degeneration. Man had divinity in him. By teaching him his worth and power, Swami Vivekananda sought to establish him as a divine being. As he said, "You are the pure one; awake and arise, O' mighty one, ...think not that you are weak and miserable. Almighty, arise and awake and manifest your own nature. It is not fitting that you are weak."[58] He also said, "You are the children of God...immortal. You divinity on earth-sinners! It is a sin to call a man so,...come up O' lion, shake off the delusions."[59] By reminding them of their spiritual worth Swami Vivekananda infused in them strong self-confidence. This spiritual consciousness, he instilled into their mind, indirectly paved the path for a democratic consciousness, leading to national regeneration.

Swami Vivekananda's concept of strength and fearlessness provided a new force to the national life of India. He treated strength and fearlessness as the very essence of every religion. As he said, "The essence of religion is strength. The religion that does not infuse strength into heart is not a religion, whether it is the Upanishad, the Gita or the Bhagabat. Strength is greater than religion. Nothing is greater than strength."[60]

When Swami Vivekananda preached the gospel of strength and fearlessness to a politically prostrate country like India, it served as a galvanic shock of strength for the country. As it is said, "...it served as the best antidote to tyranny and oppression."[61] He did not think of challenging the British imperialism face to face. But his speeches and writings inspired the people to the very core of their mind against the British. The people took a critical look towards the British and ultimately turned hostile to foreign yoke.

Beside pointing out all vices and anomalies of our national life, attempting to raise his countrymen from the abyss of lethargy and stagnation, elevating man to the pedestal of Divinity, reconciling Western science with our religion, promoting the principle of religious tolerance among the people of various faiths and sects of his country for social solidarity, synthesising Western materialism with our spiritualism as inevitable condition of life, and above all high-lighting his concept of strength and fearlessness he at the same time accelerated the spirit of Indian Renaissance to a considerable height and fostered a sense of nationalism among the people. His clarion call to his countrymen for national regeneration also galvanised the feelings of nationalism in India.

Stimulating the pride of his people in their hoary past and rich culture, Swami Vivekananda wanted to unite them for rebuilding their country with fresh zeal and energy without succumbing to any discomfiture and despair. As he said, "This national ship of ours, ye children of the immortals, my countrymen, has been playing for ages, carrying civilization and enriching the whole world with its inestimable treasures. For scores of shining centuries, this national ship of our has been ferrying across the ocean of life and has taken millions of souls to the other shore, beyond all misery. But today it may have sprung a leak and got damaged through your own fault or whatever cause it matters not...would you go about cursing it and quarrelling among yourselves! Would you not unite together and put your best efforts to stop the holes? Let us all gladly give our heart's blood to it; and if we fail in our attempt, let us all sink and die together with blessings and not curses on our lips."[62] He offered himself as the vanguard of such drive and said, "I will borrow the lantern of the Athenian sage and follow you, my brother through the cities and villages, plains and hills, and forests to show you the way to reach the goal."[63]

Swami Vivekananda wanted to awake people in every sphere of the society so as to give it the dimension of a mass movement and make the scattered forces of Indian nationalism unified and strong. With this end in view he gave his clarion call, "Let new India arise in your place. Let her arise out of the peasant's cottage, grasping the plough; out of the huts of the fisher man, the cobbler, and the sweeper. Let her spring from the grocer's shop. Let her emanate from the factory from marts and from markets. Let her emerge from the groves and forests, from hills and mountains."[64]

Swami Vivekananda made earnest appeal to his countrymen to work hard for national regeneration. Indolence and lassitude, as he said, are the greatest setbacks in the way of national regeneration. As he said, "Let us all work hard my brethren; this is no time for sleep. On our works depends the coming of new India of the future. She is there ready, waiting. She is only sleeping. Arise and awake and see her seated here, on her eternal throne, rejuvenated, more glorious than she ever was — this motherland of ours."[65]

Again he said, "My faith is in the younger generation, the modern generation, out of them will come my workers. They work out the whole problem like lions. I have formulated the idea and have given my life to it. They will spread from centre to centre until we have covered whole of India."[66]

For Swami Vivekananda, sacrifice at the alter of Motherland is a holy duty that every Indian, he said, should bear in his mind. To arouse this spirit of sacrifice for the cause of their motherland, he said, "...forget not that thy marriage, thy wealth, thy life are not for sense pleasure, are not for thy individual personal happiness; forget not that thou art born as a sacrifice to the Mother's altar."[67] He also said, "Work unto death. I am with you, when I am gone, my spirit will work with you...wealth, fame, enjoyment are only of a few days. It is better to die on the field of duty for the Motherland than to die like a worm. Advance!"[68]

Thus Swami Vivekananda not only influenced the renascent spirit of 19th century; he aroused the spirit of nationalism among the people. Hence it is rightly pointed out, "Swami Vivekananda's words, touching upon every facet of our national life, with their freshness and vigour provided answers to question that agitated both the individual and the society."[69] His dedication to the cause of national regeneration, in fact, deserves special mention. It is a great causal factor for the rise of modern Indian nationalism. Though he died young, it is said, "Hindu Renaissance and Reformation became self-conscious and adolescent with him." As in the West, the architects of Renaissance and Reformation became the harbingers of Western nationalism, Swami Vivekananda, an architect of Indian Renaissance as much as a product of it, became a prophet of Indian nationalism. Hence Romain Rolland has rightly remarked, "from his ashes, like those of the phoenix of old, has sprung anew the conscience of India — the magic bird — faith in her unity and in the Great Message, brooded over from Vedic times by the dreaming spirit of his ancient race — the message for which it must render account to the rest of mankind."[70]

Thus Swami Vivekananda's nationalism was a byproduct of his Renaissance spirit in the Indian context as was Western nationalism, in the context of Italian or Western Renaissance.

(2) Emphasis on the Principle of Self-determination

During the 19th as well as the earlier part of 20th century the principle of national self-determination developed in European politics and nationalism of the West took a different turn. National self-determination implies the right of people to determine the size and nature of the sovereign state to which they would belong and the form of government under which they would live. On the basis of this principle it was argued that each set of people has the exclusive right to lead a separate independent political life of its own. The people who feel that they have a common peculiar social heritage, shall develop itself into a nation. The principle declares that it is the birth right of each community of people to have a separate independent state of its own on the ground of a particular cultural homogeneity or affinity.

This principle of national self-determination that evolved out of the gregarious instinct of man, is purely psychological. It is a strong sentiment of man that is thoroughly instinctive. This concept that every nationality should have intrinsic right to be a self-governing state, dominated European politics right since the time of Congress of Vienna of 1815. This principle of one nation one state was given further impetus during the First World War and the idea of self-determination of the nations came to the forefront of European politics.

The propounders of this principles put forth their argument that to group together, the people of different nationalities into a single state, will lead to lack of patriotic feelings and internal dissensions, which would tell upon national integration in the long run. It is further contended that a nationality, spread over several states, can never be happy and contented and that such a nationality is like a dismembered social organism. So state must be identified with nationality.

Of course, Lord Acton and several other hold contrary views. According to Lord Acton, "the theory of nationality is more absurd and more criminal than the theory of socialism."[71] He held that identification of state with nationality must lead to political absolutism. In his view the multinational state is, "One of the chief instruments of civilization."[72] Zimmern writes, "In the long run the theory of national state will go the way of Henery VIII's and Luther's theory of national Church."[73] Bernard Joseph holds that, "One nationality one state is a dangerous principle and constitutes a chief obstacle to world progress." He argues that, "Nationality" and "State" are two different conceptions and that nationality can continue to exist even after the state had been destroyed. Hence he argues that either a single state should include more than one nationality or a nationality is spread over several states. National and state loyalty are two different things and according to Joseph they can exist side by side with each other, for all that nationality requires, is freedom for cultural and social life and a certain measure of group autonomy, particularly in communal matters. He believes that "the only hope of order in peace in world affairs is to be sought in the ultimate recognition of the principle that several nationalities may live together in harmony and co-operation within a state, each at the same time following its own national life."[74]

However domination of one nation over another is considered politically inexpedient, morally wrong, and logically unsound.[75] Woodrow Wilson declared, "That no nation should seek to extend its policy over any other nation or people but that every people should be left free to determine its own policy, its own way of development, unhindered, unthreatened, unafraid the little along with the great and powerful."[76] This principle was highly democratic. John Stuart Mill who upheld the cause of democracy, also lent his unwavering support in favour of this principle. As he writes, "It is in general a necessary condition of free institution that the boundaries of governments should coincide in the main with those of nationalities."[77] Prof. Laski is also of opinion, "Unity and independence were inevitable corollaries of this view, and it could be inferred as thinkers so different as Hegel and Mazzini inferred that the 'Nation-State' was the ultimate unit in human organisation and accordingly, the ultimate unit in human allegiance."[78]

Swami Vivekananda, an adorer of variety of world cultures like the Western advocates of nationalism championed the cause on the ground of national self-determination of every people. He acknowledged the principle of structuring of nations on the ground of their peculiarities that constitute their national heritage and believed in deep commitment of each nation to her heritage, that ensures its survival. As he said, "...each nation has its own peculiarity and individuality, with which it is born. Each represents, as it were, one peculiar note...and this is the very life, its vitality. In it is the backbone, the foundation and the bedrock of national life...."[79] He called this national peculiarity as national ideal. Different nations have different such ideals — social, political, military, commercial or spiritual. No nation can prosper if it neglects its own ideals. As he said, "No nation can rise, can become great, can work at all without enthusiastically coming under the banner of one of these great ideals...."[80]

Swami Vivekananda also held that imposition of hegemony by one people over others is very bad. Domination of one state over another is a political blunder, sure sign of bloody conflicts that invariably threatens world peace. This imposition of hegemony is a crime too against humanity. The principle of national self-determination, on the other hand, establishes equality of all states. It ensures individual right and liberty and world cultures. Oppression and exploitation of the subject nation comes to an end. The course of human liberty takes a glorious and progressive turn. Thus Swami Vivekananda who is an ardent champion of equality of all states, adoration of world cultures and individual rights and liberties, supported the cause of this principle with full heart. This principle as he felt upholds the dignity of variety of world cultures along with individual right and liberties, which are safeguarded most only in an independent sovereign state.

However since Swami Vivekananda was not a political philosopher in the traditional sense of the term he supported the cause more indirectly in a spiritual way than directly in a political way. He endeavoured to inspire and awaken the nation through spirituality. To him no nation can awake to life if its members do not awake. A nation is strong if the fibres of the nation — the individual — are strong enough and spirituality is the source of all strength for the individual and nation. Hence his exhortation to man and nation is : "Man is man so long as he is struggling to rise above nature and this nature is both internal and external.... And if we read the history of nations between the lines, we shall always find that the rise of a nation comes with an increase in the number of such men; and the fall begins when this pursuit after the infinite, however vain the utilitarian may call it, has ceased."[81] At another place, he said, "All healthy social changes are the manifestation of the spiritual forces working within and if these are strong as well as adjusted, society will arrange itself accordingly. Each individual has to work out his own salvation : there is no other way and so also with nations."[82]

By war and conquest, a nation, according to Swami Vivekananda cannot survive for all times as the glory of war and conquest is short-lived. The strength of such a nation is sure to be short-lived. Spiritual power is the perennial power to uphold the nation for ever. In support of the truth of this fact Prof. Laski has also remarked, "The spiritual life of Europe belongs not to Caesar and Napoleon, but to Christ; the civilization of the East has been more influenced by Buddha than by Ghengis Khan or Akbar. It is that truth we have to learn, if we are to survive."[83]

Thus though not a politician or a statesman yet as a great

spiritual leader and a humanist Swami Vivekananda was an advocate of the principle of national self-determination. His moral support to the cause of national self-determination, went a long way in securing national self-determination for Indian people. Hence this principle of self-determination is a common meeting ground for Western nationalism and nationalism of Swami Vivekananda. Like Western nationalists, Swami Vivekananda put much emphasis on it and made it the bed-rock of his nationalism.

(v) Difference

Though Western nationalism in its early phase emphasises on humanitarian and democratic ideology, in course of time, it acquired totalitarian tendency. As a result colonialism, imperialism, racialism, and war became the inevitable phenomena of the day. As it is said, "European nationalism tended to ally itself with parochialism, intolerance, bigotry, persecution of minorities, racialism and finally imperialism and aggression — the recoil of Pan-German, Hungarian imperialism, Japanese militarism and finally Fascism."[84] It is also said, "Now we know that nationalism far from always promoting democracy and liberty, often places these blessings in jeopardy; that it has provoked an occasion to be wholly compatible with autocracy and totalitarianism."[85] Thus there began the age of so-called totalitarian nationalism in Europe. The totalitarian tendency of Western nationalism goes against the very grain of Swami Vivekananda's concept of nationalism and exhibits some sharp difference with the latter.

(1) Religious and Spiritual Trait

So far as nationalism is concerned, spirituality and religion have played a very vital role. Therefore, H.J. Laski has aptly observed, "Broadly speaking, in fact, the idea of nationalism is essentially spiritual in character. It implies the sense of a special unity which marks off those who share in it from the rest of mankind."[86]

The religious character of nationalism can be traced to early times, when the functions of religion was one of the training its adherents to patriotic docility. Yahveh, as the God of Israel, represented the national consciousness, the hopes and aspirations of Israel. Every Greek village had its special tree or spring or shrine, devoted to the worship of some God or hero, who specially protected its people. In Japan religion is used for the consolidation of the state. Mohammed is the founder of a faith and a nation.

The cause of religion was also upheld for promoting social peace and security, leading to national solidarity. It was held that the king must be loyal to a religion and at the same time he must also try to make his subjects loyal to that religion. In so doing it was felt, the king would achieve social peace and solidarity. As Dante has said, "...if the prince follows the true religion without sham or make believe, he will be able to turn the hearts of his subjects to his religion without using violence or punishment. In so doing, he will avoid hard feelings, troubles and civil war...."[87]

However such religious or spiritual nationalism of the West did not survive long. It could not stand the test of time as the Western concept of religion is very narrow, estranged from Catholicity and universality, and is not applicable to all classes and condition of man. Besides as the West made gigantic strides in the field of science and technology, spiritual or religious nationalism ceased to hold its influence upon the people. The whole Europe is now under the heels of the mighty ogress of materialistic nationalism instead of being under the influence of spiritual nationalism. In the West politics is considered as the real religion and nationalism, the profoundest faith. The Westerners divorce religion from politics and nationalism. However whereas in the Western world, religion has long since ceased to be a force influencing nationalism, in the East, and specially in India it is still a force to be reckoned with. As Jawaharlal Nehru has observed, "In Europe there had been a fierce conflict between science and traditional religion and the cosmology of Christianity did not fit it at all with scientific theories. Science did not produce the sense of conflict in India and Indian philosophy could easily accept it without doing any vital injury to its basic conceptions."[88]

Like the erstwhile spiritual nationalism of the West, Swami Vivekananda's nationalism has spiritual tone. As a matter of fact he developed his theory of nationalism on the basis of religion and spiritualism. As he has observed, "the main spring of the strength of every race lies in its spirituality and the death of that race begins the day that spirituality wanes and materialism gains the ground."[89]

Swami Vivekananda's principal aim was to divert the Indian mind from Western areligious, secular and materialistic civilization and awaken spiritualism among the people in order to lay the foundation of spiritual nationalism in India. To convince the people he said, "In spite of the sparkle and glitter of the Western civilization, in spite of its polish and its marvellous manifestation of power, it is all vain. It is vanity of vanities. God alone lives. The soul alone lives. Spiritualism alone lives. Hold on to that."[90] To him spiritual unity or concord is the only perpetual bond that binds and keeps all men together. Spiritualism, he felt is the very life-force of the Indians. He knew that politics and other things like social regeneration, commercialism etc. would not hold together the Indians and keep them unified. "All these will roll off like water from a duck's back."[91] So he sought to make nationalism subservient to religion. Before solidifying Indian nationalism he wanted to establish the Catholicity and universality of ancient Hindu religion. On the world scenario he proved that Hinduism is beyond all dogmas, sects and creeds. It is the religion of the whole mankind. All other religious sects lost their lustre and became very dim before the radiant Catholicity and universality of old Hinduism. With Swami Vivekananda, championing the cause of Hinduism, it regained its glory, that was lost for centuries under the Western influence. India became vibrant with new force and vitality, a sense of its identity or recovery of its sense of identity. Nationalistic aspiration got fillip from his pronouncements. As it has been observed, "Vivekananda's appearance on the world scenario was the first sign of the awakening of India from the stupor into which it has fallen before and after the British conquest, into a consciousness of its identity as a nation and its importance in the comity of nations."[92]

In developing his theory of nationalism, Swami Vivekananda, like Hegel, believed that there is one all-dominating principle manifesting itself in the life of each nation. Religion for example, has been the momentous guiding principle in India's history. As he said, "In each nation as in music there is a main note, a central theme, upon which all others turn. Each nation has a theme, everything else are secondary."[93] Hence he worked hard to build the foundation of a religious theory of nationalism, which was later advocated by Bipin Chandra Pal and Aurobindo. Swami Vivekananda was the passionate advocate of the religious theory of nationalism, because, religion, he stated, had to be made the backbone of the national life. He felt that "Out of that faith and consciousness of past greatness we must build an India yet greater than what she had been."[94] The future greatness of the nation could be built on the foundation of its past greatness — the greatness of the pristine Hindu faith. He called upon the people to return to those days of the old, and build the country. As he said, "You are Vedantists, you are very orthodox. You are great Hindus and very orthodox. What I want to do is to make you more orthodox. The more orthodox the more sensible. Go back to your old orthodoxy, for in those days every sound that came from these books, every pulsation, was out of a strong, steady and sincere heart; every note was true."[95] The orthodoxy that Swami Vivekananda here harps on, is not superstitious belief, but strict adherence to religious precepts and principles in building up a mighty nation. Hence Mano Mohan Gangully has rightly pointed out that Swami Vivekananda was marked by a unison of conservatism and progress — marching forward not forgetting the past.[96]

For Swami Vivekananda to be forgetful of one's hoary past and neglectful of our religious and spiritual heritage was tantamount to negation of the very being of the nation. It meant almost the repudiation of its existence. Hence Indian nationalism had to be built on the stable foundation of its religious and spiritual cultural heritage. In the past the creativity of India, expressed itself mainly and dominantly in the sphere of religion. Religion in India had been a creative force of integration and stability and if and when the political authority had become loose and weak it imparted even to that a force of rehabilitation. Therefore, Swami Vivekananda declared that the national life should be organised on the basis of religious ideals. Spirituality or religion meant, according to him, the realisation of the eternal principle and was never to be identified with social dogmas, ecclesiastical formulation and obsolete customs. Such religion had been the basis of Indian life and all progress towards unification, and integration of the nation must come through religion, to be able to attain the adherence of the masses.

Swami Vivekananda not only spiritualised nationalism, he also identified deity-hood with motherland to make nationalism more effective and bind the people to the motherland perpetually by the silken thread of love of divinity. He always referred to India as the divine mother in all his speeches and writings that appealed to all nationalist leaders. Therefore Prof. V.P. Varma has rightly observed, "Swami Vivekananda's soul, like that of Bankim, was lit with luminous vision of mother India as a deity and this conception of India as the visible expression of the divine mother, has been the basic concept in the writings and utterances of the early Bengal Nationalists and terrorists."[97]

Hence nationalism as postulated by Swami Vivekananda is spiritual and religious, less political but deeply rooted in religion and spiritualism of the past. It is the result of deliberate effort to enthrone nationalism on the pedestal of great cultural heritage of the country. It is said about Indian nationalism, "It has had more social and cultural overtones and has been less predominantly a political creed. A traditional cultural type of nationalism, linked with religion and social attitudes of the past, has existed in India and is still a major force. Perhaps Indian nationalism is the result of conscious effort to adopt Western nationalism to the Indian scene without departing too far from tradition of the past."[98] It goes greatly to the credit of Swami Vivekananda to champion the cause of such spiritual and religious basis of nationalism and particularly Indian nationalism.

Thus, as in case of Western nationalism of the past, religion and spirituality is a special trait with Swami Vivekananda's nationalism. Though the West has swerved from the traditional path of her spiritual nationalism India still adheres to it with all sincerity.

(2) Moral Tone of Swami Vivekananda's Nationalism

The most striking difference between the Western and Swami Vivekananda's theory of nationalism is that whereas the western concept of nationalism is devoid of moral tone, nationalism of the latter is deeply steeped in it. The history of the West has come to a stage when the moral man, the complete man is more and more giving way and making room for a political and commercial man, the man of a limited purpose. This process aided by the wonderful progress of science, is assuming gigantic dimension, upsetting moral balance and obscuring the human side of man under the powerful impulse of self-interest. Lack of moral balance and loss of human value has not only penetrated into the social fibre; it has infested too the political sphere, and nationalism as the most dominant urge in the political sphere, has also come under its sway. As a consequence Western nationalism has become completely secular, completely shorn of any moral or spiritual content. Deploring this trend R.N. Tagore has observed, "This nationalism is cruel epidemic of evil that is sweeping over the human world of the present age and eating into its moral vitality."[99]

Western nationalism is not only devoid of moral tone; lack of such moral tone has made it highly materialist in nature. This materialistic nationalism of the West is now gaining ground in the whole world. Equity, propriety and fairness in politics are becoming more and more the thing of the past. In the words of R.N. Tagore, "We can well imagine what a moral havoc it is causing in a world where whole people are furiously organising themselves for gaining wealth and power."[100] Tagore has branded such Western nationalism as "organised self-interest of a whole people — an organised power for exploitation."[101] It is least human and least spiritual. It is based upon the principle of 'end justifies the means'. 'Machiavelism' is its sole method. It is least concerned with ethics, justice and fair play. In the name of nationalism and national right many heinous crimes are being committed against humanity. Therefore, Vladimir Solovyer, a

Russian philosopher has condemned nationalism and said, "It destroys a nation, for it makes it the enemy of mankind."[102]

Very often, people of Western nations have become so amoral that they identify good with what serves the interest of their own nations. They least bother about the interest of the people of other nations or of mankind as a whole. Such narrow nationalism according to Bertrand Russell is a positive menace to the happiness of the whole mankind. As he has observed, "And group feeling produces a limited and often harmful kind of morality. Men come to identify the good with what serves the interest of their own group, and the bad with what works against those interests, even if it should happen to be in the interest of the mankind as a whole. This group morality is very much in evidence during war and is taken for granted in man's ordinary thoughts. Although almost all Englishmen consider the defeat of Germany, desirable for the good of world, yet nevertheless, most of them honour a German for fighting for his country, because it has not occurred to them that his actions ought to be guided by a morality higher than that of the group."[103]

However Swami Vivekananda's nationalism is characterised by a deep moral and spiritual aspiration. He asked his countrymen to be moral and unselfish. This moral power according to him is the highest power in the possession of mankind. He, therefore, called upon his countrymen, "Be moral, be brave, be a heart-whole-man, strictly moral, brave unto desperation. Don't bother your head with religious theories. Cowards only sin, bravemen never, no, not even in the mind."[104] He further insisted, "The brave are always moral, try to be brave, try to be sympathising."[105] His sole aim was to lay the moral foundation of the character of his people and his nation. Strength of character, he felt to be the key to all types of success in life and laid stress on the formation of strong moral character. Hence, in his theory of nationalism he emphasises on morality and character. Besides, he identified immorality with selfishness. As he has observed, "That which is selfish is immoral and that which is unselfish is moral."[106] Condemning selfishness he observed, "...selfishness is the great curse of the world; that we are selfish and that therein is the curse. There should be no motive for selfishness."[107]

Swami Vivekananda was very much impressed by the moral tone of the Japanese nationalism. He attributed Japan's success in every sphere to her moral power. Hence he called upon his countrymen to follow Japan in constituting the moral rectitude as the cornerstone of their national life. As he said, "If you catch the social morality and the political morality of the Japanese, you will be as great as they are. The Japanese are ready to sacrifice everything for their country and they have become great people. But you are not."[108]

For vitalising the moral and righteous stamina of the people against all the evils of Western nationalism, Swami Vivekananda laid much stress on truth, morality and chastity of the people of all nations for their happy and peaceful co-existence in this world. He held that whole human society must be based on the bedrock of truth. It is the most unshakable base for all times. However formidable the evil force might be, it will give way before this omnipotent force of truth. People all over the world should know how to hold truth in high esteem and extol its force in cementing human relation. As he said, "Society has to pay homage to truth. Societies should be moulded on truth. The society is great where the highest truth becomes practical. It is my opinion. If society is not fit for the truth, make it so; and the sooner the better."[109] He further said that people all over the world should express their adherence and allegiance to truth at all costs. "Everything can be sacrificed for the sake of truth, but truth cannot be sacrificed for anything."[110] Truth makes man discern what is just and proper amidst all evils and superstitions. It makes man very strong both spiritually and intellectually and puts him above all superstitions.[111] So we must not be reluctant to die for the cause of truth : "To accomplish anything," said Swami Vivekananda, "We must be willing to die for truth."[112] Upholding the chastity of a nation he also said that chastity is the life-current of a nation. The moment this current ceases to flow there comes about a state of stagnation in national life, followed by fall of the nation. History abounds in such phenomena. As he said, "Do you not find in history that the first death sign of a nation has been unchastity? When that has entered, the end of race is in sight."[113]

Thus as against the Western concept of nationalism which is deeply amoral, Swami Vivekananda's nationalism is based on moral foundation.

(3) Colonialism of the West and Swami Vivekananda's Nationalism

Towards the middle of 18th century, Industrial Revolution took place in Europe, that revolutionised the whole system of production in the West. As a result competition and rivalry in the spheres of production and distribution developed among the European nations. As Prof. Laski has observed, "The English who manufactures motor cars must compete against the American, engaged in a similar effort; the Lancashire Cotton mill spins against India, and France, America, Germany and Japan. No nation could now consume all that it produces. It is compelled to find markets for its surplus goods."[114] At the same time the European countries demanded huge raw materials to feed their industries. Germany openly declared, "If Germans cannot obtain sources of raw materials, must starve."[115] So declared others like Italy and Japan to justify their cause. There began a hunt for colonies. European politics underwent tremendous change. It assumed the shape of colonialism. In the words of Prof. Laski, "It is not insignificant that there is no powerful nation in modern Europe which has not won or lost a colonial dominion. In every case that has involved either temporary or lasting tutelage for the area concerned."[116]

Industrial Revolution that gave rise to rivalry, and competition in the sphere of production, distribution and procurement of raw materials, also stimulated jealousy and hatred among the nations of Europe. There emerged very powerful nations in Europe. These powerful nations embarked upon an expansionist design. War and aggression became the common phenomena. As it is said, "The late 19th and early 20th centuries brought about growing rivalries among the great powers — rivalries for trade, for industry, for military and naval supremacy, for allies and for colonies in the great imperial scramble."[117] Analysing the international situation Geremy Bentham also believed that "Competition for colonies was at the root of all international conflict and war." Emancipate your colonies" was his advice to the government and "international conflict and war would disappear."[118]

Nationalism was thus transformed into colonialism. International goodwill, co-operation, and brotherhood began to disappear. Each nation was guided by its naked self-interest. Hence Tagore has observed, "This commercialism with all its barbarity of ugly decoration, is a terrible menace to all humanity; because it is setting up the ideal of power.... It is making the cult of self-seeking exult in its naked shamelessness."[119]

This colonialism sowed the seeds of fear, greed, suspicion and unashamed diplomacy. Mutual distrust and suspicion among the states of Europe shattered international life. As R.N. Tagore has further observed, "After centuries of civilization, nations fearing each other like the prowling wild beasts of the night time; shutting their doors of hospitality; combining only for purpose of aggression or defence, hiding in their holes their trade secrets, state secrets, secrets of their armaments : making peace offerings to each other's barking dogs with the meat which does not belong to them; holding down fallen races which struggle to stand upon their feet; with their right hands dispensing religion to weaker peoples while robbing them with their left."[120]

Now fear and suspicion gripped the whole of Europe. Each nation suspected the other and casting its nets of espionage into the slimy bottom of the other, fishing for their secrets, the treacherous secrets which brew in the oozy depth of diplomacy. As a result, kidnapping, murder, treachery, and other ugly crimes increased by leaps and bounds in the international sphere. International morality reached the degree of ludicrousness. Witnessing the precarious condition of internationalism in the West, Betrand Russell observed, "So long as hatred, suspicion, and fear dominate the feeling of man towards each other, so long as we cannot hope to escape from the tyranny of violence and brute force, man must learn to be conscious of the common interests of mankind in which all are at one, rather than of those supposed interests in which the nations are divided."[121]

But Swami Vivekananda is quite opposed to this commercial and colonial nationalism of the West. His nationalism is a reaction against foreign rules and colonialism and all that the term implied.[122] The colonialistic and imperialistic nationalism of the West met scathing attack from the preachings of Swami Vivekananda though he did not develop any theory of nationalism in defiance of the West.

Swami Vivekananda's ruthless criticism against Western colonial exploitation fell upon the European society like a bomb-shell and its effect was felt in India in terms of political consciousness and national awakening. His servere condemnation of the British as the "throat-cutter," "blood-sucker, etc. weakened the roots of British colonialism in India and also made the Indian people rise against the British. He pointed out that the British had been prosperous in all ages by exploiting other races. In the past she achieved her prosperity by cutting the throats of his fellowmen in Spain and in modern time she achieved her prosperity by keeping her feet on the neck of millions of poor, innocent Asiatics. But India would never relish her prosperity by cutting the throats and sucking the blood of her brethren.[123]

Swami Vivekananda vehemently denounced the Western policy of 'White man's burden.' To him it is but a principle to deceive the world opinion as the crafty Jackal behaves in his community to deceive others. He asserted, "No good can be done when the main idea is blood-sucking."[124] People of India produced five times their total consumption. But they were being robbed off by the British colonial policy and were left half-starved. The older regime was far better for them because there was scope for justice and liberty. It did not seek to take away every thing they had. It was less predatory than the British regime and people lived with some comforts.[125] As Swami Vivekananda writes, "There never was a time in the world's history, when there was so much robbery, high-handedness, tyranny of the strong over the weak...."[126]

Swami Vivekananda said that the terrible famines that engulfed India from time to time was the deliberate creation of the British colonial policy. Excessive exploitation of Indian economy by the British was the root cause of such famines. There occurred no such famine in India before. He has said, "There never is a famine in native state. The terrible famine that have occurred, is the inevitable consequence of the British rule."[127]

Interest of the people of India was not the concern of the British. On the contrary the Britishers let loose reign of terror to hush down the voice of the Indian masses. As Swami Vivekananda said, "For few words of innocent criticism men are being hurried to transportation for life. Others imprisoned without any trial and nobody knows when his head will be off."[128] Again he said, "English soldiers were killing our men, outraging our women...we are in terrible gloom."[129]

The British carried on ruthless exploitation on Indian people. Turning down all appeals and prayers they indulged in comfort and merriments. The misery and hardship that Indians suffered, did not touch their heart. Swami Vivekananda writes, "They ground down poor people for their own wealth. They heard not the voice of distress. They ate from gold and silver, when the Indians cried for bread."[130]

Criticing the colonial and commercial nationalism of the West Swami Vivekananda even went to the extent of saying that the Western nations are governed by a handful of Shylocks. Their democracy he said is a misnomer. Their parliament, their constitution are but farce.[131] Since Shylock, as Shakespeare described, knows not love, nor friendship, nor society nor man but money and only money — the be all and end all of life — it is a great tragedy for mankind.

Apart from criticising the Western colonial exploitation Swami Vivekananda developed his theory of nationalism for the redemption of suffering mankind — the downtrodden masses of the world. To beard the lion of colonialism, that emerged from the den of Europe, Swami Vivekananda urged the subject people of Asia, Africa and Latin America to have enormous strength and fearlessness. To infuse that sort of strength and fearlessness into the mind of the suffering mankind, he said, "The earth is enjoyed by the heroes.... Be hero. Always say 'I have no fear.' Tell this to every body. 'Have no fear.' Fear is death, fear is sin, fear is hell, fear is unrighteousness, fear is wrong life."[132] He further said, "No need of looking behind. Forward! We want infinite energy, infinite zeal, infinite courage, infinite patience, then only will great things be achieved."[133] In addition to his fervent call for resistance against injustice and oppression he talked about a more basic concept i.e., 'strength and fearlessness,' for struggle that gave a rude shock to Western colonialism. He frequently preached that strength is life, weakness is misery and fearlessness is the medicine for world diseases.[134] His gospel of 'strength and fearlessness' stimulated the politically prostrate nations to a mystical height and the suffering nations gathered enormous strength to wage war against the Western barbaric policy of colonialism.

The Western colonialism afflicted Swami Vivekananda so much that he advocated the theory of nationalism as a solution of the international problems of jealousy, hatred, fear and suspicion, that were emanations of colonialism and divided the world into several enemy camps. He delivered to the whole world in place of colonialism the Vedantic message of universal brotherhood, goodwill, co-operation and peaceful co-existence of all nations. He was almost one with Bertrand Russell when the latter said, "...international co-operation is vital to the progress of civilization. All our economic problems, all the questions of securing the rights of labour, all the hopes of freedom at home and humanity abroad, rest upon the creation of international goodwill."[135] His whole aim was to solidify the world into a single whole or one family, of one mankind with no place for colonial domination of one part over the other. In the Parliament of Religions therefore he fervently declared : "Upon the banner of every religion, will soon be written, 'Help not fight', 'Assimilation not destruction'. Harmony and peace and not dissension."[136]

Hence, as opposed to Western nationalism which is characterised by colonialism, Swami Vivekananda's nationalism is marked by its anticolonial nature.

(4) Non-Exploitative Nature of Swami Vivekananda's Nationalism

As discussed in the earlier section of this chapter, Industrial Revolution in Europe brought about a turning point in the history of Western nationalism in 18th century. Invention of different machines accelerated the process of production and there sprang up numerous industries all over Europe by leaps and bounds. The great industrial powers like Britain, Germany and France, producing huge quantity of goods flooded their home market with goods far beyond their national needs. In spite of the fact that population of these countries grew at a phenomenal rate and standard of living of the people marked an upward swing the quantum of such goods far exceeded the consumption needs of these industrialised nations. As it is said, "Population in the industrial states doubled, trebled and quadrupled. Standard of living ascended dizzily. Home market soon became glutted in spite of increasing populations and rising living standards."[137]

Farmers and manufactures turned abroad for an outlet. The great markets of the Orient and Latin America became spheres of keen competition among the rival national groups and entrepreneurs and exporters. Hence arose competition for colonies and semicolonies for the disposal of the surplus goods. Soon these nations were also faced with the problem of raw materials to feed their industries. The rich natural resources of Africa, Asia and Latin America allured the hungry eyes of European industrialists. The backward areas of the earth, rich in resources, in labour power, in consumptive capacity soon became happy hunting grounds for the profit seekers of the West. There poured forth deluge of ships, inundating Asia, Africa and Latin America states for disposal of surplus goods and capital and for purchase of raw materials.[138] There began the age of colonialistic and imperialistic exploitation of the new world. "This establishment of political control over the newly occupied regions seemed a necessary step to foster commerce and promote economic exploitation. Each European state was determined to monopolise for itself and for its subjects as many of the new opportunities as possible."[139]

The colonial powers not only exploited their colonies for dumping their surplus industrial products at a throw away price; they also exploited the cheap labour of these colonies by exporting capital to these land and shutting all doors of industrial projects in them and exploited the natural resources of these lands and their environment. That apart, the colonial powers also incurred huge expenditure for maintaining army, police and prison, which were charged upon the colonial people. As a result ruthless exploitation, brutality, misery, poverty, degradation and racial arrogance became the common phenomena in the colonies.

The colonial and imperial powers, while ruthlessly exploiting the colonial people and the imperial economy, paid little attention for improving the condition of the people over whom they were self-appointed trustees. Leonard Woolf says that in the year 1924, out of an estimated revenue of two million pounds, the Kenya government spent £44,000 on prisons and £37,000 on education. The whole policy pursued by the government was to favour some 10,000 Europeans at the expense of 25,000 Africans and 36,000 Asians. All the desirable land was reserved for them and the natives were on the road that led to their economic slavery.[140] Conditions in South and East Africa show that the fate of the native populace became much worse when entrusted to the white settlers on the spot than when it was in the hands of the colonial office in the mother country.

When we turn our attention from Africa to India, we find that the condition under the British were not very much better, although Great Britain was a better master than most other imperial powers. The economic exploitation and drainage of the wealth from this country went on apace without much let or hindrance. It is said, "The reason why the British first entered India, and the primary reason they have remained there was not to benefit India, but to benefit Great-Britain."[141] In spite of more than 175 years of British rule in India the average wage of the Indian labour was at the end, about six annas a day. The appalling poverty of the masses was still the most hideous fact that struck attention of an observer. In the words of Mahatma Gandhi : "The government established by law in British-India, is carried on for the exploitation of the masses. No sophistry, no jugglery in figures can explain away the evidence which the skeletons in many villages present to the naked eye."[142] Besides poverty, there was ignorance of the worst kind, 87% of the people having been illiterate in 1940. Public health was very poor with a high rate of mortality and high birth rate. A disproportionately large percentage of the revenue of the country was spent on an expansive army and an equally expensive civil service and a host of pensioners, with the result that nation-building departments such as education and public health were obliged to live a hand to mouth existence.

By controlling currency and the military budget and to some extent the tariff and fiscal policy of the country, England was able to favour her own people at the expense of the poverty-stricken masses of India. The indigenous cottage industries of India, which provided a living to many thousands and gave them opportunity for the expression of their personalities in creative work were practically wiped out under the stress of imperial competition.

Thus exploitation and brutality characterised Western nationalism at its colonialistic stage. Hence, Bertrand Russell has rightly observed, "Exploiting what are called inferior races has become one of the main objects of European state craft."[143] R.N. Tagore has also condemned this exploitative character of Western nationalism and has said, "It is carnivorous and cannibalistic in its tendencies. It feeds upon the resources of other peoples and tries to swallow their whole nature."[144] Bertrand Russell has condemned such exploitative tendency of Western nationalism as a crime against humanity.[145]

Swami Vivekananda's nationalism on the other hand, sought to make human society free from exploitation. His theory of nationalism envisages a society where there is abundant liberty and right of the individual, equality of opportunity for all and there is no trace of exploitation of any kind. He felt upset to see the British colonial exploitation and oppression, that were rampant in India. Poverty and starvation that hit people all-around him, shocked him very much. Out of sheer agony he said, "The British have sucked the last drop of our blood for their own pleasure. They have carried away with them millions of our money, while our people starved by villages and provinces."[146] He further said, "They, who sucked the life-blood of the people, whose very power was built on their poverty, treated the poor as slaves.... Their wives and daughters are dishonoured and their properties are robbed."[147]

Ruination of India under the British economic system became a constant source of anxiety for Swami Vivekananda. Indian industries, art and craft failed to keep pace with those of the British and began to disappear. Millions of men were thrown out of employment and finding no other means of livelihood, succumbed to slavery. It gave Swami Vivekananda much pain and anguish to express "Machines are making things cheap. One may become rich but thousands are becoming poorer and poorer and the whole mass of human beings are made slaves."[148]

Misery and hardship of the labouring class in India knew no bounds. They worked hard but did not get fair wages to make both ends meet under the socio-economic system, created by the British and lived a life of drudgery. Swami Vivekananda writes, "The peasants and the weavers and the rests who have been conquered by the foreignes...have been working silently without even getting the remuneration of their labour."[149]

Amidst the exploitation and oppression of the colonial power, Indians forgot their individuality, their manliness, their importance as human beings. They lost their reason and conscience in the colossal grip of starvation. Finding no hope for survival, as Swami Vivekananda says, they served as the drawers of water and hewers of wood.[150] His faith in Western democracy and civilization crumbled to witness that they were noting but commercial selfishness and struggle for privilege.[151]

Swami Vivekananda after having observed the country-wide phenomena of British exploitation, resolved solemnly to awake India against such exploitation by promoting a spirit of fearlessness as cult of resistance in his theory of nationalism. As he felt without strength and fearlessness we can neither preserve our individual existence nor can we fight for the vindication of our rights. Character develops through resistance to evils and resistance comes through fearlessness. This fearlessness is the best antidote to tyranny and exploitation of the foreigner. Hence he said, "It is true that fear is the sure cause of degeneration.... The moment you fear you are nobody. It is fear that is great cause of misery in the world.... It is fear that is the cause of our woes and it is the fearlessness that brings heaven in a moment. Therefore arise and awake and stop not till the goal is achieved."[152]

Explaining his concept of strength and fearlessness, Swami Vivekananda also said that fearlessness is a powerful force in man that can very effectively resist death. By firmly denying man can negate the power of poison. As he said, "Have faith in yourself. All power is in you, be conscious and bring it out, say 'I can do every thing.' Even the poison of a snake is powerless if you can firmly deny it.[153] In one of his letters to Alasingh he wrote, "If you are really my children, you will fear nothing, you will be like lions. We must rouse India and the whole world.... My children must be ready to jump into the fire, if needed to accomplish their work."[154]

Swami Vivekananda's theory of non-exploitative nationalism also envisages a new social order in which there shall be elimination of special privileges and provision for equal opportunities for all. This concept of equality is based upon the great Vedantic truth of equality of Soul and Divinity of all human beings. As he said, "Look upon all as your equal, cleanse yourself of the primal sin of inequality. We are all equal.... Equality is the sign of the free."[155] To him inequality is the curse of human society. Whenever this inequality is eliminated more and more light and progress pours forth into the society.[156] He further held that some people, through their natural aptitude and superior ability may be able to accumulate more wealth than others, but it does not mean that on account of this power to acquire more wealth, they shall be allowed to exploit and ride roughshod over those who cannot acquire so much wealth.[157] To him this goes against the canons of natural and moral law.

Swami Vivekananda not only advocated equality of all men and elimination of special privileges, for liberation of mankind from the jaws of western exploitation; he also advocated freedom of man. His call for freedom had tremendous influence upon the exploited mankind. He said that the whole universe in its constant motion represents the dominant quest for freedom. In a London lecture he said, "What is this universe? In freedom it rises, in freedom it rests."[158] Freedom is the condition of human beings in which they attain their bestselves. It is in this condition that the individual has free exercise of mind that leads to the unfoldment of all faculties, latent in him. It is the condition of growth, both spiritual and moral. Therefore he said, "Life is but tremendous assertion of freedom."[159]

In fact, Swami Vivekananda, as a nationalist, was a true spokesman of the exploited section of mankind, who visualised a new life beyond the dark horizon of slavery under foreign powers. He awakened the Indian masses against the British exploitation. He felt that colonial domination is the root of all oppression and misery of the Indian masses. It has been befittingly observed, that Swami Vivekananda saw in colonial domination not only the manifestation of national oppression in general; he saw in it the cause of monstrous poverty also and sensed the need for fighting against it.[160] Hence nonexploitative nature of Swami Vivekananda's nationalism marked it out from Western nationalism.

(5) Denunciation of War

Western nationalism is aggressive and belligerent in nature. When the Western capitalist world embarked upon an imperial design, Western nationalism became aggressive. This aggressive nature of Western nationalism has been condemned by R.N. Tagore, who has remarked. "The truth is that the spirit of conflict and conquest is the origin and is the centre of Western nation; .... It is like the pack of predatory creatures that must have its victims, with all hearts, it cannot bear to see its hunting grounds converted into cultivated fields. In fact these nations are fighting among themselves for extension of their victim."[161] Prof. Laski has also observed, "War indeed seems to have been the chief factor in building modern nations."[162]

The Western capitalistic nations assumed expansionist policy in the interest of their capital. To succeed in their mission they resorted to war and brutality. Prof. Schuman writes. "There is scarcely a single colony of any of the great power which was not won through bloodshed."[163] The capitalist powers in Europe took war as the instrument of their empire building. They thought war as the legal right of an imperial power. They not only fought wars to win empires in the backward parts of the globe; they also fought among themselves in the event of any conflict of interest. As Prof. Schuman further writes, "The most obvious results of the competitive quest for empire is war — war first between the imperial states and the backward peoples and then war among the imperial states themselves."[164]

The capitalist nations of Europe used their sovereign power as a weapon to safeguard the interest of their capital by diplomacy and war. This sovereign power as a matter of fact aggravated the aggressive nature of Western capitalistic nationalism. Prof. Laski writes, "The state in a capitalistic society needs to remain sovereign in order to protect the interest of capitalism. In the last resort, these interests have to be protected by war, which is the supreme expression of sovereignty in international relations."[165] The Western capitalistic nations even considered it as the sovereign right of every sovereign community to settle their mutual disputes by means of war. As Palmer and Perkins have remarked, "...war was considered to be a legitimate procedure for settling quarrels between sovereign states."[166] Deploring such trend Arnold Toynbee has also observed, "...we have been in the period of nationalistic...warfare, reinforced...by the combined drive of energies, generated by the recently released forces of Democracy, Industrialism and Sovereignty."[167]

A critical survey of the history of Western nationalism reveals the fact that of all the capitalistic states of Europe, Italy of Mussolini and Germany of Hitler were the greatest innovators of aggressive nationalism. They introduced the cult of war and aggression for their own prosperity and progress at the expense of other nations. Fascism and Nazism their brain children were merely the different forms of aggressive nationalism of the West. Aggressive nationalists like Mussolini and Hitler followed the Hegelian philosophy and glorification of war. They flouted international goodwill and considered war as natural, eternal and immutable. They extolled the philosophy that the world gives its glittering prizes to those who have sharp swords and stout hearts. They did not realise that "the glamour of war is unreal as the bought affection of the prostitute, that exists only in the inexperience of those who have not known its deadly furies."[168]

Fascism as a nationalist doctrine of the West is an enemy of internationalism. 'International peace', it proclaims, 'is a coward's dream.' 'Imperialism', said Mussolini, 'is eternal and immutable law of life.' Glorifying war he further said, "War alone brings up to their highest tension all human energies and put this stamp of nobility upon the peoples, who have the courage to meet it." In order to popularise the creed of war and aggression among the people of Italy he declared, "War is to man what maternity is to woman." He created war histeria and kept Italy in permanent state of war. He declared, "We are forty millions squeezed into our narrow but adorable peninsula." In order that the people of this 'adorable peninsula' may have elbow-room, Abyssinia was annexed in 1936 after a most brutal warfare. War was used to divert people's attention from the internal troubles. Fascism deliberately chose an internal policy whose external manifestation was war. It believed neither in the possibility nor in the utility of world peace. It advocated the cause of violence and falsehood and rejected all the accepted moral norms.

Similarly Nazism, it is said, "...glorified revolutionary violence,"[169] and held force and violence as the essential features of Nationhood. The Nazis stressed on the doctrine of 'Might is Right' and 'End justifies the means'. Nazism preached the glory of victorious sword. In the words of Hitler, "He who would live must fight. He who does not wish to fight in this world, has not the right to exist. Such a thing may sound harsh but that is how the matter stands." Dr. Krieck, the Head Master of the Mannheim public school said, "The task of the University is not to teach objective science, but militant, the warlike, the heroic." It was held that war is the climax of human achievement, the last phase of development in the history of mankind, the father of all things, and the most simple affirmation of life. Suppression of war was considered as the suppression of human nature. It was further held in Germany that mothers must exhaust themselves in order to give life to children and fathers must fight on the battlefield in order to secure the future for their sons. The Nazis also claimed that there is no higher or finer privilege for a woman than that of sending her children to war.

Both Italy and Germany — the two great fascist countries, embarked upon a policy of intensive rearmament and militarisation of the country. They spent huge sums of money on armaments even at the expense of food.[170] Aggressive foreign policy of the fascist countries is a necessary corollary of the internal rule of terror. It is not surprising therefore that the fascist policies were bound ultimately to bring about the catastrophe of Second World War. Fascism involves denial of the rule of law in international relations and believes in the principle that 'Might creates right.' It is evident from the politics adopted by Italy, and Germany during the years proceeding the Second World War. Prof. Laski rightly writes, "Fascism is power, built upon terror and organised and maintained by the fear of terror and hopes to which conquest gives rise.... It is the state of war, in which material law is permanent...it survives in war...it is successful in war."[171] Hans Kohn too, condemning the fascist nationalism, has also written "Nationalism in its fascist period assumed far beyond anything — an absolutist and extremist self-assertiveness, glorifying war between nations and races as the supreme and final meaning of life and history. Eventually this type of nationalism culminated in World War-II."[172]

Thus Western nationalism has brought to the world the terrible wars and vast devastation in its train. In the name of national right, national honour, national policy millions of life and billions of treasures have been wasted in war. Hayes, therefore, has rightly said that this "Nationalism paved the way of statesmen, prepared the mind of the peoples for world wars,"[173] and has condemned nationalism as "a curse."[174]

But in Swami Vivekananda's theory of nationalism, there is no place for conquest and conflict, war and aggression. Instead of glorification of force and violence, war and aggression, Swami Vivekananda a humanist, whose love for man constituted the very essence of his philosophy of life and theory of nationalism, abhorred the cult of war and aggression, force and violence and condemned as perfectly useless the attempt to govern mankind with the sword. The very centres of Europe, he felt, from which such ideas of force and violence sprang up, shall crumble to pieces, shall crumble to dust within fifty years if she does not change her position and shift her ground.[175] He further felt that the whole of the Western world, because of its faith on force and violence, war and aggression, is almost on a volcano, which may burst tomorrow, reducing all to pieces. Hence territorial gain or material aggrandisement were not the goal of Swami Vivekananda's nationalism. Instead, spiritual integration of the universe was the objective of his nationalism. According to him this spiritual integration or spiritual oneness of the whole universe is the eternal grand design, enshrined in the Vedas and the whole world will be benefited, if it is put into practice. This he felt, will enkindle not only new life among the Indians but also mankind as a whole. As he said, "It is the one great life-giving idea, which the world wants from us today and which the mute masses of India want for their uplifting, for none can regenerate this land of ours without the practical application and effective operation of this ideal of the oneness of things."[176]

Unlike Mussolini and Hitler, the two great fascist nationalists, who sought to temper their nationalism by military conquest, Swami Vivekananda endeavoured to leaven his nationalism by religious and spiritual conquest. The fascists called upon the people for territorial expansion and identified it with the law of life. But Swami Vivekananda who sought for spiritual salvation of mankind emphasised on spiritual expansion and identified it with the law of life. While in London Swami Vivekananda was asked by a lady, "What have you Hindus done? You have never conquered a single nation." From it Swami Vivekananda came to realise that the West considered conquest to be "the greatest glory that one man can have over another."[177] However much this passion for conquest may be esteemed in the West, he did not consider it an ideal to be considered by Indians. India's greatness in the past did not consist in military conquest. Rather it consisted in the very lack of it. It is of course true that Swami Vivekananda said, "We must conquer the world or die. There is no other alternative. The sign of life is expansion; we must go out and expand, show life or degrade, fester and die. There is no other alternative. Take either of these, either live or die."[178] He further said, "India must conquer the world and nothing less than that is my ideal. You have to expand or perish. This is the law of life."[179] However such conquest shall be spiritual rather than military in nature. India in the past believed in the conquest of the world through the means of religion and spirituality. She should try to adhere to her cultural heritage of spiritual rather than military conquest. Such conquest may culminate in the conquest of the whole world. As he said, "This (spiritual conquest of the world) is the great ideal before us and every one must be ready for it — the conquest of the whole world. Let foreigners come and flood the land with their armies, never mind. Up, India conquer the world with your spirituality. Ay, as has been declared on this soil first, love must conquer hatred, hatred cannot conquer itself. Materialism and all its miseries can never be conquered by materialism. Armies, when they attempt to conquer, armies only multiply and make brutes of humanity. Spirituality must conquer the world."[180]

Referring to the past history of India, he said, "There have been great conquering races in the world. We also have been great conquerors. The story of our conquest has been described by that noble Emperor of India — Ashok, as the conquest of religion and spirituality. Once more the world must be conquered by India. This is the dream of my life and I wish that each one of you have the same dream in your mind and stop not till you have realised the dream."[181] Again he said, "We must go out, we must conquer the world through our spirituality and philosophy. The only condition of our national life of awakened and vigorous national life, is the conquest of the world by Indian thought."[182]

Believing in the grand ideal of conquest by peace instead of war and love instead of hatred Swami Vivekananda called upon his people, "Wisdom and philosophy do not want to be carried on the floods of blood, wisdom and philosophy do not march upon bleeding human bodies. Do not march with violence but reach the people all over world on the wings of peace and love."[183]

Swami Vivekananda believed that whereas gift of political knowledge can be made with the blast of trumpets and march of cohorts and the gifts of secular knowledge can be made with fire and sword spiritual knowledge can be gifted away only in silence like the dew drops that fall unseen and unheard, yet quicken the process of blossoming of masses of rose buds. This has been the process of India's diffusion of spiritual knowledge in the past.[184] Very emphatically he declared, "We have never preached our thoughts with fire and sword. If there is one word in the English language to represent the gift of India to the world, if there is one word in English language to depress the effect which the literature of India produces upon mankind, it is this one word 'fascination'.[185]

The sole purpose behind the spiritual integration of the world, as envisaged in the theory of Swami Vivekananda's nationalism is to make people realise world over, the grand Vedantic ideal of 'Unity of Existence' i.e., there is but one and only one soul. This realisation will lead to the dawn of a new era — an era of universal love or brotherhood. As he has said, "This infinite oneness of soul is the eternal sanction for all morality, for through that only love or brotherhood of all living being can be established."[186] Explaining this Vedantic philosophy of oneness of soul Swami Vivekananda went a step ahead of universal brotherhood and preached love for man not as one's own brother as in Christianity but as one's own-self. "Brotherhood" he said, "should be superseded by universal selfhood."[187] He further said that 'not universal brotherhood but self-hood is our motto.'[188]

In order to make people realise world-over, the value and importance of love against the vicious effects of Western cult of force and violence, he said, "Life itself is considered beautiful and worth-living only on account of love. Without love life would not remain for a moment."[189] Very emphatically he preached that love is life and hatred is death. All nations like all individuals survive in love and die when they begin to hate other races.[190] "Love is life force of both individual and nation.

It is permanent, it is everlasting, it is the only fitting thing to survive. In it lies the strength, the longevity of life. Hatred, force, violence and brutality are but poisons that vitiate the society, kill the individual and nation."[191]

According to Swami Vivekananda all wars and aggression, waged by Western world that has flooded the earth with blood, can be averted permanently only through the realisation of the supreme Vedantic ideal of 'Unity of Soul'. When people all over, realise it, they will be bound by the silken thread of love or brotherhood. All differences of race, religion, culture etc. which are the sources of jealousy, hatred and ill-feeling, causing all bloodshed and wars, will vanish fast. Peace and progress of perennial nature will pour into the earth. Whole mankind will live in supreme peace as one family. As he intuitively said, "I am sure the day will come, when all differences will vanish and that oneness to which, we are all subjected, will become manifest, leading to a world of eternal peace, progress and brotherhood."[192]

Thus Swami Vivekananda's theory of nationalism has no place for war and aggression, force and violence like that of the Western nationalism. Instead, spiritual integration and universal brotherhood, peace and progress characterised his theory of nationalism. Humanism and universalism formed the basis of such nationalism. As it has been observed, "His humanism is unique, for which he is best known all over the world, that inspired man to make him strive for ideals of good, truth, and justice and fostered in man abhorrence for any suffering."[193]

(6) Critic of Capitalistic Greed

Western nationalism is based on greed for wealth and power. Material gain or self-aggrandisement is the guiding principle of Western nationalism. The propensity to acquire more and more wealth is the very characteristic of Western nation. Condemning this Western greed for wealth R.N. Tagore has said, "And because its genesis is greed of wealth and power it can never come to any other end but to a violent death."[194]

A critical survey of the history of Western nationalism reveals the truth of the fact that this greed for wealth and power of the Western nations has given rise to capitalism, colonialism, imperialism and jingoism or chauvinism in the long run, that have posed severe threats to world order. Western greed for money led the people of the West to accumulate wealth more and more and it assumed the form of capitalism. This capitalism enjoyed its hey-day when liberal principles, based on "Laissez Faire" theory was preponderant in European circle. State interference in the domain of individual's liberty was considered unjust, improper and imprudent. Institution of property was much respected and right to property was ensured in the state constitutions. Property or wealth was valued more than life itself.[195]

The capitalist class, obviously the ruling class in Europe began to exercise their authority always in the interest of their capital rather than in the interest of the non-capitalist class. They consequently monopolised all the privileges and opportunities of the society. As a result, society came to be divided into two antagonistic sections of people — Bourgeoisie and the Proletariat — the exploiter and the exploited. There started severe conflict between these two classes. Prof. Laski writes, "They (the capitalist) identify their own good with their own preservation. Attacks upon them they will punish as sedition. Education, justice, religious teachings are tempered to serve their interest. This is not, it should be insisted a conscious effort on their part to exclude members of the non-possessing class from a share in social benefit; it is simply the natural reaction to the material environment. But the class excluded from the privileges of possession naturally, also desires a share in them. Hence arises in every society a struggle between the classes for its control."[196]

Capitalism for its further growth spread its tentacles for exploiting the underdeveloped peoples of the other parts of the globe. Industrial Revolution in 18th century Europe, added further strength for such move by the capitalist countries. As industries developed and home markets become glutted with commodities produced, they made frantic search for markets in the underdeveloped countries of the world. As a result hunt for colonies, empire building became a common phenomena in European politics. Backward countries of Asia, Africa and Latin

America became the favourite hunting grounds of European profit seeking capitalists. Thus colonialism and imperialism evolved out of Western greed for wealth and power and western nations entered upon a new phase of territorial gain or self-aggrandisement. Prof. Schuman has rightly remarked, "Contemporary colonialism or imperialism is a phenomena of Western civilization in the age of capitalism, Bourgeois individualism, planless economy...and demagogic politics."[197]

But Swami Vivekananda abhors capitalism in toto. He showers vengeance on Western capitalistic economy. As he said, "The present merchantile civilization must die with all its pretensions and humbug."[198] To him Western administration is nothing but a mechanism of treachery. All that we hear about their constitution, government, freedom, liberty and right, are but mockery, that seeks no real welfare of the people. As he said, "The wealth and power of a country are in the hands of a few men, who do not work but manipulate the work of millions of human beings. By this power they can deluge the whole earth with blood. Religion and all things are under their feet; they rule and stand supreme. The Western world is governed by a handful of Shylocks. All the things that you hear about constitutional government, freedom, liberty and parliaments are but jokes."[199] Condemning this Western capitalist system of administration, again he said, "They, that have money have kept the government of the land under their thumb, are robbing the people and sending them as soldiers to fight and be slain on foreign shores so that in case of victory, their coffers may be full of gold brought by the blood of the subject people on the field of battle."[200]

In a capitalistic state masses are ignored, only a few powerful men run the machinery of the state. Majority rule is only a false slogan. Majority is surrendered to the will of the few powerful capitalists. Swami Vivekananda condemned it saying, "I have seen your Parliament, your Senate, your vote, majority, ballot; it is the same thing everywhere my friend. The powerful man in every country are moving society whatever way they like, and the rest are only like a flock of sheep."[201] To Swami Vivekananda glamour of commercial and material prosperity is ephemeral. It will fade away and fall very soon. He said, "The West is groaning under the tyranny of the Shylock." He warned that Europe, the centre of manifestation of material energy will crumble into dust within a short time, if she is not mindful to change her life."[202]

In capitalist system of economy property is valued more than life. Property enjoys precedence over life as capitalism is concerned only with accumulation of property. Security of property is ensured first in such a state but security of life comes next. As Prof. Laski has observed the criminal law of capitalist countries is more "severe upon offences against property than upon offences against the person, because capitalism is more tender to the interest of property than those of human life."[203] But to Swami Vivekananda life is more significant than money. Spirit is superior to matter. Hence in his theory of nationalism, he has always sought to uphold the interests of life instead of the interest of property. His entire theory of nationalism centres round the divinity of human life and the soul. Life is the subject matter of his whole philosophy. He bothered most for man and least for money. Therefore repeatedly he has said, "Men are more valuable than all the wealth of the world."[204]

As against capitalism, Swami Vivekananda upheld socialistic values. To him socialism is the only panacea for all ills in the society. He declared that he was a socialist because half a loaf is better than no bread.[205] His deep socialistic realism is revealed in his statement that India's political slavery of a thousand years is rooted in the suppression of the masses. They held the latter in contempt and humiliated them so much that they almost lost their manhood.[206] The masses, he held, to be the backbone of the country because they produce wealth of the nation.[207] When they are rejected and humiliated how shall they contribute to the growth of the national energy? Hence he said, "The one thing that is at the root of all evils in India, is the condition of the poor masses."[208] For any rejuvenation of the country, felt Swami Vivekananda, it was absolutely essential to take steps for raising the masses up. To Swami Vivekananda it was a formidable problem and, necessarily, demanded great sacrifice on the part of the educated Indians. Hence he declared, "I call him a traitor, who having been educated, nursed in luxury by the heart's blood of the downtrodden millions of toiling poor never even takes a thought for them."[209]

Swami Vivekananda mercilessly denounced the sophistication, the arrogance and wickedness of the upper classes of Indian society. They, he felt have been responsible for exploiting the millions of the masses throughout India's history. They, he felt in 19th century began to co-operate with the British imperialism and helped in strengthening the foundations of foreign political and economic system, because, that system, in its turn, permitted them to practise their own oppression on their less fortunate brethren. Hence he poured forth all his suppressed venom and deep resentment against the so-called upper classes who perpetrated all sorts of tyranny on the poor, defenceless masses in strong terms : "You the upper classes of India, do you think that you are alive? You are but mummies ten thousand years old. It is among you whom your ancestors despised as walking carrion...and it is you who are the real walking corpses.... In this world of Maya, you are the real illusions, the mystery, the real mirage in the desert...you are the upper classes of India! You are a nightmare...you are the void, the unsubstantial nonentities of the future. Denizens of the dreamland, why are you loitering any longer?...why do you not quickly reduce yourselves in to dust and disappear in the air?"[210]

Swami Vivekananda's experience during his travels in India and the West revealed to him the imperative necessity of strength and fearlessness for straightening the backbone of nation, subjected to misery, frustration, and political tragedies for over a thousand years. It is indeed a revolutionary statement from the mouth of a Sannyasi when he uttered that it is mockery to offer religion to a starving man.[211] It also sounds revolutionary when emerges from the mouth of a Indian Vendantist that India is a "country where millions of people live on flowers of the Mohua plant and million or so of Sadhus and hundred million or so of Brahmans suck the blood out of these poor people."[212]

As a social revolutionary Swami Vivekananda denounced in unmeasured terms the oppression of upper class and held the

Brahmin priesthood responsible for suppression of the lower classes in India. As he said, "The West is groaning under the tyranny of the priests."[213] Speaking about the upper castes of India he said, "...Brahmins...have thrown the country into ruin. Intent all the while on theft and wickedness, they pose as preachers of religion. They will take gifts from the people and at the same time cry, 'Don't touch me!' "[214] Hence he made fervent and eloquent appeal for the elevation of the poor masses because "the nation lies in the peasant's cottage."[215]

In the system of Marx, technology and economics which represent the substructure are more important than the superstructure of politics; in a sense they are regarded as the determinants of political conditions.[216] Marx fully realised the importance of capital, but Swami Vivekananda emphasised on the social and economic value of money and the economic causation of historical action to the same degree as the economic determinists and historical materialists do. But after his return from the West he realised the value of social organisation, and used to say that if he collected three million rupees, the salvation of Indian masses could be effected. The experiences of the materialist West even revealed to this spiritual aspirant the social significance of the demand for the conquest of hunger and poverty. He once said, "Material civilization, nay, even luxury, is necessary to create work for the poor. Bread! Bread! I do not believe in God, who cannot give me bread here, giving me eternal bliss in heaven! Pooh! India is to be raised, the poor are to be fed, education is to be spread.... More bread, more opportunity for everybody."[217]

Swami Vivekananda the great humanist not only voiced his concern for the poor and downtrodden masses of India; his concern was for the downtrodden mankind as a whole. He thought for redemption of the whole mankind. He intuitively felt the emergence of new type of a political system that would gradually envelope the whole world. As early as 1893 he prophesied that the next great political upheaval which is to bring about a new epoch will come from Russia or China.[218] He also said elsewhere, "...this raising of the Sudras will take place first in Russia and then in China. India will rise next and will play a vital role in shaping the future world."[219]

Apart from the scheme of Socialism, Swami Vivekananda's theory of nationalism also highlights the grand principle of sacrifice and renunciation as a remedy against the evils of Western greed for wealth and capitalism. This sacrifice or renunciation is not only the very watchword of Vedic philosophy but also of Swami Vivekananda's philosophy of nationalism that stands in contrast with the materialistic nationalism of the West.

Dispassion for wealth is the highest spiritual realisation upon which Indian philosophy is based. For Swami Vivekananda, such dispassion for wealth or renunciation is the very soul of our national life. It also forms the core of our national character. It is this unique feature of our national life that has brought distinction to us over other nations.

According to Swami Vivekananda, vairagya or renunciation as opposed to Western greed for wealth, is the most cardinal feature of all religions. Without renunciation there cannot be any true religion or morality. He said, "Vairagya or renunciation is the beginning of religion. How can religion or morality begin without renunciation? The Alpha and Omega is renunciation. 'Give up' says the Veda 'Give up'. That is the one way, 'Give up'."[220] Again he said, "'Give up'! that is the watchword of Indian religion."[221] According to him immortality cannot be achieved without renunciation. It is through renunciation only that immortality can be achieved.[222]

It is through this power of renunciation that the nations attain vitality. In it lies all strength of a nation. He says, "What makes our nation survive and the other die? Should love survive or hatred, should enjoyment survive or renunciation...in the struggle of life...renunciation, giving up...love, these are fittest things to survive. Giving up...makes a nation survive."[223]

India, all through her history, has adhered to this principle of renunciation and have survived in the midst of all her national catastrophe. As he has said, "This big gigantic race which had to grapple with some of the greatest problems of misfortunes, dangers and vicissitudes such as never fell upon the head of any other nation of the world, survives because it has taken the side of renunciation....[224] Renunciation he felt is the national ideal of India. It is the very essence of her literature, culture and civilization. It is the very philosophy of her life, the message that she has delivered to the world from time immemorial. As he said, "Renunciation is the flag, the banner of India, floating over the world, the one undying thought, which India sends again and again as a warning to dying races, a warning to all tyranny, as a warning to wickedness in the world."[225]

Different nations, said Swami Vivekananda, have different themes, some have politics and others have military. But the theme to India's national life is spirituality and renunciation. India subordinates everything to it. Glory, fame, wealth and enjoyments — all these are not her concern. As he writes, "...here is a nation, whose great theme of life is spirituality and renunciation, whose one watchword is that this world is all vanity and delusion of three days, and everything else, whether science or knowledge, enjoyment or power, or wealth or name or fame, must be subordinated to that one them."[226]

Emphasising on India's capacity for renunciation and charity in opposition to Western greed for wealth and power Swami Vivekananda said, "So long there is a piece of bread in the home of the beggar, he will give half of it. Such a phenomenon can be observed only in India."[227] Stressing on the need of charity as a power of sustaining nationhood he said, "No civilization can begin to lift up its head until we love charitably upon one another; and the first step towards that much-needed charity, is to look charitably and kindly upon...others."[228]

Thus socialism — the panacea for all social ills, coupled with renunciation, as advocated by Swami Vivekananda, shall serve as an effective check to Western capitalistic greed.

To sum up, Swami Vivekananda's nationalism like Western nationalism was a product of Renaissance and Reformation. The only difference being whereas Western nationalism was a product of Renaissance and Reformation in the West, Swami Vivekananda's nationalism emerged out of the impact on him of Indian Renaissance and Reform movements of 19th century.

Like Western concept of nationalism, Swami Vivekananda's nationalism is based on the principle of self-determination. But his concept of nationalism differs radically from the Western concept of nationalism. In the first place whereas the Western concept of nationalism is purely secular in tone, Swami Vivekananda's nationalism is religious and spiritual in character. Besides, whereas Western nationalism is mainly concerned with material advancement of the nation, devoid of moral tone, Swami Vivekananda's nationalism is deeply moralistic and is characterised by deep moral aspiration. That apart, whereas Western nationalism, has flourished on colonialistic and imperialistic exploitation of the economically underdeveloped parts of the world Swami Vivekananda was a critic of colonialistic and imperialistic exploitation. Above all whereas Western nationalism is aggressive and belligerent in nature and is based on capitalistic greed Swami Vivekananda denounced them. He tried to leaven his nationalism by religious and spiritual conquest and emancipation of the poor and the downtrodden.

REFERENCES

1. Charlton, J.H. Hayes, *The Historical Evolution of Modern Nationalism*, p. 289.
2. Dr. Radhakrishnan, *Recovery of Faith*, p. 51.
3. Palmer and Perkins, *International Relations*, p. 18.
4. Arnold Toynbee, *Civilization on Trail*, p. 225.
5. William Ebenstein, *Today's Isms*, p. 122.
6. Sabine, *A History of Political Theory*, p. 312.
7. W.A. Dunning, *A History of Political Theories* (from Rousseau to Spencer), p. 90.
8. W. Friedmann, *Introduction to World Politics*, p. 31.
9. Ramsay Muir, *British History, Book-1*, pp. 5-6.
10. W.A. Dunning, *A History of Political Theories* (from Rousseau to Spencer), p. 312.
11. Charlton, J.H. Hayes, *The Historical Evolution of Modern Nationalism*, p. 155.
12. W.A. Dunning, *A History of Political Theories* (from Rousseau to Spencer), pp. 311-12.
13. Schleicher, *International Relation*, p. 56.

14. Ramsay Muir, *British History, Book-1*, pp. 3-4.

15. Prof. Dunning, *A History of Political Theories* (from Rousseau to Spencer), p. 316.

16. R.G. Gettell, *Political Science*, p. 89.

17. F.L. Schuman, *International Politics*, p. 430.

18. Arnold Toynbee, *A Study of History*, pp. 283-84 (Abridgement of Vols. I-VI by D.C. Somervell).

19. Palmer and Perkins, *International Relations*, p. 24.

20. William Ebenstein, *Modern Political Thought*, p. 635.

21. F.L. Schuman, *International Politics*, p. 431.

22. Palmer and Perkins, *International Relations*, p. 24.

23. W.A. Dunning, *A History of Political Theories* (from Rousseau to Spencer), p. 294.

24. Hans J. Morgenthau, *Politics Among Nations*, p. 160.

25. W.A. Dunning, *A History of Political Theories* (from Rousseau to Spencer), p. 336.

26. *Ibid.*, p. 330.

27. F.L. Schuman, *International Politics*, p. 115.

28. John H. Randall, *Nations and Nationalism*, p. 250.

29. Bipin Chandra, Amles Tripathy and Barun Dey, *Freedom Struggle*, pp. 16-17.

30. H.G. Rawlinson, *India — A Short Cultural History*, p. 249.

31. Sri Aurobindo, *The Renaissance in India*, p. 60.

32. Bipin Chandra Pal, *Freedom Struggle*, p. 26.

33. F.L. Schuman, *International Politics*, p. 560.

34. V.P. Varma, *Modern Indian Political Thought*, p. 4.

35. *Encyclopaedia Britannica*, Vol. 19, p. 123.

36. Will Durant, *Story of the Civilization*, Vol. X, p. 4121.

37. *Encyclopaedia Britannica*, Vol. 19, p. 122.

38. M.N. Das, *World History*, p. 324.

39. Sabine, *A History of Political Theory*, p. 311.

40. *Story of the Civilization*, Vol. X, p. 4130.

41. Ramsay Muir, *British History*, Book-III, p. 143.

42. W.A. Dunning, *A History of Political Theories* (from Rousseau to Spencer), p. 47.

43. *Story of the Civilization*, Vol. XI, p. 4141.

44. R.G. Gettell, *Political Science*, p. 65.
45. V.P. Varma, *Modern Indian Political Thought*, p. 4.
46. Sri Aurobindo, *The Renaissance in India*, p. 60.
47. K.M. Panikkar, *Asia and Western Dominance*, p. 353.
48. Hans Kohn, *A History of Nationalism in the East*, p. 118.
49. *The Cultural Heritage of India*, Edited by Haridas Bhattacharyya, Vol. IV, p. 620.
50. A.R. Desai, *Social Background of Indian Nationalism*, p. 290.
51. R.N. Tagore, *Inaugurator of Modern Age in India*. Ram Mohan Roy, *The man and his work*, Cal. Ram Mohan Centenary Committee, 1933, pp. 4-5.
52. Romain Rolland, *The Life of Ramkrishna*, pp. 157-58.
53. Manomohan Ganguly, *Swami Vivekananda — A Study*, p. 24.
54. V.P. Varma, *Modern Indian Political Thought*, p. 102.
55. Quoted in Swami Vivekananda, *Religion and National Integration*, p. 3.
56. B.C. Pal, *Indian Nationalism*, p. 44.
57. *Complete Works of Swami Vivekananda*, Vol. V, pp. 227-28.
58. *Ibid.*, Vol. II, p. 304.
59. *Ibid.*, Vol. I, p. 11.
60. *Ibid.*, Vol. II, p. 699.
61. V.P. Varma, *Modern Indian Political Thought*, p. 110.
62. *Complete Works of Swami Vivekananda*, Vol. III, p. 461.
63. *Ibid.*, Vol. IV, pp. 47-48.
64. *Ibid.*, Vol. VII, pp. 327-28.
65. *Ibid.*, Vol. III, p. 154.
66. *Ibid.*, Vol. V, p. 223.
67. *Ibid.*, Vol. IV, p. 479.
68. *Ibid.*, Vol. V, p. 114.
69. Swami Budhananda, *Swami Vivekananda — His Call to the Nation*, p. 3.
70. Romain Rolland, *The Life of Swami Vivekananda*, p. 7.
71. Quoted in William Ebenstein, *Modern Political Thought*, p. 635.
72. *Ibid.*, p. 636.
73. Quoted in William Ebenstein, *Great Political Thinkers*, p. 521.
74. Bernard Joseph, *Nationality*, p. 331.

75. H.J. Laski, *A Grammar of Politics*, p. 222.
76. Address to the Senate, January 22, 1917 (By the American President Woodrow Wilson).
77. J.S. Mill, *Representative Government*, p. 2.
78. H.J. Laski, *A Grammar of Politics*, p. 222.
79. *Complete Works of Swami Vivekananda*, Vol. III, p. 148.
80. *Ibid.*, Vol. III, p. 315.
81. *Ibid.*, Vol. II, pp. 64-65.
82. *Ibid.*, Vol. V, pp. 415-16.
83. H.J. Laski, *A Grammar of Politics*, p. 289.
84. William Ebenstein, *Modern Political Thought*, p. 635.
85. Palmer and Perkins, *International Relations*, p. 24.
86. H.J. Laski, *A Grammar of Politics*, p. 219.
87. Quoted in William Ebenstein, *The Great Political Thinkers*, p. 354.
88. Nehru, *India Today and Tomorrow*, p. 13.
89. *Complete Works of Swami Vivekananda*, Vol. II, pp. 64-65.
90. *Ibid.*, Vol. III, p. 149.
91. *Ibid.*, Vol. III, p. 149.
92. *Nationalistic and Religious Lectures of Swami Vivekananda*, p. vii.
93. *Complete Works of Swami Vivekananda*, Part I, p. 140.
94. *Ibid.*, Vol. III, p. 286.
95. *Ibid.*, Vol. III, p. 346.
96. Manomohan Ganguly, *Swami Vivekananda — A Study*, p. 20.
97. V.P. Varma, *Modern Indian Political Thought*, p. 109.
98. Palmer and Perkins, *International Relations*, p. 448.
99. R.N. Tagore, *Nationalism*, p. 9.
100. *Ibid.*, p. 9.
101. *Ibid.*, p. 8.
102. Quoted in Hans Kohn, *Prophets and People*, p. 205.
103. Bertrand Russell, *Political Ideals*, p. 80.
104. *Complete Works of Swami Vivekananda*, Vol. I, p. 110.
105. *Ibid.*, Vol. V, p. 3.
106. *Ibid.*, Vol. I, p. 110.
107. *Ibid.*, Vol. III, p. 520.
108. *Ibid.*, Vol. V, p. 210.

109. *Ibid.*, Vol. II, pp. 84-85.
110. *Ibid.*, Vol. V, p. 410.
111. *Ibid.*, Vol. VIII, p. 186.
112. *Ibid.*, Vol. VIII, p. 45.
113. *Ibid.*, Vol. II, p. 111.
114. H.J. Laski, *A Grammar of Politics*, p. 223.
115. Hans J. Morgenthau, *Politics Among Nations*, p. 108.
116. H.J. Laski, *A Grammar of Politics*, p. 219.
117. Palmer and Perkins, *International Relations*, p. 25.
118. Hans J. Morgenthau, *Politics Among Nations*, p. 37.
119. R.N. Tagore, *Nationalism*, p. 78.
120. *Ibid.*, p. 51.
121. Bertrand Russell, *Political Ideals*, pp. 88-89.
122. Palmer and Perkins, *International Relations*, p. 448.
123. *Complete Works of Swami Vivekananda*, Vol. III, p. 474.
124. *Ibid.*, Vol. VIII, p. 475.
125. *Ibid.*, Vol. III, p. 475.
126. *Swami Vivekananda — Studies in Soviet Union*, Published on 150th Birth Anniversary of Sri Ramkrishna, p. 120.
127. *Complete Works of Swami Vivekananda*, Vol. III, p. 476.
128. *Ibid.*, Vol. III, p. 476.
129. *Ibid.*, Vol. III, p. 477.
130. *Ibid.*, Vol. VII, p. 279.
131. *Ibid.*, Vol. III, p. 158.
132. *Ibid.*, Vol. VII, p. 135.
133. *Ibid.*, Vol. VI, pp. 383-84.
134. *Ibid.*, Vol. II, p. 201.
135. Bertrand Russell, *Political Ideals*, p. 88.
136. *Nationalistic and Religious Lectures of Swami Vivekananda*, p. 11.
137. F.L. Schuman, *International Politics*, p. 515.
138. *Ibid.*, p. 538.
139. *Ibid.*, p. 513.
140. Leonard Woolf, *Imperialism and Civilization*, p. 86.
141. Parker T. Moon, *Imperialism and World Politics*, p. 290.
142. M.K. Gandhi, *Speeches*, p. 753.

143. Bertrand Russell, *Political Ideals*, p. 84.
144. R.N. Tagore, *Nationalism*, p. 36.
145. Bertrand Russell, *Political Ideals*, p. 84.
146. *Complete Works of Swami Vivekananda*, Vol. VII, pp. 279-80.
147. *Ibid.*, Vol. VIII, p. 330.
148. *Ibid.*, Vol. II, p. 96.
149. *Ibid*, Vol. VII, p. 358.
150. *Lectures From Colombo to Almora*, p. 95.
151. *Complete Works of Sister Nivedita*, p. 201.
152. *Complete Works of Swami Vivekananda*, Vol. III, p. 321.
153. *Ibid.*, Vol. VI, p. 274.
154. *Ibid.*, Vol. V, pp. 61-62.
155. *Ibid.*, Vol. VIII, p. 18.
156. *Ibid.*, Vol. I, p. 423.
157. *Ibid.*, Vol. I, p. 435.
158. Quoted in V.P. Varma, *Modern Indian Political Thought*, p. 117.
159. *Complete Works of Swami Vivekananda*, Vol. V, p. 287.
160. *Swami Vivekananda, Studies in Soviet Union*, Published on 150th Birth Anniversary of Sri Ramkrishna, p. 116.
161. R.N. Tagore, *Nationalism*, p. 12.
162. H.J. Laski, *A Grammar of Politics*, p. 220.
163. F.L. Schuman, *International Politics*, p. 539.
164. *Ibid.*, p. 539.
165. H.J. Laski, *The State in Theory and Practice*, p. 229.
166. Palmer and Perkins, *International Relations*, p. 187.
167. Arnold J. Toynbee, *A Study of History*, pp. 552-53 (Abridgement of Vols. I to VI, by D.C. Somervell).
168. H.J. Laski, *A Grammar of Politics*, p. 289.
169. Sabine, *A History of Political Theory*, p. 752.
170. H.J. Laski, *Reflections of Revolution of Our Time*, p. 92.
171. *Ibid.*, p. 96.
172. Hans Kohn, *Nationalism and Internationalism in 19th and 20th Centuries*, p. 210.
173. Charlton, J.H. Hayes, *Nationalism*, p. 247.
174. *Ibid.*, p. 248.

175. *Lectures From Colombo to Almora*, p. 60.
176. *Complete Works of Swami Vivekananda*, Vol. III, p. 189.
177. *Ibid.*, Vol. III, p. 273.
178. *Lectures From Colombo to Almora*, p. 227.
179. *Nationalistic and Religious Lectures of Swami Vivekananda*, p. 73.
180. *Complete Works of Swami Vivekananda*, Vol. III, p. 277.
181. *Ibid.*, Vol. III, p. 276.
182. *Ibid.*, Vol. III, p. 277.
183. *Ibid.*, Vol. III, p. 273.
184. *Lectures From Colombo to Almora*, p. 217.
185. *Ibid.*, p. 8.
186. *Nationalistic and Religious Lectures of Swami Vivekananda*, p. 39.
187. *Complete Works of Swami Vivekananda*, Vol. IV, p. 222.
188. *Ibid.*, Vol. IV, p. 222.
189. *Ibid.*, Vol. III, p. 80.
190. *Ibid.*, Vol. IV, p. 366.
191. *Ibid.*, Vol. IV, p. 180.
192. *Ibid.*, Vol. II, p. 188.
193. *Swami Vivekananda — Studies in Soviet Union*, Published on 150th Birth Anniversary of Ramkrishna, p. 209.
194. R.N. Tagore, *Nationalism*, p. 51.
195. H.J. Laski, *Communism*, p. 118.
196. *Ibid.*, p. 63.
197. F.L. Schuman, *International Politics*, p. 539.
198. *Complete Works of Swami Vivekananda*, Vol. VI, p. 144.
199. *Ibid.*, Vol. III, p. 158.
200. *Ibid.*, Vol. V, p. 462.
201. *Ibid.*, Vol. V, p. 461.
202. Swami Vivekananda, *On India and Her Problems*, p. 39.
203. H.J. Laski, *Communism*, p. 118.
204. *Complete Works of Swami Vivekananda*, Vol. V, p. 83.
205. *Ibid.*, Vol. VI, p. 381.
206. *Ibid.*, Vol. VIII, p. 307.
207. *Ibid.*, Vol. V, p. 45.
208. *Ibid.*, Vol. IV, p. 362.

209. *Ibid.*, Vol. VIII, pp. 329-30.
210. *Ibid.*, Vol. VII, pp. 326-27.
211. *The Life of Swami Vivekananda by His Western and Eastern Disciples*, Vol. IV, p. 177.
212. *Complete Works of Swami Vivekananda*, Vol. VI, p. 254.
213. *Ibid.*, Vol. III, p. 158.
214. *Ibid.*, Vol. VI, pp. 317-18.
215. *Ibid.*, Vol. VII, p. 237.
216. V.P. Varma, "Critic of Marxian Sociology," *The Calcutta Review*, March-June, 1955.
217. *Complete Works of Swami Vivekananda*, Vol. IV, p. 313.
218. Swami Vivekananda, *Proletariat! Win Equal Rights*, p. v.
219. Quoted in B.N. Datta, *Swami Vivekananda — P.V. Patriot Prophet*, p. 335.
220. *Complete Works of Swami Vivekananda*, Vol. III, p. 343.
221. *Ibid.*, Vol. III, p. 148.
222. *Ibid.*, Vol. III, p. 343.
223. *Lectures From Colombo to Almora*, p. 109.
224. *Ibid.*, p. 109.
225. *Complete Works of Swami Vivekananda*, Vol. III, p. 344.
226. *Ibid.*, Vol. III, p. 152.
227. *Lectures From Colombo to Almora*, p. 69.
228. *Ibid.*, p. 90.

7

Swami Vivekananda's Nationalism and Imperialism

(i) Introduction

Although Western Nationalism, in course of time, has developed into imperialism, nationalism as such and imperialism have oil and water relationship. As antithetical to each other, they cannot co-exist. If nationalism seeks to build nation, imperialism on the other hand, seeks to build empire, imposing the will of one nation over the other. Hence "Imperialism" as it is said, "is a policy which aims at creating, organising and maintaining an empire; that is a state of vast size composed of various more or less distinct national units and subject to a single centralised will."[1] Since it is opposed to nationalism or self-determination of every people, Charles A. Beard has condemned it as "the engines of government and diplomacy to acquire territories, protectorates or spheres of influences occupied usually by other races or peoples and to promote industrial, trade and investment opportunities."[2] Parker T. Moon, a well-known authority on the subject has similarly condemned it as "the domination of non-European native races by totally dissimilar European nations."[3] George Lichtheim with same tone has also said, "What counts is the relationship of domination and subjection, which is the essence of every imperialism."[4]

But 'Domination of one nation over another' said Prof. Laski, 'is politically inexpedient, logically unsound and morally wrong.'[5] Hence imperialism, as an institution must therefore necessarily collapse, making way for nationalism of all peoples — big or small, powerful or weak. Such collapse will not only place all nations on equal footing but make their peaceful co-existence feasible on earth. It too, will be a blessing for the whole of mankind, who, having trodden the path of peace, progress and prosperity, will reap the harvest of a wholesome civilization for the world of succeeding generations.

(ii) Nature and Vices of Imperialism

While some condemn imperialism for its economically exploitative and politically dominating nature, other extol it for its humanitarian nature, *i.e.*, the role of the advanced countries in civilizing the backward nations. This is what they call 'white man's burden'. But it is not a travesty of truth to say that humanistic nature of imperialism is only an eyewash to hoodwink the world opinion. It is nothing but a sugar-coating to conceal the ugly bitterness of the policy of territorial annéxation and exploitation by imperial powers. Subscribing to such view Hobson has observed, "It cannot be too clearly recognized that...the notion of educating and civilizing the lower races...is discredited and only survives for platform purposes when some new steps of annexation is urged upon the country."[6] It is also said, "White man's burden is a mask to clothe the enslavement of others."[7] Exploitation of weaker nations by the stronger ones, through the use of force and violence is the very essence of imperialism. It is completely devoid of any humanitarian consideration or any civilizing mission. As Prof. Schuman has rightly pointed out, "Imperialism is the imposition by force or violence of alien rule upon subject people, despite all moralising and pretensions to the contrary."[8] As he has further observed, "It is no more the purpose of imperialism to confer benefits upon its victims than to confer benefits upon the home country."[9] Prof. Hodges has also remarked, "The object of imperialism is to affect the destinies of the backward people in the interest of the more advanced from the stand-point of the world power."[10]

In ancient times imperialism was only political in nature. It meant physical control over foreign territory. It is of course true that the empires were also "tax collecting and recruit raising" agencies. However, political predominance of the imperial powers were more prominent than any other feature. But as time changed the imperial powers changed their policy to suit the need of the time. They have, of late, diverted their primary attention to economic and strategic gain rather than mere political control or political preponderance. The political power that the imperial power acquired over their empire were utilized by them for the promotion of their international trade and investment of their surplus capital. Thus the most prominent nature of imperialism is extension of political power over the weaker states for the sake of economic gain only. Hence, Prof. Laski has observed, "as power extends, nationalism becomes transformed into imperialism. The latter is most generally an economic phenomena."[11] In the same light Morgenthau has also remarked, "Whenever a country...sets out to increase its power...it is a stepping-stone to world conquest; that is manifestation of an imperialistic policy."[12] He has further observed, "A nation...whose foreign policy aims at acquiring more power, more wealth than it actually has...pursues a policy of imperialism."[13] Criticising the economic policy of British imperialism in particular, Knowles has said, "The English are not an assimilating race, their motives of expansion are almost wholly economic."[14]

The nature and inherent vices of imperialism is rooted in the predatory instinct of man. This predatory vices were found even in the early phases of human history. Different races during the time of their movement from one part of the world to another, in search of pasture and food, were compelled by this predatory nature to fight and subjugate other races. History bears ample testimony of ruthless aggression and bloody wars, carried out by different races for winning new lands.

This predatory instinct of modern man instigates him to conquer new land and expand its territory. This thirst for conquest ingrained in the human nature, compels him to indulge in competition and struggle for new lands. The inordinate desire for conquest of new territory and mastery or power over the people of other races is one of the most powerful incentives to the building up of modern imperialism. As Prof. Schuman has observed, "Modern imperialism is a new expression of the will to power and the drive for conquest."[15] It is precisely this instinct of conquest and power that made Alexander, Cecil,

Rhodes and Napoleon think for conquest of the world. This desire for conquest and power is evident in the Fascist theory of Mussolini and Nazi theory of Hitler. Mussolini himself declared in 1932 "The fascist state is a will to power and an empire." So they emphasised on the expansion of their nations and glorification of war. In this context Morgenthau writes, "The outstanding historic examples of...imperialism are the expansionist policies of Alexander the great, Rome, the Arab in 7th and 8th century, Napolean-I and Hitler. They all have in common an urge towards expansion, which knows no rational limits.... Their urge for power and mastery over the lands will not be satisfied so long as there remains anywhere a possible object of domination — a politically organised group of man, which by its very independence, challenges the conqueror's lust and power."[16] He further writes, "The most obvious the most ancient and also the crudest form of imperialism is military conquest."[17] This predatory instinct for conquest and power also led Machiavelli to stress that Republic and Monarchies both must have to expand their territory as a necessity. According to him territorial aggrandisement is of vital importance because if they do not expand they will expire. Hence predatory nature is most fundamental in imperialism of ancient and modern time.

This passion for territorial aggrandisement was treated as a sort of super-patriotism and principle of nationalism. Prof. Schuman has observed, "Patriotism and economic nationalism have contributed to policies of territorial aggrandisement on the part of the nation-states. These policies have, until recently led to most spectacular result in the backward regions of the globe, where native governments, have been unable to offer effective resistance to great powers. The latter have succeeded in partitioning most of the non-European world among themselves, some times by peaceful bargaining, some times by war."[18]

Imperialism was considered as a foremost nationalist doctrine. Power and dominion characterised the principle of nationalism of the imperial states and territorial possession was considered as a foremost national pride. As Bertrand Russell has put it, "National pride, as it exists now, is almost exclusively concerned with power and dominion, with the extent of territory that a nation owns and with its capacity for enforcing its will against the opposition of other nations."[19] Hence imperialism assumed a patriotic and nationalist nature in the process of its growth and development.

Intoxicated by the imperialistic vision, some nations in the recent past embarked upon an expansionist and annexationist policy with the argument that colonial possession was necessary for their surplus population. Japan took up this plea till 1941, because she wanted to dominate over foreign territory. Italy also claimed new territory as the narrow peninsula was unable to accommodate the teeming millions. This led to Japanese occupation of Korea, Formosa, Machuria, and the Italian conquest of Libya, Abyssinia and the Italian Somaliland. But the futility of this argument has been proved as in actual practice, a very small number of people leave their home country for settling in a colony. English men have gone to the Dominions in great numbers, but they have shown less interest in moving to colonial possessions. Of nearly 20,000,000 Europeans, who emigrated between 1880 to 1940, nearly 17,000,000 went to free nations of Western hemisphere.[20] Between 1925 and 1933 while Japan was trying to justify her cause on China with the population pressure argument less than 4% of her population increase of that period migrated to her own colonies.[21] During the last decade of her colonial empire, 1904-13, Germany sent only one out of 24,000 of her annual population increment to her colonies — in absolute numbers, about thirty persons a year.[22] Prof. Schuman writes, "Since most of the empires are located in tropical and subtropical areas, unsuitable for residence by the Europeans and since emigrants prefer to go to congenial lands of easy economic opportunity, there has been no appreciable outflow of population from the nation-states to their colonies."[23] He further writes, "The surplus population argument for imperialism has played its part in convincing patriots of the necessity of expansion, for reason, facts and logic are usually conspicuous by their absence in the mental process of emotional nationalists. It has, therefore, been utilized effectively by imperialists as a means of securing population support for their policies. But in view of the results, it can be regarded as an honestly and consciously formulated purpose behind the quest for empire only on the assumption that statesmen are imbeciles or mad men."[24] Thus annexationist nature of imperialism with its vices of exploiting and oppressing the subjugated people is quite evident from the above fact.

A critical analysis of the history of European imperialism shows that heavy industrialisation of the Western nations gave further impetus to the ugly nature of imperialism and its inherent vices. As indicated in the earlier chapter, industrial powers wanted raw materials to run their industries and side by side they also wanted to dispose off their industrial products. As Prof. Schuman has written that industrialisation led "the states to have colonies for the surplus goods and for the purchase of raw materials."[25] He has further written that "the great markets of Orient and Latin America soon become spheres of keen competition among the rival rational groups of entrepreneurs and exporters. The rich natural resources of Asia, Africa and Latin Americas were demanded in ever greater quantity to feed the seemingly insatiable hunger of the god of the machine."[26]

Keeping in view, the two problems — import of raw materials and export of finished products — the industrial powers wanted to establish colonies in the backward countries. The search for colony led the Western nations to pursue imperial policy towards the weaker and backward nations of Asia, Africa and Latin American countries. Dr. Shacht, German financier had pointed out, "The fight for raw materials played the most important part in the world politics and even greater role than before the war 1914." Of course Parker Moon holds a contrary view. He contends that no Imperial country, with the possible exception of Great Britain, can solely depend upon its colonial possessions for the supply of major portions of her raw materials. There is no truth in the fact that an imperial country receives most of the raw materials which its colonies produce. As he has written, "Raw materials in general are colourblind. They recognise no national flag. They follow the law of supply and demand and of distance and transportation costs. They obey economic rather than political control."[27]

However the great imperial powers made it their state policy to establish hegemony over the underdeveloped areas of the world and lord over the subject people for industrial and commercial gain. As Prof. Schuman has pointed out, "The backward areas of the earth — rich in resources or in labour power or in consumptive capacity, but poor in capital and underdeveloped industrially and commercially became happy hunting grounds for profit seekers of western capitalism. From Western Europe, from the U.S.A., from Western Japan, there poured forth a deluge of ships, goods and money, inundating the rest of the world."[28] Parker Moon has also observed, "Imperialism affords...marketing facilities for an industrial nation's good."[29]

An empire is required not only as an outlet for surplus goods but also as an outlet for surplus capital in the backward countries and make huge profits. As it is said, "It is not only or primarily trade that is desired, but opportunities for investment; finance is more concerned in the matter...."[30] Government agencies and diplomatic channels were used to persuade the backward countries to borrow money from advanced countries. The U.S.A. exerted a powerful influence over Central and South America as well as over other parts of the world by means of her vast investment. This kind of policy known as dollar diplomacy, was almost as effective as a foreign army of occupation. It is said that "if money talks, American dollar shouts." Almost all the backward countries of the world became the worst victims of this "dollar diplomacy" in modern times. Through the investment of huge capital, the European nations sought to control the economic and political institutions of the underdeveloped countries of the world. Speaking of this Western influence through capital investment, Morgenthau has observed, "Its outstanding modern example is what is called 'dollar diplomacy'. It has also played an important role in the history of British and French imperialism. British influence in Portugal since the beginning of the 18th century has been powerfully supported by economic control. British supremacy in the Arab world was the result of economic policies for which the term 'oil diplomacy' is not misplaced.... The predominant influence that France exercised in countries such as Rumania, in the period between two World Wars to a considerable extent, is based upon this factor."[31] Condemning it the same writer has also remarked, "Capitalistic societies...are unable to find within themselves sufficient markets for their products and sufficient investment for their capital. They have, therefore, a tendency to enslave even larger non-capitalist...areas in order to transform into markets for their surplus products and to give their surplus capital opportunities for investment."[32]

Of course it is argued that to satisfy the economic needs, the modern industrialised nations found no other alternative than pursuing imperialistic policy towards the backward countries of the world. Had they got these economic needs like place for investment of capital, markets for raw materials, fulfilled by other nations, they might not have pursued such imperialistic policies. It is said, "In our time we have heard it said that...German, Italian and Japanese imperialism was born out of economic needs, these countries would have refrained from imperialistic policies had they received loans, colonies and access to raw materials."[33]

However, it is a fact that imperialism at this stage assumed a beastly nature of falling upon the backward peoples of the globe and exploiting them in course of hunting markets for purchase of raw materials, sale of finished products and investment of surplus capital. This exploitation, the most heinous inherent vice of imperialism became a glaring phenomena of the period. Hobson, an uncompromising critic of imperialism has condemned such nature of imperialism as "rapacious and immoral."[34]

Apart from the economic nature of imperialism, as described above there is still another nature of imperialism which has received impetus from the false or vain prestige or glory of a nation. This nature of imperialism may be branded as vainglorious or vaunted nature of imperialism in which national prestige, obviously unwarranted and unreasonable, has played a significant role. Until World War-II prestige played an important role in the annexation of other people. Annexation or possession of colonies became a hallmark of respectability in the international world. It was believed that a state must achieve its "manifest destiny" or its "place in the Sun." Generations of English men gloried in the boast that "the sun never sets on British empire."[35] The English people were intoxicated by the dimension of the British empire. It is said, "Benito Mussolini loved to move his hand over the map of those expanses of African desert and hill-land that he had brought under the Italian flag. His chest expanded with his dominion."[36] Americans applauded the acquisition of territory that, at the turn of the century, made their country a world power. The European imperial powers held that land for flag flying may mean responsibility and expense rather than grandeur. But an analysis of imperialism shows that the desire for land and still more gold is the very essence of imperialism, which is embedded in the heart, from which the imperialists get optimum pleasure and pride. So their statement is nothing but a false show to hide the apparent vices, that are latent in their imperialist character. This national prestige, above all factors stimulated French imperialism of vaunted nature, in the Eastern Asia. As it is said, "The taproot French imperialism in the Far East from first to the last, was national pride — pride for culture, reputation, prestige and influence. This was the constant factor which ran through the Kaleidoscope of episodes of missionary dedication and daring, of naval coups and of private adventures."[37]

Speaking of the vices of imperialism Hans Kohn harped on the psychological distortion that the people of imperialist powers suffer from. As he has observed, "Besides the economic urge, psychological motives played a great role in imperialism — the lust for adventure and for power, the added prestige and glory which seemed to accrue from a vast colonial empire not only to the governing classes but even to the masses of the colonizing nations, the new sentiment of price and superiority which animated even the lowest members of the white races in their dealings with the backward races."[38] Thus vainglorious or vaunted nature of imperialism, which had its sway till World War-II cannot be overlooked.

To effect their ugly imperial design, the imperial powers mostly took recourse to war and aggression. They went on increasing their military power and fortifying their arsenals to reach their imperial goal. It is hence, befitting to say that imperialism is based on militarism. Hobson has rightly remarked, "The basis of imperialism is force and its instrument is military power. Imperialism and militarism support each other."[39] It has been further observed, "Militarism and imperialism clearly constitute an identical pattern of thought and behaviour."[40] This aggressive and military nature of imperialism has brought havoc to this world keeping world peace and order at stake. Laski has rightly said, "Imperialism necessarily involves war and an effective international order is incompatible with it."[41] Thus aggressive and militaristic nature of imperialism with its war and devastation, as its innate vices that has posed a severe threat to modern world, is a matter of grave concern.

Racial nature of modern imperialism, that involves the vices of hatred, ill-feeling and jealousy between the imperial powers and the subject peoples cannot be overlooked. The imperial powers look upon the subject people with much contempt and violence. To them, native races are uncivilized and barbaric. Out of such feeling they, obviously get prejudiced against the native races and feel ill at ease amidst them. The fact is evident from the statement of Elgin, "It is a terrible business, this living among the inferior races. I have seldom from man or woman since I came to East, heard a sentence which was reconcilable with the hypothesis that Christianity had ever come into the world."[42] Referring to the contemptuous attitude of the white races towards the subject people, Hans Kohn writes that the sentiment of pride and superiority animated white races in their dealing with the backward races.[43]

The policy of Apartheid or segregation, as pursued by the white races of South Africa, has driven the Negroes, Indians and other non-whites to the ghettoes. The situation worsened considerably since the end of World War-II. A few universities which were formally open to nonwhite races became increasingly closed to them. In 1958 there took place the Sharpeville massacre when 67 Negroes were shot to death in cold blood and many were seriously injured when Negroes protested against the law which compelled them to carry pass cards.

This racial policy of the imperial powers turn the native people hostile to them. In their attitude, the subject people become disrespectful and stubborn towards the white or imperial people. This was the main cause of all disaffection towards the British in India, for which a British people in India is said to have reported, "It is true that English are not loved by the native subjects in India."[44] Hence racial nature of imperialism, the source of all vices of disaffection and hatred between imperial power and the colonial people have divided the world into two enemy camps, leading to bloody wars, and violence.

The pseudo humanitarian consideration that the imperial powers claimed to express through the hackneyed phrase 'the white man's burden' or the 'imperial responsibility' as described earlier in this chapter was responsible for the rise of vices of imperialism. In 17th century, the missionary motive was an important factor of imperialism. The name of David Livingstone in Africa is the most outstanding name in the history of missionary empire builders. The London Missionary Society was closely linked up with the spread of British imperialism in Africa. Even Calvin Colidge, a former president of the U.S.A. said, "The legions which America sends forth are armed not with the sword but with the Cross."[45] General MacArthur advocated a similar policy in regard to Japan after the military defeat in 1945. Joseph Chamberlain, perhaps Britain's leading exponent of imperialism next to Disraeli declared in 1893, "It is our duty to take our share in the work of civilization in Africa."[46] Albert J. Beveridge, often regarded as the ablest defender of imperialism in the American Senate while explaining American responsibility said, "God has made us adepts in government that we may administer government among the savage and servile people to civilize them."[47]

But an analysis of imperialism today has revealed the fact that humanitarian programme of the imperial powers is nothing but a mockery to befool the anti-imperialist forces which became very active subsequently. It is often argued that the imperial nations opposed the work of humanitarian missionaries, for it might give the subject people a new dignity and consciousness against the Western imperial powers. Some times the missionaries were open or secret allies of imperialists as they received a warm welcome from the empire builders. It is also argued that humanitarianism was certainly not the original cause of imperialism but it is only an after thought. It is, in fact a programme of lip-service and dry sympathy to befool the anti-imperial section of the world. Visualising the glaring vices of pseudo-humanitarian imperialism, Prof. Schuman has observed that in imperial states profit motive and power motive are skillfully concealed in terms of humanitarianism, civilizing mission, religious conversion, and material benefits conferred upon the backward people.[48]

It is held that the imperial powers spent huge sum of money on humanitarian programme. But this is only to screen over the vices of imperialism of the Western powers. If they spent huge sums of money on humanitarian programme — on education, sanitation and general improvement of the subject people, why as per Julian Huxley's report, African infant mortality ranges from one in four to one in two, why every adult Negro is infested with one or more deadly kind of worms, usually including hook-worm and often with malaria? Why in some areas about 90% of the population suffer from venereal disease — a disease imported by the whiteman — gross malnutrition as well as vitamin deficiency? Why not even 1% of children of Africa do attend school? In the light of all these one cannot but agree with Prof. Schuman's remark that it is no more the purpose of imperialism to confer benefits upon its victims than to confer benefits upon the home country.[49] Raymond L. Buell also held the same view and declared, "It would be gross perversion of the fact to say that European and American imperialism was originally inspired by a desire to better the lives of the people, whom it forcibly subjected."[50]

Hence, despite all attempts to conceal its vices, imperialism, as a whole, stands for ruthless exploitation and political domination. Due to imperialistic design of the Western nations half the world's land area and one-third of human race had a colonial status in the mid 1920's.[51] Prof. Schuman condemned it saying "the new epoch entered upon the phase of armed combat among the empires for world supremacy."[52]

Since the sole motive of imperialism is profit, the imperial powers degrade the native people to the position of labourers and slaves with least consideration for them. As profit from colonies usually depended upon the use of native labour, imperialist powers force the natives to till the soil, dig for gold, gather rubber, hunt for ivory or collect coconuts. As it is said, "The colonial powers...through slavery, forced labour, heavy taxation, and the confiscation of land, succeeded in the mission of their profits."[53] It is also said, "Some times the natives were forced to give a share of the crops, some times the troops directed forced labour, some times a hut-tax or pol-tax was imposed, payable only in labour on in certain products. Some times native chieftains were rewarded according to their successes in mobilising their tribesmen for labour. Various types of punishment was inflicted on the native like lashing, mutilation, death, separation from wife and family, confiscation of land or exclusion from hunting grounds."[54]

The colonial people are virtually treated as slaves. The maintenance of an army and construction of prison houses are given top priority rather than the health and education of the colonial people. Raymond L. Buell has pointed out, "...the expenditure on education and health in the colonial areas are pitifully small...."[55] The white-settlers enjoy all protection and privileges to the exclusion of the local people. They occupy high military and administrative post and are paid high salaries. They too, take away the lion's share in everything and the colonial people lead a life of slavery and starvation. If the subject nations resist and revolt, they are suppressed ruthlessly. As it is remarked, "Government can only be carried on by force and tyranny. If its subjects view it with hostile eyes, they (the imperial powers) will so view...."[56]

Hence despite all defensive arguments, imperialism with its nefarious nature and hideous inherent vices, is a glaring phenomena of "domination and subjection,"[57] leading to oppression and exploitation of the backward peoples. It is a gross violation of the canons of humanism and justice that has tarnished the pages of the history of human civilization. We can best sum up its nature in the words of Hobson, who said, "...not withstanding the benefits conferred by...imperialism..., by its very nature is incompatible with democracy and self-government and little disposed to self-liquidation. The basis of imperialism is force and oppression."[58]

(iii) British Imperialism and Exploitation of India

Among all the imperial powers, the British had by far the largest imperial domain during the last two centuries. It did spread over six continents and seven seas and included within its frontiers something like one-fifth of the land area of the globe and one quarter of its population. It was then said that the British conquered an imperial domain upon which the sun never sets. The richest and the most populous unit of the empire was India,[59] which the British began to exploit without any regard for the interest of the Indians. Bipin Chandra Pal has pointed out, "The British were treating India as "Kamadhenu" or the milch cow of England."[60]

Early in the 17th century, trading ports were established along the coasts by the British East India Company, an organisation of private merchants, that received a Charter from the British Crown, giving it the monopoly of British trade with India and authorising it to rule over the natives within the sphere of its commercial operation. Since the disintegration of the empire of the Great Mogul, India had been divided into warring principalities in quarrels among whom the Europeans found an excellent opportunity for intervention. The British East India Company and the French East India Company became rivals for commercial and political supremacy, the former triumphing over the latter in the seven years war (1756-63) and taking over the functions of government in the portions of the country under its control. The British power gradually extended by conquest. In 1818 the Marahtta Confederacy of Princes was over-thrown and the Marahtta dominion in the Central and Western India was annexed by the Company. In 1849 the Sikhs of the Punjab were similarly conquered and brought under the British rule. A series of wars on the Eastern frontier culminated in the annexation of Burma in 1886. Beluchistan became a province of British India in 1903. This is how the British Empire grabbed India and made it its own crown.

As "India is by far the greatest market ever acquired as a colony by industrial empire,"[61] the British made enormous profit out of it. But she paid no heed for the material development of the people of India. She pursued a nefarious economic policy which was very regressive towards India but highly progressive for England. The whole economic set up of the country was up set. The economic development of India, particularly its masses was completely ignored. It was a period of abject poverty and starvation for India; but for England it was a period of tremendous progress. Hence during the very years after 1760 when the Britain was developing into the leading developed capitalist country of the world, India was developing into the leading backward colonial country of the world. In fact the two processes were interdependent in terms of cause and effect. The entire system of economic relationship between Britain and India involving trade, finance and technology, continuously developed India's colonial dependence and underdevelopment. India was bleeding under the British rule and whatever the British government did, did with a selfish motive.[62]

The military policy of the empire was more concerned with the security and stability of the British empire than with the maintenance of peace in India. The Indian army conducted a series of expeditions some times beyond the territory of India and the policy of expansion caused a constant rise in the military charges which was charged upon Indian exchequer. Hence it has been rightly observed, "India suffered in silence the military policies of Great Britain...the glaring fact was that much of the military needs of the whole British empire was met from the Indian resources."[63] With this extravagant military expenditure India's public debt was also mounting up. Hence, Dadabhai Naoroji, expressing his concern on India's public debt observed, "The public debt of India increased mainly due to English conquest in India and English wars abroad in the name of India.... The burden of all England's wars in Asia has been thrown on India's shoulder."[64]

The maintenance of English army in India was highly

expensive. This subject was discussed in the Congress Sessions and a comparative analysis reveals, "the German soldier costs Rs. 145/-, the French Rs. 185/- and English in England Rs. 285/- but in India Rs. 775/- a year."[65] This caused a continuous rise in India's debt.

Hence the British rule in India could never promote increasing wealth and prosperity, industrial expansion and rich harvests; neither it could provide even a full meal to each and all. Forty millions of people had only one meal a day and "the government did almost nothing to halt the growth of poverty."[66] In spite of their poverty under a very low per capita income, the people were, heavily taxed. There was a wide gap between India's per capita income and the per capita income in other countries by the end of 19th century. When the per capita income in Canada and Great Britain was £ 48 and £ 42 respectively in India it was officially estimated as £ 2.[67] the Government did not evolve any systematic method of taxation and it went on levying new taxes, the worst being the salt tax. Dadabhai Naoroji commenting on this said, "...The people were in such a wretched plight that they had nothing, the government could tax, and that government must therefore tax on absolute necessaries of life to an inordinate degree."[68]

Though the poverty of India was ascribed to many factors, such as decay of handicrafts, destruction of pre-British economic structure, disintegration of traditional social order, arrested nature of India's industrialisation, lack of enterprise etc., military policy and over taxation were the main factors.[69]

"Agriculture" says R.C. Datta, "as a source of income has not been widened under British administration". Yet as the government could not tax commerce at ease, the entire burden fell on agriculture. There was absolutely no improvement in agrarian relation nor in methods of production. The cultivators were heavily taxed, and were always on the brink of famine and starvation.[70] Moreover the method of assessment was defective. Hence it has been rightly observed, "The land tax, which was the most important source of revenue and the sheet anchor of Indian finance, was unpopular because of the mode of assessment."[71] The government even could introduce new taxes.

The rise of revenue assessment in one sub-district showed that from 66 P.C. in 1891, it was raised to 99 P.C. in the next year and 116 P.C. in the next.[72] The British introduced Zamindari and Ryotwari system in India. As a result the ordinary landowner was ruined by a triple burden, *i.e.*, tax to the government, to the Zamindar and to the moneylender — in the form of interest. Colonialism evolved a new structure of agrarian system where a number of intermediaries flourished and the cultivator at the bottom was squeezed.[73]

Industry was equally suppressed. Weaving was the main industry before the advent of the British. But here too, British interest dominated. The Indian interest was subordinated to that of Lancashire. The East India Company made a law that the silk weavers were to work for the Company only, which strangled the silk cotton industry of India.

The growth of Indian foreign trade was neither natural nor normal; it was artificially fostered to serve imperialism.[74] "The production of raw-material for British industries and the consumption of the British manufactures in India were the two-fold objects..."[75] of British commercial policy. The Indian markets were flooded with British goods. India became an exporting country of raw materials. The government to promote British interest, encouraged British export to India and discouraged Indian exports. Free trade was introduced between India and Britain. Dadabhai Naoroji commenting on this policy declared that there could be no free trade between India and England and observed, "It is like a race between a starving, exhausting, invalid and a strong man with a horse to ride on."[76] The difference between export and import which was some thing between three and four millions a year became 20 millions sterling after seventies and within 12 years of the change from company to the Crown, the economic drain from India became four-fold.[77] Hence Ranade observed that India had come to be regarded as a plantation, growing raw-products to be shipped by the British agents in British ships, to be worked into fabrics by British skill and capital and to be re-exported to the dependencies by the British farms in India and elsewhere. The infant industries of India had to compete with British products and the government did not give any protection. It was the tariff policy which convinced Indian people that British policies in India were basically guided by the British interest.[78]

After 1850 a very large amount of British capital was invested in railways and loaned to the Indian government. To render this capital secure from economic and political dangers, the British tightened its rule over India firmly than ever, which resulted in the further exploitation and oppression of the country. Not only this; the British also tried to perpetuate its rule over India to ensure repayment of its capital. This was frankly confessed by a contemporary civil servant of Bombay who wrote in 1880 that England "must keep India...because a vast amount of British capital has been sunk in the country, on the assurance of British rule being, humanly speaking, perpetual."[79]

The government was very keen on the expansion of Railways which were claimed as an index to economic development. But the Railways were not at all beneficial for India as the money invested, were borrowed from London market and the interest was charged on Indian revenues. Moreover, railways "facilitated penetration of Indian markets by foreign goods."[80] Hence it has been rightly observed, "foreign capital in Indian condition was not developing the country but exploiting it."[81]

Continuous famine added to the misery of the Indians. India passed through a series of famines, between 1897 and 1900 except in 1999. It is illustrative here to mention that between 1848 and 1878, the loss of population due to famine was nearly 20 millions.[82]

Thus when government became callous day by day and was merely talking of the bliss of the British rule, the poverty and misery of the Indian people reached the point of no return. Dadabhai Naoroji declared, "The chief cause of India's poverty, misery and all material evils is the exhaustion of its previous wealth, the continually increasing, exhausting and weakening drain from its annual production by the very excessive expenditure on the European portion of all its services and the burden of a large amount a year to be paid to foreign countries for interest in the public debt, which is chiefly caused by the British rule."[83]

The British government always followed a policy of economic exploitation, racial discrimination and autocratic administration towards India. Though the Queen's Proclamation laid much stress on "equality," in 1885, out of 900 civil servants only nine were Indians.[84] The covenanted services were of course open for Indians; but the prospects of pay and promotion were gloomy. Hence, educated Indians usually entered into the profession of law or became school teachers and clerks.

The government of India keeping the interest of cotton manufacturers of Manchester in view, abolished the cotton duties on imported textiles. Although the Manchester Chamber of Commerce alarmed by the growth of Indian cotton industries, during the Vice-royalty of Lord Northbrook pressed its demand for the abolition of such duty, it met with resistance from the government of India. The government of India, not prepared to sacrifice the revenue, contended "It is our duty to consider the subject with regard to the interest of India, that the removal of the import duty on cotton manufactures is not consistent with those interest."[85] Even Lord Northbrook protested against the insistence of the Home government to abolish it and resigned. But during the Vice-royalty of Lord Lytton, the cotton duty was abolished to the detriment of Indian interest. In this case the Viceroy over-ruled the majority decision of his Council.[86] Sir Erskin Parry has condemned the Viceroy's action as "unconstitutional and dangerous precedent."[87] Section 41 of Indian Council Act 1861, endowed the Viceroy with the power of over-ruling the Council decision only if the safety, tranquility or interests of the British-India or any part thereof, were or apprehended to be essentially affected.

The Vernacular Press Act or the Gagging Act of 1887 is another instance of anti-Indian and anti-people stand of the government of India. In order to contain, rather silence, the critical tone of the Vernacular Press that had become vociferous in publishing anti-Indian and anti-people policy of the government, magistrates were empowered with the previous sanction of the provincial government to demand of a printer or a publisher either to deposit security or to enter into a bond binding himself not to print or publish anything which is likely to incite feelings of disaffection towards the government. The government was even endowed with the authority to confiscate the plant and the deposit in the event of publication of materials that can be considered undesirable by it. Sir Erskin Parry branded it as a "retrograde and ill-conceived measure injurious to the further progress of India."[88] S.N. Banarjee described it as "A bolt from the blue."[89]

During Lord Lytton's time another anti-Indian Act was enacted, *i.e.*, Indian Arms Act, 1878. As per the Act, as far as Indians were concerned, to keep or bear or traffic in arms without licence, was considered a criminal offence, accompanied with punishment ranging to imprisonment up to a period of three years. In case of concealment or attempt at concealment, the term of imprisonment could be extended to seven years. Thus a discriminating policy in respect of Indian nationals was pursued in spite of the spirit of the Queen's Proclamation.

The Ilbert Bill controversy also revealed the discriminatory policy indulged in by the British government, and the British people in India. A bill was introduced on February 2, 1883 in the Legislative Council with the approval of the Home government to remove the racial discrimination in the matter of trial of Europeans by native judges such as district magistrates and Sessions judges outside the Presidency. Sir Ashley Eden, the Lieutenant Governor of Bengal realized, "There seems to be no sufficient reason why convenanted native civilians with the position and training of a District Magistrate or Sessions Judge should not exercise the jurisdiction over Europeans as is exercised by other member of the service."[90]

Yet there was opposition to it from the side of the merchants of Calcutta and planters of Bihar. Parties and entertainments, hosted by Lord Ripon, the then Viceroy, were boycotted by the British nationals. A 'Defence Association' was formed and donation to the sum of rupees one and half lakh[91] was raised to fight against the enactment of the Bill. Protest meetings were held and the Anglo-Indian Press notably the Englishman became hysterical. They argued, "Shall we be judged by the Nigger? Shall he send us to jail? Shall he be put in authority over us? Never, it is impossible ! Better that British rule in India should end than that we should be obliged to submit to such humiliating laws."[92] Ultimately, the bill was modified to the effect that the European offenders, when tried by the Indian District Magistrate or Sessions Judges could claim trial by a jury of which at least half the members should be Europeans or Americans.

Thus Indian masses rotted under the autocratic and despotic rule of the British. Justice and fair play for the Indians became a far cry. In every sphere of life they were looked down upon. Whenever they sought any relief, they met with utter gloom and despair. It has been rightly observed, "...the British India was ruled autocratically. At all levels from the Viceroy's Council down to the district, the system spurned any recourse to representative government...while inveighing against oriental despotism, the British had enacted one of their own."[93]

(iv) Swami Vivekananda on the Vices of Imperialism

Swami Vivekananda's world outlook went against the nefarious practices of British imperialism in India. He was not a politician, or a political philosopher but a great humanist. His humanistic bent of mind made him anti-imperialistic. The horrors of British imperialism in India overwhelmed him. Out of sheer agony he cried, "We three hundred and thirty millions of people have been ruled for about one and half centuries by a handful of foreigners who chose to walk over our prostrate bodies."[94] Again he cried, "...these few, standing on the necks of the masses of the people want to rule them."[95]

As a doyen of humanism and universalism, he believed in the basic principle of equality of all men and all nations and rejected outright domination of any nation by another. He wanted sincerely to awaken the whole mankind from ignorance and lassitude to the supreme height of divinity. As he said, "I am no preacher of any momentary social reform. I am not trying to remedy evils. I only ask you to go forward and to complete the practical realization of the scheme of human progress.... I only ask you to work to realize more and more the Vedantic ideal of the solidarity of man and his inborn divine nature.[96]

Swami Vivekananda discerned divinity in all men, irrespective of race, religion and sex. To him every man is imbued with divine nature. Divinity is inherent in man, however degraded and low he might appear to be. As he said, "The more I live the more I became convinced everyday that every human being is divine. In no man or woman, however vile, does that divinity die."[97] Addressing man again he said, "There is no God separate from you, no God higher than you. All the gods are little beings to you. All the ideas of God and Father in heaven, are but your own reflection. God Himself is your image. 'God created man after his own image.' That is wrong. Man created God after his own image. That is right. Throughout the universe we are creating gods after our own image."[98]

Swami Vivekananda was far above the dark hedges of racialism, sectarianism and personal God-head. He, rather believed in the absolute and impersonal God-head, as the only way leading to world peace and human progress. He has said, "The idea of the impersonal God-head gives the best rationale of ethics. The highest ethical doctrine teaches that we must love all men as ourselves. Now the idea of impersonal God-head teaches the solidarity of all life, the oneness of the universe and thus gives the reason why you should love all. Besides, it equips man with great strength, because he is made to stand without dependence — in the glory of his own soul, the infinite, the eternal and the deathless."[99] Hence Swami Vivekananda, condemned the narrow selfish motives like territorial expansion, racial segregation, colonial and imperialistic establishments. His aim was to submerge the whole world with the idea of oneness of soul of the universe and bridge the gulf among men and nations of the world. Unity of the universe, despite the diversity of race, religion and culture that he described as, "the highest point in every science — physical or spiritual,"[100] and "the mission and destiny of humanity"[101] was his prime concern. As Dr. I. Chelishev has rightly observed, "Vivekananda's impassioned call to the general fraternity and unity of India's people, to the abolition of religious and communal discord and of caste prejudices, were combined with an appeal for peace and friendship among all the nations of the world, which is the cornerstone of Indian tradition, the main content of Indian national character.

Urging people to be fearless and bold to fight the dark forces for their happiness and better future, Vivekananda declared that it was hopeless and useless to try and rule the world by force of arms. Vivekananda called for establishment of friendly relations between all nations, based on love of man for each other...."[102]

The outword glamour of the Western civilization, initially captivated his eyes. He thought of the West as the mine of human progress and centre of human civilization. But such high notion of the West soon turned pale and bleak, the moment he began to see the Western civilization from close quarters and in its clear perspective. In the words of Sister Nivedita, "When he (Swami Vivekananda) first landed in the West, he was greatly attracted, as his letter shows, by the apparent democracy of conditions there. Later in 1900 he had a clearer view of the underlying selfishness of capital, and struggle for privilege and confided to someone that Western life now looked to him like hell."[103] It is further pointed out, "Vivekananda's searching mind noticed many things, that were hidden under the outword glitter of Western civilization. In his public statement, Swami Vivekananda relentlessly exposed bourgeois chauvinism, capitalist competition, the quest for profit, the fabulous luxury of a handful of exploiters and disastrous impoverishment and rightlessness of the millions of toilers, religious and racial discrimination, intrigue and violence."[104]

In contrast to some Indian leaders of that age, who believed in the miracles of Western civilization, Swami Vivekananda realized its deficiencies. He pointed out that the wealth and power in the European countries are in the hands of a few, who do not work, but manipulate the works of millions of human beings. By this power, they deluge the earth with blood. "That class of people, in the name of politics" said Swami Vivekananda, "rob others and swell themselves by sucking the very blood of the masses."[105] He also pointed out that Western capitalistic system of economy provides tremendous impetus to imperialism. It tends to enslave the masses of mankind. This tendency to enslave humanity finds its fullest manifestation in imperialism. Hence he condemned capitalistic system of economy saying that "in Western capitalistic system if one becomes rich, thousands at the same time become poorer and poorer. It makes, ultimately, mass of human being mere slaves, crushed under the heels...."[106] He boldly declared that the constitutional government, the individual right and liberty and parliament are nothing but a farce or a mockery in the West. Behind everything there is but slavery of the masses. Therefore he said, "No greater upheaval for the establishment of right and liberty can be imagined than the war for abolition of slavery."[107]

During his first visit to United States, Swami Vivekananda proclaimed it to be the homeland of freedom. But coming to known more intimately the order of things in that country, underneath which the force of imperialism was latently active, he realized the shallowness and hollowness of such freedom. With his microscopic eye as he discovered the strong undercurrent of imperialism in the whole system of the country, he was soon disillusioned. He was indignant at the power of money, the unlimited rule of the financial plutocracy and its uncurbed drive for riches and political supremacy. He declared openly "Old conception of America as the future hope of emancipated mankind, were wrong."[108]

Swami Vivekananda condemned outright the Western imperialistic greed for wealth and power, their cruelty and brutality, their competition and rivalry. He said, "Europe is trying to solve the problem as to how much a man can have, how much more power a man can possess by hook or crook, by some means or other. Competition — cruel, cold and heartless — is the law of Europe."[109] He also said, "...in the West the old order of things is vanishing, giving way to a new order of things, which is worship of gold...the worship of Mammon,... competition and gold...."[110] He warned the Western states that all centres from which such ideas as amassing wealth at all costs and carrying on government by force, sprang up, will very soon become the centres of crumble and fall.[111] He also warned that "no nation, however strong can stand on such foundation and the history of the world tells us that all that has such foundations, are dead and gone."[112] He further warned that no civilization can flourish with greed, violence and brutality or on the blood of man. Bloodshed has never served as foundation of any world famous civilization. Love and charity, on the other hand, have served, in all ages, as the foundations of all great cultures and civilizations of the world. "Unless we look charitably" said Swami Vivekananda, "no civilization can lift its head." "The first step towards that" said he, "is to look charitably and kindly upon others."[113]

The imperial powers, always sought to promote their own racial or national interest. Blind to the interest of the universe, they seek their individual or personal interest in all cases. But Swami Vivekananda's world outlook and cosmopolitanism was so high that he always thought beyond his nation and race. He called upon the nation-states of Europe to feel concerned about states and races beyond their national boundary. As he said, "The solution of any problem can never be attained on racial or national or narrow grounds. Every idea has to become broad till it covers the whole of this world, every aspiration must go on increasing, till it has engulfed the whole humanity, nay, the whole of life within its scope."[114]

As a lover of mankind Swami Vivekananda decided to devote all his energies to emancipate the Indians from the slavery of the British imperialism and lift it to the height of its own glory. As a Sannyasin, he felt it to be his sole responsibility to elevate the poor and downtrodden masses of India and bring about their social, political and spiritual well being. As he said, "For the good of the many, for the happiness of the many, is the Sannyasin born. His life is all vain, indeed, who, embracing Sannyasa, forgets this ideal. The Sannyasin, verily, is born into this world to lay down his life for others...."[115] He thought that the yellow robe of a Sannyasin is the armour to put up a fight against the evils of imperialism for ameliorating the lot of the downtrodden masses. "Our yellow robe" said he, "is the robe of death on the field of battle."[116]

Swami Vivekananda realized that Western imperialism is the root-cause of all India's misery and misery of mankind as a whole. It is the foremost cause of poverty and starvation of the native people of the world. This developed his anti-imperial attitude towards the West. The Western imperialistic civilization was his main target of attack. He did not like to attack Western imperialism directly firstly because it would go against the images of a Sannyasin like him and secondly, it would draw the attention of the British imperial power, to arrest him. However, his policy was to arouse the people of India and the world as a whole and make anti-imperial forces very active against the West, behind the scene as a monk than openly on the stage as a politician or a political philosopher. As he has said, "We are to put the chemicals together, the crystallisation will be done according to the law of nature. Work hard and be steady...keep the motto before you : Elevation of the masses."[117]

Swami Vivekananda felt that century-long foreign domination and oppression had taken away the strength and fearlessness from the body and mind of the Indians. Their backbone is broken and they are like downtrodden worms. Fear and weakness had gripped them and they succumbed to British imperialism. If they overcome their fear and weakness the mighty edifice of Western imperialism that overshadowed the glory of human life, shall crumble. Only then can Indians enjoy the dawn of a new life, full of liberty and right. He was intensely devoted to the cause of the emancipation of the poor and the downtrodden, and wanted to arouse the leonine spirit in the man by encouraging the concept of strength and fearlessness. This concept of strength and fearlessness according to him was to serve as the greatest weapon against all the evils of Western imperialism. He exhorted his countrymen that strength is life, strength is felicity; weakness is constant strain and misery, weakness is death.[118]

Again he said, "Fear is the source of degradation. It is fear that brings misery, fear that brings death, fear that breeds evil."[119] He also exhorted that strength is the best anti-dote to all tyranny and oppression. It is the best medicine for all world's diseases.[120] So he fervently called upon his people, "My children, what I want is muscles of iron and nerves of steel, inside which dwells a mind of the same material, that of which the thunderbolt is made. Strength, manhood, Khatriya-Virjya + Brahma-Teja — This is what I want."[121] He also said, "We want faith in our ownselves. Strength is life, weakness is death. We are the

Almighty, deathless. It is by losing this idea that the country has gone to ruin."[122]

As a spiritual man Swami Vivekananda not only stood for spiritual freedom or emancipation of soul from the bondages of Maya, but also wanted the political emancipation from the clutches of imperialism. To him this political emancipation was an essential condition for spiritual freedom. So struggle for freedom is a conditional feature of his concept of freedom. Hence he stated, "There is to be found in every religion, the manifestation of this struggle towards freedom. It is the ground work of all morality, of selfishness, which means getting rid of idea that men are the same as their little body."[123] Thus for Swami Vivekananda political emancipation from the grip of imperialism was the basis of spiritual freedom and for the sake of spiritual freedom people must be politically free from imperialistic domination.

Swami Vivekananda's concept of strength and fearlessness along with his concept of freedom and right instilled a sense of vigour and energy into the minds of the people of India to rise against Western imperialism. They thought in terms of emancipation of their nation, shaking off the morass and prostration that beset them. In the words of I.P. Chelisheve, "...Vivekananda objectively helped to popularise among masses the idea of liberation and imparted to these ideas the nature of sacred religious duty."[124]

In the words of Sister Nivedita, "India was the queen of his adoration". Naturally, therefore, Swami Vivekananda preferred to make India, suffering under the fetters of Western imperialism, the first step for the liberation of the world. His reaction against British imperialism is his reaction against the Western imperialism as a whole, that gripped the colonial people and debased the whole mankind. All his writings and speeches, therefore, have tremendous relevance not only for India, his own country, but for the whole world as well.[125] Not only India, but the whole world was his concern. As he once said that he belonged to the world as much as he belonged to India.[126] Again he said, "the universe is my country."[127]

Swami Vivekananda's comprehensive personality could well understand the cause of India's misery and hardship. The imperial power, always guided by the profit motive, did not pay any attention to the miserable plight of the native people. He fully believed that "When a modern state asserts its title to a backward region, the property of the inhabitants is...exploited by the conquering state for its own private profit."[128] Swami Vivekananda condemned the British as the blood-sucker and said that no good can be expected when the main policy is blood-sucking.[129] Criticising bitterly the exploitative nature of British imperialism he also wrote "The British in the past achieved her prosperity by cutting the throat of her fellow-men in Spain and in modern time she achieved her prosperity by keeping her feet on the neck of millions of poor and innocent Asiatics."[130]

He felt that the earlier regimes were better for the people as it did not seek to take away everything they had. There was some justice and liberty in it.[131] But British regime, on the contrary became ruthlessly and mercilessly exploitative. Justice and liberty were misnomers under British regime. Referring to history he said, "There never was a time in the world's history when there was so much robbery, high-handedness, tyranny of the strong over the weak...."[132]

The British imperial policy was to make England prosperous at the cost of India. British industries flourished and all the indigenous industries collapsed. Crores of rupees flowed to England and India became impoverished day by day. An English official graphically summed up the situation, "Our system acts very much like a sponge drawing up all these good things from the banks of the Ganges and squeezing them, drawn on the banks of the Thames."[133] For example, from 1770, the Company sent out of Bengal nearly 35% of its net revenue in form of goods. Moreover, the officials of the Company sent out large sums of their illegal incomes, extorted from Indian merchants, officials and Zamindars. The wealth, drained out of India, played an important part in financing Britain's imperialist development. It has been estimated that it constituted nearly 2% of Britain's national income at that time. Swami Vivekananda reacted to it severely and cried out "They have sucked out blood, they have carried away with them millions of our money, while our people have starved."[134] In a fit of anger he also cursed the British : "...now the Chinaman is the vengeance that will fall upon them : if Chinese rose today and swept the English into the sea, as they well deserve, it would be no more than justice."[135]

Swami Vivekananda realized that the white-settlers enjoyed the protection and privileges to the exclusion of the native people. They occupied high military and administrative posts and were paid highly. They took away the lion-share in everything. If at all the Indians got any economic benefit, they paid it back in terms of taxes to the imperial treasury. Thus prevailed perpetual poverty among the people. Swami Vivekananda felt agitated against the British barbaric imperial policy and poured out the venoms : "By their cruelty they degraded the populace.... If a man cannot believe in the vengeance of God, he certainly cannot deny the vengeance of History. And it will soon come upon the English : they have their heels on our necks; they have sucked the last drop of our blood for their own pleasure."[136] Keeping the British in view, he also said, "God will have vengeance. You may not see it in religions, you may not see it in politics, but you must see it in history, and as it has been; it will come to pass. If you grind down the people, you will suffer."[137]

In spite of the terrible famines, that engulfed India from time to time as the fatal consequence of the British rule and its policy of exploitation, India was still a populous country. But the British imperial government paid no attention to their welfare at all. The bulk of wealth of the country was diverted to the West rather than benefiting the masses. As a result, people of India remained half-starved and half-naked. This poverty resulted in poor health, low life expectancy and infant mortality. The poverty of the people found its visible manifestation in the series of famines which ravaged the country during the second half of 19th century. Twenty years from 1860 to 1908 were the years of famine. Nearly 29 million people died during famines from 1854 to 1901. These famines revealed that poverty and chronic starvation had taken firm roots in colonial India. Swami

Vivekananda criticized this inhuman policy of British imperialism and said, "Indian labour and produce can support five times as many people as there are now in India with comfort, if the whole thing is not taken from them."[138] Thus he blamed the British for all the famines that took away heavy toll of innocent Indian lives, which was their deliberate creation.

British ruthless exploitation left the poor masses of India under the monstrous jaws of poverty and hunger. Under such perpetual strain of poverty and chronic stress of hunger, people lost their manhood, all worth and importance of life, and succumbed to slavery at the feet of the British people. Referring to it Swami Vivekananda said, "They have been compelled to be merely hewers of wood and drawers of water...they are made to believe that they are born as slaves, born as hewers of wood and drawers of water."[139]

The maintenance of imperial army and construction of prison houses were given top priorities rather than health and education of the people. War expenses were justified. These were charged upon the Indian heads on the ground that such wars were waged in the interest of India and her territory. In his speech at Mansion House on November 9, 1978, Disraeli justified the 2nd Afghan war and its expenses on the ground that "the frontier of India was haphazard and not a scientific one."[140] No attention was paid to remove illiteracy and promote education in the country. Expenses on education and health of the people of India was insignificant. Illiteracy and lack of proper education killed the incentive of the people of India in all spheres of life and they succumbed to dullness and servitude. Swami Vivekananda deplored it saying, "We have been slaves forever, it has never been given to the masses of India to express their inner light...."[141] Suggesting rejuvenation of the spirit of the Indian masses as a measure for regeneration, he said, "The only service to be done for our people is to give them education to develop their lost individuality."[142] He further said that education is the primary need of the Indians as "through education comes faith and strength in one's ownself."[143]

The British government provided only such type of education that would enable Indians to keep the imperial machinery running. Criticising such education Swami Vivekananda said that the whole system of British education in India is "bent upon getting a thirty-rupee clerkship, or at best becoming a lawyer — the height of young India's ambition...."[144] Pointing out the futility of British education in India, he further said that "fifty years of such education has not produced one original man in the three Presidencies. Every man of originality, that has been produced, has been educated elsewhere and not in this country, or they have gone to the old universities once more to cleanse themselves of superstitions."[145]

The British crushed the native resistance by force, resorted to dishonest tactics to break their unity and make them loyal to the Empire. It made a farce of popular participation in the imperial government and took every care to retain the real power in its own hand. Native culture and language were replaced by those of the West to establish and maintain their racial superiority. Dadabhai Naoroji resented it severely and expressed, "British rule was everlasting, increasing and everyday increasing foreign invasion that was utterly, though gradually, destroying the country."[146] Resenting and challenging the policy of racial superiority of the British in strong terms, Swami Vivekananda said, "Only just a while ago they were savage...the vermin crawled on the ladies bodies...and they scented themselves to disguise the abominable odour of their persons.... Most horrible! Even now, they are barely emerging from barbarism."[147] Again he said, "They are quite savage. The frightful cold, the want and privation of their northern climate has made them wild. They only think to kill."[148] Swami Vivekananda, thus wanted to demoralise the British imperialism by harping on the false sense of superiority of the British race and culture that sought to perpetuate itself on the Indian soil.

Swami Vivekananda believed like Prof. Morgenthau, "In truth military imperialism seeks military conquest; economic imperialism, economic exploitation of the people; cultural imperialism, the displacement of one culture by another — but always, as means to the same imperialistic end. That end is the overthrow of the statusquo."[149] He also fully believed that "cultural imperialism is the most subtle...the most successful of all imperialistic policies. It aims not at the conquest of territory or at the control of economic life but at the conquest of and control of minds of men..."[150] for fortification of the imperial regime. He considered the impact of Western cultural imperialism as the most unfortunate for Asian people themselves.[151] He could well imagine the fatal consequence, if the Eastern spiritual culture is replaced by the Western materialistic one. In order to make people of Asia know their spiritual culture and keep their special identity from that of the West, he said, "The voice of Asia is the voice of Religion. The voice of Europe is the voice of politics."[152] Drawing the attention of the Asian people to the merits of Eastern spiritual culture over the political culture of the West he said, "Man cannot be made virtuous by act of Parliament : the Chinese experience it before you. And that is why religion is of deeper importance than politics, since it goes to the root and deals with the essential of conduct."[153]

To Swami Vivekananda spiritual culture "is not necessarily bound up with rules and rituals, superstitions and dogmas, but it is a sublime culture, capable of giving peace and solace to the distressed and afflicted."[154] So when the whole of Europe will be tired and fade up amidst the turmoils of materialistic civilization and culture they will turn to East for spiritual solace and peace. Drinking deep the ambrosia of Eastern spiritualism, they will get their wounds, caused by the wine of Western materialistic culture, healed up.

Swami Vivekananda was confident that Western cultural imperialism can never succeed to efface the spiritual culture from the soil and transplant itself on it. Time and again "the Western conquerors, sword in hand came to demonstrate to the children of the sages that they were mere barbarians, a race of dreamers, that their religions was but mythology and God and soul and everything they had been struggling for, were mere words without meaning, that the thousands of years of struggle, the thousands of years of endless renunciation, had all been in vain...."[155] But to Swami Vivekananda it was all meaningless blusterings of the Western conquerors. It was their vainglorious shouts. History shows that India's spiritual culture is still unconquered. It is still indomitable and invincible. It has met the ravages of thousands of foreign invasions, but still it is unmoved and unchallenged. As he has said, "Wave after wave had flooded the land, breaking and crushing everything for hundreds of years. The sword flashed and the victors rent the skies of India with their shouts, but the flood of foreign culture have subsided, leaving the national culture unchanged. Indian culture cannot be killed. Deathless it stands. It will stand so long as that spiritualism remains as the background, so long as her people do not give up their spirituality."[156] He further assured that "India is immortal, her culture is immortal so long as she persists her search for God."[157]

The whole system of imperial administration was based upon the theory of punishment. Imperial laws were highly repressive. Freedom of the people was muzzled and individual right was a far cry. Swami Vivekananda was very pained to observe it and said, "For writing a few words of innocent criticism men are being hurried to transportation for life, others imprisoned without any trial; nobody knows when his body will be off."[158]

Swami Vivekananda deplored the way the imperial power did let loose the reign of terror in India to intimidate the masses and continue its imperial domination. Despotism, oppression and brutality of the imperial power tormented him. Loss of diginity and individuality at the altar of imperial slavery shocked him all the more. Monopolisation by the white-settlers of all the opportunities in every sphere was an intolerable sight for him. The brutality and atrocity heaped upon the innocent masses, for slightest error or violation of the imperial rule, caught him to the quick. As he said, "There has been reign of terror in India for years. The English soldiers are killing our men and outraging our women – only to be sent home with passage and pension at our expense. We are in a terrible gloom."[159] He further said, "For centuries people have been taught theories of degradation. They have been told that they are nothing. The masses have been told all over the world that they are not human beings. They have been so frightened for centuries, till they have nearly become animals."[160]

The imperial power loudly repeated the slogans of its civilizing mission and raising of the standard of living of the colonial people to deceive the world opinion. But its whole policy was confined to enslave the subject people by shutting all doors of enlightenment. Life of the people was altogether dull and sluggish. Describing the miserable lot of masses Dadabhai Naoroji remarked, "Indians were mere helots. They were worse than the American slaves, for the latter were at least taken care of by their masters, whose property they were."[161] The sole aim of the British was to debase the conscience and destroy and moral fibres of the people so as to continue their over-lordship over them. Marie Louis Burke condemned the so-called policy of civilizing India in strong terms, "The English used three B's — Bible, brandy and bayonets in civilizing India."[162] Swami Vivekananda resented the education policy of the British and said that the British government made huge profit in India but spent much less even than Russia on education.[163] He further said, "We do not get that education which the common people in the West do get...."[164] Criticising the achievement of the British India in educational sphere he said, "A few hundred modernized half-educated and denationalized men are all the show of modern British India — nothing else."[165]

There was no room for humanitarianism in British imperialism. The predatory instinct of the ancient wild races found its fullest manifestation in it. As it is said, "While the Christian missionaries were trying to save the souls of the people, the British officials and traders were extorting what wealth they could with little concern for the welfare of the inhabitants."[166] Heathen murdering was the legitimate pastime for them. But to deceive the world opinion, they took the plea of friendship and love with the colonial people. They appeared to be very kind and sympathetic but in their heart they were quite the opposite. They were not really so as they appeared to be. In words they seemed to be very kind and considerate but in action they were very cruel and monstrous. Referring to it Swami Vivekananda said, "It is their hunger that has civilized them.... The love of man is on their lips, in their hearts there is nothing but evil and every violence."[167] Such duplicity of the

British, has been depicted by Nehru as "We find British imperialism inclining more and more towards fascist powers, though the language it uses, as its old habits, is democratic in texture and pious in tone. And because of this contradiction between words and deeds, British prestige has sunk in Europe and the world."[168]

British imperialism created an atmosphere of suspicion, hatred and jealousy between the imperial power and the people of India. Pretention and treachery characterized the imperial administration. Swami Vivekananda observed, "There is love on their lips. But in heart there is evil and every violence. In the plea of love, they cut our throat."[169] As a lover of mankind Swami Vivekananda said that this heinous act of cut-throatism of Western imperialism would never go scott free. It would suffer vengeance of God and have its deplorable fall very soon. Subsequently Gandhi also got annoyed with the British blood-sucking policy who in a fit of anger said, "I have no doubt whatsoever that...England will have to answer, if there is God, for this crime against humanity, which is perhaps unequalled in history."[170]

Swami Vivekananda considered the British to be the worst of all imperial powers to whose attack and exploitation, India had been subjected in the past. India had been conquered time and again by several imperial powers. They came slaughtering the Hindus, but they left behind them so many beautiful places and monuments that are part of India's art and architecture. But to Swami Vivekananda the British left nothing behind them but mounds of broken brandy bottles[171] and heaps of skeletons of those who died of poverty and hunger.

To Swami Vivekananda British imperialism was best known for its cruelty and barbarity. It paid no attention to the grievances of the poor and distressed. They lived with maximum comfort and luxury when the hungry masses cried for a piece of bread. Such brutish cruelty and callousness characterised the whole system of British imperialism in India. Explaining it he said, "They ground down poor people for their own wealth. They heard not the voice of distress. They ate from the gold and silver when the Indian cried for bread."[172]

Imperialism created racial barriers, strained human relations, stunted social progress and marred human happiness. It resulted in social chaos and conflicts that divided the whole human society into various warring camps — the whites and non-whites or the Christians and the heathens. Swami Vivekananda had been much disturbed particularly by the racial discrimination of the West against the Negroes. He voiced his grave concern against it and said that though the position of the Negroes has improved after the abolition of the institution of slavery, their position in human society was still deplorable. They are treated very harshly by the white people. As he pointed out, "Their lives are of no value; they are burnt alive on mere pretences. They are shot down without any law for their murders; for they are niggers, they are not human beings, they are not even animals."[173] An ardent lover of mankind he could not tolerate such a situation. His very slogan 'free men in the free society' held out a severe threat to Western imperialism.

Swami Vivekananda hated most the diplomacy coercion and military force that are the true accompaniments to imperialism. He realized that the path of imperialism is red with blood of the victims. The imperial powers sought to impose their will over the weaker nations through force, fraud or violence. They pursued the most nefarious policy of exploitation forgetting all canons of morality and justice. War and aggression seemed to them to be the only means for the attainment of their end. All these wounded the heart of Swami Vivekananda. He expressed his mental agony after returning from a tour of an European country; "Europe resembled a military camp. Everywhere the stretch of war." His mental agony is marked further when he said, "Everyday we read of Christian nations acquiring land by bloodshed."[174] As a prophetic visionary he cautioned Europe that relished imperialism as her way of life and said, "It is hopeless and perfectly useless to attempt to govern mankind with sword. ...the very centres from which such ideas as government by force sprang up, are very first centres to degrade and degenerate and crumble to pieces. Europe...will crumble to dust...if she is not...to change her...."[175]

Thus though Swami Vivekananda was a mystic par excellence

his deep sense of humanism and universalism imbibed from the Hindu scriptures — the Vedas, the Upanishads, the Gita etc., reacted severely against the Western imperialistic policy in general and British imperialism in particular.

To sum up, Swami Vivekananda as an impassioned nationalist was a bitter critic of imperialism and condemned outright the imperialistic greed of the West. India's poverty and backwardness he considered to be the direct consequence of British imperialistic exploitation. As a lover of mankind as a whole he earnestly desired liberation of all peoples and all nations all over the world, from the clutches of imperialism. Hence he advocated shedding of fearlessness and commencement of struggle for the liberation of India from the grip of imperialism. He called upon the Indians to cultivate muscles of iron and nerves of steel to put an end to British imperialism.

REFERENCES

1. Moritz Gulia, *Encyclopaedia of Social Science*, Vol. VII, p. 605.
2. Charles A. Beard, *American Foreign Policy in the Making*, p. 113.
3. Parker T. Moon, *Imperialism and World Politics*, p. 33.
4. George Lichtheim, *Imperialism*, p. 9.
5. H.J. Laski, *A Grammar of Politics*, p. 222.
6. J.A. Hobson, *Imperialism, A Study*, p. 112.
7. William Ebenstein, *Today's Ism*, p. 637.
8. F.L. Schuman, *Imperialism and World Politics*, p. 420.
9. *Ibid.*, p. 426.
10. Charles Hodges, *The Background of International Relations*, pp. 421-22.
11. H.J. Laski, *A Grammar of Politics*, p. 283.
12. Hons J. Morgenthau, *Politics Among Nations*, p. 59.
13. *Ibid.*, p. 53.
14. L.C.A. Knowles, *Economic Development of Great Britain in 19th Century*, p. 307.
15. F.L. Schuman, *International Politics*, pp. 511-12.
16. Hans J. Morgenthau, *Politics Among Nations*, p. 69.
17. *Ibid.*, p. 72.

18. F.L. Schuman, *International Politics,* p. 511.
19. Bertrand Russell, *Political Ideals,* p. 73.
20. H. Arthursteiner, *Principles and Problems of International Relations,* pp. 145-46.
21. Grover Clark, *The Balance Sheet of Imperialism : Facts and Figures on Colonies,* p. 10.
22. L.S. Amery, *The German Colonial Claim,* p. 79.
23. F.L. Schuman, *International Politics,* p. 536.
24. *Ibid.,* p. 536.
25. *Ibid.,* p. 538.
26. *Ibid.,* p. 515.
27. Parker T. Moon, *Imperialism and World Politics,* p. 349.
28. F.L. Schuman, *International Politics,* p. 516.
29. Parker T. Moon, *Imperialism and World Politics,* p. 349.
30. Bertrand Russell, *Political Ideals,* p. 72.
31. Hans J. Morgenthau, *Politics Among Nations,* p. 72.
32. *Ibid.,* p. 62.
33. *Ibid.,* p. 66.
34. J.A. Hobson, *Imperialism, A Study,* p. 285.
35. The English Workers of 19th Century at times preferred to speak of "the empire on which the sun never sets and wages never rise."
36. Quoted in Palmer and Perkins, *International Relations,* p. 164.
37. John F. Cady, *The Roots of French Imperialism in Eastern Asia,* pp. 294-95.
38. Quoted in Palmer and Perkins, *International Relations,* p. 164.
39. J.A. Hobson, *Imperialism, A Study,* p. 287.
40. Winslow, *The Pattern of Imperialism,* p. 227.
41. H.J. Laski, *The State in Theory and Practice,* p. 243.
42. Lord Elgin, *Report,* p. 30
43. Quoted in Palmer and Perkins, *International Relations,* p. 164.
44. Quoted in Dr. Tarachand, *History of Freedom Movement,* Vol. II, p. 493.
45. Quoted in Palmer and Perkins, *International Relations,* p. 186.
46. *Ibid.,* p. 186.
47. Speech in the Senate, January 9, 1900, *The Record of American Diplomacy,* New York, Alfred A. Knopf, 1964, p. 385.

48. F.L. Schuman, *International Politics*, p. 535.
49. F.L. Schuman, *Imperialism and World Politics*, p. 426.
50. Raymond L. Buell, *International Relation*, p. 318.
51. Parker T. Moon, *Imperialism and World Politics*, p. 553.
52. F.L. Schuman, *International Politics*, p. 516.
53. Palmer and Perkins, *International Relations*, p. 173.
54. *Ibid.*, p. 174.
55. Raymond L. Buell, *International Relations*, p. 353.
56. Bertrand Russell, *Political Ideals*, p. 69.
57. George Lichtheim, *Imperialism*, p. 9.
58. J.A. Hobson, *Imperialism, A Study*, p. 287.
59. F.L. Schuman, *International Politics*, p. 517.
60. B.C. Pal, *The Rise and Growth of Economic Nationalism in India*, p. 41.
61. Parker T. Moon, *Imperialism in World Politics*, p. 520.
62. Bipin Chandra and Others, *Freedom Struggle*, pp. 16-17.
63. M.N. Das, *Indian National Congress Vrs. The British*, Vol. I, pp. 6-7.
64. Dadabhai Naoroji, *Poverty and UnBritish Rule in India*, p. 185.
65. Pattabhi Sitaramaya, *The History of Indian National Congress*, Vol. I, p. 13.
66. M.N. Das, *Indian National Congress Vrs. The British*, Vol. I, p. 16.
67. R.C. Datta, *The Economic History of India*, Vol. II, p. vii.
68. Dadabhai Naoroji, *Poverty and UnBritish Rule in India*, p. 190.
69. M.N. Das, *Indian National Congress Vrs. The British*, p. 6.
70. R.C. Datta, *The Economic History of India*, Vol. II, p. 10.
71. M.N. Das, *Indian National Congress Vrs, The British*, Vol. I, p. 9.
72. Pattabhi Sitaramaya, *The History of Indian National Congress*, Vol. I, p. 43.
73. B.C. Pal, *Freedom Struggle*, p. 19.
74. *Ibid.*, p. 21.
75. R.C. Datta, *The Economic History of India*, p. 7.
76. Dadabhai Naoroji, *Poverty and UnBritish Rule in India*, Vol. II, pp. 248-49.
77. R.C. Datta, *The Economic History of India*, Vol. II, pp. 248-49.
78. M.G. Ranade, *Essays in Indian Economics*, p. 150.
79. Quoted in Bipin Chandra, *Freedom Struggle*, p. 14.

80. Bipin Chandra, *Nationalism and Colonialism in Modern India*, p. 108.
81. *Ibid.*, p. 110.
82. M.N. Das, *Indian National Congress Vrs. The British*, Vol. I, p. 16.
83. Dadabhai Naoroji, *Poverty and UnBritish Rule in India*, p. 133.
84. M.N. Das, *Indian National Congress Vrs. The British*, Vol. I, p. 16.
85. Culled from B.L. Grover, *A New Look on Modern Indian History*, p. 275.
86. *Ibid.*, p. 276.
87. *Ibid.*, p. 276.
88. *Ibid.*, p. 278.
89. *Ibid.*, p. 278.
90. *Ibid.*, p. 285.
91. *Ibid.*, p. 284.
92. *Ibid.*, p. 285.
93. Anil Seal, *The Emergence of Indian Nationalism*, pp. 5-6.
94. *Lectures From Colombo to Almora*, p. 93.
95. *Ibid.*, p. 58.
96. *Ibid.*, p. 99.
97. *Complete Works of Swami Vivekananda*, Vol. III, p. 186.
98. *Ibid.*, p. 24.
99. *Nationalistic and Religious Lectures of Swami Vivekananda*, p. 22.
100. *Complete Works of Swami Vivekananda*, Vol. III, p. 439.
101. *Ibid.*, p. 202.
102. *Swami Vivekananda — Studies in Soviet Union*, Published on 150th Birth Anniversary of Ramkrishna, p. 217.
103. *Complete Works of Sister Nivedita*, Vol. I, p. 201.
104. *Swami Vivekananda — Studies in Soviet Union*, p. 215.
105. *Complete Works of Swami Vivekananda*, Vol. III, p. 158.
106. *Ibid.*, Vol. II, p. 96.
107. *Lectures From Colombo to Almora*, p. 119.
108. *Swami Vivekananda, Studies in Soviet Union*, p. 216.
109. *Lectures From Colombo to Almora*, p. 109.
110. *Ibid.*, p. 353.
111. *Ibid.*, p. 60

112. *Ibid.*, p. 353.
113. *Ibid.*, p. 90.
114. *Ibid.*, p. 177.
115. *Complete Works of Swami Vivekananda,* Vol. VI, p. 511.
116. *Ibid.*, Vol. VIII, p. 522.
117. *Ibid.*, Vol. V, p. 29.
118. *Ibid.*, Vol. II, p. 3.
119. *Ibid.*, Vol. III, 160.
120. *Ibid.*, Vol. II, p. 201.
121. *Ibid.*, Vol. V, p. 117.
122. *Ibid.*, Vol. V, p. 332.
123. Quoted in *Swami Vivekananda — Studies of Soviet Union,* p. 219.
124. *Swami Vivekananda — Studies of Soviet Union,* p. 34.
125. *Proletariat! Win Equal Rights,* p. VI.
126. *Complete Works of Swami Vivekananda,* Vol. V, pp. 95-96.
127. *Ibid.*, Vol. V, p. 92.
128. F.L. Schuman, *International Politics,* p. 535.
129. *Complete Works of Swami Vivekananda,* Vol. VIII, p. 476.
130. *Ibid.*, Vol. III, p. 474.
131. *Ibid.*, Vol. VIII, p. 476.
132. *Swami Vivekananda — Studies of Soviet Union,* p. 120.
133. Peter Heehs, *Freedom Struggle,* p. 20.
134. *Complete Works of Swami Vivekananda,* Vol. VII, p. 280.
135. *Ibid.*, Vol. VII, p. 280.
136. *Ibid.*, Vol. VII, p. 280.
137. *Ibid.*, Vol. VII, p. 279.
138. *Ibid.*, Vol. VIII, p. 476.
139. *Lectures from Colombo to Almora,* pp. 94-95.
140. Hans J. Morgenthau, *Politics Among Nations,* p. 46.
141. *Complete Works of Swami Vivekananda,* Vol. IV, p. 481.
142. *Ibid.*, Vol. IV, p. 362.
143. *Ibid.*, Vol. IV, p. 433.
144. *Ibid.*, Vol. V, p. 10.
145. *Ibid.*, Vol. III, p. 301.
146. Dadabhai Naoroji, *Poverty and UnBritish Rule in India,* p. 60.

147. *Complete Works of Swami Vivekananda,* Vol. VII, p. 278.
148. *Ibid.,* Vol. VII, p. 279.
149. Hans J. Morgenthau, *Politics Among Nations,* pp. 71-72.
150. *Ibid.,* p. 74.
151. K.M. Panikkar, *Asia and Western Dominance,* p. 50.
152. Swami Gambhirananda, *Life of Swami Vivekananda,* p. 114.
153. *Complete Works of Swami Vivekananda,* Vol. V, p. 200.
154. *Ibid.,* Vol. III, p. 169.
155. *Ibid.,* Vol. IV, p. 158.
156. *Ibid.,* Vol. IV, pp. 159-60.
157. Swami Gambhirananda, *Life of Swami Vivekananda,* p. 114.
158. *Complete Works of Swami Vivekananda,* Vol. VIII, p. 476.
159. *Ibid.,* Vol. VIII, p. 477.
160. *Ibid.,* Vol. III, p. 224.
161. Dadabhai Naoroji, *Poverty and UnBritish Rule in India,* p. 60.
162. Marie Louis Burke, *Swami Vivekananda in America,* p. 535.
163. *Complete Works of Swami Vivekananda,* Vol. III, p. 290.
164. *Ibid.,* Vol. V, pp. 461-62.
165. *Ibid.,* Vol. VIII, pp. 475-76.
166. Palmer and Perkins, *International Relations,* p. 437.
167. *Complete Works of Swami Vivekananda,* Vol. VII, p. 278.
168. Nehru, *Indian Independence and Social Revolution,* p. 52.
169. *Complete Works of Swami Vivekananda,* Vol. VIII, p. 279.
170. Quoted in P.T. Moon, *Imperialism in World Politics,* p. 290.
171. *Complete Works of Swami Vivekananda,* Vol. VIII, pp. 279-80.
172. *Ibid.,* Vol. VII, p. 279.
173. Quoted in Swami Vivekananda — *Studies in Soviet Union,* Published on 150th Birth Anniversary of Sri Ramkrishna, p. 216.
174. *Complete Works of Swami Vivekananda,* Vol. II, p. 483.
175. *Lectures From Colombo to Almora,* p. 60.

8

Nationalism of Swami Vivekananda, Aurobindo and Gandhi

(i) Introduction

Modern Indian history is replete with the struggle of many great champions of nationalism of the soil. But all those who championed the cause of nationalism and spearheaded the national movement did not have an identical objective, nor subscribed to identical technique. The moderate nationalists who espoused the cause of nationalism in India through the Indian National Congress had a moderate objective and they sought to lead the National Movement to a destination, opposed to that of the extremists or militant nationalists. The moderate nationalists made it their destination to please and placate, to petition, pray the British so as to get their blessing in form of some reformation in the system of British rule in India. While pining for India's progress and prosperity they did not look beyond the reformed and expanded Governor General's and Governors' Council and introduction of popular representation. Besides, their vision was limited by paltry concessions in the form of simultaneous conduct of civil service examination in London and India, reduction of salt-duty, curtailment of military and civil expenditure, and separation of executive from judiciary etc.[1] W.C. Banarjee the first President of the Indian National Congress expressing his objective in his Presidential address said, "All we ask is that the basis of the government should be widened and the people should have proper and legitimate share in it."[2] This pining for paltry reforms is further evident from the observation of Sir S.N. Banarjee, who said, "It is not Home Rule or parliamentary institutions we want, our humble prayer is that we should be associated with our rulers and only with a limited measure with the government of the country."[3]

As against the moderates the extremists of the militant nationalists pitched their ambition on Swaraj or complete self-government. As political realists they realized that a colonial and imperial power, accustomed to the privileges of governing colonies and exploiting their economy, cannot be expected to renounce its privileges. Such expectation on the part of the colonies will seal their own doom. Hence they put forth their goal of Swaraj or Purna Swaraj. B.G. Tilak one of the extremist nationalists gave the slogan, "Swaraj is my birth-right and I shall have it."[4] Aurobindo another stalwart of extremism also voiced, "Our ideal is Swaraj or absolute autonomy, freedom from foreign control.... We reject the claim of aliens to force upon us...."[5] Thus, the ambition for Swaraj became the burning passion of all extremist nationalists who championed the cause of "Home Rule." They considered Swaraj or self-rule as a moral necessity and the Dharma of all self-respecting man. Without Swaraj, they felt, right ordering of society could never be attained. Without Swaraj life was not worth-while and the enrichment of the community was next to impossible. As they said, "We demand Swaraj as it is the foundation...of our future prosperity."[6]

Thus, the moderate and the extremist nationalists of India had no identical objective. Their aim and objective differed and differed their plan of action.

(ii) Identical Objective

Swami Vivekananda, Aurobindo and Gandhi — the three stalwarts of Indian national movement had identical aim and objective. Though they belonged to three different periods and phases of the growth of Indian nationalism — Swami Vivekananda of pre-moderate period, Aurobindo of extremist phase and Gandhi of Gandhian age, all of them had an identical objective. They cherished in the core of their heart the goal of complete Swaraj or full-freedom for India — their motherland and worked for the same mission. According to them freedom or Swaraj is the birth-right of every nation. It is needed for the proliferation of national energy and fulfilment of national ideal.

It is too as they held, the social, political and spiritual necessity for man to have a wholesome and balanced life.

Swami Vivekananda the earliest of these nationalists, in order to arouse passions for freedom among his people said that freedom is the sole craving of the universe. Whole universe in its constant motion represents the dominant quest for freedom.[7] Freedom is the life-force, the essence of the universe. 'It is the motive of the universe, it is the goal of the universe'.[8] Various sounds and sights of the universe are the manifestations of its craze to reach its goal of freedom.

Everything and every being according to Swami Vivekananda are the manifestation of freedom and they feel unremitting urge to be free. Freedom is the destination towards which everything moves. As he said, "Everything that we perceive around us is struggling towards freedom, from the atom to the man, from the insentient lifeless particle of matter to the highest existence on earth, the human soul. The universe is in fact the result of this struggle for freedom."[9] Hence, freedom is the ultimate goal of nature and consciously or unconsciously everything sentient or insentient is struggling for the attainment of this goal.

What is true of all sentient and insentient beings is more true of man. Man, according to him is the final manifestation of passion for freedom. As he said, "The universal struggle for freedom attains its highest expression in man, in the conscious desire to be free."[10] Not only man is the highest expression of freedom and is fired by consummate desire to be free; he aspires for complete freedom. Complete freedom is essential for the attainment of perfection of man. Accordingly Swami Vivekananda said, "To be more free is the goal of all our efforts, for only in perfect freedom can there be perfection."[11]

Highlighting this individual freedom Swami Vivekananda said that it is indispensable for the realisation of one's personality in social, political and economic spheres. He, therefore, wanted to make freedom as the natural possession of all individuals. He desired that every individual must cultivate a free body, mind and spirit. As he said, "Liberty does not certainly mean the absence of obstacles in the path of misappropriation of wealth etc. by you and me, but it is our natural right to be allowed to use our own body, intelligence or wealth according to our will without doing any harm to others and all the members of the society ought to have same opportunity for obtaining wealth, education or knowledge."[12]

Swami Vivekananda regarded liberty or freedom as the only condition of growth.[13] He said, "To advance towards freedom — physical, mental and spiritual and help others to do so is the supreme prize of man. Those social rules which stand in the way of the unfoldment of this freedom are injurious and steps should be taken to destroy them speedily. Those institutions should be encouraged by which men advance in the path of freedom."[14]

This freedom, according to Swami Vivekananda in all spheres — physical, mental and spiritual is the watchword of the Upanishads. He wanted to inspire his countrymen with this message of the Upanishads and said, "Freedom is the watchword. Be free! a free body, a free mind and a free soul! That is what I have felt all my life."[15]

Swami Vivekananda thus not only aroused passion for freedom among his countrymen; he also made them realise the fact that freedom of the individual in social, political and economic spheres is not possible without political freedom of the country. Political freedom of the country is the root of all liberty and right of the individual. So Swami Vivekananda in his plan of nationalism visualised political freedom of the country as his sole aim and objective. It was not only his avowed goal; he fervently sought to make it also the goal of his countrymen and inspired them to reach the goal. As he said, "Arise and awake and stop not till the goal is reached. Arise and awake! Awake from the hypnotism of weakness..... Too much of inactivity, too much of weakness, too much of hypnotism has been and is upon our race. O ye modern Hindus, dehypnotise yourself...power will come, glory will come and everything that is excellent will come...."[16] Again he said, "Arise, awake, sleep no more; within each of you there is the power to remove all wants and miseries.... If you think that infinite power...indomitable energy lie within you, you can reach the goal."[17]

To Swami Vivekananda, freedom is the life-force of every

race or nation. In freedom lies its longevity. Without freedom no race, no nation can survive on earth. As he said, "Liberty in thought and action is the only condition of life, growth and well-being; where it does not exist the man, the race, the nation must go down."[18] As an impassioned humanist he earnestly hoped that the freedom which dawned in America on 4th July 1776 would become universal in the world.

According to Swami Vivekananda India is the fountainhead of spiritualism for the whole world. In all ages of history India has played her spiritual role as a spiritual guide of the whole humanity. But since India suffers from her political degeneration under British imperialism she has forgotten her traditional role. In order to resume her role of the glorious past said Swami Vivekananda, she must be awakened and led to reach the goal of her national freedom. Without her political freedom she cannot play her role for the world.

Whole world according to Swami Vivekananda, is under the severe stress of materialism of the West, and eagerly awaits India for solace. So it is high time for India to study the world phenomena and be ready to pick up again her age-old customary duty of supplying spiritual solace to the world. He said, "The eyes of the whole world are now turned towards this land of India for spiritual food; and India has to provide it for all the races. Here alone is the best ideal for mankind; and the Western scholars are now striving to grasp the ideal, enshrined in our Sanskrit literature and philosophy and which has been the characteristic of India all through the ages."[19] Hence, Swami Vivekananda cherished the goal of national freedom of India as much for herself as for the world as a whole.

According to Swami Vivekananda, the way to reach the goal of national freedom is full of hazards and hurdles. It involves the problems of life and death. Yet, we must be up and doing on our way to reach the goal. On the way we must not succumb to despair. As he said, "Be not in despair, the way is very difficult like walking on the edge of a razor; yet despair not, arise, awake and find the goal."[20]

Aurobindo, though younger to Swami Vivekananda by almost a decade outlived him by almost a half century. He developed his flair for patriotism and nationalism from his Cambridge days. But he was deeply committed to the cause of Swaraj right since the partition of Bengal in 1905. The central theme of his nationalism was the extinction of the British rule from the soil of India. Hence, his political goal was Swaraj or self-rule *i.e.,* absolute freedom of the country.

Aurobindo like Swami Vivekananda believed that Swaraj or national independence is the social political and religious necessity of the people of India. The realisation of this Swaraj will infuse new life into the nation, changing her whole fabric. All ills that crippled her will be soon eradicated and India, as a nation, will recover her soul, arise once again to her pristine glory and greatness, occupying the most esteemed place in the hierarchy of nations of the world. As he said, "Swaraj is the life-belt, Swaraj the pilot, Swaraj the star of guidance.... She must change the rags of the past so that her beauty may be re-adorned. She must alter her bodily appearance so that her soul may be newly expressed."[21]

As Swami Vivekananda so also Aurobindo believed that India had an appointed mission to lead the world. But she cannot fulfil this mission "Overshadowed by the foreign power and foreign civilization." He believed that India had not only a glorious past and a rich and dazzling heritage; an equally glorious future awaits her. This glorious future consisted in providing spiritual leadership to the world. But this spiritual leadership she cannot provide to the world, herself in bondage, in the grip of political subjugation. Therefore, in the interest of the humanity she must be free. As he said, "God has set apart India as the fountain-head of holy spirituality and he will never suffer that fountain to run dry. Therefore, Swaraj has been revealed to us. By our political freedom, we shall once more recover our spiritual freedom. Once more in the land of the saints and sages will burn up the fire of ancient Yogo and the hearts of her people will be lifted up into the neighbourhood of the eternal."[22] He further said, "If India does not become free, men will not be free. People of other countries think only of their own interests : people of India even when they think about India, think of the whole world."[23]

Besides, Aurobindo like Swami Vivekananda pitched his ambition on Swaraj as stated previously, on the ground that individual, social and national development are inconceivable without Swaraj. Swaraj held the key to all types and forms of development and progress. India can be rescued from the state of decline and decadence, poverty and underdevelopment, misery and exploitation and ushered into a better world and better life with a brighter future only through Swaraj. Hence, he pined for "Swaraj as the object of political endeavour — Swaraj as the only remedy for all our ills — Swaraj as the one demand nothing sort of which will satisfy the people."[24]

Aurobindo was much concerned with Swaraj, the national freedom, the ultimate end of which as he explained to his people, was "entire and radical change of the system of government", acquisition of political power, attainment of self-government, "substitution for the autocratic bureaucracy," "Perfect national liberty," "...full, vigorous and noble realisation of its national existence" and "a free national government unhampered even in the least degree by foreign control."[25]

Aurobindo felt concerned about Swaraj because like Swami Vivekananda he believed that national liberty is the precondition of individual liberty. Aurobindo also, in this light went a step further and said that national liberty is not only the precondition of individual liberty; it is also the precondition of the liberty of the whole world. Neither individual nor liberty on the global scale can be conceived without national liberty or Swaraj. National liberty or Swaraj promotes on the one hand individual liberty and on the other, liberty at the international level. National liberty or Swaraj makes possible life of the individual, his unrestrained development and the development of an international community. As he said, "We advocate the struggle for Swaraj first because liberty is in itself a necessity of national life; secondly because liberty is the first indispensable condition of national development; thirdly because in the next great stage in human progress, it is not a material but a spiritual, moral and physical advance that has to be made and for this a free Asia and in Asia a free India must take the lead and liberty is, therefore worth-striving for, for the world's sake. India must have Swaraj in order to live; she must have Swaraj in order to live well and happily; she must have Swaraj in order to live for the world; not as a slave for the material and political benefit of a single purse-proud and selfish nation but as a free people for the spiritual and intellectual benefit of the human race."[26]

Like Swami Vivekananda, Aurobindo, highlighting liberty as the vital force of national life held that "Liberty is the life-breath of a nation."[27] Again he held that "liberty is the first requisite for the sound health and vigorous life of nation."[28] But a foreign despotism said Aurobindo is an unnatural condition that bring about unhealthy and unnatural condition among the subject people that lead to fatal decay and disorganisation of the nation."[29]

Like Swami Vivekananda Aurobindo also exhorted his people that the way leading to Swaraj is not strewn with flowers but with deadly thorns causing bloodshed and death. So, to pluck the flower of Swaraj involves sacrifice and fortitude at the altar of the motherland. As he said, "The work of national emancipation is a great holy Yajna — liberty is the fruit we seek from the sacrifice and the motherland, the great goddess to whom we offer it."[30]

Thus Aurobindo and Swami Vivekananda held identical objective on Swaraj or national freedom. Their whole theory of nationalism centres round this objective, that inspired the people of pre-independent India to the very core of their heart, paving the path for National Freedom in the long run.

Gandhi is considered as the father of the nation — Indian nation. He was more than half a decade younger to Swami Vivekananda but a few years older to Aurobindo, like both passionately yearned for the termination of British rule over India and India's attainment of nationhood. Gandhi of course remained a loyalist till 1919. He assisted the British government in times of war and got *Kaisar-i-Hind* Gold Medal and other war decorations. He acted as the recruiting sergeant during the First World War. On his return to India in 1915, he met Lord Wellingdon the then Governor of Bombay, at latter's invitation and was said, "I ask nothing of you. I would like you to come and see me whenever you propose to take any step concerning the government."[31] Mr. Edwin S. Montague after his interview with Gandhi in November 1917 entered in his diary about Gandhi, "All he wants is that we should get India on our side. He wants the millions of India to leap to the assistance of the British throne."[32] He believed in British sense of justice and fair play and aspired to win British favour for India as a part of British empire. Declaring his loyalty to British Raj he said, "It gives me the greatest pleasure to redeclare my loyalty to this British empire and my loyalty is based on very selfish grounds. I discovered that the British empire had certain ideals with which I have fallen in love and one of these ideals is that every subject of the British empire has fresh scope possible for his energies and honour and whatever he thinks due to his conscience...and I have more than once said, the government is best which governs least. And I have found that it is possible for me to be governed least under the British Empire."[33] In 1918 Gandhi extending his helping hand to the Empire said, "To help the Empire was to help India on the road to independence."[34] He rebelled against the British Empire only in 1919, after the Amritsar massacre and the British policy on Khilafat issue.

However, Gandhi gave a serious thought to the question of Swaraj in 1908 in his book "Hind Swaraj or Indian Home Rule." But the Swaraj as the goal of his nationalism during those days differed from Swami Vivekananda and Aurobindo. Whereas Swami Vivekananda and Aurobindo thought of Swaraj in the sense of complete freedom from foreign domination and political power in the hands of the Indian people, Gandhi in his Hind Swaraj observed, "It is Swaraj when we learn to rule ourselves.... It is not necessary for us to have as our goal and expulsion of the English. If the English become Indianised we can accommodate them."[35] He of course said, "Real Home-Rule is self-rule or self-control," but he qualified it by the rider "What we want to do should be done not because we object to English or because we want to retaliate but because it is our duty to do so.... I bear no enmity towards the English."[36]

Even when Gandhi started his Non-cooperation Movement against the British imperialistic rule, he did not think in terms of completely snapping all relationship with the British authorities : his ambition during those days were "self-government within British Empire, if possible, and without it, if necessary." Even at the Calcutta Session of the Congress in 1928 Gandhi was not prepared to make complete independence or severance of all British connection, the goal of the party. Dominion status or self-government within the British empire still had its appeal for him. It was only at Amritsar in the year 1929 that Gandhi moved the resolution on complete independence or Purna Swaraj. However, once this decision was taken by the Congress, Gandhi became very serious and sincere for winning independence or Swaraj. During his conversation with Louis Fischer he said emphatically, "I am not interested in independence after the war, I want independence now."[37] Since then the issue of independence or Swaraj as the goal of his nationalism became almost an obsession with him that changed his plan of action to a considerable extent. He accepted the truth of the famous Mantra given by Tilak that Swaraj is the birth right of the Indians. He declared that "Spreading disaffection against the British government in India was the Dharma of Indians"[38] and with a great psychological insight he also warned the imperialist countries that domination over others would jeopardize the moral fibre of great powers."

Gandhi felt that nationhood could not be achieved with the efforts of a few nationalist leaders and the rich, educated elites. Unless the poor masses — the teeming millions of India awake, India cannot reach the goal of freedom. So to arouse the passion for nationhood among the poor masses, he insisted on "Poorman's Swaraj" that recognises no discrimination nor any differentiation between man and man, but establishes popular sovereignty, *i.e.*, power to the people at large. He also believed that true nationhood could not be achieved unless the mass is awakened to a state of dignity and democratic consciousness of their right and privileges. Keeping these facts in view he wrote in 1930, "The Swaraj of my dream recognises no race or religious distinction. Nor it is to be the monopoly of the lettered persons nor yet of moneyed men. Swaraj is to be for all including the farmer, emphatically including the maimed, the starving toiling millions"[39] He also wrote in 1931 "The Swaraj of my dream is the poor man's Swaraj. The necessaries of life should be enjoyed by you in common with those enjoyed by the princes and the moneyed man.... You ought to get all the ordinary amenities of life that a richman enjoys. I have not the slightest doubt that Swaraj is not Purna Swaraj until these amenities are guaranteed to you under it."[40]

Drawing the attention of the people to the prevailing British injustice and for strengthening the forces of Swaraj in India, he also said, "A government that does not ensure this much of privilege, is not government. It is anarchy. Such government must be resisted."[41] Thus, Swaraj as the goal of Gandhi's nationalism seeks welfare of the downtrodden — the starving masses in order that the mass will take interest in it and rise against British imperialism. Regarding the welfare scheme of Gandhi's Swaraj, V.P. Varma has observed, "Swaraj of Gandhi's nationalism is to champion the interest of the downtrodden and starving millions."[42]

While thinking of nationhood of India, Gandhi laid much stress on economic freedom rather than mere political freedom of the country. He felt that political freedom has no meaning for the people, if they go about naked and starving. This political freedom is bound to remain mere philosophical abstraction unless the vast masses have some gainful employment.[43] So there should be adequate work for the workless. He stressed on the basic economic fact that man must have to eat. Freedom from want was the first article of his economic theory and he worked throughout his life to free Indians from the degeneration of poverty.[44]

Gandhi also felt that acquisition of nationhood does not only mean abolition of foreign domination from India, but throwing off, all shackles by every section of people and in every sphere of society. As he said, "I am not interested in freeing India merely from the British yoke. I am bent upon freeing India from any yoke whatsoever. I have no desire to exchange King Log for King Stork."[45]

Gandhi like Swami Vivekananda and Aurobindo also advocated individual freedom as a stimulus for national freedom.

He declared, "Individual freedom alone can make society progressive. If it is wrested from him, he becomes an automaton and society is ruined. No society can possibly be built on a denial of individual freedom. It is contrary to the very nature of man."[46] Again he declared, "The person or a citizen must be held inviolate. It can only be touched to arrest or the prevent violence."[47] He also highlighted freedom of speech as a part of individual liberty that instigated the people for national freedom. In 1940 when India had been made a party to the European war against her will, Gandhi strongly pleaded for freedom, freedom of speech during war time, because he felt that, "Freedom of speech of the individual is the foundation of Swaraj."[48]

Gandhi, like both Swami Vivekananda and Aurobindo exhorted his countrymen that without suffering and sacrifice attainment of nationhood is a day-dream. Intense suffering and prolonged struggle is the only way to national emancipation. It would be chimerical to believe that nationhood can be acquired as a gift. As he said, "Nations are born out of travail and suffering."[49] He also frequently said, "Freedom is the fruit of suffering."[50] Glorifying death and incarceration for the cause of national liberation he also said, "Death in the fight is a deliverance and prison gate way to liberty."[51]

Thus national freedom that Gandhi accepted as "the part of Truth which is God"[52] was also the goal of nationalism of Swami Vivekananda and Aurobindo. These outstanding trio of Indian National Movement accepted attainment of nationhood by India as a great gospel and did their best for the fulfilment of this goal.

(iii) Spiritual Basis of Nationalism

'Nationalism' as Prof. Laski has pointed out, 'implies the sense of a special unity, which marks off those who share in it from the rest of mankind.'[53] This special unity must be of universal importance. It must be conducive to high moral social life to attain such universality. But unless nationalism has a sound moral basis, which is consistent with the very ideals of human existence, it cannot achieve universality nor can the nation thrive long. History abounds with the phenomena of meteoric fall of many great nations, that moved R.N. Tagore to write, "As I look back on the stretch of past years, I find the crumbling ruins of a proud civilization lying heaped as garbage out of history!...."[54] But Indian nationalism on the other hand, based on spiritualism — the very essential vitality of human existence — becomes universal despite time and space. During different ages of history devastating storms of terrible dimension have swept over the nation, but it has not hurt the very soul or spirit of India. In spite of barbaric foreign invasions that brought in its train unprecedented oppression and massacre, India has retained her spirit ever clear and ever clean. However what India has sustained is external injury to her national life, which she has recouped in no time. Therefore, Jawaharlal Nehru writes, "India has been throughout the ages distinctively Indian, with the same national heritage and the same set of moral and mental qualities."[55] He further writes, "Overwhelmed again and again, her spirit was never conquered even today when she appears to be a play thing of a proud conqueror, she remains unsubdued and unconquered."[56]

The great trio-Swami Vivekananda, Aurobindo and Gandhi believed in the spiritual heritage of India. They advocated spiritualism that forms the very core of Indian national life, as the basis of Indian nationalism. Swami Vivekananda said that "Each nation has its own peculiarity and individuality, with which it is born. In it lies the backbone, the foundation or the bedrock of its national life. Religion and spirituality form that foundation and national backbone of India."[57] He further said that politics, military power, commercial supremacy, mechanical genius etc. are the fields of specialisation for different nations. But spirituality has always been the way of life in India.[58]

Explaining the above facts Swami Vivekananda said that the Indians understand religion more than anything else. They can understand even politics only if it is given through religion. Religious sentiment of the people of India is very soft and sensitive. It reacts at very slightest stroke. Religion is a matter of special interest for them. From time immemorial the religious ideal has been dominating India in every sphere of life. "This is the line of life : this is the line of growth and this is the line of well-being in India."[59] So uplift of India is to be attempted through vitalising her religion that forms the very soul of the nation. If attempt is made to throw off religion from India and assume politics as the centre of national life, the consequence will be the total extinction of nation. So Swami Vivekananda, emphasised on the influence of spirit over politics. He said, "Great indeed are the manifestations of muscular power and marvellous the manifestations of intellect expressing themselves through machines by the appliances of science; yet none of these is more potent than the influence which the spirit exerts upon the world."[60] So politics is to be made subordinate to spiritualism in India. He asked all the nationalist leaders to deluge India with spiritual ideas before flooding India with politics. He said, "We may be degraded and degenerated now, but however degraded and degenerated we may be we can become great if only we begin to work in right earnest on behalf of our religion."[61] Hence according to him spirituality but not politics, is our national ideal; in it lies the vitality of our nation. As long as we keep faith in this spirituality as the life-force of our nation, no force on earth can subdue us or kill. As he said, "This, therefore, the vitality of the race and so long as that remains, there is no power under the sun that can kill the race."[62]

According to Swami Vivekananda our motherland is the land of religion and spirituality. India is still the first and foremost of all the nations of the world in this respect.[63] Down the ages India has become faithful to her national ideal and that is why the Hindus have still survived as a nation in spite of numerous calamities and foreign invasions in the past. As he said, "Wave after wave of barbarian conquest has rolled over this devoted land of ours. "Allah Ho Akbar!" has rent the skies for hundreds of years and no Hindu knew what moment would be his last. This is the most suffering and the most subjugated of all the historic lands of the world. Yet we still stand practically the same race...."[64]

He further said that our ancestors, finding that the quest for nature through external investigation is useless, turned their attention inward. They focused their attention on this inward quest, which is grander, infinitely higher, infinitely more blissful till it has become our sacred nature. Thus the name of religion and Hindu have become one. This is our national characteristic, the source of all vitality of the race.[65]

Swami Vivekananda realised that spirituality is the only unifying force in India — a land of diverse faith, belief, sect and creed. If all religious forces stand united on the point of spirituality, national unity will be strengthened. That is why he said, "National Union in India must be gathering up of its scattered spiritual forces. A nation in India must be a union of those whose hearts beat to the same tune."[66]

In his plan of nationalism Swami Vivekananda sought to deluge the world with spiritualism to bring new life and new vitality to the West and other nations of the world, groaning under the materialistic civilization of the West. As he said, "In this land are, still, religion and spirituality, the foundations which will have to over-flow and flood the world to bring new life and new vitality to the Western and other nations, which are now almost borne down, half killed, and degraded by political ambitions and social scheming."[67]

If we analyse the life of Aurobindo, we find that during the first phase of his life as a nationalist, he thought of unifying India through politics and made politics to be the basis of his nationalism. That's why, he took active part in struggle against the British Empire. He believed it to be a means to the end. But towards 1909 his view of life changed. As M.N. Roy writes, "A year and half in jail (1908-1909) brought the philosopher and ascetic in Aurobindo Ghose...but he practically retired from politics."[68] R.R. Diwakar has also observed, "Aurobindo emerged from Alipore a changed man,.... Jail had not only given him a vision of God but had also transformed him from a flaming agitator into a mature and serene political philosopher."[69] He realised that political unification of India is impossible without spiritual unification. Like Swami Vivekananda he believed that religion and spirituality is the very backbone of Indian national life. So if India is to awake, she is to awake through her vital force of religion and spirituality. Since then he quietly retired from the arena of Indian politics to Pondicherry for spiritual practices and sadhana.

On the issue of spiritualism as the basis of Indian nationalism Aurobindo reached the acme of glory. As M.N. Roy writes, "What child birth was to North cliff 'Spiritualism is to our political anchorite'. Aurobindo Ghose...of course the cult of spiritualism is no monopoly of Aurobindo. In India apostle of this cult are as plentiful as its devotees. But Aurobindo represents the acme of the cult so much so that he is not content with the quixotic programme of spiritualising politics, but would make socio-political progress of the Indian people conditional upon attaining 'Supramental State'."[70]

Aurobindo like Swami Vivekananda, identified Hinduism with Indian nationalism. Ramsay Mac Donald observed, "Aurobindo Ghose has made the connection between his devout Hinduism and his strenuous nationalism clear. Man has to fulfil God, he has written, and that is only possible fulfilling himself, this again being possible only through nationality. On this religious conception rests his belief in Swadeshi and his desire to see the English predominance in India ended."[71]

Swami Vivekananda subordinated politics to religion. As he said "If you succeed to throw off religion from India and take up politics then extinction of the nation will be the consequence. To prevent this you have to vitalise your religion first and subordinate everything else to it."[72] He further said, "Before flooding India with...political ideas first deluge the land with spiritual ideas."[73] Aurobindo like him gave precedence to religion and spiritualism over politics and said, "It is the spirit alone that saves and only by becoming great and free in heart that we can become politically great and free."[74] That is why he remained faithful to the high ideals of spirituality and universal love as a leader of the revolutionary movement in India.

Aurobindo raised politics to the plane of spirituality. He interpreted political freedom in terms of spiritual perfection. So nationalism to him was not merely a patriotic sentiment or an intellectual conception, but a deep religious sadhana. He identified Hindu nationalism with religion and said that nationalism is not mere a political programme. It is a religion that has come from God.

Aurobindo differentiated nationalism from patriotism. He

said that no man dare call himself a nationalist if he does so merely with a sort of intellectual pride, thinking that he is patriotic, thinking that he is something higher than those who do not call themselves by that name. If one is going to be a nationalist, if one is going to assent to the religion of nationalism, one must do it in a religious spirit. He also said, "Nationalism is a religion that has come from God,.... It has not been crushed. It is not going to be crushed. Nationalism survives in the strength of God and it is not possible to crush it, whatever weapon are brought against it. Nationalism is immortal, nationalism cannot die because it is not a human thing, it is God.... God cannot be killed, God cannot be sent to Jail.... This great nation will rise again and become once more what it was in the days of spiritual greatness."[75]

Aurobindo identified nationalism with Sanatana Dharma. He said, "The Hindu nation was born with Sanatana Dharma, with it, it moves and with it, it grows. When Sanatana Dharma declines then the nation declines and if Sanatana Dharma were capable of perishing with the nation, it would perish. The Sanatana Dharma, that is nationalism."[76]

Swami Vivekananda called upon his compatriots to work for national emancipation, which would facilitate the work of diffusing spiritual knowledge in the world for the welfare of humanity at large. As he said, "This nationalship of ours, ye children of the immortals, my countrymen, has been playing for ages, carrying civilization and enriching the whole world with its inestimable treasures. For scores of shining centuries, this nationalship of ours has been ferrying across the ocean of life and has taken millions of souls to the other shore, beyond all misery. But today it may have sprung a leak and got damaged, through your own fault or whatever cause it matters not.... Would you not all unite together and put your best efforts to stop the holes ? Let us all give our heart's blood to do it...."[77]

Like Swami Vivekananda, Aurobindo wanted Indian freedom from British imperialism and like him also in the freedom of India Aurobindo saw the hopes of freedom of the entire world. As he said, "India awakes not for herself but for the humanity." He further said, "...function of India is to supply the world with a perennial source of light and renovation.... She sends forth a light from her bosom which floods the earth and the heavens, and mankind bathes in it.... The world needs India and needs her free."[78]

Thus like Swami Vivekananda, Aurobindo gave a spiritual direction to Indian politics and nationalism. His interpretation of Indian spiritual nationalism excelled that of other spiritual nationalist of the age. In fact Aurobindo went much ahead of them in this respect and he is rightly acclaimed as the prophet of Neo-Nationalism in India. In the words of Dr. Karan Singh, "His concept of spiritual Nationalism and the divinity of motherland which imparted an esoteric significance to the movement for India's liberation,"[79] is a great contribution to Modern Indian Political Thought.

Like Swami Vivekananda and Aurobindo, Gandhi, "the last link in the chain of great nationalists of the past and the first in that of the great nationalists of the future"[80] felt properly the pulse of Indian national life and sought to give a spiritual basis to Indian nationalism. He was a highly spiritual person and for him religion meant emphasis on moral and ethical values. His religion was identified with morality and ethics. He always spoke in terms of ethical idealism. To quote him, "For me morals, ethics and religion are convertible terms. A moral life without reference to religion is like a house built upon sand. A religion divorced from morality is like a sounding brass gong only for making noise and breaking heads."[81] In this context he has also said, "I reject any religious doctrine that does not appeal to reason and is in conflict with morality."[82] He felt that as soon as the moral basis of religion is lost it ceases to be religion. Thus, he was a great believer in the dynamic force of religion in human history in bringing about social solidarity and national coherence. He felt that French nationalism, established by the French Revolution soon degenerated into despotic imperialism of Napoleon I and III and that the Russian slogan of dictatorship of the proletariat got perverted into dictatorship of a manipulating group — 'the vanguard' because they lacked religious foundation. It so happened, because the nationalism of the two countries were not ethically and morally inspired and had no rock like spiritual foundation. He felt that ethics and morality as preached by all the religions are indispensable for the development of genuine nationalism. Hence he condemned the Godlessness and violence of Bolshevic nationalism.[83]

Gandhi also condemned the Western materialistic nationalism very bitterly since it pays no regard for religion and spiritualism. Regardless of morality and ethics, it believes in limitless expansion of capitalism that has resulted in exploitation of the weaker peoples. In most cases it has resorted to Fascist technique. He said, "Western nationalism as it functions today is undiluted Nazism and Fascism. At best it is merely a cloak to hide the Nazi and Fascist tendencies of imperialism."[84] He frankly stated that it was through immoral and unethical method that the British conquered India for their selfish end. He warned the Western nations that for such crime against humanity they have to answer one day.[85]

Hence, for Gandhi, a spiritual nationalist, nationalism was not merely a political fact, but a spiritual necessity. As a humanist he never tolerated or compromised with injustice, wrong, tyranny and authoritarianism. So unlike the Western materialistic nationalists his nationalism was founded on the bedrock of spiritualism — source of all morality and ethics — so that it will never get perverted nor degenerated come what may. He had firm conviction that India not only lives for herself but lives for the whole world. Welfare of humanity at large was the goal of her nationalism. Secular nationalism cannot inspire its people to reach such an avowed goal. So he wanted to organise Indian spiritual nationalism for the benefit and service of whole humanity. He wrote, "Indian nationalism is not exclusive, nor aggressive nor destructive. It is health-giving, religious, spiritual and therefore humanitarian. India must learn to live before she can aspire to die for humanity."[86]

To Gandhi, in India's freedom lies the welfare of mankind.[87] So as a great humanist, he took up the cause of Swaraj for India with great zeal and enthusiasm for the furtherance of service to mankind. To arouse passion for Swaraj among his countrymen and quicken the forces of Swaraj in India he wanted to spiritualise politics. When he found that the Indian masses preferred religion to politics, remained aloof from politics and Indian freedom movement, he felt that it hindered the achievement of the goal of Swaraj. As Vinoba Bhave has written, "Gandhi transformed the work for Swaraj into work for the service of mankind. He gave politics a religious and spiritual hue so that the movement for Swaraj would become more than a political movement with millions taking part in it who had no interest in politics. Babu himself was not interested in politics. Even though he had to grapple with political issues right up to the moment of his death, the whole struggle was for him part of a wider spiritual Sadhana : the quest for truth."[88]

Gandhi did not give much importance to politics as distinct from ethics, spiritualism and religion. Hence like Swami Vivekananda and Aurobindo he based his politics on religion. In this respect he also went a step ahead of them to recognise Truth and Non-violence as his only religion saying that "politics should be governed by truth and non-violence."[89] In his opinion politics cannot be separated from religion since both stand for the same ideal *i.e.*, service of mankind. He said, "Those who say that religion has nothing to do with politics, do not know what religion means.... He does not know what patriotism or feelings for one's own country is, who does not know true duty or religion."[90] He also said, "If I take part in politics, it is only because politics today encircles us like the coil of the snake.... I am trying to introduce religion into politics."[91] It is clear from the above statements that Gandhi like the Western nationalists did not divorce religion from politics. Moreover, he fervently sought to unite them for the furtherance of spiritual nationalism of the country.

To Gandhi, public life, which is obviously related to national life was always concerned with religion and morality. So, from public life, religion — the source of all morality — cannot be separated. If there is separation, the consequence will be very terrible. Therefore he insisted to introduce religion into public life and said, "At the back of every word that I have uttered since I have known that public life in India is and every act that I have done, there had been a religious consciousness and down right religious motive."[92] Thus by stressing on religion and morality in Indian public life that has obvious relation with national life, he intended to strengthen the cause of spiritual nationalism in India.

Religion and Politics, therefore, to Gandhi are inseparable. Both of them are useful for the society. They are meant for identical purpose *i.e.*, the purpose of human welfare. So he declared, "For me politics, bereft of religion is absolute dirt ever to be shunned."[93] Again he said, "...there are no politics devoid of religion.... Politics bereft of religion are a death-trap, because they kill the soul."[94]

Gandhi not only spiritualised politics : he apprehended worst to follow if politics dominates over religion. So in order to forestall domination of politics over religion he sought subordination of politics to religion. In this respect he probably followed the foot-prints of Swami Vivekananda and Aurobindo. However his primary intention was to build up the edifice of Indian nationalism on the basis of religion and spirituality. As Romain Rolland has observed, "To understand Gandhi's activities it should be realised that his doctrine is like a huge edifice, composed of two different floors or grades. Below is the solid ground work, the basic foundation of religion. On this vast and unshakable foundation is based the political and national campaign."[95]

Thus spiritual basis of nationalism is one of the common traits of three great nationalists of India — Swami Vivekananda, Aurobindo and Gandhi.

(iv) National Education

British system of education, in course of time, gave rise to severe discontentment in India. Many political associations sprouted up to ventilate people's wounded feelings, of whom the Indian National Congress was at the forefront. Year after year it passed resolutions hammering people's demand, but British authority paid no heed to it. Hence a cloud of disillusionment hovered over the Indian scene.[96] At such a juncture a nationalistic public opinion was taking shape and Swami Vivekananda, Aurobindo and Gandhi, three great nationalists advocated scrapping of English system of education in India and introduction of a nationalistic system. They realised that education is the strongest force to regenerate the country by awakening self-consciousness among the masses. So they strongly resented the prevailing system of British education in India that sought to destroy the seeds of national self-consciousness in its very embryo and demanded vigorously a national system of education for the Indian masses, based on national language and culture. This novel type of education will arouse a sense of nationalism among the people which will strengthen national unity. This stress on national education is another point of semblance in the nationalism of the Swarajist trio like Swami Vivekananda, Aurobindo and Gandhi.

Swami Vivekananda as a nationalist, realised the enormous importance of education in the building up of a nation. He felt that education is a positive means by which human nature can be shaped in the right direction of national consciousness to produce a unified harmonious state. It too, makes man realise his own importance and worth and causes him to react against the prevailing injustice and oppression that always tend to pull him downwards. So stressing the need of mass education he declared that "the only service to be done for our poor masses is to give them education, to develop their lost individuality. That is the only help they require and then the rest must follow as the effect."[97] He also declared, "We want that education by which character is formed, strength of mind is increased, the intellect is expanded and by which we can stand on our own feet."[98]

Swami Vivekananda was completely disgusted with the prevailing system of education in India. He said, "The present system of education is all wrong. The mind is crammed with facts before it knows how to think."[99] He criticised the prevailing system of education as useless that rarely produced an original man in the country during the last fifty years.[100] The system of education was meant to make us fit only for a thirty-rupees clerkship or at best a lawyer, but did not help us to reach the height of our ambition in life.[101] It was because of this that the system of education was negative in character, and had no bearing on the culture and habit of the people. As he said, "The education that you are now getting is not man-making education, it is merely and entirely a negative education. A negative education is worse than death. The child is taken to school and the first thing he learns is that his father is a fool, the second thing that his grandfather is a lunatic, the third thing that all his teachers are hypocrites, the fourth that all the sacred books are lies! By the time he is sixteen, he is a mass of negation, lifeless and boneless."[102]

According to Swami Vivekananda the system of education in which Indian culture and customs did not find any place, had proved abortive for the people of India. It was altogether a meaningless education to be rejected forthwith. Pouring out his heart-felt anger and deep-seated resentment against it, he said, "Is there not water enough in the sea to drown you, books, gowns, university diplomas and all?"[103] Again he said, "Customs of the country, customs of the people must be adhered to. No compromise, no white washing, nothing else. Throw away such texts, the customs of the people have to be followed."[104]

Hence according to Swami Vivekananda, education in India must be based on the culture of the country. Education in order to be life-building, man-making, and character-making" should conform to its national tradition or culture.[105] As he said, "Knowledge without culture is only skin-deep."[106] "For raising the masses," he said, "interpretation of scriptures in the regional languages and at the same time popularisation of sanskrit are necessary."[107]

Swami Vivekananda not only condemned the British system of education on the ground that it was based on foreign culture; he also condemned it on the ground that it was also imparted through a foreign language. To him education, in order to be very effective must be imparted in one's own language. As he said, "The language in which we naturally express ourselves, in which we communicate our anger, grief or love etc. — there cannot be fitter language than that. We must stick to that idea, that manner of expression, that diction and all. No foreign language can ever have that force, that expression or admit of being given any turn you please as that country language."[108] When education is given in the language of the nation, the language flourishes and side by side it brings about a sort of lingual unity among the countrymen that serves as a stimulus to national unity. As he said, "...language is the chief means and index of a nation's progress and unity."[109] He further said, "...the more strength is infused into the national life, the more will language...become spontaneously instinct with ideas and life."[110]

Defying the argument of some Westernised teachers, who held that modern science and technology could not be imparted through the country's language except English, Swami Vivekananda said, "Every man is capable of receiving education if it is imparted in his own language. A teacher who cannot convince others should weep on account of his own inability to teach the pupil in their own language, instead of cursing them and dooming them to live in ignorance and superstition, setting up the plea that the higher knowledge is not for them."[111] Again he said, "The greatness of a teacher consists in the simplicity of his language. If he expresses himself in the common language of the people he is the only worthy teacher."[112]

Thus Swami Vivekananda highlighting the defects of the British system of education in India demanded a national system of education, based on indigenous culture and language and asked the contemporary social reformers to spread such education among the poor masses in order to quicken the process of national regeneration. Drawing the attention of the social workers and reformers to it, he said that ever since education began to flow in among the poor masses, Europe began to advance.[113] So the poor and lower class people in India must be educated to make the nation worth-living. But if the poor people, depending on daily wages for their subsistence, do not turn up to education, the only alternative before them is that education should reach them. He said, "If the mountain does not come to Mohammed, Mohammed must go to the mountain. If the poor cannot come to education, education must reach them at the plough, in the factory, every where."[114]

Thus Swami Vivekananda, emphasised on national education for the poor masses of India.

Aurobindo, a brilliant product of Western system of education also emerged as a bitter critic of that system and like Swami Vivekananda became an impassioned advocate of national education right since his Borada days. His Borada days developed in him tremendous weakness for cultural heritage of India. It is rightly said, "In fact Borada became for him the starting point for new studies regarding everything Indian and Western."[115] He branded the British education in India as anti-national[116] and took a plunge in National Education Movement.

Aurobindo joined the Bengal National College with his primary purpose to convert the whole educational system into a vehicle of patriotism and nationalism, to be wielded as a weapon to win Swaraj. Education, as he felt, shall act as a catalystic agent against colonialism and imperialism. The aim of his plan of education was to inculcate a sense of nationalism among the educated people, in a very short period who will inspire the masses immediately. As he said, "Nationalism having once taken possession of the educated class, must immediately proceed to invade the masses."[117] That apart, the syllabus of such study also should not be very complicated. The syllabus should cover such topics as would inspire the people to work and suffer for the motherland rather than opening careers for earning a livelihood.[118] S.C. Sengupta has rightly remarked, "His syllabus of national education was very simple, straightforward and not very difficult to teach."[119] It is also said, "It (The Syllabus) attempted to achieve a healthy intellectual and moral development of the student according to the highest national ideas."[120]

While advocating boycott as a part of his Doctrine of Passive Resistance, Aurobindo condemned the British system of education in India and said, "We are dissatisfied...with the condition under which education is imparted in this country, its calculated poverty and insufficiency, its anti-national character, its subordination to the government and the use made of that subordination for the discouragement of patriotism, and the inculcation of loyalty."[121] The objective behind Educational Boycott, according to Aurobindo, was to make "the control of its youthful minds pass out of the hands of the foreigners"[122] so that the government shall not get any scope to throttle the growth of nationalistic and patriotic sentiment of the young mind and instill in them a sense of loyalty for the imperial power so that the mind shall be free from the poverty or insufficiency of intellectual commitment to nobler ideals like love of the nation and loyalty for the land and the people.

Aurobindo like Swami Vivekananda said that education in India must be based upon its culture, its literature, history and philosophy.[123] To him national education cannot take itself adrift from its roots, its heritage. Since spiritualism constitutes the back-bone of Indian culture and heritage, such education cannot afford to neglect spiritual basis. As he wrote in Karmayogin, "What was the secret of the great gigantic intellectuality, spirituality and superhuman moral force which we see pulsating in the Ramayana and Mahabharat, in the ancient philosophy, in the supreme poetry, art, sculpture and architecture of India? What was at the basis of the incomparable public works and engineering achievements, the opulent and exquisite industries, the great triumph of science, scholarship, jurisprudence, logic, meta-physics, the unique social structure? What supported the heroism and self-abandonment of the Kshatriya, the Sikh and the Rajput, the unconquerable national vitality and endurance? What was it that stood behind that civilization second to none in the massiveness of its outlines or the perfection of its details? Without a great and unique discipline involving perfect education of soul and mind a result so immense and persistent would have been impossible."[124]

Aurobindo believed that a nation is an integrated whole deeply steeped in its past and growing out of it and obtaining sustenance from it. If India has to win its nationhood, revivified into the glory and greatness that is its legacy and fulfil its national destiny, it must bank upon its inheritance. Any dream of building up India into a robust and enviable nation, by cutting itself adrift from its ancient heritage, is foredoomed to failure. Hence he said, "Whoever wishes to cut off the nation from its past is no friend of our national growth."[125] Thus it is evident that Aurobindo in his scheme of national education followed the foot-prints of Swami Vivekananda who put emphasis primarily on Indian culture as the basis of national education for India.

Aurobindo also believed that the system of national education shall be so designed that it shall instill in the young a sense of self-confidence and self-reliance. He realised that the English system of education, prevailing in India made the educated people too much reliant on the imperial power. Besides it also stunted their courage, their manliness and their individuality and failed them in cultivating a sense of commitment to higher values of life. That also dwarfed their capacity to take risk, patriotism and the spirit of nationalism. As he said, "He, trained by present system of education even when it is somewhat above the average, is almost invariably deficient in practicality and the robustness to shake off cherished superstitions and face and recognise facts."[126] Hence national education apart from making the youth self-reliant and robust in spirit shall endow them with manly courage, nationalistic and patriotic fervour, spirit of adventure and the strength and stamina to take risks for nobler causes. As he wrote, "National education shall be a system which will be impregnated with the spirit of self-reliance so as to build up man, national man, able men, men fit to carve out a career for themselves by their own brain power, fit to meet the shocks of life and breast the waves of adventure. So shall the Indian people cease to sleep and become once more a people of heroes, patriots, so shall it became a nation and no longer a disorganised mass of men."[127]

Swami Vivekananda stressed that national education must be imparted through national language, the common language of the masses. But Aurobindo went much further and said that the entire system of national education must be manned and managed by the Indians, rather than the British people in India. To him national education must be a completely autonomous system, controlled absolutely by the Indians. As he writes, "It means an education...absolutely by the Indians."[128] Putting stress on autonomy of the system of national education again he said, "Independence is the first condition and any scheme which disregards it is doomed to failure."[129]

Thus Aurobindo also like Swami Vivekananda emphasised

on national education to inspire and prepare the people of India for nationalism and national unity.

Like Swami Vivekananda and Aurobindo, Gandhi as a nationalist also emphasised on national education. He also condemned the prevailing English system of education in India, which according to him did not help the people in their being and becoming. For him, "a nation's culture resides in the heart and the soul of the people."[130] So education for a nation, in order to be effective, must be based on its culture. Since the existing system of education was not founded on its culture it was of no use for Indians. Condemning it he said, "The existing system of education is defective...it is based upon foreign culture to the almost entire exclusion of indigenous culture."[131]

Explaining the glaring defects of the system of education he said that the textbooks, dealt not with indigenous culture, but exclusively with that of the West, making Indian boys and girls foreigners in their homeland. All Western phenomena that embody themselves in the textbooks produce little effect upon the minds of the Indian people in unfolding their mental faculty and making themselves discern the light and life in their homeland. The more they were educated the more they became strangers in their home country. They failed to take pride in their own surrounding and the culture of their own land. All charms and pleasures of their indigeneous culture remained sealed to them forever. Describing this woeful scene he wrote, "His own civilization is presented to him as imbecile, barbarous, superstitious and useless for all practical purpose. His education is calculated to wean him from his traditional culture and if the mass of educated youths are not entirely denationalised, it is because the ancient culture to too deeply imbedded in them to be altogether uprooted even by an education, adverse to its growth."[132]

Gandhi was very much struck with owe by the evils of such education. He expressed his extreme resentment and severe discontentment saying that "if I had my way, I would certainly destroy the majority of the present textbooks and cause to be written textbooks which have a bearing on the correspondence with home-life, so that a boy as he learns may react upon his immediate surrounding."[133]

Like Swami Vivekananda and Aurobindo, Gandhi was also dead against the English medium of education. As he said, "Real education is impossible through a foreign medium."[134] Highlighting the defect of English medium he said, "The foreign medium has caused brain fag, put an undue strain upon the nerves of our children, made them crammers and imitators, unfitted them for original work and thought and disabled them for filtrating their learning to the family or the masses. The foreign medium has made our children practically foreigners in their own land. It is the greatest tragedy of existing system."[135]

Some Indians felt inclined towards English medium of education and sought to groom their children in English fashion. But Gandhi asked such Indians to give up such inclination towards a foreign language saying that such undesirable habit of fascination would keep our own languages ever backward under the supremacy of foreign language. As he said, "If we seek the pleasure of English language, our language will remain poor, which means that we shall remain a poor people. The habit of deriving enjoyment only from a foreign language is, I must say, if you will pardon me the simile, like the thief's habit of deriving pleasure from stolen goods."[136]

Preference for a foreign medium will also result in the extinction of our own literature. He was so much overwhelmed by the evils of English medium, that sought to threaten the very existence of our vernaculars, that he ventilated his wounded feeling by saying, "The foreign medium has prevented the growth of our vernaculars. If I have the powers of a despot, I should today stop the tuition of our boys and girls through foreign medium and require all the teachers and professors on pain of dismissal to introduce the change forthwith.... It is an evil that needs summary remedy."[137]

Gandhi was, in fact, against English education, including the English medium in Indian system of education. As he said, "I have come to the conclusion that in the ordinary course of our life neither our men nor our women need necessarily have any knowledge of English."[138] Of course he had no hostility to

English language and literature. His uncompromising opposition to English education does not mean that he was completely averse to foreign literature and culture. As he said, "English is the language of international commerce and diplomacy and therefore I consider its knowledge on the part of some of us as essential. As it contains some of the richest treasures of thought and literature, I should certainly encourage its careful study among those who have linguistic talent and expect them to translate these treasures for the nation in its vernaculars."[139]

Gandhi was opposed to Western system of education as it has no contribution for the building up of the character of the individual. His view was that education must promote a sound moral character among the people. So like Swami Vivekananda and Aurobindo, who believed in man-making and character building education...Gandhi also said, "Literary education is of no value if it is not able to build up a sound moral character."[140]

Gandhi in his scheme of national education not only put emphasis on the literary education based on Indian culture and tradition; he also put emphasis on the training in manual labour. He held a very strong view that since India is mainly an agricultural country and for 80% people, cultivation is the mainstay of their subsistence, Indian students should be made to acquaint themselves with physical labour. As he said, "Whatever may be true of other nations, in India at any rate where more than eighty per cent of the population is agricultural…it is a crime to make education merely literary and to unfit boys and Girls for manual work in after-life. Indeed I hold that as the larger part of our time is devoted to labour for earning our bread, our children must from their infancy be taught the dignity of such labour. Our children should not be so taught as to despise labour."[141] Again he said, "The introduction of manual training…will teach them an occupation on which they can fall back in after-life, if they choose, for earning a living. Such a system shall make our children self-reliant. Nothing will demoralise the nation so much as that we should learn to despise labour."[142]

Gandhi's scheme of national education has a special reference to education of women. Emphasing the need of female education he said, "It is no exaggeration to say that a human being without education is not far removed from an animal. Education therefore, is as necessary for woman as it is for man."[143] But as the prevailing system of education was unsuitable for Indian women, he asked them to give up such education. As he said, "Our present system of education is full of error and productive of harm in many respects. It should be eschewed by men and women alike. Even if it were free from its present blemishes, I would not regard it as proper for women for all points of view."[144] Gandhi was much pleased to see the excellent activities of some women in Champaran district of the Tirhut division in Bihar, in waking up their backward sisters to freedom, both individual and national. Appreciating their role he said, "Women...are doing excellent work in Champaran. They are waking up their extremely backward sisters to freedom."[145]

Thus like Swami Vivekananda and Aurobindo, Gandhi also condemned the British system of education in India and stressed the need of national education based on indigenous culture and language for the promotion of national consciousness and unity in India.

(v) Humanistic Basis of Nationalism

Humanism is the finest flower of Indian culture. The Veda and Upanishads that constitute the very core of Indian Culture, look upon the whole universe as one family and prays for divine blessing for it as, "Let all be happy, let all be immune from disease, let all be gentle, and let not they be ever afflicted with sorrow."[146] Love for all men, for all creatures and for the creation as a whole is the main theme of Indian culture. "Let the Earth, the Sky, the Water and the Trees and the Medicines etc. be tranquil and tranquiliser."[147] This has been prayed in our Veda Mantra. Thus love for all creatures and entire creation, is the core of Indian spiritualism.

Down the ages different prophets and visionaries of India like Buddha, Chaitanaya, Sankaracharya, Ramanuja etc. have upheld the cause of humanism and have laid down their lives upholding this ideal. In the light of this philosophy the great humanist poet R.N. Tagore writes, "Civilization must be judged and prized not by the amount of power it has developed, but by how much it has evolved and given expression to, by its laws and institutions, the love of humanity."[148]

But under the impact of the materialistic civilization of the West that gave rise to colonialism and imperialism and brought India under the sway of British imperialism, the lofty humanistic philosophy was strangled. The humanistic value like dignity of human life and right and liberty of the individual were trampled under the heels of the imperialist power. Man was subordinated to money and degraded to servitude. The humanistic culture reached the saddest point in human history. M.N. Roy, has accordingly written, "The eclipse of the humanist tradition is the curse of this degeneration and decay. Modern civilization stood at the head of the declining plane of decay the moment it broke away from the tradition of humanism — subordinated man to the institutions."[149] However, the 19th century witnessed the emergence of a galaxy of great souls in India who initiated revival of interest in humanistic values. Of them Swami Vivekananda, Aurobindo and Gandhi were the three spiritual figures, who apart from being patriots and nationalists, were deeply inspired by humanistic values.

Swami Vivekananda's humanism as discussed earlier in Chapter 4 of this dissertation, is based upon the philosophy of Upanishads and the teachings of Sri Ramkrishan. He had renounced the world not for the purpose of seeking his own salvation but for finding a way out for the world, dominated by all kinds of miseries — both material and spiritual. He followed the foot-prints of Lord Buddha, who renounced his royal estate, not for his personal salvation but for mitigating the sorrows and sufferings of the world. As he said, "Gautama Buddha...did not believe in personal God, nor a personal soul, never asked about them, but was a perfect agnostic and yet was ready to lay down his life for any one and worked all his life for the good of all and thought only of the good of all."[150]

Swami Vivekananda was a true lover of man. The more he came closer to man, the more he enjoyed the nearness to God. Like Tagore, who said, "In the vessel of man's affection I taste his divine nectar,"[151] Swami Vivekananda enjoyed his God in his affection for man. His love for man was so great that he identified man with God. As Annie Besant declared, "To know man is to know God,"[152] Swami Vivekananda also said, "every body is divine, is God."[153]

Jesus Christ asked to love all men as brothers, but Swami Vivekananda went a step ahead and said, "Love every man as your own self and not as your brother as in Christianity. Brotherhood should be superseded by universal self-hood. Not universal brother-hood but universal self-hood is our motto."[154] He believed in the worship of Man-God and criticized the worship of God in the temples.[155] To him it is perfect lunacy to place edibles before images of God leaving the true God, the Man-God behind.

Swami Vivekananda's conception of universal religion was based on the belief that God manifests Himself through living beings. He gave a call to the people of India to work for the welfare of humanity. He always exhorted people to seek God in fellow human beings. He often gave a call to serve man in order to find God.[156] He expressed his desire to be born again and suffer thousands of miseries so that he could worship the only God, the sum total of all souls.[157]

Swami Vivekananda's love for man was so great that his heart bled to see the suffering of the poor man. He called them "Daridra Narayan" and called upon his followers to serve the poor the downtrodden with great care and love. His love for mankind reached the climax when he visited England. Although as an Indian patriot, he deeply resented the rule of the foreigners, as a lover of mankind, he entertained no ill-will towards the people of Great Britain. As he said, "There is no more among you, who loves the English people more than I do now."[158] He found in England "a nation of heroes, a true Kshatriya."[159]

As a true lover of mankind, Swami Vivekananda emphasised on the right, liberty and equality of all individuals. These are the conditions in which the individual attains his best-self and perfection of life. According to Dr. Y. Chelysev, Swami Vivekananda founded his society on the lofty ideals of freedom and equality.[160]

Swami Vivekananda's love for man made him a staunch individualist. He stood for right and liberty of man. He would perhaps say, "Every state is known by rights that it maintains. Our method of judging its character lies, above all, in the constitution that it makes to the substance of man's happiness."[161] He did not allow any state interference in individual's right and liberty. To him state interference hinders the growth of the individual. So state should not make any law to limit the individual's liberty. As he felt too many laws are sure sign of death.[162]

Swami Vivekananda exhorts that the law that impedes the growth of individual, should be thrown away outright and he appreciated the ability to break such laws. As he said, "It is not law that we want, but ability to break the law."[163]

This intense sense of humanism of Swami Vivekananda turned him to a nationalist. His nationalism is the product of his humanism. As a spiritual personality he had no concern for nationalism and political freedom of the country. But his love for man made him realise the value and importance of nationalism and national unity. When he saw the Indian masses rotting in misery and hardship under British imperialism, his sense of humanism revolted against it. He fervently called on his country-men to rise against all such injustice and exploitation. He said, "India must rise, the masses, the poor are to be fed and made happy...."[164] Again to awake his countrymen nationally he said, "We as a nation have lost our individuality and that is the chief cause of all mischief of British imperialism in India. We have to give back to the nation its lost individuality and raise the masses."[165] Encouraging a mass rising he also said, "The only hope of India is from the masses."[166] Thus the nationalism of Swami Vivekananda has a humanistic basis. His nationalism is the manifestation of his tender feeling of love and affection for the people of India. However his nationalism is not narrow nationalism confined to the interest of people of India alone, but to the humanity at large.[167] Interest of humanity as a whole was his chief concern.

This very sense of humanism made Swami Vivekananda think in terms of internationalism also and "he called for the establishment of friendly relations between all nations, based on love of man for each other."[168] So his nationalism, the product of his humanism is but universalism or cosmopolitanism, that embodies in itself the principles of peaceful co-existence of the nations on the basis of universal brotherhood. It is above regionalism, capitalist chauvinism and exclusiveness that characterise the Western nationalism of Germany, Italy etc. Based on sacrifice, and renunciation, it abhors greed for wealth, power and fabulous luxury of the West. Unlike the Western concept of nationalism Swami Vivekananda's nationalism conforms to the canons of morality, ethics and humanism. It does not accept military conquest or territorial aggrandisement as signs of national prestige; rather it believes in spiritual conquest for spiritualisation of the world. As he said, "India must conquer the world and nothing less than this is my ideal."[169]

Swami Vivekananda wanted to synthesise the West and the East in the interest of international understanding and welfare of the humanity at large. He sought to integrate the world spiritually to achieve solidarity of the universe. In fact his scheme of the union of the East and the West and spiritual integration of the world — the greatest landmark in the history of internationalism — is the outcome of his strong sense of love for humanity at large.

Modern age is the age of complexity. International situation has become very vexed and complicated. Problems of each nation cannot be solved at national level. So Swami Vivekananda earnestly aspired for international organisations and international laws. As he said, "Even in politics and sociology, problems that were only national twenty years ago can no more be solved on national grounds only. They are assuming huge proportions and gigantic shapes. They can only be solved when looked at in the broader light of international grounds. International organisations, international combinations, international laws, are the cry of the day."[170] His international outlook left deep marks on Nehru, who wrote in his *Discovery of India* "progressively Swami Vivekananda grew more international in outlook...."[171]

Thus Swami Vivekananda's humanism not only seeks the unity of India for national freedom; it also seeks promotion of international peace and brotherhood. It has been befittingly observed, "Swami Vivekananda's impassioned call for general fraternity and unity of India's people...were combined with an appeal for peace and friendship among the nations of the world, which is the cornerstone of Indian tradition, the main concept of Indian-national character."[172] Hence, humanism inspired Swami Vivekananda to ba a nationalist and internationalist and, provided a basis to his theory of nationalism.

Aurobindo, who like Swami Vivekananda, sought to regenerate India, also made humanism the basis of his nationalism. Among the contemporary humanists he occupies a unique place. His humanist approach to nationalism has made him a man, belonging to all nations and all ages, eternal or Sanatana in character. Unlike Gandhi and Nehru he could not, of course, influence the vast masses. Even then those who go through his philosophy are bound to note his burning optimism about the future of human race. His realistic approach to the problems of life and his grand vision of human perfectibility to achieve world unity as envisaged in his theory of nationalism, gives new hope to the bewildered mankind.

It is a fact to be reckoned with that like Swami Vivekananda, Aurobindo was primarily a humanist. Love for man was his innate philosophy. British imperialism that brought about social morass and political prostration in India, bringing in its wake poverty and starvation among the masses, told severely upon his sense of humanism. Reacting against this imperial injustice and oppression, he said, "I assert as our first and holiest duty, the elevation and enlightenment of the poor masses."[173] For ameliorating the lot of the Indian masses he sought to arouse a sense of nationalism. It is said, "Aurobindo evinced a keen interest in the rehabilitation of the condition of the masses.... He felt...that greatness of India could only be brought out if national spirit among the masses was roused...."[174] Thus Aurobindo's national leadership was shaped by his humanistic philosophy.

Aurobindo's love for his motherland was not motivated by narrow nationalism. To him nationalism was spiritual Sadhana — a moral endeavour. So his nationalism is not selfish nationalism blind to the interest of humanity. On the contrary, like that of Swami Vivekananda it reflects an exuberant spirit of humanism, that makes it acceptable world over despite the diversities of world religion, race and geography.

He thought not only for India, its people, but for the whole world, the mankind. Indians were not only his concern; his concern was for the whole humanity also. In the freedom of India he saw the hope of the freedom of the entire world. Therefore, he repeatedly said, "Indian awakes not for herself, but for the humanity."[175] He said that India must be reborn because her rebirth is demanded by the future of the world. Thus we find that political freedom of India and his nationalism has a humanistic purpose.

Aurobindo's love for man was so great that he was in his life time ever prepared to lend his helping hand to every faltering being. He was confident that he could do it. As he said, "I am confident that I have the strength in me to bring salvation to these fallen people."[176]

In his love for man, Aurobindo, like Swami Vivekananda recognised divinity in all man. To him "Man is Divine spirit on earth."[177] He said, "Mankind on earth is one foremost self-expression of Divine Being in His Cosmic self unfolding."[178] Again he said, "Mankind in godhead to be worshipped and served...the respect, the service, the progress of human being and human life are the chief duty and chief aim of the human spirit. No other idol, neither the nation, the state, the family, nor anything else ought to take its place; they are only worthy of respect...they are the images of Divine Spirit and enshrine its presence and its self manifestation."[179]

Like Swami Vivekananda, a great humanist who considered human body as a holy temple, Aurobindo also glorified it and held it in high esteem. To him, human body, mind and soul, all are great objects of profound respect and deep veneration. People of all nations, should make it their motto. As he said, "The body of man must be respected, made immune from violence and outrage, fortified by science against disease and preventable death. The life of man is to be held sacred, preserved, strengthened, and ennobled, uplifted. The heart of man is to be held sacred also, given scope, protected from violation, from suppression, from mechanisation. All this is not to be held as abstract or pious sentiment but given full and practical recognition in the persons of men, nations and mankind."[180]

Like Swami Vivekananda, who felt the importance of individual liberty and equality as the basis of human society, as discussed in chapters 2 and 3, Aurobindo also stressed the need of liberty, equality and fraternity in the perfection of human society. He says that a perfect society is based upon these three ideals. If the society failed to promote these essential ideas it cannot perfect its individuals. As a result the state they constitute fails to reach the goal. As he said, "The perfect society will be that which most entirely favours the perfection of the individual; the perfection of the individual will be incomplete if it does not help him towards the perfect state of the social aggregate to which he belongs."[181] Hence Aurobindo as a humanist, believed in individual liberty and equality to be the criteria of a state. M.N. Roy has observed, "...the merit of any pattern of social organization or political institution is to be judged by the actual measure of freedom it affords to individual."[182] That was Aurobindo's attitude towards liberty of the individual.

Sri Aurobindo felt that we have not been able to achieve any of these ideals. Liberty of which there is so much talk has been achieved only in outward sense — it is only unreal, mechanical liberty. Similarly equality of which the modern democrats talk so loudly is also achieved in a formal sense. There is no real equality. Fraternity is yet thought of as impracticable. These ideals cannot be achieved so long as man lives in his individual and communal ego. Only through the power of human brotherhood these can be achieved. But brotherhood exists only in the soul and in recognition of same soul in others. As Annie Besant said, "The recognition of the one self, dwelling equally in all, is the one sure foundation of brotherhood."[183] That is why Aurobindo emphasised the need of spiritual unification of mankind. Only unification in a spiritual and divine sense could be permanent, while unity brought about through world organisation such as U.N.O. would not be stable and real. Explaining it Aurobindo said, "A spiritual oneness which would create a psychological oneness not dependent upon any intellectual or outward uniformity and compel oneness of life not bound up with its mechanical means of unification, but ready always to enrich its secure unity by a free inner variation and free varied outer self-expression — this would be the basis of a higher type of human existence."[184]

Sri Aurobindo, though "the founder and precursor of the divine race of man"[185] for the good of humanity, made a compromise with the materialistic West. As humanist and a realist he thought of the synthesis of Eastern and Western ideals — spiritualism and materialism in the interest of mankind. "While asking the Indians for abandoning a slavish imitation of the West and depreciating the excess of materialism, he also condemned superstitions and dogmatism in Indian spirituality. He said, "The exaggerated spirituality of the Indian effort has also registered a bankruptcy; we have seen how high individuals can rise by it, but we have seen also how low a race can fall which in its eagerness to seek after God ignores His intentions in humanity."[186] Thus he advised to take a balanced view of both the Eastern and Western attitudes and ideals.

In the interest of humanity, Aurobindo repudiated the view that the West was purely materialistic and the East was exclusively spiritualistic. Both had materialism and spiritualism. In the past they met closely and influenced each other powerfully. Therefore, his message was not to think of the West as different from the East. He said, "It has been customary to dwell on the division and difference these two (East and West) sections of human family and even oppose them to each other, but for myself I would rather be disposed to dwell on oneness and unity than on division and difference."[187] At another place he said, "The safety of Europe has to be sought in the recognition of the spiritual aim of human existence, otherwise she will be crushed by the weight of her own unillumined knowledge of soulless organisation. The safety of Asia lies in the recognition of the material mould and mental conditions in which that aim has to be worked out."[188] All these clearly show that he was equally concerned for both and for the whole human race. Charles A. Moore has befittingly said, "Sri Aurobindo's philosophy provides two great needs of the time, namely a virtual synthesis of East and West, looking towards a philosophy acceptable to all mankind for its welfare and second, a richful interpretation of Indian thought correcting abuses and aberrations, thus providing a point of view."[189]

Aurobindo in his love for man, like Swami Vivekananda as discussed in chapter 6 of this dissertation advocated the cause of self-determination *i.e.*, free grouping of mankind. According to him the people of world must be allowed to group themselves according to their free will and their natural unity and affinity. As he said, "Unity would be the largest principle of life but freedom would be its foundation stone."[190] According to Aurobindo such free grouping will avert all wars and establish equal right of all nations, because he said, "The elimination of war and recognition of equal right of all peoples are intimately bound up with each other."[191]

Aurobindo's love for man was not confined to the mankind in India but to humanity at large. So his nationalism like Swami Vivekananda was not narrow and fanatical but had a cosmopolitan character. Universalism is the most cardinal feature of his nationalism that makes way for perfect international relation. Hence in his love for mankind, he envisaged a World Union for humanity. In such a World State, there would be no discrimination of any sort on the ground of wealth and power among the nations, that shall put an end to domination of the powerful nations over the weaker nations. As he wrote, "The ultimate result must be the formation of a World State and the most desirable form of it would be a federation of free nationalities in which all subjection or forced inequality and subordination of one to another would have disappeared and, though some might preserve a greater natural influence, all would have an equal status. A confederacy would give the greatest freedom to the nations, constituting the World State."[192]

Aurobindo's profound sense of humanism is reflected on his theory of spiritual evolution of man. In his theory he refuses to accept the world of matter as an illusion, a dream or Maya. On the other hand he emphasised that "it is the sense of evolutionary unfolding of being which moves towards the relations of supreme spiritual light and power and joy and oneness."[193] The theory helps to transform an individual from mere physical and mental being into a spiritual being — a divine being. It establishes that every man is a fragment of Divinity, clothed in matter. Aurobindo himself said, "Evolution is nothing but a progressive unfolding of spirit out of the density of material consciousness and the gradual self-revelation of God out of this apparent animal being."[194] The fact is that man is often ignorant of divinity and is unable to foresee the future possibilities. But Aurobindo's theory of spiritual evolution, dispels such ignorance and leads man to Divinity. "Spiritual evolution," as said Aurobindo, "is the transformation of life of ignorance in the divine life of truth conscious spirit."[195] Hence Aurobindo's theory of spiritual evolution, reflecting tremendous humanistic optimism serves as a solace to the bewildered mankind.

Thus, as in case of Swami Vivekananda, so also in case of Aurobindo, humanism is the basis of his theory of nationalism. His whole theory of nationalism seeks welfare of the humanity at large. Even though he directed his nationalism against the British exploitation and oppression of the Indian people, his love for the British people was little affected by it. Like Swami Vivekananda, he was so much devoted to the cause of humanism in his theory of nationalism that he never conceived of any prejudice against the British people. He had no jealousy nor hatred against them. But all that he did was to condemn and criticise their imperialistic mentality and exploitative temperament. That apart, he had no hatred or ill-feeling against the British race. As he said, "It is interest warring against interest and hatred is directed not really against the race, but against the adverse interest. If the British exploitation were to cease tomorrow, the hatred against the British race would disappear in a moment.... No hatred against the foreigners but antipathy to evils of foreign exploitation...."[196]

Like Swami Vivekananda and Aurodindo, Gandhi was also a

great humanist. Humanism the most cardinal feature of Gandhi's philosophy of life, is also the basis of his theory of nationalism. He was first a humanist and then a nationalist. His love for man, subsequently turned him to a nationalist. As Swami Vivekananda and Aurobindo, moved by imperial oppression and exploitation of India, turned nationalist, so also turned Gandhi a nationalist. His love for man compelled him to involve himself in the politics of the country and the struggle for national freedom. As he said, "For it was not politics, but work for awaking public spirit. The work of securing freedom for an enslaved nation is not politics but service."[197] Vinoba has accordingly remarked, "Gandhi never practised politics....what he pursued, could be called service of the people.... Gandhi took politics because at the time the main task before the country was the securing of freedom.[198] Hence Gandhi's theory of nationalism is characterised by a strong sense of humanism.

Gandhi accepted the most important Western criterion of human well-being — justice. By justice he meant devotion to the cause of elevation of the oppressed and the outcaste. He decided to fight against British rule in India because it led to the degradation of the poor[199] and created an unjust society. Similarly he considered it to be his foremost duty to uplift the untouchable because thereby they would get social justice. Like Swami Vivekananda Gandhi launched vigorous crusade for their social and economic emancipation. In the words of F.R. Moraes, "Posterity in assessing the place of Mahatma Gandhi will rank him higher as a humanist than as a politician and nationalist."[200]

As a humanist Gandhi had tremendous faith in the goodness of man. As he said, "Man's nature is not essentially evil. Brute nature has been known to yield to the influence of love. You must never despair human nature."[201] Like Rousseau he never considered man a born sinner. His faith in the inherent goodness of human nature is the basis of his humanism. As he declared, "The most practical the most dignified way of going on in the world is to take people at their word, when you have no positive reason to the contrary. I refuse to believe that the tendency of human nature is always downward."[202]

Gandhi's faith in mankind was so great that even bloody

communal riots could not shake his faith in man. It could not make him a pessimist. He wrote to Amrit Kaur, "You must not lose faith in humanity. Humanity is an ocean. If few drops of ocean are dirty, the ocean does not become dirty."[203] The very statement established the truth of the fact that Gandhi's love for mankind was deep-rooted and unmoved.

Gandhi like Swami Vivekananda and Aurobindo, recognised divinity in man. The nationalist trio believed, "Of all the manifestations of the Divine, man is incomparable. The human self is unique, because in it God reveals Himself in a special manner."[204] Gandhi himself said, "If I could persuade myself that I should find Him in a Himalayan cave, I would proceed there immediately. But I know that I cannot find Him apart from humanity."[205]

Gandhism is the philosophy of love. Gandhi not only accepted the lines of Bible, 'Love thy neighbour as thyself' but he added his own version to this line that every living being is thy neighbour. Hence love of man was the creed of his political philosophy. In the words of Sarojini Naidu, "He shared with Christ the gospel of love and with the Great Mohammed, the gospel of brotherhood, and equality of all man."[206]

Gandhi even loved the British people though he revolted against British exploitation and oppression. This is really a special trait of his humanistic approach like that of Swami Vivekananda and Aurobindo as discussed earlier. His love for the British people was so great that he warned the Indians not to humiliate the British even for the sake of national independence.[207] Prescribing the duty of a Satyagrahi, he also said that a Satyagrahi should never harbour any hatred or ill-feeling against his opponent or the evil doer.[208]

Like Swami Vivekananda and Aurobindo, Gandhi a humanist, had tremendous faith in the inherent equality of all men. Gandhi condemned such inequality as a crime against man and Swami Vivekananda as a social curse or sin. They recognised no inequality on the ground of caste, creed, colour and wealth. They opposed untouchability as a social superstition. Swami Vivekananda deplored Hinduism losing its Vedantic ideology and being reduced to narrow sectarian Don't touchism.

He overwhelmingly exclaimed, "We are neither Vedantists...nor Puranics nor Tantrics. We are just "Don't touchists."[209] He strove hard to do away with this superstition and restore Hinduism to its grand majestic form. Similarly Gandhi expressed his grave concern to reform the society and its religion by abolishing such ugly superstition. He said, "I believe that if untouchability is really rooted out, it will not only purge Hinduism of a terrible blot but its repercussions will be world-wide. My fight against untouchability is a fight against the impure of humanity."[210]

Gandhi's concern for the people of India was the same as his concern for mankind of the world. By serving the people of India, he wanted to serve the people of the whole world. As he said, "I am a humble servant of India and in trying to serve India I serve humanity at large."[211] In his opinion his service to the world will be incomplete, if his service to India is not complete. He wrote, "God has cast my lot in the midst of the people of India. I should be untrue to my Master, if I fail to serve them. If I do not know how to serve them I shall never know how to serve humanity."[212]

Gandhi looked upon humanity as the children of one family, like branches of a same tree. He asked his countrymen to develop a sense of love for humanity. He went much ahead of his contemporary nationalists when he sought to infuse into Indian minds the love for humanity and share their sorrows and sufferings.

Hence, like Swami Vivekananda and Aurobindo, Gandhi was universalistic and cosmopolitan in his outlook. His theory of nationalism is deeply rooted in universalism and humanism. He has rightly said that "Indian nationalism is neither exclusive nor aggressive. It is health giving and humanitarian."[213] "Indian nationalism" he has also said, "wants to organise itself or to find full self-expression for the benefit or service of the humanity at large."[214]

Like Swami Vivekananda and Aurobindo, Gandhi thought that India under fetters of British imperialism, could not serve humanity, her age-long mission. So India must be free to take up her responsibility of human welfare. He declared, 'India under Swaraj must serve the world.' But as he saw "An India, prostrate at the feet of Europe can give no hope to humanity. An India, awakened and free has a message of peace, goodwill and brotherhood to the groaning world."[215] He frankly declared, "My mission is not merely brotherhood of Indian humanity. My mission is not merely the freedom of India. But through realisation of freedom of India, I hope to realise and carry on the mission of the brotherhood of man."[216]

Like Swami Vivekananda and Aurobindo, Gandhi belonged to all times and entire mankind. He bent is energies for the upliftment of humanity. He belonged not to India but to the whole world. He belonged not only to our generation but to posterity as well. Since Gandhi's profound humanism inspired him to serve entire humanity, Dr. Rajendra Prasad has aptly compared his life with river Ganges which serves all who seek to make use of her. "If we want peace and happiness and to live as a human being we must follow the path, chalked out by Gandhiji, for in it lies our own good and that of the world."[217]

Thus the concept of nationalism of Swami Vivekananda and Aurobindo and Gandhi is based on the solid foundation of humanism.

(vi) Secularistic Nationalism

Swami Vivekananda, Aurobindo and Gandhi as nationalists were deeply committed to secularism. All the three were spiritual personalities yet all of them were deeply secular.

Swami Vivekananda was a religious personality. Yet he was enamoured of India partly because of her spirit of religious toleration in all ages of history, and felt proud to proclaim his country as 'the glorious land of religious toleration'.[218] He at the same time criticised the Western countries for their religious persecution and hostility, which is still in vogue.[219]

Swami Vivekananda sought to eliminate the outward differences between religions and show that all religions are but one that leads man to the same goal *i.e.,* Moksha or Salvation. As Khan Abdul Ghaffar Khan has observed, "The fundamental principle of all religions are the same though details differ because faith takes the colour and flavour of the soil from which it springs."[220]

However, Swami Vivekananda's secularism went much beyond the principle of religious toleration, harmony and unity. He elevated secularism beyond mere religion and spiritualism and brought it to the world of hard realities of work-a-day world, which is chiefly concerned with stomach rather than the soul or spirit and declared that what India needs is more of spirituality but at the same time she needs bread. The material demands of the poor is as important as the spiritual demands. So Swami Vivekananda stood for the complete separation of religion and social laws. As he said, "Social laws are created by the economic condition...the terrible mistake of religion was to interfere in social matters. What we want is that religion should not be a social reformer, but we insist at the same time that society has no right to become a religious law-giver. Hands off! keep yourself to our own bounds and everything would come right."[221]

To Swami Vivekananda religion is meaningless to a starving man. Man's mind is guided by stomach. If his stomach is full everything will impress his mind but if it is empty his mind will catch nothing. All preachings and philosophy will fall in deaf ears and fail to have any hold upon him. Religion will stand supreme if it has an economic background. As he said, "Whenever any religion succeeds, it must have economic value. Thousands of similar sects will be struggling for power, but only those who meet the real economic problem will have it."[222] He further said, "You may preach a religion that may not be perfect in every detail but if there is an economic background to it...you can convince the whole country."[223]

Aurobindo, like Swami Vivekananda felt that religion is a great shaping force. It moulds every individual and society in the direction of social solidarity and national unity. He said, "To make all life religious and to govern all activities by the religious idea would seem to be the right way to the development of the ideal individual and ideal society."[224] However he was an advocate of a secular conception of religion that does not identify itself with any creed, sect, faith, cult, church or dogma. He believed that the purpose of all religions is one *i.e.,* "lifting the whole life of man into the Divine."[225] As a secularist, he did not even hesitate to condemn Indian dogmatic spirituality and said that "the exaggerated spirituality of Indian efforts registered a bankruptcy."[226] He advised the Hindus to take a secular view of their religion and also said, "If the conservative mind in this country opens itself sufficiently to the necessity of secularism, the resulting culture, born of a resurgent India, may well bring about a profound modification in the future civilization of the world."[227]

Aurobindo as a secularist, apart from being a nationalist had little faith in sects and creeds, faiths and dogmas. He considered them as the greatest disintegrating forces in human history. But he believed in spirituality as the greatest integrating and unifying force in human society. So he said, "Our aim is not to found a religious faith or a school of philosophy or a school of Yogo but to create a ground of spiritual growth."[228] Hence it is obvious that Aurobindo like Swami Vivekananda was a spiritual personality, very much concerned with secularism, rather than religious sectarianism or fanaticism.

Aurobindo as a secularist, distinguished between true religion and religionism. The first is spiritual or secular religion, which informs all beings about the higher light, the law of spirit. The second entrenches itself in some narrow pietistic exaltation and rests on some fixed moral code. As religion must be able to spiritualise mankind for unity and common brotherhood, it must be a bonafide and lived religion. As he said, "Religion has to be lived not learned as a creed. No religious teaching is of any value unless it is lived."[229] He defended ancient Indian religion and culture because it held that man could become conscious of the eternal and he could spiritualise and divinise himself by self-knowledge. It filled the purpose of true secular religion.

To Aurobindo, religions may be different but the inner spirit of all religions is same. This inner spirit of all religions is meant for inspiring and influencing man for divinisation. As he said, "A religion of humanity means the growing realisation that there is one secret spirit in all religions, a divine spirit, in which we all get a lift."[230] Hence Aurobindo's secularist nationalism upholds the cause of religious toleration and abhors all communal discords leading to religious persecution and bloodshed.

Aurobindo, like Swami Vivekananda not only believed in religious unity; he also believed in the unity of godhead. To him there is but one God for people of all religions, though He differs in name and form. Some call Him God, some others may call Him Allah and some others say Him Krishna. But He is the same God everywhere, assuming different names for different sects of people. As he said, "All...is one...not a separate existence... separate in names and forms only."[231]

Aurobindo's secularistic religion served as a stimulus for the growth of nationalism in India. By secularising religion and eliminating all communal discords he developed a harmonious and unified living among the people of India that eventually galvanised the sense of national unity. Aurobindo described it as "Divine Unity in the nation,"[232] which is not marred by any fanaticism or sectarianism. Commenting on it, it is said, "Aurobindo's creed of nationalism is not narrow and fanatical, but had a cosmopolitan character."[233]

Aurobindo's secularistic ideology is more explicit in his synthesis of East and West. By secularising the religions of East he could succeed to bring about such a unique synthesis. But for such new philosophy *i.e.,* secularisation of spirit, coupled with spiritualisation of matter, the two divergent ideals could not have been reconciled. Hence it is said, "Aurobindo hoped that Indian spiritualism and European secularism and materialism could be reconciled and felt that this was possible only by the creation of a new secular philosophy which gives equal importance to the claims of both spirit and matter."[234] Charles A. Moore has also remarked, "Aurobindo's new philosophy (secularism) provides two great needs of the time, namely, a virtual synthesis of East and West, looking towards a philosophy, acceptable to all mankind and second a richful interpretation of Indian religion, correcting abuses and aberrations...."[235] However Aurobindo's secularism like that of Swami Vivekananda went much beyond the frontiers of religion and spirituality. He raised secularism to its status of materialism which is the prime concern of day-to-day world. He did not like to downgrade materialism, which, as he felt, has equal value and importance like spiritualism for the balanced improvement of the world. He felt that material needs of the poor is as important as the spiritual needs. Besides, amidst wretchedness, poverty and starvation it is too difficult to preach Advaitism and realise the grand dream of Universal Unity. So he decided that the poor must be given bread first and then religion. A hungry stomach knows no religion nor philosophy, nor anything else but bread and bread only. When his stomach is full, the world for him is O.K. or else it is a devil's workshop. Such consideration made Aurobindo a critic of the modern capitalism, which is characterised by oppression and exploitation of the poorer sections of the people. He criticised the imperialistic drain of wealth from the backward parts of the globe and its piling up in the capitalistic areas of the West that causes poverty and starvation in one part and plentitude in another part of the world.[236]

Like Swami Vivekananda and Aurobindo, Gandhi also advocated that secularism adds strength to a nation of diverse faiths. As a practical spiritualist, he realised very well the evils of religion. Religious spirit no doubt serves as a unifying factor of a nation but if there is overemphasis on religion it acts as the greatest disintegrating force. Hindu-Muslim communal conflicts opened his eyes to it. He considered communalism as the worst social evil in India. Communalism meant a fight between two different faiths for their respective supremacy. A truly spiritual man is always secular in his outlook. But most of the time religion is misinterpreted and misunderstood by the orthodox and fanatic section of the people who take religion in a narrower sense. So in order to help both the section of people like Hindu and Muslim to live peacefully he suggested the ideal of secularism.

Like Swami Vivekananda and Aurobindo, Gandhi also laid stress on the principle of religious toleration, harmony, co-operation and unity. To him these principles are the only road to happy and peaceful co-existence of the people of various faiths of a country. He explained that "religious toleration and harmony consists in our having a common purpose, common goal and common sorrows. It is best promoted by co-operating with each...by sharing one another's sorrows and by mutual tolerations."[237]

Like Swami Vivekananda and Aurobindo, he glorified India for her grand principle of religious toleration and hoped that after independence, India would stand as a great example of it to the world. As he said, "India of the near future stands for perfect toleration of all religions."[238]

Like Swami Vivekananda, who said "God is one but sages call Him differently." Gandhi also believed in the unity of Godhead. As he said, "There is one God, who is everywhere."[239] He also believed in the principle of equality of all religions. He considered different religion as different roads leading to the same destination *i.e.,* Moksha or Salvation. Brotherhood and friendship but not enmity, as he said to Dr. Iqbal, is the true essence of all religions.[240]

Gandhi fervently appealed to the people of all sects and faiths to forget religious bickerings and develop universal brotherhood for the cause of our motherland. He frequently laid stress on the unity of all religions for unity of India despite our various faiths and beliefs. As he said, "Let all of us Muslim, Parsis, Sikhs, Christians live amicably as Indians, pleaded to live and die for our motherland. Let it be our ambition to live as the children of same mother, retaining our individual faiths and yet being one, like the countless leaves of one tree."[241]

Gandhi's toleration for all religious faiths made him an advocate of secularism or a nation based on secular foundations. As he said, "The state should undoubtedly be secular."[242]

His secular attitude was best expressed in his address to All India Congress Committee on August 8, 1942 when he said, "The Congress does not believe in the domination of any group or any community. It believes in democracy which includes in its orbit Muslims, Hindus, Christians — every one of the communities, inhabiting this vast country."[243]

As a staunch secularist, he favoured neutrality of state in the matter of religion. India should not accord any preference to any particular religion. In matters of religion she must maintain strict neutrality. All religions will be treated equal. As he said, "In free India every religion should prosper on terms of equality unlike what is happening today. Christianity being the nominal religion of the rulers, it receives favours which other religions enjoy. A government responsible to the people dare not favour one religion over another."[244]

The state shall not accord any priority or preference to any particular religion. Instead it shall show eqnal respect to all religions. Religions shall not become the cause of discord among members of a nation. Therefore, he said, "I hold it to be utterly wrong to divide man on the ground of religion. What conflict of interest can there be in the matter of revenue, sanitation, police, justice or the use of public conveniences? The difference can only be in religious usages and observances with which a secular state has no concern."[245]

Gandhi said that a state has nothing to do with any religious matter. As he said, "In matters of religion I am against any state interference."[246]

Thus Swami Vivekananda, Aurobindo and Gandhi were secularists apart from being nationalists. Their nationalism emits secularistic fervour.

To sum up Swami Vivekananda, Sri Aurobindo Ghosh and Mahatma Gandhi had, as opposed to the moderate nationalists, identical objective in the sense that all the three had as the end of their nationalism, Swaraj for the country. For them Swaraj was the birth-right of every people and every nation. All the three were basically spiritual personalities and believed in the rich spiritual heritage of India. Hence their nationalism is spiritual in tone and temper. They felt that India has a spiritual mission for the whole world and that mission can be fulfilled only when India attains her nationhood. They realised the tremendous importance of education for building up a mighty nation and advocated Indianisation of educational system with its emphasis on spiritual basis of education and education through the medium of mother-tongue. All the three were great humanists apart from being nationalists. As a matter of fact their nationalism emanated from their deep sense of humanism. Hence their nationalism did not suffer from narrowness and exclusiveness but is marked by universalistic fervour and intense desire for effecting welfare of mankind. Although all the three were spiritual personalities, their nationalism is secular in nature in the sense that all believed in the spirit of mutual toleration by people of different faiths. That they felt shall strengthen the nation by unifying people of different religious belief.

REFERENCES

1. B.P. Sittaramayya, *History of Indian National Congress*, Vol. I, pp. 23-58.
2. Indian National Congress, *Presidential Address*, 1985-86.
3. *Bengalee*, 8 January, 1889, (*A Weekly*, Ed. By S.N. Banarjee).
4. B.G. Tilak's speech at Akola on 2nd May, 1908.
5. Aurobindo Ghose, *Speeches*, pp. 73-74.
6. B.G. Tilak, *His Writings and Speeches*, p. 164.
7. *Complete Works of Swami Vivekananda*, Vol. II, p. 125.
8. *Ibid.*, Vol. V, p. 434.
9. *Ibid.*, Vol. I, p. 108.
10. *Ibid.*, Vol. I, p. 108.
11. *Ibid.*, Vol. I, p. 333.
12. *Ibid.*, Vol. V, p. 145.
13. Quoted in Manomohan Ganguly, *Swami Vivekananda — A Study*, p. 60.
14. *Life of Swami Vivekananda*, Vol. II, p. 753.
15. *Complete Works of Swami Vivekananda*, Vol. V, p. 145.
16. *Lectures From Colombo to Almora*, p. 96.
17. *Complete Works of Swami Vivekananda*, Vol. VI, p. 454.
18. Quoted in Manomohan Ganguly, *Swami Vivekananda — A Study*, p. 60.
19. *Lectures From Colombo to Almora*, p. 38.
20. *Complete Works of Swami Vivekananda*, Vol. II, p. 124.
21. *Bande Mataram*, 5 March, 1908.
22. *Ibid.*, 23 February, 1908.
23. A.B. Purani, *The Life of Sri Aurobindo*, p. 126.
24. Sri Aurobindio, *The Doctrine of Passive Resistance*, p. 2.
25. *Ibid.*, p. 21.

26. *Bande Mataram*, 3 July, 1907.
27. Sri Aurobindo, *The Doctrine of Passive Resistance*, p. 21.
28. *Bande Mataram*, 27 April, 1907.
29. *Ibid.*, 27 April, 1907.
30. *Ibid.*, 21st July, 1908.
31. G.D. Tendulkar, *Mahatma Gandhi*, Vol. 1, p. 158.
32. Edwin S. Montague, *An Indian Diary*, Ed. by Venetia Montague, p. 58.
33. M.K. Gandhi, *Speeches and Writings*, p. 310.
34. Simon Panter Brick, *Gandhi against Machiavellism*, p. 67.
35. M.K. Gandhi, *Hind Swaraj and Indian Home Rule*, p. 65.
36. *Ibid.*, p. 104.
37. Louis Fischer, *The Life of Mahatma Gandhi*, Vol. II, p. 127.
38. Quoted in V.P. Varma, *Modern Indian Political Thought*, p. 355.
39. Nirmal Kumar Bose, *Selections from Gandhi*, p. 111.
40. *Ibid.*, p. 111.
41. *Harijan*, June 9, 1946.
42. V.P. Varma, *Modern Indian Poltical Thought*, p. 355.
43. *Harijan*, 9 May 1946.
44. F.R. Moraes, *Gandhi, the Humanist*, 75th Birthday Volume, 1944, pp. 19-20.
45. M.K. Gandhi, *Hind Swaraj and Indian Home Rule*, p. 60.
46. *Harijan*, Feb. 3, 1942.
47. *Young India*, April 24, 1930.
48. *Ibid.*, August 24, 1945.
49. *Ibid.*, November 19, 1920.
50. *Ibid.*, October 13, 1921.
51. *Ibid.*, April 7, 1927.
52. *Ibid.*, April 3, 1924.
53. H.J. Laski, *A Grammar of Politics*, p. 219.
54. R.N. Tagore, *Towards Univerisal Man*, p. 350.
55. Pandit Nehru, *Discovery of India*, p. 45.
56. *Ibid.*, pp. 536-37.
57. *Complete Works of Swami Vivekananda*, Vol. III, p. 148.
58. *Ibid.*, Vol. III, p. 137.
59. *Ibid.*, Vol. III, p. 179.

60. *Complete Works of Swami Vivekananda,* Vol. III, p. 137.
61. *Ibid.,* Vol. III, p. 139.
62. *Ibid.,* Vol. III, p. 371.
63. *Ibid.,* Vol. III, p. 147.
64. *Ibid.,*Vol. III, p. 370.
65. *Nationalistic and Religious Lectures of Swami Vivekananda,* pp. 85-86.
66. *Complete Works of Swami Vivekananda,*Vol. III, p. 371.
67. *Ibid.,* Vol. III, p. 148.
68. M.N. Roy, *Selected Works,* Vol. I, p. 338.
69. R.R. Diwakar, *Mohayogi Sri Aurobindo,* p. 63.
70. *Selected Works of M.N. Roy,* Vol. II, p. 165.
71. J. Ramsay Mac Donald, *The Awakening of India,* p. 182.
72. *Nationalistic and Religious Lectures of Swami Vivekananda,* p. 44.
73. *Complete Works of Swami Vivekananda,* Vol. III, p. 221.
74. Essays in *Karmayogin, Sir Aurobindo.*
75. *Speeches, Sir Aurobindo,* pp. 7-9.
76. *Uttar Para Speech,* Sri Aurobindo, p. 20.
77. *Complete Works of Swami Vivekananda,* Vol. III, p. 461.
78. *Bande Materam,* 1 May, 1908.
79. Dr. Karan Singh, *Prophet of Indian Nationalism,* p. 142.
80. *Vinoba on Gandhi,* p. 6.
81. *Young India,* October 7, 1924.
82. Nirmal Kumar Bose, *Selection from Gandhi,* p. 225.
83. M.K. Gandhi, *Non-Violence in Peace and War,* Vol. I, p. 138.
84. *Harijan,* May 18, 1940.
85. M.K. Gandhi, *Speeches,* p. 753.
86. Nirmal Kumar Bose, *Selection from Gandhi,* p. 113.
87. R.K. Prabhu and U.R. Rao, *The Mind of Mahatma Gandhi,* p. 135.
88. *Vinoba on Gandhi,* p. 26.
89. *Ibid.,* p. 30.
90. *Conversation of Gandhi,* Ed. C.S. Sukla, p. 14.
91. *Young India,* May 8, 1920.
92. *Harijan,* 7 November, 1921.
93. *Young India,* November 27, 1924.

94. N.B. Sen, *Glorious Thoughts of Gandhi*, p. 230.
95. Romain Rolland, *Mahatma Gandhi*, p. 144.
96. A.R. Desai, *Social Background of Indian Nationalism*, p. 158.
97. *Complete Works of Swami Vivekananda*, Vol. IV, p. 362.
98. *Ibid.*, Vol. V, p. 342.
99. *Ibid.*, Vol. VIII, p. 280.
100. *Ibid.*, Vol. III, p. 103.
101. *Ibid.*, Vol. V, p. 10.
102. *Ibid.*, Vol. III, p. 301.
103. *Ibid.*, Vol. V, p. 10.
104. *Ibid.*, Vol. V, p. 264.
105. *Ibid.*, Vol. III, p. 302.
106. *Nationalistic and Religious Lectures of Vivekananda*, p. 62.
107. *Ibid.*, p. 62.
108. *Complete Works of Swami Vivekananda*, Vol. VI, p. 187.
109. *Ibid.*, Vol. VI, p. 188.
110. *Ibid.*, Vol. VI, p. 189.
111. *Ibid.*, Vol. V, p. 362.
112. *Ibid.*, Vol. V, p. 106.
113. *Ibid.*, Vol. VII, p. 372.
114. *Ibid.*, Vol. VIII, p. 308.
115. R.R. Diwakar, *Mahayogi Sri Aurobindo*, p. 30.
116. *Bande Mataram*, 17 April, 1907.
117. Quoted in S.C. Sengupta, *Swami Vivekananda and Indian Nationalism*, p. 101.
118. Sri Aurobindo's speeches, p. 3.
119. S.C. Sengupta, *Swami Vivekananda and Indian Nationalism*, p. 101.
120. Haridas and Uma Mukherjee, *Origin of the National Education Movement*, p. 50.
121. *Bande Mataram*, 17 April, 1907.
122. *Ibid.*, 17 April, 1907.
123. R.C. Majumdar, *History of Freedom Movement in India*, Vol. II, p. 78.
124. Sri Aurobindo, *The Brain of India*, pp. 9-10.
125. *Bande Matram*, 24 February, 1908.
126. *Ibid.*, 13 July, 1907.

127. *Bande Matram*, 24 February, 1908.
128. *Ibid.*, 26 June, 1907.
129. *Ibid.*, 13 July, 1907.
130. *Harijan*, January 28, 1909.
131. *Collected Works of Mahatma Gandhi*, Vol. XXVIII, p. 329.
132. *Ibid.*
133. *Ibid.*
134. *Ibid.*
135. *Ibid.*, p. 330.
136. *Ibid.*, Vol. XIV, p. 208.
137. *Ibid.*, Vol. XXVIII, p. 329.
138. *Ibid.*, Vol. XIV, p. 207.
139. *Ibid.*, Vol. XXVIII, p. 330.
140. *Speeches and Writings of Mahatma Gandhi*, p. 224.
141. *Collected Works of Mahatma Gandhi*, Vol. XXVIII, p. 329.
142. *Ibid.*, Vol. XXVIII, p. 329.
143. *Ibid.*, Vol. XIV, p. 207.
144. *Ibid.*
145. *Ibid.*, Vol. XIV, p. 206.
146. *Bruhadaranyak Upanishad*, *Shantipatha*, Sloka-1.
147. *Yajurveda*, Chapter 36, *Mantra*-10.
148. R.N. Tagore, *Sadhana*, p. 108.
149. M.N. Roy, *Reason, Romanticism and Revolution*, p. 105.
150. Swami Vivekananda, *Practical Vedanta*, p. 105.
151. R.N. Tagore, *Arogya*, p. 29.
152. Annie Besant, *The Self and its Sheaths*, p. 1.
153. *Complete Works of Swami Vivekananda*, Vol. IV, p. 356.
154. *Ibid.*, Vol. IV, p. 122.
155. *Ibid.*, Vol. VI, p. 264.
156. Romain Rolland, *The Life of Swami Vivekananda and Universal Gospel*, p. 11.
157. *Life of Swami Vivekananda*, Vol. III, p. 178 (by his Eastern and Western Disciple).
158. Romain Rolland, *The Life of Swami Vivekananda*, p. 88.
159. *Ibid.*, p. 89.

160. Swami Vivekananda, *A Centenary Volume*, p. 150.
161. H.J. Laski, *A Grammar of Politics*, p. 89.
162. *Complete Works of Swami Vivekananda*, Vol. V, p. 287.
163. *Ibid.*, Vol. V, p. 289.
164. *The Life of Swami Vivekananda*, Vol. VI, p. 55.
165. *Ibid.*, Vol. I, pp. 306-07.
166. *Complete Works of Swami Vivekananda*, Vol. V, p. 106.
167. Swami Vivekananda very often said, "I know my mission in life and no chauvinism about me; I belong as much to India as to the world...."
168. Swami Vivekananda, *Studies in Soviet Union*, p. 216 (A Centenary Volume).
169. *Nationalistic and Religious Lectures of Swami Vivekananda*, p. 73.
170. *Complete Works of Swami Vivekananda*, Vol. III, p. 241.
171. Jawaharlal Nehru, *Discovery of India*, p. 316.
172. Swami Vivekananda, *Studies in Soviet Union*, p. 217 (A Centenary Volume).
173. Indu Prakash, December 4, 1895.
174. V.P. Varma, *Modern Indian Political Thought*, p. 304.
175. Quoted in Karan Singh, *Prophet of Indian Nationalism*, p. 80.
176. R.R. Diwakar, *Maha Yogi Sri Aurobindo*, p. 147.
177. Sri Aurobindo, *The Ideal of Human Unity*, p. 773.
178. Sri Aurobindo, *The Human Cycle*, p. 85.
179. Sri Aurobindo, *The Ideal of Human Unity*, p. 7.
180. *Ibid.*, p. 733.
181. *The Integral Philosophy of Sri Aurobindo*, Ed. by H. Chaudhury, p. 314.
182. M.N. Roy, *Reason Romanticism and Revolution*, Vol. II, p. 227.
183. Annie Besant, *The Ancient Wisdom*, pp. 189-90.
184. Sri Aurobindo, *The Essential Ideals of All Mankind*, p. 97.
185. *The Integral Philosophy of Sri Aurobindo*, Ed. by H. Chaudhury, p. 312.
186. Sri Aurobindo, *Ideals and Progress*, p. 44
187. *Sri Aurobindo and Mother on the Essential Ideals of All Mankind*, p. 85.
188. Sri Aurobindo, *Ideals and Progress*, p. 45.
189. C.A. Moore, *The Integral Philosophy of Sri Aurobindo*, p. 108.

190. Sri Aurobindo, *The Ideal of Human Unity*, p. 723.
191. *Ibid.*, p. 723.
192. *Ibid.*, pp. 399-400.
193. Sri Aurobindo, *The Life Divine*, p. 606.
194. Sri Aurobindo, *A Practical Guide to Integral Yoga*, p. 236.
195. Sri Aurobindo, *The Life Divine*, p. 660.
196. Sri Aurobindo, *Bande Mataram, Early Political Writings*, p. 126.
197. Quoted in *Vinoba on Gandhi*, p. 31.
198. *Ibid.*, p. 29.
199. F.R. Moraes, *Gandhi, The Humanist*, pp. 19-20.
200. Quoted in Louis Fischer, *The Life of Gandhi*, Part-II, p. 286.
201. *Young India*, November 5, 1938.
202. *Ibid.*, December 26, 1926.
203. *Collected Works of Mahatma Gandhi*, Vol. VI, p. 401.
204. R.N. Tagore, *Sadhana*, p. 41.
205. Quoted in D.G. Tendulkar, *Mahatma*, Vol. IV, p. 109.
206. *Ibid.*, Vol. VIII, p. 142.
207. *Harijan*, August 4, 1940.
208. *Young India*, August 8, 1929.
209. *Complete Works of Swami Vivekananda*, Vol. III, p. 167.
210. D.G. Tendulkar, *Mahatma*, Vol. II, p. 168.
211. *Young India*, November 7, 1933.
212. *Ibid.*, June 18, 1925.
213. *Young India*, October 13, 1921.
214. *Ibid.*, June 18, 1948.
215. *Ibid.*, March 12, 1931.
216. R.K. Prabhu and U.R. Roa, *The Mind of Mahatma Gandhi*, p. 49.
217. Dr. Rajendra Prasad, *Legacy of Gandhi*, p. 65.
218. *Lectures From Colombo to Almora*, p. 89.
219. *Complete Works of Swami Vivekananda*, Vol. III, p. 114.
220. Quoted in Peter Heehs, *India's Freedom Struggle*, p. 156.
221. *Complete Works of Swami Vivekananda*, Vol. III, p. 480.
222. *Letters of Swami Vivekananda*, p. 454.
223. *Proletariat! Win Equal Rights*, p. 57.
224. Shri Aurobindo, *The Human Cycle*, p. 232.

225. *Ibid.*, p. 223.
226. Sri Aurobindo, *Ideals and Progress*, p. 44.
227. *Ibid.*, p. 38.
228. Sri Aurobindo, *A Practical Guide to Integral Yogo*, p. 56.
229. *Ibid.*, p. 224.
230. Sri Aurobindo, *The Ideal of Human Unity*, p. 775.
231. Sri Aurobindo, *Life Divine*, p. 136.
232. *Bande Mataram*, September 22, 1907.
233. V.P. Varma, *Modern Indian Political Thought*, p. 307.
234. *Ibid.*, p. 300.
235. C.A. Moore, *The Integral Philosophy of Sri Aurobindo*, p. 106.
236. V.P. Varma, *Modern Indian Political Thought*, p. 308.
237. *Young India*, February 25, 1930.
238. *Ibid.*, December 12, 1922.
239. Chandra Sekhar Sukla, *Conversation of Gandhi*, p. 28.
240. M.K. Gandhi, *Non-violence in Peace and War*, Vol. II, p. 249.
241. *Young India*, April 23, 1931.
242. *Harijan*, August 29, 1947.
243. Quoted in D.G. Tendulkar, *Mahatma*, Vol. VI, p. 59.
244. *Harijan*, December 30, 1939.
245. Quoted in Peter Heehs, *India's Freedom Struggle*, p. 155.
246. *Young India*, July 7, 1927.

Bibliography

(a) PRIMARY SOURCES

(i) Books by Swami Vivekananda

The Complete Works, Vol. I to Vol. VIII, Mayavati Memorial Edition, Advaita Ashram, Calcutta, 1972.

Lectures from Colombo to Almora, Mayavati Memorial Edition, Advaita Ashram, Calcutta, 1975.

The East and West, Mayavati Memorial Edition, Advaita Ashram, Calcutta, 1946.

Modern India, Mayavati Memorial Edition, Advaita Ashram, Calcutta, 1946.

On India and Her Problems, Advaita Ashram, Almora, 1946.

India's Message to the World, Advaita Ashram, Almora, 1946.

Our Duty to the Masses, Advaita Ashram, Almora, 1946.

A Plan of Work for India, Advaita Ashram, Almora, 1946.

To the Awakened India, Advaita Ashram, Almora, 1946.

The Education that India Needs, Advaita Ashram, Almora, 1946.

Proletariat! Win Equal Rights, Advaita Ashram, Mayavati, 1984.

Our Present Social Problems, Advaita Ashram, Almora, 1946.

Practical Vedanta, Advaita Ashram, Calcutta, 1958.

Idea of Universal Religion (Selected Works), Advaita Ashram, Calcutta, 1958.

The Way to the Realisation of Universal Religion, Advaita Ashram, Calcutta, 1958.

The Great Teachers of the World, Advaita Ashram, Calcutta, 1958.

Is India a Benighted Country? Advaita Ashram, Calcutta, 1958.

The Future of India, Advaita Ashram, Calcutta, 1958.

The Mission of Vedanta, Advaita Ashram, Calcutta, 1958.

My Plan of Campaign, Advaita Ashram, Calcutta, 1958.

Sri Ramkrishna, *The Great Master*, Advaita Ashram, Calcutta, 1958.

To the Youths of India, Advaita Ashram, Almora, 1963.

The Man-Making Message for the College Students, Sri Ramkrishna Tapovanam,Tiruchinapalli, 1972.

Caste, Culture and Socialism, Advaita Ashram, Almora, 1963.

Karma Yogo, Advaita Ashram, Calcutta, 1970.

Vedanta : Voice of Freedom, Advaita Ashram, Calcutta, 1970.

Hinduism, Advaita Ashram, Calcutta, 1928.

Women of India, Advaita Ashram, Calcutta, 1928.

What Religion Is, Advaita Ashram, Calcutta, 1928.

Spiritual Heritage of India, Ramkrishna Math, Mylapore, Madras, 1956.

Chicago Address, Advaita Ashram, Calcutta, 1946.

My Life and Mission, Advaita Ashram, Calcutta, 1946.

The Science and Philosophy of Religion, Udbodhan Series, Baghabazar, Calcutta, 1923.

Religion of Love, Udbodhan Series, Baghabazar, Calcutta, 1923.

A Study of Religion, Udbodhan Series, Baghabazar, Calcutta, 1923.

(ii) Books on Swami Vivekananda

Abhedananda, Swami, *Swami Vivekananda and His Activities*, Advaita Ashram, Calcutta, 1960.

Arora, V.K., *The Social Political Philosophy of Swami Vivekananda*, Punthi Pustak, Calcutta-4, 1968.

Budhananda, Swami, *Swami Vivekananda, His Call to the Nation*, Advaita Ashram, Calcutta-14, 1971.

Burke, Marie Louis, *Swami Vivekananda in America : New Discoveries*, Advaita Ashram, Calcutta-14, 1958.

Dhaban, S.N., *Comprehensive Biography of Swami Vivekananda*, Vivekananda Prakashan Kendra, Madras-5, 1975.

Datta, B.N., *Swami Vivekananda : Patriot-Prophet,* Calcutta Navbharat Publisher, 1954.

Dev, G.C., *Swami Vivekananda's Ethics of Religion and Service,* Vivekananda Centenary Volume, Advaita Ashram, Calcutta, 1963.

Eastern & Western Disciples, *Life of Swami Vivekananda,* Advaita Ashram, Almora, 1933.

Eastern & Western Admirers, *Reminiscences of Swami Vivekananda,* Advaita Ashram, Mayabati, 1983.

Ganguly, Manomohan, *Swami Vivekananda — A Study,* Contemporary Publishers Pvt. Ltd., Calcutta-3, 1962.

Gambhirananda, Swami, *A Short Life of Swami Vivekananda,* Advaita Ashram, Calcutta, 1958.

Jitatmananda, Swami, *Swami Vivekananda : Prophet & Pathfinder,* Ramkrishna Math, Mylapore, Madras, 1985.

Lokeswarananda, Swami, (Ed.), *Studies in Soviet Union,* (Centenary Volume), Ramkrishna Mission, Institute of Culture, Golpark, Calcutta, 1987.

Mujumdar, R.C., *Vivekananda : A Historical Review,* Advaita Ashram, Calcutta, 1965.

Mukherjee, S.L., *Social and Political Ideas of Swami Vivekananda,* Cultural Institute, Ramkrishna Mission, Golpark, Calcutta, 1986.

Mukherjee, Hiren, *Vivekananda and Indian Freedom,* Cultural Institute, Ramkrishna Mission, Golpark, Calcutta, 1986.

Nivedita, Sister, *The Master As I Saw Him,* Udbodhan Office, Baghabazar, Calcutta, 1923.

Nivedita, Sister, *Notes of Some Wonderings With Swami Vivekananda,* Udbodhan Office, Baghabazar, Calcutta, 1923.

Nikhilananda, Swami, *A Biography of Swami Vivekananda,* Advaita Ashram, Calcutta, 1923.

Rolland, Romain, *Life of Swami Vivekananda and the Universal Gospel,* Advaita Ashram, Almora, 1953.

Ramkrishnan, R., *Swami Vivekananda : Awakener of Modern India,* Ramkrishna Math, New Delhi, 1979.

Rao, V.K.R.V., *Swami Vivekananda : The Prophet of Vedantic Socialism*, New Delhi, 1979.

Ranganathananda, Swami, *Swami Vivekananda : His Humanism*, Advaita Ashram, Calcutta, 1970.

Roy, B.K., *Socio-Political Views of Swami Vivekananda*, New Delhi, 1970.

Sengupta, S.C., *Swami Vivekananda and Indian Nationalism*, Sahitya Sansad Pvt. Ltd., Calcutta, 1984.

Tapasyananda, Swami, *Swami Vivekananda : His Life & Legacy*, Ramkrishna Matha, Mylapore, Madras, 1985.

——, *Nationalistic & Religious Lectures of Swami Vivekananda*, Ramkrishna Matha, Mylapore, Madras, 1989.

Tajesananda, Swami, *A Short Life of Swami Vivekananda*, Advaita Ashram, Calcutta, 1942.

Vaswani, T.L., *The Voice of Vivekananda*, East and West Series, Connaught Road, Poona, 1959.

(b) SECONDARY SOURCES

Agrov, Daniel, *Moderates and Extremists in Indian National Movements (1883-1920)*, Calcutta, Asia Publishing House, 1934.

Ahluwalia, M.M., *Freedom Struggle in India (1858-1909)*, Delhi Ranjit Printers and Publishers, 1965.

Aiyar, S. Kailasam, *The Present Situation in India*, London, 1909.

Allen, J.T. Wolseley Haig & H.H. Dodwell (Ed.), *Cambridge History of India*, Bombay, Bharatiya Vidyabhawan, 1964.

Allen, J.W., *A History of Political Thought in Sixth Century*, London, 1942.

Amery, L.S., *The German Colonial Claim*, London, 1939.

Andrews, C.F., *Mahatma Gandhi's Ideas*, London, George Allen & Unwin, 1949.

——, *The Renaissance in India*, London, 1912.

Arthursteiner, H., *Principles and Problems of International Relations*, New York : Harper, 1940.

Aurobindo, Sri, *The Renaissance in India*, Pondicherry, Sri Aurobindo Ashram, 1920.

——, *The Doctrine of Passive Resistance*, Pondicherry, Sri Aurobindo Ashram, 1955.

——, *Speeches*, Calcutta, 1922.

——, *Uttarpara Speeches*, Pondicherry, Sri Aurobindo Ashram, 1950.

——, *The Ideal of Human Unity*, Pondicherry, Sri Aurobindo Ashram, 1962.

——, *The Essential Ideals of All Mankind*, Pondicherry, Sri Aurobindo Ashram, 1962.

——, *Ideals and Progress*, Pondicherry, Sri Aurobindo Ashram, 1918.

——, *The Life Divine*, Pondicherry, Sri Aurobindo Ashram, 1940.

——, *Essay on Gita*, New York, Sri Aurobindo Library, 1950.

——, *The Foundation of Indian Culture*, New York, Sri Aurobindo Library, 1953.

——, *On Nationalism*, Pondicherry, Sri Aurobindo Ashram, 1965.

——, *A System of National Education*, Pondicherry, Sri Aurobindo Ashram, 1921.

——, *Bande Mataram : Early Political Writings*, Vol. I, Pondicherry, Sri Aurobindo Ashram, 1972.

——, *Karmayogin : Early Political Writings*, Vol. II, Pondicherry, Sri Aurobindo Ashram, 1972.

——, *Present Situation in India*, Madras, 1909.

Barker, Ernest, *Political Thought in England from 1849 to 1914*, London, Oxford University Press, 1915.

Bali, D.R., *Modern Indian Thought*, Sterling Publisher Pvt. Ltd., New Delhi, 1988.

Bakshi, S.R., *Gandhi and Concept of Swaraj*, Criterion Publication, New Delhi, 1988.

——, *Gandhi and the Mass Movement*, Atlantic Publisher, New Delhi, 1990.

Bandopadhyya, J., *Social and Political Thoughts of Gandhi*, Delhi Allied Publishers, 1956.

Basu, B.D. (Maj.), *Ruin of India's Trade and Industries*, Calcutta, 1935.

Bayly, C.A., *The Local Roots of Indian Politics*, Oxford, Clarendon Press, 1975.

Banarjee, Surendra Nath, *A Nation in the Making*, Calcutta, 1925.

Bevan, Edwyn, *Indian Nationalism*, London, 1913.

Besant, Annie, *The Self and its Sheaths*, London, Theosophical Publishing Society, 1884.

——, *The Education of Indian Girls*, London, T.P.H., 1904.

——, *The Ancient Wisdom, Madras*, T.P.H., 1959.

——, *The Wisdom of Upanishads*, Madras, T.P.H., 1952.

——, *Autobiography*, Madras, T.P.H., 1939.

——, *Wake Up, India*, Madras, 1913.

——, *Hinduism*, Madras, T.P.H., 1915.

——, *The Bhagvad Gita*, Madras, T.P.H., 1916.

Beard, Charles, *American Foreign Policy in the Making (1932-40)*, New Heaven : Yale University Press, 1946.

Bhattacharyya, Haridas (Ed.), *The Cultural Heritage of India*, Vol. III & IV, R.K. Mission, Institute of Culture, Golpark, Calcutta, 1966.

Bhaktivedanta Swami, A.C., *Bruhadaranyaka Upanishad*, London : Macmillan Publisher, 1974.

——, *Ishopanishad*, London : Macmillan Publisher, 1976.

——, *Yajurveda*, London : Macmillan Publisher, 1980.

——, *Rigveda*, London : Macmillan Publisher, 1980.

Bipin Chandra, *Nationalism and Colonialism in Modern India*, New Delhi, Orient Longman, 1979.

Bipin Chandra Amles Tripathi & Barun De, *Freedom Struggle*, National Book Trust, India, New Delhi, 1972.

Bose, Nemaisadhan, *The Indian National Movement*, Calcutta, 1965.

Bosu, Sankariprasad, *Letters of Sister Nivedita*, Vol. I, Udbodhan Office, Baghabazar, Calcutta, 1916.

Brick, Siman Panter, *Gandhi against Machiavellism*, Bombay, Asia Publishing House, 1966.

Bose, Nirmal Kumar, *Selections From Gandhi*, Ahmedabad, N.P.H., 1948.

Bose, S.C., *Indian Struggle*, London, 1935.

Buell, L. Raymond, *International Relations*, New York : Holt, 1929.

Burnes, Leonard, *Future of Colonies*, London : Hogarth & Co., 1941.

Burns, E.M., *Ideas in Conflict*, New York : W.W. Norton & Co., 1941.

Bush, M.A., *Rise and Growth of Indian Militant Nationalism*, Baroda, 1940.

Bryce, Lord, *International Relations*, London : Macmillan, 1942.

Cady, John F., The *Roots of French Imperialism in Eastern Asia*, Ithaca : Cornell University Press, 1954.

Cantor, Norman F., *The Age of Protest*, London : Allen & Unwin, 1970.

Chatterjee, Nandalal, *India's Freedom Struggle*, Allahabad, 1958.

Chowdhary, Sukhbir, *Indian People Fight for National Liberation*, Srijanee Prakashan, New Delhi, 1972.

Chirol, Valentine, *Indian Unrest*, Light and Life Publisher, New Delhi, 1979.

Crawford, Arthur, *The Unrest in India*, Publication Division, Govt. of India, New Delhi, 1978.

Clark, Grover, *The Balance Sheet of Imperialism : Facts and Figures on Colonies*, New York : Columbia University Press, 1936.

Das, M.N., *World History*, Vidyapuri, Bhubaneswar, 1980.

——, *Modern Indian History*, Vidyapuri, Bhubaneswar, 1980.

——, *Indian National Congress Vrs The British*, Vol. I, Delhi, 1978.

Datta, R.C., *The Economic History of India*, Vol. II, Government of India Press, Delhi, 1963.

——, *The Economic History of India Under Early British Rule*, Vol. I, Trubner and Co. Ltd., 1903.

Datta, K.K., *Dawn of Renascent India*, Nagpur, 1950.

Das, Hari and Uma Mukherjee, *Origin of National Educational Movement*, Jadavpur, Calcutta, 1957.

Desai, A.R., *Social Background of Indian Nationalism*, Bombay : Popular Prakashan, 1966

——, *Recent Trends in Indian Nationalism*, Bombay : Popular Book Depot, 1960.

Deussen, Paul, *The Philosophy of Upanishads*, T and T. Clark, Edenburgh, 1908.

De Rein Court, Amaury, *The Soul of India*, New York, 1960, Harper (Bros.).

Diwakar, R.R., *Mohayogi Aurobind*, Bharatiya Vidya Bhawan, (Bombay), 1964.

——, *Paramahansa Sri Ramkrishna*, Bharatiya Vidya Bhawan, (Bombay), 1965.

Dunning, W.A., *History of Political Theories* (from Rousseau to Spencer), Central Publishing House, Allahabad, 1989.

Ebenstein, William, *Today's Ism*, Prentice Hall, I.N.C., England, Woodcliff New Jersey, 1973.

——, *Modern Political Thought*, New York, McGraw Hill, 1978.

——, *Great Political Thinkers*, Oxford and I.P.H. Publishing Company, Calcutta, 1975.

Edwin, Arnold, *The Song Celestial*, London, 1912.

Encyclopaedia Britannica, Vol. 19, U.S.A., R.R. Donnelley & Sons Co., 1973.

Encyclopaedia of Social Science, Vol. VII, *The Song Celestial*, New York, The Macmillan Company, 1937.

Fischer, Louis, *The Life of Mahatma Gandhi*, Bombay, Bharatiya Vidya Bhawan, 1955.

Friedman, W., *Introduction to World Politics*, London : Macmillan Company, 1943.

Gandhi, M.K., *Speeches and Writings*, Madras, G.A. Natesan & Co., 1918.

——, *Hind Swaraj and Indian Home Rule*, Ahmedabad : Navjivan Publishing House, 1948.

——, *Non-Violence in Peace and War*, Ahmedabad : Navjivan Publishing House, 1948.

——, *The Story of my Experiment with Truth*, Ahmedabad : Navjivan Publishing House, 1956.

——, *Collected Works*, Vol. XXVIII, Vol. XIX, Vol. VI, Publication Division, New Delhi, 1982.

Gambhirananda, Swami, *History of Ramkrishna Math and Mission*, Ramkrishna Mission, Calcutta, 1957.

Gettell, R.G., *Political Science*, London : Ginn, 1949.

——, *History of Political Thought*, London : Allen and Unwin, 1940.

Grover, B.L., *A New Look on Modern Indian History*, S. Chand & Co. Ltd., New Delhi, 1984.

——, *A Documentary Study of British Policy towards Indian Nationalism (1888-1909)*, Delhi, 1967.

Hayes, Charlton J.H., *The Historical Evolution of Modern Nationalism*, Peterborough, N.H., The Richard R. Smith Co., 1931.

——, *Nationalism*, New York : The Macmillan Company, 1948.

——, *Nationalism, A Religion*, New York : The Macmillan Company, 1960.

Heehs, Peter, *India's Freedom Struggle*, Pondicherry, Sri Aurobindo Ashram, 1950.

Hobson, J.H., *Imperialism : A Study*, London : George Allen and Unwin, 1938.

Hobbes, Thomas, *Levianthan*, Part I, London : Oxford University Press, 1916.

Hodges, Charles, *The Background of International Relations*, New York, John Wiley & Sons, 1932.

Inge, W.R., *Mysticism in Religion*, London, 1947.

Ingham, Kenneth, *Reforms in India*, Macmillan, Calcutta, 1956.

Jagindar, P.R., *M.G. Ranade*, Nasik, 1971.

Joseph, Bernard, *Nationality*, London : George Allen & Unwin, 1950.

Joad, C.E.M., *Introduction to Modern Political Theory*, Oxford University Press, Walton Street, 1987.

Keith, A.B., *The Religion and Philosophy of the Vedas and the Upanishads*, Harvard University Press, 1925.

Kohn, Hans, *Reflections on Colonialism*, New York : Frederick A. Praeger, 1958.

——, *Nationalism and Internationalism*, New York : Macmillan Co., 1937.

——, *A History of Nationalism in the East*, New York : Macmillan Co., 1931.

——, *Prophets and People*, New York : Macmillan Co., 1946.

Knowles, L.C., *Economic Development of Great Britain in 19th Century*, Harvard University Press, 1925.

Laski, H.J., *The State in Theory and Practice*, London : George Allen & Unwin, 1951.

——, *Reflections and Revolutions of Our Time*, London : George Allen & Unwin, 1950.

——, *Communism*, London : George Allen & Unwin, 1967.

——, *A Grammar of Politics*, London : George Allen & Unwin, 1960.

Lattimore, Owen, *Situation in Asia*, Boston : Little Brown and Company, 1949.

Lichtheim, George, *Imperialism*, Alen Lane, The Penguin Press, London, 1971.

Luniya, B.N., *Evolution of Indian Culture*, Laxminarayan Agarwal, Educational Publishers, Agra, 1983.

Macnicol, N., *The Making of Modern India*, Oxford University Press, 1924.

Macdonald, J. Ramsay, *The Awakening of India*, London, 1911.

Macaulay, Lord, *Speeches with His Minute on Indian Education*, London : G.M. Young, 1935.

Masani, R.P., *Dadabhai Naoroji*, New Delhi Publication Division, 1975.

——, *Britain in India*, Bombay : Oxford University Press, 1962.

Marx and Angles, Vol. I, Foreign Languages Moscow Publishing House, 1949.

Mazumdar, A.C., *Indian National Evolution*, Madras, 1917.

Mill, J.S., *Representative Government*, New York, 1875.

Moraes, F.R., *Gandhi — The Humanist*, Bombay : Asia Publishing House, 1967.

Moon, P.T., *Imperialism and World Politics*, New York : The Macmillan Co., 1926.

Moor, C.A., *The Integral Philosophy of Sri Aurobindo*, Jaico Publishing House, Bombay, 1954.

Morgenthau, Hans J., *Politics Among Nations*, Kalyani Publisher, New Delhi, 1991.

Mujumdar, R.C., *History of Freedom Movement in India*, Vol. II, Bombay : Bharatiya Vidya Bhawan, 1958.

——, *History and Culture of Indian People*, Vol. I & Vol. VI, Bombay : Bharatiya Vidya Bhawan, 1960.

Mukherjee, Radhakumud, *The Fundamental Unity of India*, Calcutta, 1925.

Mukherjee, Hiren, *Gandhi — A Study*, New Delhi : People's Publishing House, 1960.

Mukherjee, S.N., *History of Education in India*, Baroda Acharya Book Depot, 1955.

Muir, Ramsay, *The British History*, Book I to Book III, Capital Book House, Jawahar Nagar, Delhi.

Narvane, V.S., *Modern Indian Thought*, People's Publishing House, New Delhi, 1960.

Naoroji, Dadabhai, *The Essays, Speeches and Writings*, Bombay, 1892.

——, *Poverty and Un-British Rule in India*, Nasik, 1962.

Nehru, Jawaharlal, *Discovery of India*, Signet Press, Calcutta, 1946.

——, *India Today and Tomorrow*, New Age Printing Press, Jhansi Road, New Delhi, 1960.

——, *Indian Independence and Social Revolution*, Vikash Publishing House Pvt. Ltd., New Delhi, 1984.

Nikhilanda, Swami, *The Gospel of Sri Ramkrishna*, Vol. I & II, (Translation from Bengali) Ramkrishna Math, Mylapore, Madras, 1985.

Nivedita, Sister, *Complete Works*, Udbodhan Office, Baghabazar, Calcutta, 1950.

——, *Aggressive Hinduism*, Udbodhan Office, Baghabazar, Calcutta, 1952.

——, *The Web of Indian Life*, Udbodhan Office, Baghabazar, Calcutta, 1950.

——, *Civic and National Ideals*, Udbodhan Office, Baghabazar, Calcutta, 1949.

Pal, B.C., *Rise and Growth of Economic Nationalism in India*, Calcutta Jagajatri Prakashan, 1954.

——, *The Memoirs of My Life and Time*, Calcutta, 1932.

——, *Indian Nationalism*, Calcutta : Jagajatri Prakashan, 1932.

Palmer & Perkins, *International Relations*, Jain Bhawan, Bholanath Nagar, Delhi, 1955.

Panikkar, K.M., *Asia and Western Dominance*, Bombay : Asia Publishing House, 1955.

Payne Robert, *The Revolt of Asia*, New York : The John Day Co., 1947.

Perkins, Dexter, *The American Approach to Foreign Policy*, Cambridge, Mass. : Harvard University Press, 1952.

——, *The United States and Latin America*, Baton Rough Louisiana State University Press, 1961.

Pool, John J., *Famous Women of India*, London, 1962.

Prabhu, R.K. and Roa, U.R., *The Mind of Mahatma Gandhi*, Oxford University Press, 1945.

Purani, A.B., *Studies in Vedic Interpretation*, Varanasi : Chowkhamba Sanskrit Series, 1963.

Purohit, B.R., *Hindu Revivalism and Indian Nationalism*, Lucknow : Sethi Prakashan, 1965.

Rao, Vyas, *Foundation of Indian Swaraj*, Madras : V.R. Sastrulu and Sons, 1925.

Radhakrishnan, *Recovery of Faith*, Hind Pocket Book (P) Ltd., G.T. Road, Delhi, 1960.

——, *The Bhagvad Gita*, George Allen and Unwin, 1958.

——, *Education Politics and War*, George Allen and Unwin, 1961.

——, *Religion in Transition*, George Allen and Unwin, 1960.

Ranganathananda, Swami, *Essential Values for Changing Society*, Calcutta : Advaita Ashram, 1958.

——, *Science and Religion*, Calcutta : Advaita Ashram, 1952.

Ramgopal, *Life of Balgangadhar Tilak*, Bombay : Book Centre Pvt. Ltd., 1967.

——, *How India Struggled for Freedom*, Bombay : Book Centre Pvt. Ltd. 1965.

Rawlinson, H.G., *India : A Short Cultural History*, Penguin Press, London, 1971.

——, *Intercourse between India and Western World*, Penguin Press, London, 1971.

Rapson, E.G., *The Cambridge History of India*, Vol. I, London : Allen and Unwin, 1924.

Renou, Louis, *Religions of Ancient India*, University of London, 1953.

——, *Hinduism*, Prentice, Hall Inernational, London, 1961.

Risley, Sir Herbert, *People of India*, Prentice Hall International, London, 1951.

Rajendra Prasad, *Legacy of Gandhi*, Delhi : Shiv Lal Agarwal Co., 1962.

Ranade, M.G., *Essays in Indian Economics*, Nasik, 1962.

Rolland, Romain, *Mahatma Gandhi*, Bharatiya Vidya Bhawan, Bombay, 1985.

Rousseau, *Social Contract*, Oxford University Press, 1946.

Roy, M.N., *Reason, Romanticism & Revolution*, Vols. I & II, Calcutta : Renaissance Publisher, 1952.

——, *New Humanism*, Calcutta : Renaissance Publisher, 1961.

——, *Indian in Transition*, Ajanta Publication, Jawahar Nagar, Delhi, 1989.

——, *Selected Works*, Vol. I & Vol. II, Oxford University Press, New York, 1960.

Russell, Bertrand, *Political Ideals*, London : George Allen & Unwin, 1919.

——, *Roads to Freedom*, London : George Allen & Unwin, 1937.

Sabine, G.H., *A History of Political Theory*, Holt, New York, 1961.

Sarkar, J.N., *India Through the Ages*, Allied Publishers, 1964.

Seal, Anil, *The Emergence of Indian Nationalism*, Cambridge University Press, 1969.

Sen, Amit, *Notes on the Bengal Renaissance*, Calcutta, 1957.

Sen, N.B., *Glorious Thoughts of Gandhi*, New Delhi : New Book Society of India, 1948.

Seaver, Geroge, *Albert Schweitzer*, London : Macmillan, 1962.

Schuman, F.L., *International Politics*, New York : McGraw Hill Book Company, 1948.

——, *Imperialsim and World Politics*, New York : McGraw Hill Book Company, 1948.

Schleicher, *International Relation*, London : Macmillan Co., 1942.

Sharma, B.S., *Gandhi as a Political Thinker*, Allahabad, Indian Press, 1956.

Sharma, D.S., *Hinduism Through the Ages*, Bombay : Bharatiya Vidya Bhawan, 1955.

Shah, Kantilal (Ed.), *Vinobha on Gandhi*, Sarva Seva Sangha Prakashan, Rajghat Varanasi, India, 1972.

Singh, Karan, *Prophet of Indian Nationalism*, George Allen and Unwin, 1963.

Sitarammaya Pattavi, *The History of Indian National Congress*, Vol. I, Bomaby : Padama Publication, 1952.

Smith, V.A., *The Early History of India*, New Heaven, 1938.

Smit, W.R., *Nationalism and Reform in India*, New Heaven, 1938.

Snyder, Louis, *The Meaning of Nationalism*, New Brunswick, N.J. Rutgers University Press, 1954.

Sundaram, Lanka, *A Secular State for India*, Bomaby, 1970.

Sukla, C.S., *Conversation of Gandhi*, New Delhi : New Book Society of India, 1948.

Surendranath, *Terrorism in India*, New Delhi : National Publishing House, 1980.

Tagore, R.N., *Nationalism*, Macmillan India Limited, Madras, 1950.

——, *Sadhana*, London : Macmillan & Co., 1954.

——, *Towards Universal Man*, Bombay : Asia Publishing House, 1962.

Tarachand, *History of the Freedom Movement in India*, Vol. II, New Delhi Publication Division, 1967.

Tilak, B.G., *Gita Rahasya or the Science of Karma Yogo*, Poona, 1971.

——, *Writings and Speeches*, Madras : Ganesh, 1919.

Tendulkar, G.D., *Mahatma Gandhi*, Vol. I, Vol. II, and Vol. VI, New Delhi Publication Division, Govt. of India, 1961.

Toynbee, Arnold, *Civilization in Trial*, New York : Oxford University Press, 1948.

——, *Study of History*, Vol. I to VI, London : Oxford University Press, 1933.

——, *War and Civilization*, New York : Oxford University Press, 1951.

Tripathy, Amales, *The Extremist Challenge*, Bombay : Orient Longman, 1967.

Varma, V.P., *Modern Indian Political Thought,* Laxmi Narayan Agarwal, Educational Publishers, Agra, 1991.

Vinacke Herold, M., *Far Eastern Policies in the Post War Period,* New York : Appleton Century Crofts, 1956.

Vireswarananda, Swami, *Religion and National Integration,* Ramkrishna Math Mylapore, Madras, 1986.

——, *Our Duty Towards the Motherland,* Ramkrishna Math, Mylapore, Madras, 1984.

Vyas, K.C., *Social Renaissance in India,* Bombay : Vora and Co. Ltd., 1957.

Whitehead, *Religion in the Making,* London, 1926.

Will Durant, *Story of the Civilization,* Vol. X and Vol. XI, Cosmos Publicaitons, Genesis Publishing Pvt. Ltd., Delhi, 1991.

Winslow, *The Pattern of Imperialism,* New York : Columbia University Press, 1948.

Works of William Law, Vol. VIII, London, 1928.

Younghusband, Sir Francis, *Dawn in India : British Purpose and Indian Aspiration,* London, 1930.

Zacharies, H.C.E., *Renascent India,* London, 1933.

(c) JOURNALS, PERIODICALS AND REPORTS

Bulletin of the Ramkrishna Institute of Culture, Calcutta, December, 1966.

Bulletin of the Ramkrishna Institute of Culture, Calcutta, April, 1967.

Bulletin of the Ramkrishna Institute of Culture, Calcutta, May, 1967.

Bulletin of the Ramkrishna Institute of Culture, Calcutta, August, 1967.

Bulletin of the Ramkrishna Institute of Culture, Calcutta, January, 1968 etc.

The Calcutta Review, March-June, 1955, Article — "Critique of Marxian Sociology" by V.P. Varma.

Patna College Megazine, September, 1946, Article — "Vivekananda : The Hero Prophet of Modern World" by V.P. Varma.

Sunday Times, London, 1896, Aritcle — "India's Mission" by Swami Vivekananda.

Bengalee, 8th January 1889, 10 April 1890, 18 May 1895, 22 March 1896 etc.

Bande Mataram, 22 September 1907, 17 April 1907, 21 July 1908, 27 April 1907, 13 July 1907, 23 February 1908, 24 February 1908, 5 March 1908, 1 May 1908, etc.

Indu Prakash, 4 December 1895, 25 December 1895, 6 March 1896 etc.

Young India, Issues between 13 October 1921 to 24 August 1945.

Harijan, 7 November 1921, 13 December 1934, 18 May 1940, 4 August 1940, 3 February 1942, 9 June 1946, 9 May 1946, 29 August 1947 etc.

Report of the Calcutta Police Commissioner (Tergart), 1914.

Rowlatt Committee Report, 1918.

Report of Indian National Congress, 1885-86.

Report of Indian National Congress, 1917.

Report of Indian National Congress, 1942.

INDEX